JAMES B. HUNT

JAMES B. HUNT

A North Carolina Progressive

by Wayne Grimsley

McFarland & Company, Inc., Publishers
Jefferson, North Carolina, and London

Library of Congress Cataloguing-in-Publication Data

Grimsley, Wayne, 1964–
    James B. Hunt : a North Carolina progressive / by
Wayne Grimsley.
        p.   cm.
    Includes bibliographical references and index.

    ISBN 0-7864-1607-6 (softcover: 50# alkaline paper)

    1. Hunt, James B., 1937–   2. Governors—North Carolina—
Biography.   3. North Carolina—Politics and government—
1951–   4. Progressivism (United States politics)   5. North
Carolina—Social policy.   I. Title.
F260.42.H86G75   2003
975.6'043'092—dc21   2003008661

British Library cataloguing data are available

Cover image: Hunt addresses a crowd at his 1981 inauguration (*North
Carolina Office of Archives and History*). Background ©2003 PhotoSpin

Manufactured in the United States of America

*McFarland & Company, Inc., Publishers
    Box 611, Jefferson, North Carolina 28640
    www.mcfarlandpub.com*

To
Joseph Wayne Grimsley, Sr.

Acknowledgments

This author expresses sincere gratitude to the many who gave selfless assistance in the completion of this work. The book was originally a dissertation that I wrote to receive my Ph.D. in American history at Mississippi State University. Foremost, I thank Dr. Robert Jenkins, my committee chairman, for guiding and assisting me throughout the difficult dissertation process. I also appreciate the aid of other members of my dissertation committee, namely, Dr. Stanly Godbold, the second reader who had a strong expertise on the presidency of Jimmy Carter, Dr. John Marszalek, Dr. Johnpeter Grill, and Dr. Mfanya Tryman. I also owe a debt to Peggy Bonner, a secretary at MSU who typed the final draft.

I also would like to thank my family for their support. I spent the years 1999 and 2000 working busily in libraries, archives, and historical collections. I also thank Dr. Ted Gasper and Laura Buffalo at Halifax Community College for allowing me the time to work on this project.

I am also indebted to all the people who aided my research. Many of them played major roles in the Hunt administration. Their willingness to help, and their honesty and valuable recollections, made this a far better study. This is especially true of the insight I received from Joseph Grimsley, Sr., my late father, a top-level Hunt aide. I had no idea that my interviews with my father would be his final discussions about the man that he loyally served for fourteen years. I did not always agree with my father, and often brought up the opinions of Hunt opponents, which he deflected with his own arguments. I regret that Dad did not get to see the finished manuscript, but I am very happy that I interviewed him several times before his premature death.

Others who provided valuable information through interviews

include Gordon Allen, Bert Bennett, Jr., Phil Carlton, Rob Christensen, Thomas Ellis, Paul Essex, David Flaherty, William Friday, Thomas Gilmore, Linda Grimsley, Ferrel Guillory, Carl Henley, James B. Holshouser, Abraham Holtzman, James B. Hunt, Jr., James B. Hunt, Sr., Patricia Hunt, Robert Hunt, Edward Knox, I. Beverly Lake, Jr., Howard Lee, Quentin Lindsey, William Link, Paul Luebke, Donald Mathews, Betty McCain, Betty Owen, Robert Scott, John Webb, and Carter Wrenn. I also wish to thank the librarians and research guides who helped me at the A. H. Hill Library at North Carolina State University, the Jimmy Carter Presidential Library, the North Carolina Archives, the North Carolina State University Record Center, the North Carolina Old Records Center, the Wilson County Public Library, the Southern Historical Collection and the North Carolina Collection at Louis Wilson Library at the University of North Carolina at Chapel Hill, and the graduate and law libraries at that same university. Although I did not gain access to former Governor Hunt's private papers at East Carolina University because the governor wished those documents to be used solely by his personal biographer, Governor Hunt assisted me by granting me a personal interview and reviewing the final manuscript.

Table of Contents

Preface

In early 1989, I entered the law office of James B. Hunt, Jr., the former governor of North Carolina, wanting some advice on a career. After struggling as a news reporter for the previous few years, I did not know what to do next. Hunt reminded me of my adolescence that, during my difficult time, seemed like the good old days. In the years between 1972 and 1983, I moved from elementary school to college, Hunt won three consecutive elections, and my father, Joe Grimsley, served as his campaign manager, legislative aide, and secretary of two cabinet departments. I recalled handing out paper fans and printed material, eating lots of barbecue and hearing bluegrass music at rallies, celebrating happy November election results, braving cold January inaugurals, and feeling positive about this politician. As we talked in his law office in 1989, I asked him what I should do with my life. I believe that he said, "Why don't you become a teacher?" I confess that I wasn't too enthusiastic about that idea at the time.

Thirteen years later, in the spring of 2002, I graduated with a Ph.D. in history from Mississippi State University after teaching for several years and writing a dissertation on Jim Hunt. Three years earlier, in 1999, I wasn't sure about what my dissertation topic should be. Dr. Stanley Godbold, a professor of southern history at MSU, suggested that I choose Jim Hunt as a topic since my father had worked on his campaign and I would have plenty of help in getting firsthand material. I debated this suggestion, since Hunt was not yet a man of the past — indeed, he was still serving a fourth term as governor. Thinking about it carefully, I got excited about the idea of examining the man who deeply influenced the lives of my family members and the rest of the families of my native state.

At first, I wanted to cover Hunt's life from his birth to 1984, when he ended his second term as governor after Jesse Helms defeated him in a United States Senate race. (His two gubernatorial terms in the 1990s occurred too recently to be considered history.) As my research progressed in 1999 and 2000, I realized that I had an overabundant amount of material about his youth, lieutenant gubernatorial years, and his first term as governor. I changed the end of my study period from 1984 to 1980, the last victorious campaign that my father ran for him.

This study focuses on Jim Hunt's rise to power and examines his fundamental political beliefs. Since my childhood, I have been told how the clean-cut young man from Rock Ridge studied hard to achieve the state's top political position. Senator Jesse Helms told a different story in his reelection race against Hunt in 1984, saying that the governor was an extremely ambitious politician with no sense of ideology (unless it was secretly liberal) and that he did anything to get elected. Despite my efforts to aid the governor, the amount of televised propaganda even made me question things. What was Jim Hunt's ideology? Did he only care about getting higher office? In this study, I look at both his political career and his viewpoints to understand the answers.

I researched this work with the help of many people, including my late father. Before he died in July 2001, Joe Grimsley, Sr., provided tremendous help by confirming background information about Hunt's career in the 1970s and helping me get an interview with Hunt while he was still a sitting governor. Through my own efforts, I was able to get interviews with key persons in his childhood, college years, and early political career. I also spent a lot of time in libraries, going through archives, newspaper files, and historical collections to come up with the first study of North Carolina's only four-term governor in the twentieth century. I believe that this is an accurate account of Hunt's early life and political career, but I accept any errors in the book as my own.

I knew that I would have to challenge previous biases by talking to people who were not part of Hunt's inner circle. I interviewed several of his Republican critics, including I. Beverly Lake, Jr., Carter Wrenn, and Tom Ellis. I also talked to James Holshouser and Gordon Allen, who sometimes challenged Hunt while he was lieutenant governor, and former allies like Eddie Knox who sometimes felt betrayed by the governor. I corresponded with Hunt's liberal critics. I studied hundreds of articles, letters, and tapes about Jim Hunt, both negative and positive, and dealt with administration scandals during his first term.

I still conclude that James B. Hunt, Jr., served the state well during the 1970s and beyond. He not only fit the mold of a progressive tradition of earlier North Carolina governors, but he transformed the tradition to include a concern for minorities, women's rights, and consumer issues. He had high ambitions, sometimes straddled the progressive course during conservative times, often practiced a powerful sense of political caution, and could abandon a political ally who embarrassed him or did not serve his purposes. Yet, he worked extremely hard in his early political career, remained highly moral in his personal life, fought hard for good causes such as education, crime prevention, and industrial development, and did much good for North Carolina.

1

Before Jim Hunt: The Birth of the Tar Heel Progressive Myth

North Carolina acquired a progressive reputation long before the birth of James B. Hunt, Jr,. in 1937. The future governor modeled himself after progressive predecessors who favored the use of the state government to build good roads and provide a decent education to its citizens. When Governor Hunt talked about improvements to the state highway system, he sometimes mentioned Governor John Morehead's establishment of a state railroad in the 1840s. When Hunt sought passage of education bills, he often spoke of Charles Aycock, governor from 1901 to 1905, who promoted a strong public school system. Both of these governors wore the label of "progressive." They were not New Deal liberals who sought economic redistribution to end poverty, nor did they fight ardently for the civil rights of oppressed minorities. Instead, they backed pragmatic reforms that benefitted the rising industries in North Carolina. Hunt admired these men and maintained their traditions during his four terms as governor.

The roots of Hunt's progressivism and his nineteenth and twentieth century predecessors go deep in North Carolina history. Even by the standards of the North Carolinian elite of the early twentieth century, however, the first leaders following American independence in 1776 seemed conservative. Suspicious of central government after royal governors spent extravagantly in New Bern, the first general assemblies kept the state governors weak and the taxes low. Dominated by conservative eastern North Carolinian planters, the legislatures refused to spend dollars on internal improvements or education except for the University of North Carolina

(UNC), the nation's first public university dedicated to training the state's most privileged young men. Indifference to reform caused many North Carolinians to leave "The Rip Van Winkle State."[1]

During the prosperous period after the War of 1812, western legislator Archibald Murphey introduced the first extensive progressive program for North Carolina, and it revolutionized the political and social thinking of the state. Murphey, an affluent planter, won election to the state senate and served on a board recommending internal improvements to make the rivers more navigable. In a series of reports, Murphey backed a dynamic program for public school education and transportation projects, convincing the General Assembly to buy stock in transportation companies in 1815 and to create a state board of agriculture in 1822. Fearing reform would allow westerners to empty the state treasury, the eastern elite rejected Murphey's other proposals, including the financing of public education. The Tar Heel legislator died in 1832 before witnessing the completion of his reform proposals.[2]

Influenced by Murphey, the frustrated citizens of western North Carolina worked for constitutional reform in 1835. Lacking adequate representation, the westerners resented an antidemocratic system dominated by eastern planters. Historian Charles Sydnor said the western citizens wanted to revise the constitution, but "the eastern counties, being strong through overrepresentation, obstructed the march of democracy."[3]

Joining with coastal North Carolinians who desired internal improvements, the westerners backed an 1835 constitutional convention that endorsed suffrage for all white males. The western progressives also promoted the funding of transportation projects and public education for poor white children. Many voters appreciated these reforms and voted for these progressives who tended to belong to the Whig party.[4]

This new generation of so-called reformers was least progressive on the race issue. The state constitution that allowed poor whites to vote for governor in 1835 also disfranchised all free black males. Whigs, who had once backed gradual emancipation as a means to end the peculiar institution permanently, began to defend slavery in the aftermath of the 1831 Nat Turner rebellion. Often, commitment to economic reform and support of slavery did not conflict. The Whigs argued that internal improvements could get plantation crops more quickly to market, while education for poor whites ensured the differences between races. They supported efforts to censure abolitionist literature and backed the expulsion of a university professor who supported the 1856 Republican ticket. Despite disagreements with conservative planters, they rallied for slavery even before Fort Sumter. Historian Eugene Genovese concluded that white southern reformers discovered no contradictions between slaveholding and "progress" because the latter term was so loosely defined.[5]

The state's antebellum reformers also showed no sympathy for the emerging women's rights movement or the Native American population. Like most American men, they treated the efforts of northern feminists Elizabeth Cady Stanton and Susan B. Anthony to seek gender equality with ridicule and contempt. "Before secession, North Carolina women, like their sisters throughout the South, had been distant observers of Northern feminism, which was identified with the radical wing of abolitionism," historians Donald G. Mathews and Jane Sherron De Hart wrote. "They believed that women should confine themselves to raising children and taking care of the home, while men dominated the business and political arenas."[6] Few North Carolina women publicly disagreed with the men until the creation of the first state women's suffrage club in the 1890s. The antebellum reformers had even less concern for the Indian population. Since many reformers came from the West, they did not frown upon the removal of land from Cherokee Indians.

North Carolinians elected a series of Whig governors who contributed to Murphey's vision of progress. In the late 1830s, David Swain initiated constitutional reform that allowed poor white males without property to vote, and Ed Dudley backed the Public School Law of 1839 providing the first state funds to county schools. In the early 1840s, John Motley Morehead successfully pushed for internal improvements and state schools for the deaf, the mute, and the insane. Biographer Burton Alva Konkle praised Morehead for helping to create the state-funded North Carolina Railroad and a system of roads extending from Beaufort to Charlotte and from Salisbury to the Tennessee line.[7]

At times, the Whig governors were motivated less by progressive instincts than noblesse oblige for those they considered their inferiors. Historian Thomas Jeffrey downplayed the progressivism of the North Carolina Whigs, arguing that they adopted minimum efforts for transportation and public education. Although the Whigs initiated reform, they respected the average North Carolinian's hostility to tax increases. Instead of financing internal improvements through taxes, they funded the programs through federal redistribution of land sale profits. Jeffrey said state tax revenue from 1840 to 1858 increased only from $79,548 to $99,328, a small amount for progressive reforms.[8]

Realizing that the Democratic party failed to win elections because of its rejection of reform, a younger generation of Democrats supported progressive goals in the 1850s. William Holden, editor of the Raleigh *Standard,* strongly promoted a reform agenda for the party. Convincing voters that the Whigs had relaxed their zeal for reform and became the guardians of wealth, privilege, and culture, Holden helped elect David Reid governor in 1850 and 1852. Despite opposition by conservative Democrats who still favored limited government and class distinctions, Reid backed the old Whig program of aid to schools, internal improvements, and humanitarian reform. The Democratic reformers centralized the school system under one superintendent and made the school system one of the best in the antebellum South.[9]

Secessionist tensions and civil war temporarily stopped efforts at educational and economic progress between 1860 and 1867. Political divisions instead focused on the North Carolinians who supported the southern nationalism of Confederate President Jefferson Davis against the state-rights philosophy of former Whig Congressman Zebulon Vance. He and former Democratic editor William Holden mobilized the "Conservative" party to win the gubernatorial election for Vance in 1862. As the tide turned against the Confederacy in 1863, Holden began a peace movement in the state that Governor Vance refused to support. Their alliance shattered, Holden challenged Vance in the 1864 gubernatorial election. The governor defeated the peace candidate by visiting "Tar Heel" soldiers at the front (a nickname that came from the fact that many North Carolina soldiers had no shoes to wear during their marches) and by appealing to the eastern slave owners who once opposed him. With war preoccupying all matters, Vance neglected educational and industrial reform.[10]

The Civil War left defeated North Carolinians in a severe financial crisis. Land values plummeted, and the state had no funds to open the abandoned University of North Carolina. Moreover, the General Assembly did not have much money for public schools, and was less inclined to revive them if the federal government forced blacks to attend. However, in the next fifty years, North Carolina returned to its reform-oriented path because, according to political scientist V. O. Key, Jr., the state seemed less shackled than her southern neighbors on lost grandeur; poor before the war, "it had less grandeur to lose."[11]

Congressional Reconstruction became the first major attempt in North Carolina to blend race and educational progressivism. Desperate for equality, the freed slaves strongly backed the education denied to them during slavery. At first, they sought the help of northern teachers who came South. In 1867, congressional radicals replaced President Andrew Johnson's mild Reconstruction program with a new plan that allowed African-American men to vote. The freedmen joined northern carpetbaggers and native whites to form a state Republican party dedicated to public education, civil rights, and industrial expansion. Backed by northern education-minded migrants like Albion Tourgee, North Carolina Republicans called for a public school system for both races in the 1868 constitution, which for the first time in North Carolina also gave wives complete control over their personal property. The following year, the Republican General Assembly approved a public school law requiring schools to be open at least four months a year.[12]

The Republican reformers faced insurmountable challenges. Many of the state's whites resisted the efforts of the freedmen to vote. The Ku Klux Klan rose in power, frightening Republicans away from the polls with violence and murder. The Conservative party took control of the legislature in 1870, vowing to end expensive reforms. They resisted the efforts of Governor William Holden, who had switched parties, but who continued to call for spending on education. The governor's attempt to suppress the Ku Klux Klan in Alamance County led to his impeachment and removal from office in 1871. A rising generation of economically progressive eastern Democrats forgot Holden's support for education over three decades and remembered his service to "Negro rule."[13]

The Conservatives took over the North Carolina Democratic party, nominated former Civil War hero Zebulon Vance for governor, and endorsed a mild reform program in 1876. Vance backed funding for public schools, supported the creation of an agricultural college, and approved of a state department of agriculture. Once a Whig who supported the limited reforms of the antebellum era, Vance attracted young progressive Democrats such as future Raleigh *News and Observer* editor Josephus Daniels and future North Carolina governor Charles Aycock by promising reform. True to his word, Vance pushed through the state's first agricultural department to aid the state's struggling farmers.[14]

The attempt to appease rural whites ebbed in the 1880s as the Democratic governors and legislatures replaced mild reform with conservatism. After the legislature selected Vance to the United States Senate in 1878, his gubernatorial successor Thomas Jarvis rejected aid to public schools and farmers. Historian Elgiva Watson claimed that Jarvis's use of party machinery and patronage, his support for the sale of the state's railroads to northern interests, and his enthusiasm for state control of county government must all have lessened his appeal for those Democrats who joined the Farmer's Alliances.[15]

Raleigh newspaper editor Walter Hines Page represented the spirit of urban progressivism in North Carolina during the 1880s. He backed the Democratic leaders on industrial progress, but criticized their lack of support for education and faulted them for not allowing the state's average citizens to have a chance at intellectual growth. Despite conservative opposition, Page successfully lobbied for the creation of an agricultural and industrial school in 1889 that later became North Carolina State College.[16]

Two attempts by reformers to challenge the state Democrats in the 1880s failed. The Liberal Anti-Prohibition party and the Knights of Labor union each elected a United States congressman, but both political efforts soon faded into oblivion. John Nichols, elected with the Knights' support to a seat in the Fourth District, angered farmers by backing high tariffs, supporting Union veteran pensions, and favoring a liberal racial policy. Historian Melton McLaurin claimed that the North Carolina Knights of Labor failed because of a surplus labor market, the racial issue, ignorance of the labor force about the principles of unionism, and a power structure militantly hostile to labor unions. Such factors continued to hurt the state's unions in the twentieth century.[17]

The most successful effort at reform in the late nineteenth century came from the farmers frustrated over the railroads, banks, and politicians that ignored their economic difficulties. Farmers supported Leonidas L. Polk, a former Confederate colonel, who resigned his post as state agricultural commissioner to protest the failure of the state to back the agrarian cause. Polk edited *The Progressive Farmer*, a newspaper promoting radical measures that included government control of the railroads. By the time he served as president of the Southern Farmers' Alliance in 1890, he had won a large rural following.[18]

Two years before his unexpected death, Leonidas Polk backed a successful effort by agrarians in 1890 to control the North Carolina General Assembly. Agrarians received support from educators Edwin Alderman and Charles McIver, both graduates of the University of North Carolina, who dedicated themselves to ending the state's high illiteracy rate. Alderman and McIver toured the state in 1889 and discovered rural backwardness. Understanding the desire of poor farmers to educate their children, the two educators encouraged the "Farmer's Legislature" to back dramatic reforms. The assembly approved a woman's college at Greensboro that McIver successfully administered for nearly two decades. The legislature also backed funding for the University of North Carolina after President Alderman promised to open the university to average citizens, and approved a black agricultural college in Greensboro, partly to win needed federal funds.[19]

After conservative Democrats defeated the agrarians in several 1892 legislative elections and took control of the General Assembly, many rural North Carolinians broke from their traditional loyalties to the party of Andrew Jackson and supported the Populists, a third party dedicated to agrarian reforms. The state Populist platform, strongly backed by State

Senator Marion Butler of Sampson County, demanded economy, tax reform, election reform, a ten-hour day for labor, and a limitation of six percent on interest charges. Butler, once a loyal eastern white supremacist Democrat who edited *The Caucasian* newspaper, turned against the party in 1892. As a Populist leader of the Farmers' Alliance, Butler conspired to "fuse" with the Republicans in a successful coalition that captured the legislature two years later.[20]

The Republicans and Populists of the 1895 General Assembly discovered that cooperation was difficult. "Fusion was a misnomer," historian Allen Trelease later said. "Republicans and Populists never merged. Most Republicans were pro-business while Populists sought business regulation, Republicans favored the gold standard while Populists advocated silver inflation, and Republican policy reflected the party's dependence on Negro support while the Populists tended toward white supremacy."[21] However, they still attempted to find common ground. The fusionist legislature removed state control over county offices which allowed blacks to control some counties, selected Butler for the United States Senate, backed Alderman as UNC president, and supported funding for the public schools. The coalition strained to keep blacks allied with racist whites and radical agrarians allied with conservatives.[22]

In 1898, Democrats defeated "fusion rule" with a violent white supremacy campaign. Led by Democratic party chairman Furnifold Simmons, a New Bern resident and former United States congressman who had lost his seat to an African-American candidate in 1886, the Democrats called for whites to unite against the second coming of "Negro rule." Using racist campaign techniques, Simmons brought forth a Democratic legislative victory that led to celebrations and a Wilmington riot that forced black and white Republicans to flee the city in terror. Although a conservative, Simmons won the support of economic liberals like Josephus Daniels, the white supremacist editor of the Raleigh *News and Observer*, the newspaper that became the predominant progressive organ for the Democratic party.[23]

African Americans hardly thought that a new era of progress existed. Following 1898, the Democrats successfully backed efforts to segregate state facilities and to disenfranchise black voters. "Denied the vote and physically separated from whites residentially and in public accommodations, African Americans struggled to earn a living, to educate their children in under-funded and inferior facilities, and to contest the limits placed on their social, economic, and political lives," historian Jeffrey Crow wrote.[24] George White, the last black United States Congressman from North Carolina until 1993, correctly predicted in 1901 that blacks would return to take their proper place in Congress. Although many North Carolina blacks achieved success at black businesses, especially at Durham's North Carolina Mutual Life Insurance Company, their political role remained submerged for decades.[25]

The white supremacy campaign of 1898 actually provided an opportunity to Democrats who claimed to be progressive regarding education. Understanding that whites had left the Democratic party in droves because of the conservatism of its leaders, the progressives developed a reform agenda. To retain the white poor, Furnifold Simmons backed progressive candidate Charles Aycock as the Democratic gubernatorial nominee in 1900. The former Goldsboro attorney provided the state with a program of public education and state development, a concern for the welfare of the common man, and a greater responsiveness to the needs of a growing state. At times, Aycock advocated measures that annoyed the conservative Democrats, although they muted their criticism because of the governor's popularity. He proclaimed that he wanted to put a public school house in every district of the state and to insure that all children, black and white, would be able to read and write. According to educator Edwin Alderman, Aycock turned a tax-hating people suspicious of progress into one convinced that ignorance could not remedy anything.[26]

Following Aycock's term in office, Governor Robert Glynn promoted an agenda that borrowed from the national progressive movement. With the backing of Speaker Edward Justice, who presided over a General Assembly that historian Joseph Steelman called the most progressive body to deal with the state problems in the first twenty years of the twentieth century, the 1907 assembly enacted significant antitrust and anti-lobby legislation, provided for a statewide system of public schools, reformed the tax system, and approved consumer protection and child labor laws. Glynn also pushed for a teacher-training school in Greenville to win over those easterners who still opposed public funding of education. This school would expand dramatically in the twentieth century under the new name of East Carolina University.[27]

Following the success of the 1907 assembly, North Carolina progressives experienced a series of setbacks. Aycock, probably the only educational progressive who could successfully challenge United States Senator Furnifold Simmons's control over the Democratic party, died in 1912, uttering his final word, "education," before dropping dead of a heart attack during a speech in Birmingham, Alabama. That year, Simmons successfully defeated a progressive challenger and helped to elect an ally to the governor's mansion. Another progressive North Carolina era for poor whites seemed at an end.[28]

State progressives succeeded better at the national level. Josephus Daniels, North Carolina Supreme Court Justice Walter Clark, and other Tar Heel progressives helped New Jersey Governor Woodrow Wilson, a southern-born politician who spent some time in the Tar Heel State in his youth, win the Democratic presidential nomination in 1912. Wilson won the presidency and repaid the favor by selecting Daniels as his Secretary of the Navy and Walter Hines Page as his ambassador to England. Wilson's popularity in North Carolina influenced Simmons to sponsor a low tariff act in 1913 that allowed for a progressive income tax. A year later, North Carolina progressives initiated their own state convention in 1914 to back a state utilities commission, a state highway department, rural credit system for farmers, free public school textbooks, and regulation of deceptive advertising. Despite having a friend in the White House, the North Carolina progressives failed to persuade the conservative state Democratic establishment to support reform.[29]

At first, these Tar Heel progressives ignored or opposed the issue of woman's suffrage. Beginning as small urban groups of middle-class women, the state's suffragettes slowly gained ground. Historians Donald G. Mathews and Jane Sherron De Hart said that the idea that North Carolina women should participate in politics was so outrageous that even the progressives dared not damage their appeal to male voters by including the issue in the "People's Platform" of their 1914 convention. By that time, female activists had organized numerous chapters across the state and formed the North Carolina Woman's Suffrage Association. Despite gaining a few progressive male legislators to their cause, the suffragettes suffered numerous defeats in the General Assembly. White supremacists opposed woman's suffrage because they feared the reform would spur the latent desire of blacks to vote. Cotton and textile employers did not want to see women vote, fearing that their female employees might support pro-union candidates. Even a few conservative women believed that voting would disrupt family life and possibly lead to an increase in divorces. Without North Carolina's help, the nation ratified the Nineteenth Amendment in 1920.[30]

A progressive crusade more popular with the industrialists was the effort to create better North Carolina roads. Backed by state geologist Richard Hyde Pratt, who called upon a statewide highway system for the rising automobile industry, the good-roads movement won a following among urban dwellers. Pratt also backed the convict lease system as a way to pave the streets, arguing that such efforts improved both the roads and the morale of prison laborers. Pratt's "good roads" progressivism successfully challenged the desires of other reformers who wanted to end the convict lease system. Even in the late twentieth century, North Carolina governors approved prisoners to build roads.[31]

In the early 1920s, Governor Cameron Morrison won legislative support to create a state highway system. Although he belonged to Senator Simmons's conservative wing of the Democratic party, Morrison reached out to the state's progressives in his 1921 inaugural address by proclaiming that "progressive democracy" should "challenge the reactionary and unprogressive forces of our state."[32] Because of prosperity and numerous tax revenues, the governor asked the legislature for lavish spending on highways and education. Morrison won backing for the University of North Carolina, where President Harry Woodburn Chase supported a program of enlarging physical facilities, bringing more faculty members to Chapel Hill, and enlisting the support of students, alumni, and the General Assembly. Under Morrison and his successor Angus McLean, the state increased its annual appropriation to its colleges to more than two million dollars a year during the 1920s.[33]

Morrison revealed his conservatism on racial and religious matters. He informed black teachers asking for more funds that their people received "as much education as you are ready for. You cannot use the highly organized system that is provided by whites."[34] He backed the state's fundamentalists when they went into politics to halt the teaching of evolution, vetoing two biology texts because he did not want his daughter to "have to study a book that prints pictures of a monkey and a man on the same page."[35] Despite the governor's opposition, University of North Carolina President Harry Woodburn Chase took the lead in fighting to preserve Darwinism in the classrooms. With help from state legislator Sam Erwin, Chase defeated the fundamentalists in the General Assembly.[36]

The next challenge between Tar Heel progressives and conservatives came in the bitter 1928 United States presidential contest. The conservatives, led by United States Senator Furnifold Simmons, refused to back Democratic presidential nominee Al Smith in the general election because of his Roman Catholicism and his opposition to Prohibition. Economically progressive Democrats remained faithful to the party (often by linking a Republican victory to renewed black voting), but a majority of North Carolinians supported Republican presidential candidate Herbert Hoover — the first time that the GOP carried the state since Reconstruction. Two years later, when the Great Depression damaged Hoover's popularity, Josiah Bailey defeated Senator Simmons in the 1930 Democratic primary.[37]

This event signified the replacement of the Simmons machine with Governor Max Gardner's "Shelby Dynasty." Although he arose from the progressive wing of the state Democratic party and loyally supported the ticket when running for governor in 1928, the North Carolina State College graduate often took stands that alienated his base. During the 1929 Gastonia textile strike, for example, Gardner sided with management in suppressing the strikers, even though a few progressives and the League of Women Voters opposed his actions. A Communist leader called him the "mill-owning, slave driving, capitalist governor"[38] of North Carolina. As the Great Depression grew worse in the state, Gardner made more unpopular decisions. Instead of increasing government expenditures, he slashed the school budgets and consolidated the university system. "I am by nature an optimist and at heart a progressive," Gardner said, "yet I have been forced into the position of taking my place in the minds of a great many of my dearest friends as a reactionary."[39] While some historians criticized Gardner for his limited vision of North Carolina progressivism, others credit the governor for bringing modern administrative techniques to the state and for appointing esteemed liberal Frank Porter Graham to the presidency of the university system.

Before the 1930s, Tar Heels had forged many of the progressive traditions of North Carolina that molded the political career of North Carolina Governor James B. Hunt, Jr. Since Archibald Murphey proposed his reforms, progressive North Carolinians moved the state away from its status as the "Rip Van Winkle State" toward a commitment to public schools, paved roads, industrialization, and improved education. In the antebellum era, a rising generation of Whigs and Democrats established a limited commitment to public education and internal improvements. After the Civil War, reform was frustrated by the devastation to educational institutions, the lack of support for racially progressive Republican reformers, and the rise of a conservative Democratic elite hostile to spending programs. These Democrats resisted all but industrial progress until a farmer revolt destroyed party solidarity in the 1890s. To win back the small farmers, the progressive wing of the Democratic party elected candidates dedicated to better public schools, easier access to higher education, and improved roads. However, these politicians rejected reform on race, organized labor, and women's rights issues so often that political scientists Jack Bass and Walter DeVries have argued that they were not true reformers; the state's native leadership accepted a "progressive myth" unsupported by the facts.[40] Despite the faults of the early North Carolina progressives, however, they influenced strongly Governor Jim Hunt in the late twentieth century.

2

Jimmy Hunt of Rock Ridge

The family of James Baxter Hunt helped him become governor of North Carolina. Arising from generations of moderately successful North Carolinians, Jim Hunt's parents had beliefs that he accepted as a youth. "Jimmy" Hunt abided by their faith in community participation as a way to practice Christianity. They taught him that hard, strenuous work on behalf of other people, combined with a high sense of personal morality, led to future success. He understood his mother's belief that education stimulated character; he became the valedictorian of his high school class. He honored his father's faith in fair competition by competing fiercely in speaking and athletic events. Since Jimmy learned from his parents that elected leaders produced the most good for the people, he began to think about a life in public service.

The Hunts settled in North Carolina in the eighteenth century. Nearly two hundred years before Jimmy Hunt had moved to tobacco-rich Wilson County, his direct paternal ancestor Henry Hunt had migrated to the North Carolina colony from Virginia in 1742, bringing African slaves to harvest the tobacco on his 150-acre farm in Edgecombe County. By 1747, Hunt owned 450 acres in northeastern North Carolina. Three years later, Henry wrote a will giving his wife Agnes "the plantation where I now dwell during the life and she has the use of all the Negroes."[1] He gave property to each of his three sons, including a slave and a tract of land at Buffalo Creek to James, the "negro woman Jenny and all her increase" to John, and Jenny's unborn child to George.[2] Henry Hunt's son John settled in the Buffalo Creek area of Granville County, North Carolina, operating a 370-acre tobacco plantation where his children and grandchildren remained for several decades. John Hunt's son Jonathan married Dicey

Smith in 1792, giving her husband several children including Moses Park, who first appeared on poll tax rolls in 1816, indicating that he probably reached age twenty-one that year. Moses Park married Nancy Lee Overton, began operating a farm, and built a grist mill for the manufacture of cornmeal. Nancy gave him two sons, Sam Garrett Hunt and the future governor's great-grandfather, Moses James Hunt. One morning in 1827, Nancy and the boys noticed that the elder Moses failed to return for breakfast. They found him dead in the mill after his coat got caught in the gears of the mill and pulled his body through the cycle of wheels.[3]

To deal with such tragedies, Moses James Hunt adhered closely to the Bible. He became a circuit riding Methodist preacher while still farming on his Granville County land. By 1860, he made a profit producing wheat, Indian corn, and tobacco. The 1860 census listed him as owning two horses, three cows, ten hogs, and a carriage that he used to bring the faith to farmers, residing in their homes when visiting a rural community. The census indicated that he owned no slaves, even though leaders of his southern Methodist faith condoned slavery as an acceptable practice.[4]

The controversy over slavery led to the American Civil War and Reconstruction, and these eras had a deep impact on Moses Hunt. Land and property values rose briefly at the beginning of the war, only to decrease dramatically. Later on, Moses's brother Sam enlisted as a Confederate substitute at age fifty, and witnessed bloody carnage at Antietam, the battle that prompted Lincoln's Emancipation Proclamation. Captured in the Wilderness campaign on May 12, 1864, Sam later died in a Union prison in Maryland. To add to this tragedy, Moses' wife Jennie died from illness as Union troops entered North Carolina in 1865. During Reconstruction, Moses' Granville County farm continually decreased in value. Despite hardships, he married a woman who gave him more children, including James B. Hunt's grandfather William, born on February 7, 1869. Three years later, Moses sold his farm for a mere $425 to a neighbor and moved his family to Kernersville in central North Carolina to make the ministry his fulltime profession.[5]

Jim Hunt's grandfather, William Baker Hunt, worked as a contractor in Greensboro, teaching his father's values to his children, including James Baxter Hunt, Sr. William helped design the state's first women's college in Greensboro after the General Assembly approved funding for the project in 1891. He lived close to his brothers, Robert, a Methodist minister, and Joe, a plumbing contractor whose son later became a speaker of the state House of Representatives. Their father, Moses James, died in 1901 at the age of 77 while visiting them in Greensboro. William inherited his father's land in nearby Fentress, where he lived with his wife Mary

Leticia Ross Hunt, a fervent Methodist, until their move to nearby Pleasant Garden around 1920. He and Mary had seven children, including James Baxter, who learned to be a good Methodist, which included abstaining from alcohol.[6]

The family of James B. Hunt Jr.'s mother, Elsie Brame, first settled in the American colonies in the seventeenth century. She descended from John Brame, an English immigrant who moved to Christ's Church, Virginia, to escape Oliver Cromwell's Puritan dictatorship in 1657. Several generations later in the early nineteenth century, Elsie's grandfather Samuel Brame left Virginia to farm in Granville County in the North Carolina tobacco belt. Samuel's son, Charles Ernest Brame, born a year after the Civil War ended, moved west to Wilson County, named in the 1850s after Mexican American War hero Louis Wilson. With knowledge about tobacco farming, Charles taught the inexperienced farmers how to cure bright leaf tobacco. He became a highly regarded farmer, justice of the peace, church elder, and owner of an agricultural business at the "Brame home place." He lived profitably off the land that Elsie Brame Hunt inherited in the 1930s.[7]

Charles Brame eventually met James Thomas Renfrow, an affluent farmer and country store owner whose descendants had owned land in Wilson County for five generations. Charles got along well with "Tom," a man "so hospitable that he would take store customers home with him for lunch."[8] Charles also became acquainted with James's wife Celia and his five daughters Rebecca, Ellie, Senie, Euzelia, and Pollie Ann. He fell in love with Pollie Ann and married her on September 14, 1892 at the Marsh Swamp Free Will Baptist Church in Rock Ridge. "Miss Pollie" gave birth to Clarence, Edgar, Elsie, Paul, and Kermit Brame, all eventually to become graduates of Rock Ridge High School. As Pollie cared for the children, Charles served on the Wilson County Board of Education, sometimes driving with his daughter Elsie in a horse and buggy to attend the meetings in Wilson. From her father Charles, Elsie learned the importance of receiving a good education.[9]

After graduating from Rock Ridge High School in 1922, Elsie Brame decided to become a teacher. Despite existing prejudices against educating women, she went to college just like her brothers. In 1926, she received a teaching degree from the Woman's College at Greensboro, where she attended classes with Susie Sharp, who nearly fifty years later would administer the oath of office as governor to her son. After graduation, Elsie taught at Corinth-Holders High School in Johnston County, beginning a forty-year career with the North Carolina public school system. People described young Elsie as an extraordinarily kind person dedicated to the belief that education could strengthen the moral character of children from even the poorest families.[10]

As the nation entered the Great Depression, James B. Hunt courted Elsie Brame. In 1929, Elsie started teaching public school in Pleasant Garden, where William and Mary Hunt participated in the annual community meetings with the teachers. They often brought their son James Hunt, who in the early 1930s prepared for an agricultural education career at North Carolina State College. James and Elsie met at one of these meetings; she was 31 and he was 23, and they fell in love, even though thinking about their age difference made her feel uncomfortable. After James graduated with an agricultural degree in May 1934, he married Elsie at the Marsh Swamp Free Will Baptist Church. Afterwards, they lived with Hunt's parents while James worked for the United States Department of Agriculture (USDA).[11]

In his new federal job, James Hunt became an advocate of President Franklin Delano Roosevelt's New Deal programs transforming agricultural practices in the South. After the United States Supreme Court rejected the first Agricultural Adjustment Act, the president backed the Soil Conservation Service as a way to establish production limits. James transferred to that department and stayed for thirty years, helping to implement the federal tobacco program in North Carolina. He revered that effort, defending the program against criticism that federal subsidies benefited landowning farmers and wealthy warehouse owners while displacing predominantly African-American sharecroppers and other landless tenants.[12]

The year 1936 brought great changes to the family. The federal government ordered James to begin soil conservation work in Burlington, a textile-manufacturing center several miles east of Greensboro. Although the couple mourned the death of Elsie's father Charles, who succumbed to illness in July, they were elated in November when President Roosevelt was reelected in an overwhelming landslide over Republican candidate Alf Landon. By this time, Elsie discovered that she was expecting their first child. Because she believed that her older age meant a risky pregnancy, she approved a medical specialist to deliver her baby.[13]

On May 16, 1937, in a Greensboro hospital, Elsie gave birth to their first son whom she and James named after his father. In the first three years of the life of James Baxter Hunt, Jr., his father James moved the family to Shelby and Raleigh, where he lived near the governor's mansion. In that city in 1940, Elsie gave birth to their second son, Robert. The family then relocated to Wilson County, where James completed a house in 1941 on land that had belonged to the Renfrows for five generations. They lived near Elsie's relatives in Rock Ridge, a community named after a nineteenth-century school located near a ridge of stones. While James kept busy with soil conservation, Elsie taught English at the local high school and managed the school's library. Her mother, Pollie Ann Brame, a tiny, thin woman known to her grandson as "Miss Pollie," stayed with the Hunts. "When I was a boy," Hunt reflected later, "[she] lived in our house," and she was part of the Hunt family.[14]

Since the late nineteenth century, Rock Ridge had been a prosperous community from an intellectual as well as an economic standpoint. When the high school burned down in 1939, the community contributed generously to the creation of a new facility that seemed modern by the time Jimmy and Robert Hunt attended it in the early 1950s. The *Wilson Daily Times* declared the school in 1955 to be one of the most modern rural school buildings in the state. Renowned Hollywood actress Ava Gardner vouched for the seriousness of the Rock Ridge educators. They demanded that the future actress find room in her schedule for most of the subjects that she had skipped at an earlier high school

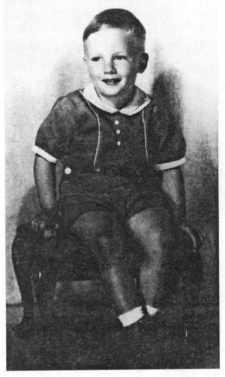

As a young child, Jimmy Hunt moved with his family from Greensboro to Raleigh to Rock Ridge, North Carolina. In Raleigh, he lived only a mile from the governor's mansion. The family moved to Rock Ridge partly to be near Hunt's mother's family. (Courtesy of the North Carolina Office of Archives and History)

in order to get her diploma. Hunt said of his own experience in Rock Ridge that education was "highly prized" and "my parents would make any sacrifice to help their children have it. I was always expected to go to college and to do my best."[15]

In Rock Ridge, James Baxter Hunt, Jr., nicknamed "Jimmy," learned how people cooperated for the common good. "The community has given me a sense of roots, a sense of belonging and of the goodness of neighbors that you can really depend on," he said. "That's important for stability, happiness and security."[16] His mother's family shared this spirit of mixing business with community service. Jimmy's uncle, Clarence Brame, managed the office at Banner Tobacco Warehouse, provided income tax return assistance to local farm families, co-founded both the local medical clinic and the electric company, and served two short stints as county commissioner. When he was not working on his tobacco farm, Uncle Kermit Brame served on the board of deacons at the Marsh Swamp Free Will Baptist Church. In Jimmy's own household, his father advised the local farmers on soil matters and the tobacco quota allotment system. Robert Hunt, Jimmy's brother, who later became a social worker and aided Vietnam War veterans and psychiatric patients in Virginia and North Carolina, said that his parents stressed public service as the only honorable way to pursue life. "We grew up thinking somehow that just making money was not honorable," he said.[17]

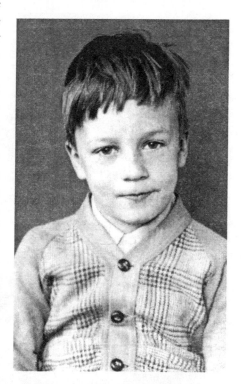

Like the Brames, the Hunts remained active in many organizations. Robert recalled that his father went to a meeting almost every night. Realizing the absence of politically organized farmers, James helped a Goldsboro legislator create the Wilson County Grange chapter in 1943. Later, he and his wife developed Grange clubs in the Wilson County communities of Saratoga, Elm City, Lucama, and Gardners. As a Grange deputy, James visited meetings across the county, using his color slides to describe how best to preserve the soil. His various roles included service as assistant chaplain and chairman of the rural electrification, transportation, and communications committees. The Grange often commended James B. Hunt, Sr., for improving irrigation by getting water holes and farm ponds dug, working to secure tobacco allotments, and helping small farmers cultivate more acreage. The father often took his son Jimmy to Grange meetings

Jimmy Hunt began first grade in Rock Ridge with the benefit of a father, James B. Hunt, Sr., who demanded excellence, and a mother, Elsie Brame Hunt, who prized education. This is Hunt's first-grade photograph. (Courtesy of the North Carolina Office of Archives and History)

where the six-year-old would fall asleep listening to tobacco farmers declare how President Franklin Roosevelt and the federal government had saved them from financial ruin. Jimmy and Robert later served as officers in the Grange Youth. "The Hunts were never ones to just sit around and talk," Jim Hunt recalled. "We were ones to get involved and change things." Inspired by his family, the future governor joined numerous activities as a youth.[18]

During World War II, when German prisoners picked tobacco in Wilson County, Jimmy Hunt participated in childish pursuits. He was too young to remember Governor Clyde Hoey, who backed the first free textbooks for elementary schools in 1939, or Governor Melville Broughton, who created a retirement plan for teachers and state employees, equalized the salaries of black and white teachers, and extended the public school year to nine months. He did, however, remember the blackouts when everyone had their lights off and people got excited about a plane crossing in the sky. He recalled the day he heard the local WPTF radio station announce the death of President Roosevelt, an event which caused his mother to sob. He had happier war memories like riding his shaggy-haired pony Birdie over the dirt paths and roads near his home.[19]

Jim Hunt used to ride his pony Birdie on the Hunt farm in Rock Ridge. As a young boy, he wanted to be a cowboy. (Courtesy of the North Carolina Office of Archives and History)

Jimmy learned about religious values from the Marsh Swamp Free Will Baptist Church. His family had attended Methodist churches in Burlington and Raleigh, but because he liked the congregation, James accepted membership in Elsie's family church, despite the protest of his Methodist mother. At Marsh Swamp, James served as superintendent of the Sunday school, demanding his son Jimmy and other students learn Bible verses by repeating them. Once a year, James told the congregation why God expected farmers to take care of the soil. His sons Jimmy and Robert participated in many Marsh Swamp activities, including the planting of shrubbery behind the church.[20]

Jim Hunt later described the Free Will Baptists as being divided between "foot washing" fundamentalists and "education-minded" evangelists. The Hunts allied with the Reverend R. L. Johnson and the evangelists to keep the fundamentalists from controlling the church. Such divisions did not hurt the faith of Jimmy Hunt, who accepted a premise that all Free Will Baptists agreed upon: people had a choice between heaven and hell if they resisted temptation. Jim Hunt recalled, "We took the free will seriously."[21] One Sunday, Jimmy answered a call to be saved and came down the aisle to announce he was giving his life to Jesus. The minister later baptized Jimmy in a farm pond. Hunt described his religious beliefs as an idea that "God expects obedience and that there is punishment," but the "essence of God is love."[22]

Being a good Christian meant working hard at the dairy and tobacco farm in Rock Ridge. "I grew up milking cows," Hunt said. "In the summer, we'd harvest tobacco all day long and milk the cows again at night. We'd get about four hours sleep and then we'd get up and do it all over again."[23] Jimmy's father expected him to work hard to get the tobacco to market. Jimmy learned how to plant the bed, disk, and harrow the soil in the first three months of the year, pull plants in April, hoe in May, cultivate in June, top and sucker in July, harvest and cure in August, and finally sell the tobacco in September and October. His cousin, Carl Henley, said that Uncle James Hunt was a slave driver who would swat him and Jimmy on the rear end if the two boys overslept on a working day.[24]

The tobacco-growing Hunts discouraged youthful smoking. Long before the Surgeon General's report warned of the dangers regarding cigarettes, many thought smoking made youths appear morally bankrupt. Because he and his brother Robert refrained from smoking, they won the price of a pack and a half of cigarettes weekly to be used for vacation and travel. James Hunt also promised his son Jimmy a $1,000 life insurance policy on his sixteenth birthday if he did not smoke. The Hunts also disapproved of alcohol. "The only time I ever drank was as a high school senior in 1955 on a trip to a college basketball tournament," he once told a reporter. "Some friends were drinking beer. I had one taste. It just tasted bad. I never had any problem with [drinking] after that."[25] As for courting young women, Hunt's future stepmother, Pearl Johnson Hunt, recalled James telling his sons to "be good. Always remember who you are."[26]

Elsie Hunt also strongly influenced her son Jimmy. As a teacher at Rock Ridge High School, she took the toughest and most troublesome kids who failed English, brought them over to her house, and tutored them on her own time. "Toughest guys in the school," Jim Hunt recalled. "And they learned."[27] Elsie encouraged her sons to do their homework after sports practice and pursue an intellectual life by reading history and literature.

The Hunt brothers had a typical sibling relationship mixed with love and quarrels. "We fought all the time when we were kids," Robert Hunt recalled. "I thought he picked on me."[28] At other times, Jim treated his brother well; as scouts at a camp, Jimmy let his younger brother stay in his tent on rainy nights. Sometimes a thorn in the side, Robert argued with his older brother over use of the family car. If Jimmy did much to please his father, Robert often rebelled against the competitive ethic by not working as hard. "I did not try as hard academically because I could not measure up to this guy that attained so much," he said.[29] While his father loved him, the younger brother recalled, he worshipped his son Jimmy.

Jim Hunt and his brother Robert, pictured here in 1945, had a typical sibling relationship that mixed brotherly love with occasional quarrels. Robert never tried to imitate the great success of his brother, yet he also became a public servant, working in veterans' hospitals. Like his brother, Robert Hunt was encouraged by his parents to make a career that went beyond making money. (Courtesy of the North Carolina Office of Archives and History)

The older boy liked to be around his cousin, Carl Henley, the son of James's sister Mary Hunt Henley and her husband Herbert C. Henley, Sr., of Chatham County. Besides hunting squirrels together, Carl worked strenuously with Jimmy in the tobacco fields, including times when James paid them a dime every time they picked 100 "pitter" weeds. Carl remembered one freezing Christmas day when James bet Jimmy and Carl that they would not go naked into the Hunt pond. After the boys stripped off their clothes and went into the chilly water, the father snatched their clothes and locked them out of the house, causing them to run naked in the cold; Jimmy's mother, Elsie, let them in.[30]

It took time for Jimmy to share his father's passion for politics. James B. Hunt, Sr., might have run for office had it not been for two factors—his outspokenness, which would have cost him votes, and his adherence to the Hatch Act, which prohibited federal employees from participating in political campaigns. "I tell folks that if I did my politics, it had to be under the shade tree (rather) than in a public meeting," he said.[31] James often used the Grange as a way to challenge "the machine," the politicians who came to power with Governor O. Max Gardner and who backed the businessmen over the small farmers. Political scientist V. O. Key studied these men and wrote about the state's "progressive plutocracy" in his 1949 book, *Southern Politics in State and Nation*. He concluded:

> The state is run largely by lawyers. While many of its governors may have been stodgy or conservative, they have never been scoundrels or nincompoops. It would be inaccurate to portray a direct line of authority, or even of communication, from the skyscraper offices of industrial magnates to the state capitol. It would be inaccurate to suggest that North Carolina's top politicians and policy makers have been other than generally independent, conscientious citizens in execution of their charges. The effectiveness of the oligarchy's control has been achieved through the elevation to office of persons fundamentally in harmony with its viewpoint. Its interests, which are often the interests of the state, are served without prompting.[32]

A year before Key published his study, Kerr Scott, a farmer without legal experience, broke the power of the machine's progressive plutocracy. The Haw River native graduated from North Carolina State College where he had roomed with Elsie's older brother, Clarence Brame. Serving as master of the state Grange, Scott defeated a conservative incumbent in the 1936 race for Secretary of Agriculture. Twelve years later, he stunned observers by defeating the machine's candidate in the Democratic gubernatorial primary. "The race went into a runoff," Hunt recalled, "and we remember the happy smiles of the farmers we saw the night that the election returns came in."[33] James and Elsie cheered when Scott and President Harry S. Truman triumphed in November 1948. Despite his Democratic background, Jimmy Hunt liked Republican presidential candidate Thomas

Dewey after reading a comic book portraying the New York governor as a heroic crime fighter. Jimmy recalled being shocked that his parents strongly backed Truman. Eventually, Jimmy shared his father's view that every major reform for the good of the common man came from the Democratic party.[34]

As governor, the "Squire of Haw River" created his own progressive plutocracy, inspiring future governors Terry Sanford, James B. Hunt, and his son Robert Scott. Kerr Scott persuaded the state to back secondary road construction and the repair of school buildings. He voiced support for organized labor in a right-to-work state and became the first Tar Heel governor since William Holden to prosecute the Ku Klux Klan. James Hunt Sr., did all he could for Kerr Scott, promoting road bonds at the legislature and urging farmers to vote for the referendum. His son Jimmy recalled the cries of Wilson "town folks"[35] against the funding of the rural roads. "Those of us who lived in the country started going to town to buy, rather than just down to the country store,"[36] Jimmy Hunt wrote years later. Eventually, the town merchants realized that they benefited the most from the new roads.

Jim Hunt credited the "Squire of Haw River" with improving living conditions in North Carolina. The gravel road near the Hunt farm had ruts so deep that cars got stuck in the winter and dust made travel unbearable in the summer. "To get your road paved was the most important thing in your life," Hunt recalled.[37] One day in 1950, Jimmy watched a machine spread hot concrete over the gravel. "It's a scene I'll never forget," he said. "It burned into my memory."[38] Kerr Scott paved his road, which added to Jimmy's sense that Scott represented the best type of political leader. No one owned him; his only allegiance was to the people. Scott promised he would bring rural North Carolinians electric lights, telephones, and paved roads—and he delivered, allowing Jimmy's aunt in Chatham County to live in the modern age. Kerr Scott proved that the state government could directly improve the lives of the citizens.[39]

The Hunt family's efforts on behalf of the governor increased their bond with the Scotts. Robert Scott, son of the governor, recalled meeting young Jimmy long before either one of them got into politics. He remembered each boy worked hard on the farm, served actively in the Grange, and prized education since their mothers taught school. Governor Scott's greatest favor to the Hunts came on May 7, 1949, when he appointed Elsie Brame Hunt as the first female member of the North Carolina Board of Health. In an article with a banner headline, the Wilson Daily Times reporter described Elsie as an active member of the state Grange who had a lifetime "A" grade teaching certificate and did "outstanding" work for the Home Demonstration clubs. "The mother of two boys," the *Times* said, "Jimmy, aged 12, and Robert, aged nine, Mrs. Hunt was the founder of five of the six Grange groups in Wilson County."[40] The local health director said he could "think of no finer or better citizen, with the welfare of the state of North Carolina in their heart," than Mrs. Hunt, who was "well qualified" for the position.[41]

Scott also won the praise of the Hunts by appointing UNC President Frank Porter Graham to a United States Senate seat, although this event led to a 1950 senate race that highlighted the limits of North Carolina progressivism. The state's few liberals adored Senator Graham for his commitment to better wages for workers and better treatment for African Americans. When Raleigh attorney Willis Smith challenged Graham for the Democratic nomination in 1950, Jesse Helms and other conservatives attacked the senator for his alleged softness on segregation and communism. Jimmy's mother Elsie cried after Graham lost in the runoff primary.[42]

By that time, Jimmy Hunt, influenced by his competitive father, had already won numerous agricultural contests. While still in grade school, he won his first medal in a county contest involving dairy calves. "I had the only dairy calf project, so naturally I won," Hunt Jr., recalled.[43] He said James taught him to be a fighter, "to fight for what was right, particularly for the farmer. I've seen him stand up in meetings when a lot of other people were saying, 'Play it safe and don't antagonize the big companies.'"[44] James desired to compete, and his son emulated that trait. Robert Hunt recalled that Jimmy received a wonderful blend of personality traits from an assertive father and a kind mother.[45]

Receiving academic skills from his mother and leadership skills from his father, Jimmy Hunt became a marvelous high school student. He mastered public speaking, parliamentary procedure, livestock judging, shop, and welding. One teacher had the young sophomore moved up a grade in one class because, he said, "he is teaching my class for me. I can't teach him; he knows more than I do."[46] James, Sr., recalled that Jimmy moved into a senior class and "that lil' ole young'un had to stretch up to those seniors,"[47] meaning that he worked hard to compete academically with older students. Jimmy spent time after school practicing speeches while riding a tractor and while milking cows. Once a passerby thought Jimmy was talking to the cows, but he was just rehearsing a speech.[48]

The Hunts credited Jimmy's agricultural teacher Dewey Sheffield with their son's academic success. Born in Moore County in 1899, Sheffield served as a principal at a farm-life academy after graduating from North Carolina State College. In 1934, he arrived at Rock Ridge High School to begin its first vocational agricultural department. Sheffield introduced hybrid corn, registered hogs, commercial orchards, purebred poultry, and permanent pastures to the community. Every year that he served as a teacher, the school won Future Farmers of America (FFA) contests. Jim Hunt, Jr., later called him a no-nonsense, "get-the-job-done" champion of the Grange and the local Democratic party, who aided small farmers whenever they needed to castrate pigs, dehorn cattle, or select improved crops. "Everybody followed him," James Hunt, Sr., remembered.[49] Hunt, Jr., remembered Sheffield winning the attention of even the most uninterested students, including two illiterate twins who loved to hunt deer and bears. Sheffield talked about hunting first to grab their attention, and then proceeded to teach his subject matter. The Hunts admired the teacher greatly. When Sheffield died in 1982, James, Sr., credited Sheffield with the training that allowed his son to become governor.[50]

In 1953 and 1954, Rock Ridge High School students elected Jimmy Hunt, Jr., junior and senior class president, respectively, which some observers later believed indicated Hunt's desire for future political office. His political opponents later claimed that Hunt had wanted to run for governor since high school, or even earlier; therefore, his ambition overrode everything. Hunt denied that he ever considered running for the state's highest office before attending college, reminding people that the class presidency carried no administrative duties. However, Carl Henley claimed that Jimmy, as a teenager, told him that he wanted to be governor, an idea that made his cousin laugh hysterically.[51]

As class president, Jimmy had no student government to run, so he had time to serve as football quarterback, captain of the basketball team, yearbook editor, and class valedictorian. He played the trumpet in the school's growing band of thirty-six musicians under Sam Keen, who had the students in the 1955 annual concert play "The Rambling Wreck from Georgia Tech," Hank Williams's "Hey Good Looking," and a tribute to bandleader Glenn Miller. In his senior year, Jimmy portrayed Sir Robert Laurie of Maxwellton in Rock Ridge's production of "Annie Laurie," using his home to entertain the actors and actresses with dancing and refreshments after the play. He also served as editor-in-chief of *The Pebble*, the high school yearbook, which said in the caption beside his photograph, "The more a man knows, the more he is worth."[52]

During his high school years, Jimmy also participated successfully in several competitions. He won the FFA's annual Tobacco Federation speaking contest for Wilson and Greene counties with an essay describing how tobacco price supports aided the public welfare. Naming cows after his girlfriends (which caused a commotion at the Wilson County Fair when a

cow named after an ex-girl-
friend defeated a cow named
after his then-current girlfriend) and political heroes
(including agrarian advocates
Kerr Scott and United States
Senator Hubert Humphrey of
Minnesota), he entered them
into statewide contests and
won. Jimmy also won elec-
tion to many club offices,
including the presidency of
the Youth Grange and governor of the 1954 Boys State
convention at the University
of North Carolina. Claiming
later to be unenlightened
politically before attending
the Boys State meetings, he
learned the effectiveness of
parties from a speech by
North Carolina Agricultural
Secretary Thad Eure, whose

long government service
made him one of the best
experts on state politics. By
his senior year, Jimmy won
the presidency of the state
FFA and earned the National
FFA American Farm Degree.[53]

Jim Hunt, pictured here playing the violin in
1948, participated in many activities. At Rock
Ridge High School, he belonged to the band.
He also acted in plays, served in the Future
Farmers of America, edited the school year-
book, served as high school president, and
played on the football and basketball teams.
(Courtesy of the North Carolina Office of
Archives and History)

Only in athletics did
Jimmy not fulfill his dreams.
He did not have the physique for a career in football. He wanted to join
Everett Case's basketball team at North Carolina State College, express-
ing his desire in a winning national Juvenile Grange essay about how he
planned to play basketball with the Wolfpack. "I was as committed to basketball as anything in the world," Hunt recalled. "I ate and drank it."[54]
Jimmy often did well as both an offensive and defensive player. After one
good showing, the town rewarded the team with a free barbecue meal at
Parker's Restaurant. However, Jimmy never made the all-conference high
school team and he never tried out for the basketball squad at North

Carolina State College, realizing that the Wolfpack players were "out of my league."[55]

His basketball and football coach, Onnie Cockerell, remembered one incident about Hunt that revealed much about his character. When Rock Ridge High School played its main rival, Lucama High School, Jimmy asked at halftime for the scorekeeper to tell him how many fouls each player had. The scorekeeper said Hunt had two fouls. Jimmy came up to the coach and said, "Coach, they got me wrong. I have three fouls."[56] Cockerell was amazed that Jimmy would admit this fact. "I don't remember whether he fouled out," Cockerell recalled, "and I don't remember who won the game. But I'll never forget that boy standing up and saying he had three fouls."[57] Cockerell understood that his fierce drive to win came with a spirit of good sportsmanship.

Jim Hunt graduated from Rock Ridge High School in 1955. He excelled in all his classes, especially parliamentary procedure and public speaking. Hunt was the class valedictorian and is pictured here with the Leon B. Taylor Scholarship award. (Courtesy of the North Carolina Office of Archives and History)

Hunt graduated from Rock Ridge High School in June 1955 after listening to the head of East Carolina College's education department demand that students fight intellectual laziness. "Nobody's going to put a trained mind in your back pocket," commencement speaker J. K. Long said. "That is something you will have to strive for and acquire yourselves."[58] After the speech, the high school principal handed Jimmy Hunt the Leon B. Taylor Scholarship award for his scholastic average during four years of high school. He was also recognized as Rock Ridge High School's outstanding vocational agricultural student. At age eighteen, he appeared to have a great future ahead of him.[59]

By 1955, James B. Hunt, Jr., possessed many qualities for future success. He owed much of his traits to his mother Elsie

Brame Hunt, who taught him to use education as the best way to improve himself. However, the son mainly imitated his father James Hunt, Sr., who adhered to strict personal moral standards passed down through two generations from his grandfather Moses James Hunt. James expected Jimmy to be a tough competitor, a hard worker, a pious Christian, a farmer's advocate, and a progressive Democrat. The son used all of these roles in later life to become the most dominant North Carolina politician of the late twentieth century.

3

The Political Education
of Jim Hunt

Jim Hunt learned much about politics as a student at North Carolina State College (NCSC). He earned two degrees from the college, becoming a leading expert on the federal tobacco program by the time that he completed his masters degree in 1962. Yet, an informal political education overshadowed his agricultural education. He participated in many political activities, making invaluable contacts in the Young Democratic clubs and the State College student government. Hunt served an unprecedented two years as student body president, giving him experience in initiating legislation, meeting with constituencies, and practicing leadership skills. Most importantly, he used his education at the state's capital to acquire a good understanding of the nature of North Carolina politics.

In 1955, Jimmy Hunt decided to follow his father's example and attend NCSC as an agricultural major. Visiting the campus several times as a boy, the Rock Ridge native recalled "always wanting to go to State."[1] An avid "Wolfpacker," Jimmy went with his father to State football games and the Dixie Classic basketball tournament. He listened on the radio to nearly every basketball and football game, knowing "all the players, all the statistics."[2] His fervor for the college and its 4,000-member student body was apparent almost from the moment of his enrollment.[3]

Jimmy Hunt planned to use his education to become a successful dairy farmer. To earn money to buy Holsteins, he worked in the summers for the United States Department of Agriculture measuring federal tobacco allotments. To help his son get a farm, James Hunt, Sr., advertised for "the worst, eroded farm within fifty miles of Raleigh with no tobacco acreage."[4] The father spent $8,000 on land in Clayton, where he planned to develop

32

the soil for the dairy farm of his oldest son, who planned to major in agricultural science.

Before he arrived at North Carolina State College, Jimmy knew whom he wanted to marry. In high school, he had attended the national Grange Youth Conference in Hamilton, Ohio, where he met Carolyn Joyce Leonard of Mingo, Iowa, a youth committee leader. Carolyn came from a corn-and-beef farm family who expected the future Equal Rights Amendment advocate not only to bake pies and dress chickens, but to shell corn, drive a tractor, wring chicken necks, and do whatever else needed to be done on the farm. Carolyn was impressed by Jimmy. "He seemed to have a lot of goals," she recalled. "He knew that he wanted this degree in this, and that degree in that, because he thought someday he might run for political office."[5]

Jim Hunt, pictured with this cow, originally desired to be a dairy farmer. Jimmy's father bought land in Clayton for his son. At North Carolina State College, Hunt turned away from this goal and turned his attention toward agricultural economics and state politics. (Courtesy of the North Carolina Office of Archives and History)

When Jimmy said that he would write to her, she thought she might have to wait weeks. His first letter arrived three days later. His brother Robert remembered Jimmy's returning home and telling his mother that he had met the "sweetest, cutest and prettiest girl" with beautiful brown eyes and a beautiful light blue camel-haired coat. His father James Hunt and his cousin Carl Henley recalled Jimmy saying that he had met his future wife.[6]

In his first two years of undergraduate education at North Carolina State, Jimmy, dressed in a good suit in order to get rides, hitchhiked to

Iowa, often traveling thirty-six hours one way to see Carolyn. He took many safety precautions when he hitchhiked. "I had it down to a fine science," he said. "I would sleep in a car once I was satisfied (that) the driver was safe,"[7] although he would never tell drivers about the switchblade that he carried in his pocket for self-defense. Jimmy once arrived in Iowa so tired that when he joined the Leonards at church, he fell asleep in the middle of the front pew. The Leonards forgave him for that embarrassing incident because they found him generally to be congenial company. During one winter visit, he offered to shell corn outside with the Leonards. "It was cold as could be," Carolyn's brother Gene Leonard recalled. "He never got warm the whole time he was here."[8]

Jimmy entered NCSC when the college enrolled only white students. The freshman approved of the segregation of the state university system as best for both races, and opposed the 1954 United States Supreme Court decision *Brown vs. Board of Education* that supported public school integration. In his 1955 senior paper, Jimmy was the only Rock Ridge High School student to write about the subject of integration, arguing for the fairness of separate and equal education for the two races. While he did not support integration in 1955 (as some later biographical accounts inaccurately reported), he stressed equality within segregated institutions. He never perceived segregation to be bad for African Americans, whom his parents taught him to treat kindly. "You don't mistreat people," Hunt learned from James and Elsie. "You don't hurt people. You help people and give them a fair chance."[9] The Hunts helped any African American who came to their door seeking food or other assistance. James, Sr., once got angry at a local tobacco farmer who mistreated his black tenants. Jimmy remembered growing up in a family where "you get a whipping if you used the word 'nigger'."[10] Robert Hunt recalled using that derogatory word once. His mother Elsie jerked him into their house and lectured him about the era of slavery, when children were separated from their mothers and never saw them again. "She had me crying," Robert said. "I'm sure she did the same with my brother."[11]

Despite their kindness toward African Americans, the Hunts accepted segregation as the correct way to handle the southern race question and approved of North Carolina Governor Luther Hodges's efforts to circumvent the *Brown* decision. While the governor did not call for people to disobey the court decision, he practiced what historian William Chafe called the "guise of moderation" to fight integration. He backed the Pearsall Plan, which authorized expenditures of state money to any white student threatened with integration who wished to attend a private school. To the disgust of the National Association for the Advancement of Colored People

(NAACP), the Supreme Court approved this "voluntary segregation" plan, leaving most of the state's school systems segregated in the 1960s. A Little Rock, Arkansas, school official wrote, "You North Carolinians have devised one of the cleverest techniques for perpetuating segregation that we have seen."[12] Such efforts made Hodges popular in North Carolina. The former lieutenant governor assumed the high office following the death of Governor William Umstead in 1954 and was elected to a full term in 1956. Hodges also won praise for backing improvements in higher education and charitable institutions, and for establishing the Research Triangle Park in the Raleigh-Durham area to recruit technical industry into the state. Because of these efforts, Governor Hodges could claim to be progressive on industrial recruitment while challenging *Brown* at the same time.[13]

As Hodges dealt with those matters, Jimmy Hunt attended North Carolina State College. In his freshman year, he lived on the first floor of Syme dormitory with Bill Sharp and Joe Hamrick, who remembered Hunt wearing dungarees and a FFA jacket as he dashed off to join student committees. However, if Joe wanted to sit down and talk with Jimmy, he was always available. "He had a lot of things he was interested in," Hamrick recalled. "But he didn't want to offend anybody. He wanted to be a good roommate. He wanted our relationship to serve a purpose."[14] Jimmy's friend Phil Carlton recalled that the Rock Ridge native did not get caught up in the "social whirl," abstaining from alcohol and remaining faithful to his girlfriend Carolyn in Iowa. Instead, Jimmy and his friends favored entertainment like attending Wolfpack sporting events and eating downtown at Red Ballantine's, the S&W Cafeteria, or Gino's. Carlton said that Hunt wore a coat and a tie nearly every day, and sometimes he had an old-fashioned hat and a briefcase. Jimmy may have looked strange to some students, but his friends understood that the appearance revealed his serious demeanor.[15]

Professor V. A. Rice's introductory agricultural class intrigued Jimmy in his first semester. Jimmy recalled that Rice was a short, stocky man who wore a mustache, kept his tie comfortably loosened, and spoke with a "Yankee" accent. The professor had served as an agricultural school dean at the University of Massachusetts for several years before teaching at State College. Rice seemed so removed from rural North Carolina traditions that Jimmy wondered if he was an atheist, since "we knew darn well he was an integrationist!"[16] Although North Carolina State College called his class "Introduction to Agriculture," students nicknamed the course "Introduction to the Future of the World." Rice used his classroom as a forum to connect agriculture with the world's problems by asking "really stumping" questions. The professor predicted that natural resources would dry up and the world might revert to an agrarian culture for millions of years. To prevent such a disaster, Rice said, civilization needed a world federation to manage all natural resources. If Hunt disagreed with Rice's assessment, he appreciated the professor for making him understand how economics and politics were intertwined.[17]

In his sophomore year, Jimmy roomed at Syme with his cousin Carl Henley and discovered that the two of them had entirely different values. Although Jimmy and Carl disobeyed dormitory rules by secretly heating the Hunt farm's popcorn seeds in an electric popper, Jimmy drew the line at further violations. While Carl and his friends went out to "get plastered on Friday night," Jimmy refused.[18] Instead, Jimmy joined several activities including the Athletic Council, the Agricultural Club, the Publications Board, and *The Agriculturalist,* the agricultural department's student journal. After one day of busy activities, Jimmy turned on the lights and the television in his dorm room at 11:00 p.m. as Carl attempted to sleep. Angrily, Carl shoved his cousin Jimmy into the closet. While they later made up, it was clear that Jimmy Hunt sought a more serious life than his fun-loving cousin.[19]

As an *Agriculturalist* writer, Jimmy dedicated himself to calling for an end to the continuing decline of the American agricultural community. In his editorials, he called for North Carolina farmers to "wake up" and "join our farm organizations and stand together"[20] against better organized business and labor organizations. He endorsed the establishment of a NCSC Grange, and called for farmers to hire public relations firms to inform the public of the agrarian viewpoint. Jimmy condemned difficult entrance exams that potentially drained the Agricultural Department of rural boys who wanted to go to State College. He also argued that young men should continue to major in agriculture despite the fear that they could not break into farming without inherited land. He predicted mass population increases would make it necessary for every farmer in the world to produce the maximum just to feed "the teeming billions"[21] around the world. Mainly, he wanted farmers to cooperate with each other for political ends, just as he witnessed agrarians united in his hometown of Rock Ridge. "Whenever one man had a barn to raise or a crib of corn to shuck, he called in his neighbors for their help and cooperation," he wrote. "He, in turn, later helped them with some of their work. They found that working as a group at their various takes, they could accomplish a great deal more than they ever could have as individuals."[22]

Jimmy continued to participate in Grange activities, winning election as state FFA president. In 1956, he attended the national FFA convention in Kansas City, where he received his American Farmer Degree and made an unsuccessful bid for the national FFA presidency. After losing the election, Jimmy thought about running again for FFA president the following year. By that time, however, he was preoccupied with NCSC student politics. In his sophomore year, agricultural majors elected him to the student legislature. Since he knew so much about parliamentary procedure, he won the chairmanship to the rules committee. Even though his cousin Carl Henley said that Hunt decided on a political career during his high school years, Hunt claimed that he first considered public service as a future goal after participating in NCSC campus politics.[23]

As a student at North Carolina State College, Jimmy Hunt served as editor of the *Agriculturalist*. He encouraged students to pursue farming as a career and urged agrarians to organize to defend their interests. (Courtesy of North Carolina State University Archives)

Jimmy Hunt became a diligent student legislator. Taking his student government duties seriously, he recommended that the student newspaper, the *Technician*, publish the names of absentee committeemen. He appeared more lenient toward student absenteeism, authoring a resolution that condemned the university's new cut-system allowing students to have personal absences only because of a death in the immediate family. In the spring of 1957, Jimmy ran for student body vice-president, promising a "willingness and ability to coordinate a progressive, efficiently operated student government legislature—a legislature working for you."[24] He easily defeated industrial engineering major Bob Harris by a thousand votes.

Good fortune occurred to Jimmy at the beginning of his junior year. Encouraged by her boyfriend Jimmy, Carolyn Leonard moved to Raleigh where she worked in the textile laboratory, took courses at NCSC, and rented a room on St. Mary's Street. As Jimmy Hunt settled into his roles as student vice-president and editor of the *Agriculturalist*, Student Body

President Fred Houtz dropped out of college by failing to meet academic requirements. A startled vice-president asked for the "the cooperation of all in undertaking the responsibilities of the presidency." In his junior year, Jimmy suddenly occupied the most important office in student government.[25]

Acting Student Government President Jimmy Hunt realized that he had to win over many people — especially the seniors — who did not appreciate a junior in the role as State's most prominent student leader. The serious-minded president worked with Houtz's appointments, including two students who did not feel accountable to Hunt. After Hunt experienced a hard time getting them to fulfill his objectives, he removed them. "You had to make sure the people who worked with you and served you were loyal," he said.[26] In Jimmy's second month in the new role, the *Technician* blasted him for opposing a motion to allow a senior class committee to decide on the diploma design. Editor David Barnhardt said that Hunt "could not have possibly represented the students,"[27] because unlike the senior class president, he made no effort to find out their views. Hunt learned from his error and became known for demanding that NCSC student legislators meet with their constituencies.

By the end of 1957, Hunt had established strong control over the student government with the help of his student allies. From his bad experience with the Houtz-appointed students, Jimmy understood that he had to have a loyal team to carry out his goals. He enlisted agricultural majors who shared his loyalty to the Future Farmers of America and the progressive wing of the Democratic party. They included Eddie Knox, Phil Carlton, and Tom Gilmore, all of whom played important roles when Hunt became the North Carolina Democratic party leader in the 1970s.

Eddie Knox helped Student Government President Hunt. Reared in Davidson, a small town twenty miles from Charlotte, Eddie knew as much about farming as Hunt. Knox and his nine siblings had planted cotton and vegetables, and had raised cattle and pigs on their father's farm. In high school, he had become president of North High School's FFA chapter, and had attended FFA meetings where he had first encountered Jimmy Hunt. The same age as Jimmy, Knox had spent his eighteenth year taking care of the Davidson farm because his father had died before he was to enter State College. He entered the college a year later and decided to join the agricultural majors involved in politics. While Hunt attended North Carolina State as an undergraduate, Knox served as vice-president of his freshman class, president of the sophomores, and student body vice president. The year after Jimmy graduated, students elected Knox the NCSC student government president. Like Jimmy, Eddie Knox belonged to three major

Jim Hunt (standing, first on left) served in several organizations as student body president of North Carolina State College, including the consolidated university student council, pictured here. His closest allies were Phil Carlton (standing, fourth from right), Tom Gilmore (standing, third from right), and Eddie Knox (sitting, first on right.) With their help, President Hunt ran the student government for two years. (Courtesy of North Carolina State University Archives)

honor fraternities and chaired delegations to national student conventions. He also shared some of Jimmy's concerns about ending poverty in North Carolina. "We thought we were going to change the world," Knox recalled.[28]

Phil Carlton also joined this group of young student politicians in charge of student government. Born in 1938 and reared by a wealthy tobacco farm family in Pinetops, about twenty-five miles north of Rock Ridge, he had attended South Edgecombe High School where students elected him student body president. Carlton served in FFA competitions where, like Knox, he had first encountered Jimmy Hunt. When the Pinetops native entered State College, Jimmy persuaded him to enter student politics. Carlton won elections as freshman representative and student senator, serving as the welfare committee chairman, student government secretary, and chairman of a special committee dealing with student fees. He shared Hunt's interest in politics, visiting the legislature, attending Young Democratic Club (YDC) meetings, and meeting with North Carolina Governor Luther Hodges about student legislative matters.[29]

Hunt also had the loyal support of Tom Gilmore, a native of Julian, North Carolina, near Greensboro. As the son of a tree nursery owner, Gilmore had spent his early life growing trees, picking tobacco, and raising chickens. Receiving an appointment to West Point upon his graduation from high school in 1955, he had decided that he would rather study agricultural science at NCSC. He and Jimmy Hunt became good friends, serving together in the student government, on the *Agriculturalist*, and in the North Carolina Student Legislature (NCSL), a statewide student legislative assembly that participated in mock debates on subjects such as school integration, state fiscal policy, and the gubernatorial veto. In the NCSL, Gilmore defended gubernatorial succession in North Carolina, an issue that the Julian native introduced in the state House twenty years later as a legislator supporting Governor Hunt's right to a second term. Hunt and Gilmore also cooperated as College Young Democrats. After the NCSC Young Democrats elected Gilmore as its president, he relied on its vice president, Hunt, to turn the club into the most successful in the state, winning the O. Max Gardner Award for the largest increase in college memberships.[30]

Many observers were not surprised that Jimmy Hunt, Tom Gilmore, Phil Carlton, and Eddie Knox played prominent political roles in North Carolina twenty years later. Hunt's former North Carolina State College political science professor recalled that these agricultural students virtually ran the student government.[31] They did such a good job that Jimmy Hunt boasted that the trustees thought that the State students were a more mature group than the student governments at Duke or the University of North Carolina (UNC). William Friday, the former president of the university system, later said of them, "You knew they were going to be leaders of the state."[32]

After a rough start, Jimmy's service as student government president improved. In the spring of 1958, he announced that he would run for the office that he had assumed the previous semester. He promised to pave the sidewalks on campus, supported pre-registration to curtail registration lines, backed freshman student parking privileges, promoted more student representation within the College Union administration, and favored cheap date tickets to athletic events. He ran against George Thomason, an older Army veteran promoted by his friends as the sophisticated candidate who did not make false promises. Hunt's friends called Jimmy "a wonderful Christian" and "conscientious worker" who had the experience for the job.[33]

As Jimmy Hunt sought reelection in April 1958, he learned of the death of his political hero Kerr Scott, a graduate of North Carolina State College who had championed rural road building as governor in the early 1950s and had supported tobacco interests as a United States Senator in 1954. Hunt's family attended the funeral. "As we traveled up to Haw River on that beautiful morning that they laid him to rest, it seemed that a little part of our own heart and spirit were gone," Hunt wrote in the *Agriculturalist*. "North Carolina, and farmers in particular, will miss him."[34] Hunt lost his greatest political role model, a farmer-politician with a State College agricultural degree who fought for progressive reforms. The late senator's success proved that a farmer could triumph over the lawyers produced by the University of North Carolina, and so Hunt remained in agricultural education — until 1961, when UNC law school graduate Terry Sanford became his new political hero.

On April 23, 1958, Hunt defeated Thomason by more than a thousand votes, 1,645 to 455. In a written statement, he announced to fellow students that he was finally *"your* president."[35] Bolstered by this victory, he achieved changes in the college constitution in the final month of his acting presidency that allowed for an honor code board and a men's campus code board, completing a process of transferring disciplinary functions from the faculty to the students.[36]

During the summer recess in 1958, Jimmy married Carolyn at the Mingo Methodist Church in Mingo, Iowa. The bride prepared at home for the nuptials as James drove Elsie, Jimmy, Robert, and Carl in a small Ford on the long trip toward her Iowa home. Carrying a white Bible topped with a white orchard, Carolyn married her longtime boyfriend. Jimmy and Carolyn used the Ford for a three-day honeymoon in Iowa, then rode in a packed automobile with the family back to North Carolina. After the reception in his parents' house at Rock Ridge, Jim and Carolyn moved into married student housing at State College and began a long, successful marriage. Carolyn later said that the relationship worked because their backgrounds were similar. "We understand each other," she said.[37] A year and a half after their wedding, Carolyn gave birth to their first child, Rebecca Hunt.

As he entered his senior year, Jimmy learned more lessons about how to govern. Several students complained when the administration dropped the Old English letters on the diploma for a more modern style. Senior Class President Aaron Capel argued that Hunt failed to persuade the faculty on a diploma committee to accept the old design. Hunt replied in the *Technician*, "We did not succeed in returning to the old style diploma possibly desired by the majority of students, but neither did we go overboard for a radical new style desired by some faculty members on the committee. It was a compromise as most committee decisions must be. Compromise is not easy nor (is it) politically popular."[38] Hunt also learned how to get along with his political opponents. At the end of the year, Hunt met with the *Technician* editor over coffee for nearly five hours and discovered that they had much in common. The two had been at odds for some time. He recalled that his problem "had been a failure to communicate — just assuming that guy was a bad guy because he didn't agree with me."[39] Early in his political career, Hunt learned about the importance of compromises and the rejection of personal grudges.

President Hunt used his position to applaud the Wolfpack teams, defend the integrity of the athletic department, and condemn bad sportsmanship. Morale declined in 1956 after the National Collegiate Athletic Association (NCAA) placed NCSC athletic programs on four years of probation because of suspected recruiting violations by Everett Case's basketball coaching staff. For most of Hunt's undergraduate years, the basketball team could not participate in the NCAA basketball tournament. To make matters worse, the police arrested twenty-seven NCSC students during a riot that followed the first game of the 1957 Dixie Classic basketball tournament. Carl Henley said that the riot started when Syme dormitory students witnessed people parking cars on the street that blocked the student cars from leaving. Henley and other Syme residents decided to let the air out of the blocking automobiles, but Jimmy refused to participate in the riot. He watched from his dormitory window as the police arrived to stop the tire slashing by firing tear gas and arresting rock-throwing students.[40]

With the help of the administration, Student Body President Hunt repaired State's battered reputation by promoting sportsmanship and other efforts to build the character of the students. In his first year as NCSC student president, he wrote an open letter to the *Technician* saying that the absence of booing at sporting events would build the college's prestige immensely. When the NCSC and UNC football teams met at a Wolfpack home game in 1958, he said, "If we win, feel free to tear down the goal posts. Should we lose, let's stay off the field and allow the Carolina students to take them."[41] The president urged that his fellow students at a State-Carolina basketball game practice clapping and cheering for their own team rather than booing the Carolina team. In addition to a concern about sportsmanship, Hunt also used the bully pulpit of the student body presidency to condemn apathy, focusing on the lack of participation in student publications, radio, and student politics. As a participant himself in numerous activities, he had no patience for those who did nothing but take college courses.[42]

During his senior year, Hunt dealt with a struggle between student government officials and the College Union student administrators. Since 1955, a Union board of students and faculty managed fifteen dollars of the $43 yearly activity fee to be used for dances, lectures, movies, and exhibits.

After students complained that the Union used the money improperly, Hunt urged them in the *Technician* to attend a special hearing or quit griping about the money. Despite Hunt's warning, only fourteen visitors attended when Hunt questioned College Union President Paul Essex about the fees. Afterwards, the student government requested that President Hunt negotiate with the chancellor to force the College Union's board of directors to include elected student officials. By the end of the 1959 spring semester, Hunt forged a compromise that allowed the student government to have a voice in College Union activities.[43]

Jimmy Hunt's experience as student body president increased his interest in politics. Strongly partisan, he served a year as vice president of the State College Democrats and also belonged to the North Carolina Student Legislature. One man who noticed Hunt's interest in politics was Political Science Professor Abraham Holtzman, a California-born academic who had participated in Democratic campaigns. After getting a Ph.D. at Harvard, he had accepted a position at the "cow college" following a desperate job search in 1955. According to Hunt, Holtzman turned him into a serious political thinker. The professor recalled that Jimmy was already politically oriented. "If I influenced him at all, I accentuated the positives in Jimmy," he said.[44] The Rock Ridge native took Holtzman's courses on political parties, interest groups, and political theory. The professor realized that Hunt enjoyed the subjects as much as another prized pupil, Nicholas Ardito-Barietta, a Hunt friend and an outspoken Panamanian who later served as that nation's president.[45]

Others noticed Jimmy Hunt's intense interest in state politics. Phil Carlton said that Hunt constantly read about politics and government, kept an elaborate filing system of stories about state and national affairs, and read every newspaper he could find. Every Sunday, Hunt clipped newspaper articles and put them in a big thick file cabinet in his trailer in married student housing. Carlton considered him more issue-oriented and better read than the average State College student. "He read the *New York Times* when I was reading *Playboy*," his friend recalled.[46] In Raleigh, Jimmy Hunt visited the General Assembly and listened to legislative debates. As student government president, he lobbied against college budget cuts, urging every State student, alumni, and friend to express a desire for adequate funding. He also took interest in the state's poverty, telling Eddie Knox "about North Carolina being too poor, (and) that changes needed to be made."[47]

Students and professors described Jimmy Hunt as a serious, intense student who analyzed problems well. Tom Gilmore claimed that he worked eighteen to twenty hours a day in college. Jimmy rarely smiled and did not seem to have a sense of humor. Holtzman feared that this trait would hurt him in politics where human contact won votes. However, Carlton believed Hunt's seriousness was an asset since he appeared "ready to be governor by the time he was a junior in college."[48] NCSU Vice Chancellor Banks Talley claimed in 1976 that Jimmy's seriousness indicated a desire for achievement and a master plan toward a distant political goal. Bill Friday, former president of the university system, recalled that one could see the beginnings of what was going to happen to him.[49]

Hunt graduated from North Carolina State College in May 1959 after winning the award of "Top Senior." Looking back twenty-two years later, Hunt believed that he achieved a lot as an undergraduate. "We changed the constitution, tried to make the parking situation better, worked on improving married student housing, and worked with the student union," he recalled.[50] He also achieved an impressive resume for a future career.

Student columnist Roger Faulkner wrote in January 1959, "For his personal plans, Mr. Hunt is going to the University of North Carolina and hopes someday to go into politics, perhaps (becoming) president?"[51] Actually, nothing was certain about Hunt's future in 1959. Despite what Faulkner heard, Jimmy had not decided on UNC graduate school, or even Duke University, which later offered him a scholarship. This uncertainty over his future direction began as an undergraduate, when he changed his focus toward agricultural education when the chemistry courses in the dairy husbandry major proved to be too difficult. After he received his bachelor's degree in agricultural education, he decided to pursue a Masters of Science in agricultural economics and eventually get a Ph.D. in that field. To finance his graduate education, he sold his cows at the Clayton farm and received a National Defense Education Act grant.[52]

During his time in NCSC graduate school from 1959 to 1961, he took economic courses from Quentin Lindsey, a Nebraska-born Harvard-educated professor who praised Keynesian economics for giving government a positive role in creating a stable economy. Even before Jimmy attended State College, Lindsey recalled meeting Jimmy's father James Hunt, who had remarked in full seriousness that his son would be governor some day. Lindsey may have believed that prophecy after Jimmy demonstrated strong organizational skills in the professor's national economic policy class.[53]

In graduate school, Jimmy Hunt worked for the gubernatorial campaign of North Carolina State Senator Terry Sanford. Hunt had long admired Sanford. At a banquet in April 1959, Jim Hunt attended a tribute for the candidate. He praised the state senator's service as a former president of the Young Democrats, a World War II paratrooper, a Federal Bureau of Investigation (FBI) agent, and the campaign manager to Kerr

Scott's successful 1954 bid for the United States Senate. By the end of 1959, Sanford welcomed the young man to head his college efforts in his run for governor. The candidate wrote James Hunt, Sr., "Jimmy is doing a mighty fine job for us. It is certainly encouraging to me to see so many of our young people take an active part in our campaign."[54] The Sanford campaign changed Hunt more than any other event during his time at NCSC graduate school.

In 1961, Hunt finished his courses in agricultural economics. His thesis, completed in 1962, was entitled "Acreage Controls and Poundage Controls; Their Effects on Most Profitable Production Practices for flue Cured Tobacco." The study determined what levels and combinations of production would be most profitable for individual flue-cured tobacco farmers under both an acreage program and a poundage control program, describing the effects of "76 different combinations of product practices to determine their profitability under the controls."[55] Approved by Agricultural Economics Professor William Douglas Touissant, his thesis ranked as one of the three best in North America by the American Farm Economics Association. The United States Department of Agriculture used the thesis to develop an acreage-poundage program about the same time that a Surgeon General's report first linked North Carolina's most profitable crop with lung cancer.[56]

James Baxter Hunt's experience at North Carolina State College from 1955 to 1961 helped turn him into a successful politician. Certainly, his knowledge of agriculture benefited him in a state that still had a significant agrarian population. More importantly, he learned legislative skills as a student senator and developed leadership skills as student president. His connections in the College Young Democrats, Future Farmers of America, and North Carolina Student Legislature built the seeds of a future political network. As an undergraduate and a graduate student, he made important friends and political allies on campus, in farm organizations, and within the North Carolina Democratic party. Slowly abandoning the nickname Jimmy, the student prepared himself for future political education under the name of Jim Hunt.

4

Jim Hunt, Terry Sanford, and the Limits of Tar Heel Progressivism, 1960–1967

Jim Hunt transferred his energies from agricultural education to law in the 1960s, becoming an insider in Tar Heel progressive politics. He worked hard on the successful 1960 gubernatorial campaign of North Carolina senator Terry Sanford, endorsing his efforts to promote public education and to improve racial harmony. Viewing Governor Sanford as a role model, he received a law degree at the University of North Carolina just like Sanford did in the 1940s. Many Tar Heels did not adore the governor, however, and rejected his handpicked heir Richardson Preyer to succeed him in 1964. Disillusioned by the failure of the campaign, Hunt worked in Nepal for two years, returning in 1966 to pass the bar exam, win the presidency of the state Young Democrats, and combine his own vision of Tar Heel progressivism with a stronger sense of political caution than Sanford ever practiced.

Jim Hunt's most important political connection was Bert Bennett, Jr., Sanford's campaign manager in 1960. The wealthy businessman learned the art of behind-the-scenes politics from his father, Quality Oil co-founder Bert Bennett, Sr., who worked quietly for Democratic candidates in Winston-Salem. Elected UNC student body president in 1939, young Bert developed a friendship with classmate Sanford, who shared with Hunt that "burning gut desire"[1] to win elections and the long range desire to be governor. After the nation entered World War II, Bennett joined the Navy, serving on a naval ship carrying troops during the invasion of Normandy as his friend Terry parachuted nearby for the Airborne. After the war,

Bennett studied law at the University of North Carolina for a year before deciding to stay with the family oil business as a partner. His activities as chairman of the Forsyth County Democrats attracted his friend Terry, who wanted a businessman to run his campaign.

Bert Bennett, through hard work, outstanding management skills acquired from his business affairs, and his own wealth, created a loyal statewide political organization for his UNC friend. He worked for the campaign without money and paid rent for the campaign office out of his own pocket. He contacted Sanford's friends from the University of North Carolina, Federal Bureau of Investigation, National Guard, United Methodist Church, and Young Democrats to enlist their support. Bennett also recruited influential sheriffs, labor leaders, and African-American ministers who supposedly had the power to carry entire counties if they received adequate financial support. Through his efforts to get votes, Bennett inspired tremendous loyalty from his followers. His friend Richardson Preyer recalled key people would "follow Bert in the flames. He has that kind of personal loyalty."[2] Bennett attracted student volunteer Jim Hunt, who after winning student elections using the most honorable means, adapted to a tough campaign manager who said "you fight with everything you've got to fight with. This was part of the tactics, right or wrong."[3] Bennett introduced Hunt to serious statewide political campaigning and unknowingly laid the groundwork for Hunt's future political organization.

Three days before Sanford filed for the governor's race, the volatile civil rights issue ignited in Greensboro, the city of Jim Hunt's birth. On February 1, 1960, four North Carolina Agricultural and Technology (A&T) students held a sit-in at the Greensboro Woolworth's department store, which led to a dramatic surge in student protests throughout the state. While the event, along with several Durham sit-ins, revitalized the civil rights movement, it also awakened North Carolina segregationists' fears about the possible end of their way of life. With little money and the sympathy of large numbers of eastern whites, former assistant attorney general I. Beverly Lake ran against Sanford on a platform dedicated to preserving segregation. After Lake finished second in the first gubernatorial primary in May 1960 and called for a runoff, Bennett feared an ugly campaign similar to the 1950 race between United States Senator Frank Porter Graham and challenger Willis Smith. Ten years earlier, Smith had run a successful race-baiting campaign against the senator who had refused to respond negatively against his opponent. Bennett vowed Sanford would not go down meekly like Graham did. Instead, the Sanford campaign took the offensive, arguing that if Lake won, he would shut down the school system and hinder industrial progress in North Carolina.[4]

As college students protested against segregation, Hunt gradually changed his mind on the race question after he had an "epiphany" at a National Student Association (NSA) meeting at Ohio State University while listening to Allard Lowenstein. Born in Newark, New Jersey, to Lithuanian Jewish immigrants, Lowenstein arrived at the University of North Carolina where he worked for several liberal causes in the early 1950s. As NSA president, he urged liberals to oppose both Stalinist Communism and Jim Crow segregation. His eloquence on civil rights was legendary. Lowenstein moved Vassar College students so much with a description of white supremacist brutality toward black southern demonstrators that they picketed the Woolworth's in New York City. Historian William Chafe wrote, "Soon it became clear that, on predominantly white campuses especially, Lowenstein was a charismatic point man for the movement, someone who could use his talents for energizing students to enlarge and lead the ranks of white civil rights demonstrators."[5] Jim Hunt recalled, "I heard Al Lowenstein speak. It opened my eyes. A light went on."[6] Hunt finally understood that segregation demeaned African Americans. However, he did not join the sit-ins as his future Administration Secretary Jane Patterson did; like Sanford, he wanted to change the system from within.

During the second primary, Sanford handled the civil rights issue carefully. According to biographers Howard Covington and Marion Ellis, "Sanford was caught between saying what he believed to be the right course for the state and being the one setting that course for the next four years."[7] He portrayed himself as a responsible segregationist who endorsed North Carolina Governor Luther Hodges's plan which retained rural segregation by allowing token integration in selected urban schools. Hunt completely understood the candidate's strategy, remembering that Sanford, while committed to racial equality, had the "smarts" not to challenge the dominant attitude toward segregation, since an integrationist stance would have cost him the election. By disguising his sympathies for civil rights, Sanford won a 50,000-vote victory against Lake and rewarded Bert Bennett with the state party chairmanship.[8]

Because of his close relationship with Sanford and Bennett, Jim Hunt became a strong supporter of Democratic presidential candidate John F. Kennedy of Massachusetts. Observers described the United States Senator as young, handsome, progressive, charismatic, articulate, and telegenic — all qualities that Democratic politicians like Hunt later emulated. Against the wishes of North Carolina delegates who wanted a southern Protestant as their presidential nominee, Sanford endorsed his fellow World War II veteran at the 1960 National Democratic Convention. Hunt also supported the Catholic candidate, once taking his daughter Rebecca to a Cary town hall meeting with a JFK "Leadership for the '60s" button on one lapel, and a "Students for Sanford" button on the other. After Kennedy carried the state, his team rewarded Sanford Democrats by appointing Henry Hall Wilson to a White House post and approving Jim Hunt for a Democratic National Committee position in 1962.[9]

Hunt campaigned hard for Terry Sanford in the general election. The volunteer marveled at the way that Sanford focused on minor details, such as driving back to a farmers market after he remembered that he called someone there by the wrong name. Sanford, with the help of Bennett, planned the county campaign organizations carefully. "Frankly," Hunt said, "it (the Sanford organization) is the kind of model I've used in my own efforts as I built an organization in North Carolina."[10] Sanford's organizational skills paid off in November 1960 when he defeated Republican gubernatorial candidate John Gavin.

After winning the general election, Sanford introduced a progressive program to the legislature. "In 1961," Historian Numan Bartley wrote, "the General Assembly enacted more far reaching legislation than any similar body in the twentieth century."[11] Sanford backed higher funds for teacher salaries, school improvements, and a higher minimum wage. He favored an unpopular food tax to support public education. "The reason I got excited about him was because he was about education, quality schools, and had the courage to put on a food tax," Hunt recalled.[12] He also praised Sanford for race moderation at a time when Deep South governors resisted the federal government.

Sanford received reluctant support from Joseph Hunt, speaker of the North Carolina house and a grandson of Jim's great-grandfather Moses James Hunt. Backed by Greensboro's conservative Democrats, he won elections to the legislature and was elected to the top position in early 1961. The speaker reluctantly backed Sanford's unpopular tax proposals, and blamed the governor when a Republican candidate defeated him in 1962. Never enthusiastic about Sanford, Joe Hunt had little influence over the progressive Rock Ridge Hunts, and he did not participate in Wilson County activities like the 1961 funerals of Jim Hunt's maternal grandmother Polly Ann Brame and her son Clarence Brame. Family political divisions would heal a decade later, however, as Joe Hunt backed his younger cousin Jim Hunt for statewide office.[13]

Even on matters where Sanford failed, Hunt sided with the governor. Despite the backing of education and business leaders, Sanford could not persuade a majority of North Carolinians to pass a bond issue for community colleges and capital improvements in 1961. Two years later, conservative Democrats, angry over the rise of student civil rights protests, targeted the universities with the Speaker Ban Law, banning Communist speakers from state-supported schools. The state constitution did not allow Sanford to veto the bill. However, he encouraged Consolidated University President Bill Friday to challenge the law, which resulted in its modification in 1965 after a regional organization threatened to remove accreditation from the university. As a law student and later as a young lawyer, Hunt silently approved of efforts that led to a federal court declaring the legislation unconstitutional in 1968.[14]

In late 1961, Jim Hunt started his first year in law school at the University of North Carolina after believing that law provided a better avenue to a political career than agricultural studies. He took a course from UNC law professor Albert Coates, "a gruff, demanding, sometimes profane, and single-minded man who operated under the curious notion that all of North Carolina was his classroom."[15] When Hunt arrived, Coates was in his twenty-ninth year as the director of the Institute of Government, dedicated to the training of professionals to run state and local governments. According to Hunt, the law professor realized that North Carolina politicians would not solve complex problems "unless we developed a high degree of professional administration at the local level."[16] He learned concepts that Terry Sanford, one of "Albert's Boys," had accepted two decades earlier.

As Hunt focused on his law studies, he gained a political opportunity from the national Democrats. After taking criminal justice and torts classes during his first year of law school in 1962, Hunt received his first paying political job. Aided by his Sanford connections and his reputation as a hard-working partisan, Hunt received an appointment from the Democratic National Committee (DNC) as national college director. Following the appointment, DNC Chairman John M. Bailey, a tall, tough, Irish American who ran the Connecticut Democratic party in the 1950s, praised Hunt as one of the outstanding young college-educated Democrats in the United States. A DNC bulletin said that Hunt planned to continue his law studies at night, and return to his home county to practice law in about two years.[17]

As Hunt worked at DNC headquarters in Washington, he began his second year of law school at George Washington University. By the end of their stay, Carolyn and Jim had a son named James Baxter Hunt III, whom they called "Baxter." The college director often left his family to visit locations vital to the Democrats, including a tour of North Carolina with Vice-President Lyndon B. Johnson and visits to congressional districts in Louisville, Kentucky, where he learned a tremendous amount about how to organize a political campaign. Hunt's experience with the national

Democratic organization in the early 1960s began his role as a political insider within the entire party.[18]

Jim Hunt continued to support President Kennedy after he backed dramatic civil rights legislation that alienated many white North Carolinians. Following Birmingham Police Commissioner Eugene "Bull" Conner's violent suppression of civil rights protesters in 1963, Kennedy publicly supported legislation calling for the end of segregation in public businesses. "The people at home were not coming along with this as far as they should have," Hunt recalled.[19] Indeed, his father still believed in segregation. Jim gave James Hunt, Sr., a copy of John Howard Griffin's *Black Like Me*, that depicted the white author, disguised as an African American, traveling in the South and receiving miserable treatment because of his color. "He never said much about it, but I can tell it affected him," the son said.[20] His father's support of segregation became more muted after reading the book.

In August 1963, Jim Hunt returned to Chapel Hill, settled in a house on Daniels Road, began his final year of law school, and considered further political activity. He pledged an honorary law fraternity, but was blackballed in a secret vote because, his friends said, Hunt associated with African-American students. Such incidents only intensified his efforts for Democratic reformers, including his old mentor Bert Bennett, the Democratic Party Chairman since 1960. After the death of North Carolina Lieutenant Governor Clyde Philpott, who was Sanford's favorite choice to succeed him as governor, Bennett feared that no serious Democrat would challenge I. Beverly Lake for the Democratic gubernatorial nomination. If Lake won, Bennett reasoned, a Republican challenger such as Congressman Charles Jonas might defeat him. For a brief time, Bert Bennett seriously considered a run for governor. Hunt's former North Carolina State College classmate Phil Carlton, manager of Sanford's gubernatorial appointments, planned the Winston-Salem businessman's prospective campaign. Hunt wanted to be involved and said nice things about Bennett in a Raleigh newspaper. Bennett wrote Hunt to thank him for the remarks and to say that he looked forward to "seeing you regarding the fall campaign."[21]

By the end of the summer, Bennett decided to drop out of the gubernatorial race. He later said that he did not have the desire required for a successful effort. Instead, he urged his young supporters to back Federal Judge Richardson Preyer, a progressive candidate from Greensboro. Bennett resigned from the chairmanship and worked diligently for the campaign, counseling the dignified judge to fight hard for the nomination. Bennett told his aide Phil Carlton that Rich should get "a little meaner" and start "knocking some heads."[22] He even urged an aide to keep Preyer off the radio since his "voice is rather high and that does not make a good impression when you do not see him."[23] Urging toughness, Bennett told Preyer to hammer against the "Lake type of government" that would bring federal bayonets, closed schools, and closed businesses to the state. At the same time, Bennett secretly funneled money to the Lake campaign to insure a reactionary adversary in the Democratic primary runoff.[24]

Bennett downplayed any connection between Dick Preyer and John F. Kennedy because of the president's civil rights policies. Such efforts ended on November 22, 1963. As Bert Bennett lunched with Governor Sanford and newspapermen in Winston-Salem, a reporter told them that President Kennedy had been shot and killed in Dallas. Bennett tried to put the best face on losing a friend and contact in the White House. "If Rich Preyer is successful, the Governor and myself will have the same relationship, I think, with President (Lyndon) Johnson as we had with Kennedy," he wrote.[25] Bennett was saddened at the loss of a political hero, yet hoped that the southern president could help Preyer in 1964.

Two months after Kennedy's assassination, the Surgeon General issued a report linking tobacco, the most prosperous crop in the state, with lung cancer. The tobacco companies and North Carolina Democrats condemned the report as highly speculative. Bennett urged Judge Preyer to associate himself with the maligned crop. Bennett recommended one-minute television spots defending tobacco in eastern North Carolina. He said that Preyer should file his candidacy in the presence of a tobacco ware-houseman and a tobacco grower in overalls, a symbolic gesture illustrating "to all of the tobacco people and to North Carolina the importance we are putting on tobacco and all its problems."[26] As a son of a tobacco farmer, Jim Hunt completely understood this strategy.

Bennett gave many assignments to Jim Hunt. In February 1964, he urged Hunt to go to Washington to ask the Democratic National Committee for suggestions regarding the campaign. "Certainly we ought to pick up one or two things that would be advantageous to Richardson Preyer," Bennett said.[27] He told Hunt to work with Wilson County political leader Conner Vick to win that county. When a key Preyer supporter's son ran for student body president at North Carolina State College, Bennett urged Hunt and his friends to do all they could to elect the young man.[28]

Bennett was pleased with Hunt's actions. He praised "Jim Hunt and several of his friends" for going "to town on a sound truck" to get a key financial supporter's son elected student body president at North Carolina State College.[29] He said that Hunt did an outstanding job at a college rally, attracting a large attendance and an enthusiastic crowd. "Jimmie Hunt," Bennett told Conner Vick, "is extremely capable, has a lot of influence around the state, (is) a dedicated worker, and is from Wilson, North Carolina. Again I just wanted to let you know how much I thought of Jim in case he sees you or you run into him."[30] By the end of the campaign, most progressives in the North Carolina Democratic party learned of the hard-working volunteer from Rock Ridge.

Hunt's strenuous efforts did not create the desired outcome in the first Democratic primary. Although Preyer finished in first place, he did not avoid a runoff with Judge Dan K. Moore, a moderate conservative with support from United States Senator Sam Erwin and North Carolina's business community. Bennett later said that he thought the election was over the night of the first primary, since Preyer could not attract Lake's supporters, although Moore could win them by linking Preyer with civil rights. While Bennett and Preyer privately agreed with the national Democratic party on the race issue, they distanced themselves from President Johnson's efforts to pass the Civil Rights Act of 1964. Governor Sanford called in black leaders who agreed to prevent any demonstrations, while Bennett urged them to dissuade African Americans from handing out Preyer literature to whites. "You had to," he recalled. "We were going to get that vote. But we didn't want to alienate solidly the white vote. Any good black would realize that."[31] He wrote the White House to find a summer job for "a Jesse Jackson," the North Carolina Agricultural and Technology State College student body president "who was keeping an eye on the home front to be sure that the Negroes do not demonstrate to help Preyer."[32] John Webb, Preyer's Wilson County operative, remembered how a meeting between a Preyer aide and African Americans in Washington, North Carolina, hurt efforts to attract white votes.

As Bennett expected, Moore attracted enough Lake voters to defeat Preyer and win the Democratic nomination. In November 1964, Moore defeated the Republican candidate as President Johnson won a landslide victory. Lake portrayed Moore's victory as a repudiation of Governor Sanford and his liberal political organization. Bennett rejected that notion, telling the *Winston-Salem Journal* in the summer of 1964 that his organization survived the ordeal. "We're stronger than ever," he said. "If we were dead, we would have been dead the night after the first primary. It just wasn't our time. But we'll be in there tomorrow trying as hard and harder. You're just not going to beat this group down."[33]

While the Bennett political apparatus did not die, it hibernated for the remainder of the decade. Back at Quality Oil, Bennett failed to win a state senate seat in 1966 and prepared no candidate to run for governor two years later. Perhaps, Bennett would wait for former aides Phil Carlton and Hunt to be ready, but that time seemed a long way off in 1964.[34]

Hunt suffered another setback that year. The law student spent the Preyer campaign neglecting his studies and failed the state bar examination. "I'm sure I didn't study as much as I should have," he later admitted.[35] He still could not believe what happened. Despite all his work for Preyer, he maintained a high grade point average. "I was in the law equivalent of Phi Beta Kappa," he said. "I wrote for the law review. I graduated eleventh or twelfth in a class of a 130 or so. I didn't see any reason why I shouldn't pass."[36] In the span of a few short months, he worked for a losing opponent and failed his bar exam.

All was not hopeless, however. Wilson attorney John Webb offered him a job in his law office for a year, but Hunt wanted to see the world and he thought he had found the right vehicle in the Peace Corps. Many young persons served in the Peace Corps established by President Kennedy to send educated Americans to aid Third World countries. For a brief time, Hunt trained volunteers as a Peace Corps consultant in Hilo, Hawaii, and Davis, California. Unfortunately, the organization did not accept married couples with children for overseas assignments in 1964. Hunt had to look elsewhere for international work.[37]

Hunt soon discovered another option. In the early 1960s, his former economic professor, Quentin Lindsey, joined the Ford Foundation to work with the government of Nepal to establish land reform. Ever since King Prithwi Narayan Shah had unified the small country in the eighteenth century, the nation located between India and China remained a feudal society. The decline of the monarchy and the nation's control by prime ministers of the Bahadur family did not dramatically change the economic situation. Poor conditions under the Bahadurs eventually led to a revolution against the prime ministers, the creation of a democratically elected government, and the restoration of the royal family in 1951. Four years after the revolution, King Mahendra succeeded his father to the throne. After criticizing the chaos of democratic rule, he dissolved the government in 1960 and created the panchayat system, which gave the monarchy the strongest role in Nepal.[38]

During the Cold War, American policymakers worried more about Nepal's integration with neighboring Communist China than its commitment to democracy. Mahendra and many Americans realized that Nepal's feudal system, which contained a small number of landowners and a large number of peasants, could energize Communists to overthrow the government. Jim Hunt described the land as economically and politically the "epitome" of the undeveloped nation, since the government failed to give most Nepalese what Americans took for granted. King Mahendra backed an agricultural reform program financed by aid from Britain, China, Switzerland, and the United States. He also received help from the Ford Foundation, which sent Professor Lindsey to Nepal in 1960 to establish a pilot land reform project in the village of Budabari.[39]

Thinking of his best former students, Lindsey sent a telegram inviting Hunt to help him. At first Hunt declined, saying that he worked for Democratic gubernatorial candidate Richardson Preyer and expected to have a major role in the Preyer administration. According to Lindsey, Hunt decided to accept the offer after Preyer lost the election, but Hunt remembered otherwise, saying that he planned to go to Nepal before the candidate's defeat. The Hunts left in 1964 for the South Asian country where they remained for two years. Partly inspired by a book called *The Fabulous Flemings of Katmandu*, which described the first American medical missionaries in Nepal, Hunt desired to help the nation's citizens learn about agriculture. "We had that sense of service that went back to the missionaries," he said.[40]

Hunt tried to sell the king's economic program to peasants and landlords. For centuries, the Nepalese kings transferred the land to victorious generals who allowed peasants to farm the land in exchange for a rented shelter. Mahendra backed legislation in 1965 that ended feudal customs, encouraging advisors like Hunt to convince the landowners and tillers of corn, jute, millet, rice, sugar cane, tobacco, and raisers of cattle and water buffalo to approve the king's reforms. Aided by Hunt, Lindsey's four-man team hiked into remote villages, talking to people along the trail to find out about the area's economic needs and identifying village leaders to help them. Using an interpreter, Hunt asked the landlords to reduce their rents and end exorbitant interest rates for tenant farmers. Such activities caused Hunt to understand better the world outside of North Carolina.[41]

Hunt also helped the Ministry of Economic Planning create a tax program to finance local development in Nepal. To fulfill this goal, he and the Ford Foundation examined the implications of various tax rates and policies, wrote tax regulations, established the administrative machinery to enforce the tax, and supervised the collection of the Nepalese currency. The American advisors believed tax reform could provide funds for roads, canals, development projects, and schools, which closed in 1965 because of a drop in landlord contributions. "Here in Nepal," Hunt wrote, "we are having the novel experience of taking a society just beginning to develop, having a government willing to pass experimental laws and policies, and testing our theories and ideas for rapid economic development in a free society."[42] He knew that the road to Nepalese development would be "long and hard," but he felt satisfied "if we can help even a little."[43]

Home life differed dramatically from North Carolina. As Jim hiked in rural Nepal, Carolyn taught in a school whose student body consisted of pupils of many nationalities. In 1965, she gave birth to their second daughter, Rachel, at a missionary hospital in the old palace of Katmandu. "All I knew is that every time we moved, we had a baby," Hunt recalled.[44] Carolyn and Jim avoided the health hazards in the city ghettos to protect their three children. The Hunts lived in a house that had no television, radio, or electric stove. They heated their home with kerosene space heaters and used flickering light bulbs to illuminate the rooms. However, Carolyn recalled that the Hunts had more family life together in Nepal than they had experienced when he studied law, while Jim remembered that modern conveniences were missing, "but you learn that you can get along without them."[45]

Hunt took law books to Nepal to study for the bar exam. On January 1, 1966, he established a strong program of studying two hours every morning for six months in the royal palace at Katmandu. "People came to work at nine 'o'clock," Hunt said. "From seven to nine, I was studying for the bar exam."[46] Usually, the weather was cold until the sun came up. The Ford Foundation employee brought a special kerosene heater into the office to keep warm.

Hunt found his knowledge of law useful when a Ford Foundation employee got in trouble with the law. Quentin Lindsey remembered that a British secretary from the Ford Foundation ran her car into a cow, an animal considered sacred by Nepal's Hindus. After people gathered around to curse her, a policeman came by and arrested her. Since Hunt had legal training, he went to the jail and talked to the police. He convinced them to release the secretary by saying that the woman had accidentally killed the animal. The incident led Lindsey to claim that Hunt won his first legal case in Nepal.[47]

In 1966, Hunt returned home with his future on his mind. Bert Bennett said that they had stayed in touch constantly with letters dealing with the North Carolina political situation. Warren Ashby, a University of North Carolina philosophy professor, recalled a visit to Nepal during which Hunt said that he planned to run for governor of the state. He first needed to pass the bar exam, however. As Carolyn and her children stayed with their family in Iowa, Hunt took a bar exam preparation course at Duke University. In 1966, he finally passed. Flunking the examination the first time embarrassed him deeply, but the experience taught him to get back on his feet and move forward. After getting his law license, he accepted a job from his old friend John Webb.[48]

The son of a tobacco buyer and a Wilson attorney, Webb knew the young man well from previous political campaigns. He had first met Hunt in 1962 when the law student helped him organize a delegation backing Doug Graham for North Carolina Young Democratic Club president, and Al House for national YDC president at the state Democratic convention. Webb recalled that Hunt "knew how to organize and get people to do things."[49] Even before Hunt passed the bar exam, Webb wanted Hunt to join his Wilson law firm.[50]

Hunt proved himself in general practice, winning many cases from 1966 to 1971 for his clients. He once restored a teacher whom a school board wanted to fire. "To be honest," said law partner Russell Kirby, who also served as a state senate chairman of the finance committee in the North Carolina General Assembly, "I was rather shocked that he could step in and do the job he did."[51] Webb recalled that he was "the hardest working man I've ever been associated with."[52] Not long after he began practicing law, he officially became a law partner of Kirby, Hunt, and Webb.

Hunt's law firm encouraged his participation in Democratic political organizations. "He knew more about politics than anybody I'd ever talked to," said Webb.[53] Using his friends and political contacts, Hunt was elected president of the Wilson County Young Democrats in 1967. News reporter Ginny Carroll said that Hunt expanded his contacts from the Sanford and Preyer campaigns into a nucleus of his own grassroots organization to win the Young Democratic Club presidency. He had the support of North Carolina Lieutenant Governor Robert Scott, the son of his idol Kerr Scott, the progressive governor of the state from 1949 to 1953. In January 1968, nearly eight hundred Democrats attended Hunt's inauguration in Wilson where he pledged to keep faith in the Democratic party, maintain enthusiasm for the tasks that lie ahead, and "be ever determined that we shall win in November." He made no references to controversial issues— including civil rights, Vietnam, economic liberalism, and feminism — that deeply divided the state Democrats. Hunt focused more on county precinct administration than on ideology, understanding that the lessons of the Sanford-Bennett-Preyer organization taught him that Tar Heel candidates could not be perceived as too progressive – especially on the race issue.[54]

With the exception of his stay in Nepal, James B. Hunt, Jr., worked hard as an activist in progressive North Carolina politics between 1960 and 1967. Hunt combined idealistic goals of ending poverty and racism with an ambition to make public service his own profession. At this time, no politician influenced him more than Governor Terry Sanford. The volunteer accepted Sanford's premise that education would provide the poor with a way of achieving affluence, and that the state must insure equality to every white and black citizen. The governor became Hunt's new role model; the activist even entered the University of North Carolina law school like Sanford did a generation earlier. The limits of Sanford's political influence in the state became apparent after 1964 when Richardson Preyer, a progressive heir to Sanford, lost the gubernatorial race despite rigorous campaigning by Hunt. The young man knew that Preyer was defeated because of the controversial race issue, combined with antipathy toward Sanford because of the governor's 1961 food tax. While not abandoning progressive principles, Hunt understood the danger of taking too many unpopular progressive positions. As Young Democratic Club President, he practiced caution on controversial issues, an approach that he continued throughout his political career. While understanding his political debt to Terry Sanford, Jim Hunt realized that the governor's unabashed progressivism and unrestrained loyalty for national liberals no longer attracted a majority following and therefore the young activist searched for a new vision of Tar Heel progressivism to appeal to the conservative whites who were abandoning the party.

5

Jim Hunt and the Political Transformation of the American South, 1968–1971

James B. Hunt, Jr., considered his first run for statewide office during the greatest political transformation of the South since the Democratic party monopolized power at the turn of the twentieth century. This revolution of the early 1970s included two important developments: the flight of white conservatives from the Democrats into the rising southern Republican party, and the southern Democratic party's efforts to address the concerns of young people, women, and African Americans. The latter development provided a new group of political role models for Hunt, including Jimmy Carter of Georgia, John West of South Carolina, Reubin Askew of Florida, and Dale Bumpers of Arkansas. From these "New South" governors, Hunt learned much about political leadership.

Hunt understood the rifts in the Democratic party as he assumed the North Carolina Young Democratic Club (YDC) presidency in early 1968. In the interest of promoting party unity, he ignored the divisions. He had many rifts to ignore. The unpopular Vietnam War separated the national party into "doves," the followers of peace presidential candidates Robert F. Kennedy and Eugene McCarthy, and the "hawks," the supporters of President Lyndon Johnson and Vice-President Hubert Humphrey. The civil rights movement still created gaps between North Carolina Democrats and the national party that led many conservatives to support former Alabama Governor George Wallace's third-party candidacy in the fall. Democrats also debated the wisdom of Johnson's antipoverty programs. Hunt believed that he should not divide North Carolina Democrats over national issues, but rally them to victory by emphasizing shared beliefs and party loyalty. He refrained from stating public opinions on the Vietnam War, and he did not even discuss them with his law partner, John Webb.[1]

In contrast to the rising counterculture among the large baby-boom generation that was at least ten years younger than Hunt, the YDC president practiced a conservative social life style in Wilson, North Carolina. He paid men to construct a house on farmland near his father's home in Rock Ridge. His wife Carolyn stayed home with the children while organizing Wilson County church groups to tutor in the schools. Wishing to avoid the theological battles at the Marsh Swamp Free Will Baptist Church which he had attended as a teenager, Jim Hunt joined the First Presbyterian Church after an exhaustive search for a church home, a study that included reading the sermons of the ministers whose services he attended. Although he no longer was a member of his parents' church, he still maintained close ties with his father James and his mother Elsie. After James Hunt retired from the federal government in 1966, he worked for Mount Olive College, the Tobacco Marketing Committee, and the Coastal Plains Regional Commission. Each parent remained in good health, with James surviving heart problems in the early 1960s and Elsie recovering from an automobile accident in early 1968. That same spring, Jim and Carolyn celebrated the birth of their fourth child, Elizabeth.[2]

In Wilson, Hunt developed strategies for North Carolina Democratic party victories. In one newspaper article, he endorsed a four-point plan that called for reorganization of inactive Young Democratic Club chapters, a YDC worker for every state precinct, and YDC aid in the training of precinct leaders. "Fourth, we must work!" he said. "Each of us must knock on doors, and do the menial jobs as well as the exciting."[3] Hunt wrote his plans to promote grassroots Democratic efforts in the state manual "Rally Around the Precinct." Staying up late at nights after practicing law all day, he completed a useful manual for the state party. Such calls for hard work stirred no controversy among the party's factions divided over civil rights, the Great Society, and the Vietnam War.[4]

The desire to avoid controversy seemed natural enough for a man who wanted a career in public service. In April 1968, Jim Hunt made one major exception. Few persons stirred more intense debate among white North Carolinians than the Reverend Martin Luther King, Jr. While many southern blacks appreciated King for his leadership in the civil rights movement, many white segregationists, including Raleigh television commentator Jesse Helms, condemned the Baptist minister as a troublemaker, a promoter of racial violence, and a communist sympathizer. They also despised King for his opposition to the Vietnam War and his call for radical economic justice. Federal Bureau of Investigation (FBI) Director J. Edgar Hoover, considered a hero to many Americans, tried to destroy the minister's reputation. Even after his assassination in Memphis on April 4, 1968, King remained a despised figure to many white conservatives.

King's assassination sparked African-American violence across the nation, including cities and towns in North Carolina. Governor Dan Moore suspended liquor sales after rioters destroyed the rescue mission in downtown Raleigh, and black students smashed windows and threw rocks at Shaw University. In Wilson, vandals struck several businesses during a spree of glass-breaking and minor looting. The city commissioners responded with a nighttime curfew, the arrest of many suspects and a successful appeal to bring in the National Guard.[5]

Meanwhile, the Reverend J. D. Ellis, pastor of Wilson's Jackson Chapel First Baptist Church, the most affluent African-American church in town, planned a memorial service at the chapel and a silent procession from the black church to the courthouse. Some Wilson leaders feared that the march might turn violent and become a spectacle of militant "black power." Other white Wilson leaders, including Hunt, disagreed. As the chairman of the city's Human Relations Commission, Hunt believed that if whites marched with Ellis, they could keep the vigil nonviolent.[6]

On April 7, 1968, Hunt attended a church filled with African Americans as other blacks stood outside the packed building. The Reverend Ellis preached about King's concern for all human beings, "black and white."[7] After the service, Ellis, Hunt, the white mayor of the city of Wilson, and a mostly African-American crowd of approximately 1,800 people marched in a candlelight parade to the Wilson County courthouse. National guardsmen and city police watched the march as young black men kept the people orderly. Asked later why he marched, Hunt said, "You do what needs to be done for your community."[8]

Although the *Wilson Daily Times* did not mention the white leaders who participated in the march, possibly for fear that they would be socially rebuked, photographers took pictures of Hunt marching with blacks. Those photos became politically controversial during Hunt's early efforts for political office. In his lieutenant gubernatorial campaign in 1972, one opponent began a whispering campaign saying that Hunt marched in a procession *with* Martin Luther King, Jr., and this rumor lingered well beyond that election. Fearful in 1976 that the stories would damage his candidacy for governor, Hunt wrote a letter describing his involvement in the march. He said that the mayor of Wilson asked him and his fellow members on the Human Relations Commission to join the march to maintain nonviolence. It was a just reason, Hunt wrote, and he was pleased to comply with the mayor's request.[9]

The King march would not be the last time that Hunt involved himself in a Wilson County matter that stirred racial unrest. The young attorney championed a move to consolidate the three school systems within the county against many white citizens who feared this would mean higher taxes and undesired racial integration. With the backing of prominent city leaders, he promoted a referendum in 1969 that called for the merger of the three separate school systems. Hunt's efforts failed to persuade the majority of county voters, including most rural whites who did not want their children to integrate with African American urban youths.[10]

If Hunt took a few courageous stands in Wilson, he refrained from controversial statements as a delegate with one half of a vote at the 1968 Democratic National Convention. As YDC president with procedural experience dating from his days in Future Farmers of America, Hunt chaired the committee on rules and order of business. In this role, he dealt with few divisive issues. As antiwar demonstrators and police clashed in the streets of Chicago, and delegates in the halls vigorously debated the Vietnam War, Hunt presented the minority report proposing that the Democratic National Committee add state party chairmen and state YDC presidents to national convention delegations.[11]

The division within the state Democratic delegation added to the national spectacle. Unhappy with the liberal presidential candidates, Governor Dan Moore announced that he would run for president as a favorite son, winning the backing of the delegation's conservative Democrats. Meanwhile, Reginald Hawkins, a black dentist who ran unsuccessfully for governor in the 1968 Democratic primary, challenged the North Carolina delegation for being unrepresentative because it included only token "establishment" African Americans. To make matters worse, the area outside the convention became a battlefield between "hippie" protesters and angry Chicago policemen. To the disgust of both antiwar delegates and conservative Moore supporters, the convention nominated Vice-President Hubert Humphrey for president. North Carolina Democratic Party Chairman Jimmy Johnson said, "This was my first convention, and I wasn't too impressed."[12] Many Democrats thought that the convention cost Humphrey any chance at victory.

Attorney John Webb said that a conversation with Jim Hunt about the Chicago convention may have influenced his law partner's political future. Webb recalled talking to Hunt about United States Senator Edward M. Kennedy, who turned down the Democratic presidential nomination two months after the assassination of his brother Robert. "Kennedy made a mistake for not taking that nomination," Webb told Hunt. "He thinks he can have it any time he wants it. Just wait a few years. You never know what's going to happen."[13] Webb seemed prophetic after Kennedy lost popularity because of his involvement in a woman's accidental drowning at Chappaquiddick, Massachusetts, in 1969. When Hunt debated about running for state office as a young man, Webb said, "Remember what I said about Ted Kennedy. When it looks like the brass ring is coming your way, you better take it."[14]

As North Carolina YDC president, Hunt helped to elect Robert Scott governor. Just like his father Kerr Scott, whose service as governor from 1949 to 1953 brought rural road construction to farmers, including the Hunt family, Robert served in the Grange, farmed in Alamance County, and shared his father's progressive views. Elected lieutenant governor in 1964, Scott used the part-time position to revive the progressive rural coalition that had elected his father. Times had changed, however. Mechanization and urbanization meant fewer agrarian supporters than in the 1940s. The Republicans, a moribund state party in Kerr Scott's lifetime, increased their support among eastern North Carolinians distressed over Democratic liberalism. As Richard Nixon carried the state against Hubert Humphrey (the first GOP presidential win since 1928) and won the presidency, Scott narrowly defeated Republican candidate James Gardner in the closest general election for governor since 1896.[15]

Governor Scott, who hoped to focus exclusively on progressive issues, had to deal with violent radicals, racial tensions, and Vietnam protests. As governor, he ordered the National Guard to put down an uprising at North Carolina A&T University in Greensboro and a 1971 riot in Wilmington. The latter event resulted in the trial of the "Wilmington Ten," nine black men and one women charged with arson, whose legal difficulties dragged on into Governor Hunt's first term in the late 1970s. Despite these distractions, Scott persuaded the legislature to back consumer protection legislation, government reorganization, teacher salary increases, and a state zoo. Declaring that tobacco was no longer king in North Carolina, Scott successfully pushed for a tobacco tax increase to fund these measures. Although tobacco farmer James Hunt, Sr., opposed the tax, his son Jim backed the governor.[16]

Governor Scott and North Carolina Democratic Party Chairman Jimmy Johnson created opportunities for Jim Hunt in 1969. Naming him as his assistant, Johnson had the Wilson attorney coordinate the visits of Democratic politicians, including United States Senators Edmund Muskie of Maine and Fritz Hollings of South Carolina. Johnson also gave Hunt the chairmanship of the 1969 Jefferson-Jackson dinner, where YDC

President Charlie Rose said he "did his usual good job in getting things done properly."[17] By age 32, Hunt had completed his transition from a hardworking campaign volunteer to an insider in North Carolina Democratic politics.

In 1969, the Wilson attorney served as a member of the party's rules commission that proposed changes in future Democratic National conventions. With his new clout, he demanded that the national Democrats appeal to the large college-age baby boom generation. Although Hunt believed that the younger Democrats working for Democratic national chairman Fred Harris were very naive about how things worked practically, he understood the importance of bringing millions of young college students into the party. Only a handful resort to violence, Hunt said; most young people were idealistic and committed to a better state and nation.[18]

In July 1969, Hunt testified to a Democratic commission chaired by Senator George McGovern of South Dakota seeking to broaden the party's base in the wake of charges that party bosses played too large a role in nominating Vice-President Hubert Humphrey. Hunt called for substantial youth representation in the highest councils of the party, the end to discrimination against minorities during delegate selection, and the participation of the South in influencing presidential candidacies and party platforms. "The fact that none of our delegates favored George Wallace, who got 31.3 percent of the vote in North Carolina, Governor Lester Maddox, or other conservative candidates is very clear evidence that much of our party's membership did not have a voice," Hunt said.[19] Although the McGovern commission ignored his call to attract conservative southerners, commissioners backed measures to include youth, women, and minorities in the delegate selection process. Chairman McGovern used the knowledge of the new rules to become the party's presidential nominee in 1972.

In North Carolina, Hunt favored similar efforts to broaden the party. In a newsletter, the attorney suggested that the Democrats authorize a commission to study party reorganization as a way to attract younger members. "I believe we ought to prescribe that a certain percentage of our Democratic precinct, county and state committee positions be held by young people under the age of 30," Hunt said.[20] In the summer of 1969, he urged the party chairman to appoint a commission to study how to broaden the Democratic base.

Later in 1969, Hunt received a position that gave the young attorney his first statewide publicity. That fall, Governor Robert Scott chose Jim Hunt to head a commission to rewrite the state party rules. Chairman Johnson said that he honored Hunt with the appointment for the good job he had done as his assistant. Scott recalled years later that the appointment had little to do with helping Hunt's future political career. At a ceremony introducing the commission, Scott said that Hunt's commission would guarantee young people a voice in the affairs of the party and set about bringing the organization's rules and regulations in line with modern concepts. Hunt's panel included lawyers, lawmakers, educators, students, labor leaders, and businessmen of different ages and races. The diverse group included former party chairman Bert Bennett, who managed Hunt in two gubernatorial campaigns; Southport insurance agent Margaret Harper, whose 1968 run for lieutenant governor signaled the rise of female candidates running seriously for statewide office; state American Federation of Labor–Congress of Industrial Organizations (AFL-CIO) leader Wilbur Hobby; progressive legislators George Wood, Liston Ramsey, and Henry Frye, the first African American elected to the General Assembly since the 1890s; and black leaders Eva Clayton of eastern North Carolina and John Winters of Raleigh. Because of his new position, Hunt traveled within the state, holding hearings and meeting with friends.[21]

Hunt told Scott that he would use the commission to broaden the base of the state Democratic party. Hunt sought to bring in more responsible young people, create more democratic operations, and adopt more modernized rules. During the fall of 1969, his commission held four meetings. In one session, black attorney James Ferguson lamented the fact that blacks felt they had no voice in the counsels of either the state government or the Democratic party organization. Hunt also heard from the party's females, students, and conservative white males. "Although some of the testimony we received was from the fringe, most of it was well thought out, based on experience and existing situations, and presented in a sympathetic manner," Hunt wrote Democrats in December 1969.[22]

A month later, Hunt's commission issued its final report, which advocated the inclusion of more women, young people, and minorities into Democratic politics. To increase the number of blacks in precinct leadership roles, he called for three vice chairpersons with one female member and one minority member, and one "a young person thirty years of age or under."[23] He also urged the party to simplify its procedures. Governor Scott praised the report for providing for substantial improvements without favoring radical changes in party organization, and he commended Hunt for his countless hours of work. After the North Carolina Democratic Executive Committee approved the Hunt plan, United States Senator George McGovern hailed it as a model for state parties across the nation.[24]

Hunt understood that the Democratic party needed to be reformed to compete with the rising southern Republicans. Conservative southern Democrats, a party bloc who felt alienated for more than two decades from the national party, began finding a home in the GOP. The solid Democratic South had ended in 1948 when President Harry Truman endorsed a civil rights plank in the party platform and sparked a short-lived revolt by the "Dixiecrats." President Dwight D. Eisenhower made inroads among border-state Republicans with 1952 victories in Virginia, Tennessee, Florida, and Texas. Twelve years later, Republican presidential candidate Barry Goldwater won Deep South states by opposing civil rights legislation that protected the rights of African Americans. Conservative southern Democrats abandoned the party of their grandfathers and increasingly voted for GOP candidates.[25]

By 1970, Hunt understood that President Richard Nixon was trying to attract southern Democrats with a clever "southern strategy." To achieve this goal, Nixon carefully appealed to segregationists. He told his advisors to "quit bragging about school desegregation. We do what the law requires— nothing more."[26] In one speech, Nixon demanded that the South not be treated as a second-class part of the nation. To the consternation of moderate Republicans in his own administration, he urged that the Justice Department slow down the pace of school integration. Later, the president announced his opposition to the involuntary busing of school children away from their neighborhoods for the purpose of racial balance. He nominated conservative southerners Clement Haynsworth and Harold Carswell to the Supreme Court, despite their segregationist backgrounds. When they were rejected, he condemned the United States Senate for attacking the South. Nixon was determined to create a GOP base in the region.[27]

George Wallace of Alabama, the symbol of southern defiance, thwarted Nixon's efforts to attract southern conservative votes. In the 1940s, Wallace had entered Democratic politics to fight for the underprivileged citizens of Alabama. After the 1958 gubernatorial race, he turned to race politics after being "outniggered" by a segregationist opponent. He won the office in 1962. Wallace mixed his resistance to civil rights with populist appeals condemning federal bureaucrats and New Left radicals, a strategy that won him a national following. In 1968, he ran for president on the American party ticket, siphoning off conservative votes that might have gone to Nixon.[28]

In early 1970, Wallace desired a base to run for president again. In the Democratic gubernatorial primary, he challenged Alabama Governor Albert Brewer, who took a moderate approach on racial matters and concentrated on economic development. Despite his pledge to focus on economic issues and acquiring secret aid from the Nixon administration, Brewer could not withstand Wallace's racist appeals. Defeating Brewer by a narrow margin, Wallace proved that race prejudice could still win elections in the Deep South.[29]

Wallace's victory over Brewer, along with the defeats of Senators Al Gore, Sr., of Tennessee and Ralph Yarborough of Texas in 1970, encouraged Jim Hunt to avoid appearing too liberal on social and racial issues. Gore belonged to a progressive Democratic faction in Tennessee that had included United States Senator Estes Kefauver and Governor Frank Clement. Political scientists Jack Bass and Walter DeVries described Kefauver as a man ahead of his time who put together a coalition supported by African Americans, labor, urban low-income whites, small farmers and urban liberals. Brought to national prominence after chairing televised hearings on organized crime, he served as Democratic presidential candidate Adlai Stevenson's running mate in 1956. Like Kefauver, Gore had used this coalition to win successive elections to the United States Senate. By 1970, the Tennessee Republicans, a state party that had already proven its political strength since the Civil War because of its eastern mountain base, sensed the possibility of defeating the senator. Gore's opposition to the Vietnam War, his support for civil rights legislation, and his rejection of Nixon's Supreme Court nominees made him many enemies. Biographer Bob Zelnick said that Gore's record was "tailor-made to be ground into mincemeat by the Nixon-Agnew team and its newly minted 'southern strategy.'"[30] Vice-President Spiro Agnew proclaimed Gore to be the number-one target of the Nixon administration. The attack campaign helped Republican Congressman Bill Brock defeat Gore, an event which encouraged younger southern Democrats, including Hunt and the Senator's son Al Gore, Jr., to avoid the liberal label when running for office.

The defeat of Senator Ralph Yarborough of Texas also increased Hunt's sense that southerners rejected liberal candidates. Both Republicans and conservative Democrats hoped to oust Senator Yarborough because of his support of civil rights and the Great Society. President Nixon urged Congressman George Bush of Houston to run against Yarborough, believing that he could succeed despite his failure to defeat the senator in 1964. However, conservative candidate Lloyd Bentsen defeated Yarborough in the Democratic primary. Bush, who hoped to challenge the liberal Democrat, faced an opponent who opposed busing, high taxes, and liquor sold by the drink. In November 1970, Bentsen defeated the future president in the general election. The election again confirmed to Hunt that southern liberal candidates often failed in achieving victories in elections involving social issues.[31]

At the same time, Hunt realized that Democrats could lose elections by completely ignoring the increasing African American vote in the South. Because Virginia's conservative Democratic Byrd regime forced the schools to close to prevent integration, Republican gubernatorial candidate Lynwood Holton won inroads among African Americans in Virginia because many of them no longer viewed the Democrats as their friends. He proclaimed at his inaugural that "the era of defiance is behind us. Let our goal in Virginia be an aristocracy of ability, regardless of race, creed, or color."[32] In Arkansas, Republican candidate Winthrop Rockefeller created a similar coalition among white liberals, Republicans, and African Americans who rejected the segregationist regime of Democratic governor Orval Faubus.

The main insight that Hunt gained in the southern elections of 1970 and 1971 was the success of politicians who were liberal on race and gender issues, but who were moderate or conservative on economic matters. These politicians understood that black voter registration had increased dramatically because of the Voting Rights Act, totaling 3.5 million voters by 1975. Jack Bass and Walter DeVries described these politicians in *The Transformation of Southern Politics:*

> A wave of "New South" Democratic governors in the 1970s—men such as Dale Bumpers and David Pryor in Arkansas, Reubin Askew of Florida, Jimmy Carter and George Busbee of Georgia, John West of South Carolina, [Edwin] Edwards of Louisiana, and William Waller of Mississippi showed varying degrees of responsiveness to the interest of blacks, and also the interests of working class whites.... Few of the new governors dealt daily with problems that directly affected blacks and that segment of the population — white and black — with incomes below the poverty level. There was more emphasis on people's programs, such as expansion of public kindergartens, prison reform, consumer and environmental programs, governmental reorganization, and an end to the divisive racial politics exemplified by [Governor] Lester Maddox in Georgia and [Governor] John Bell Williams in Mississippi. The new governors by and large were moderates, but not liberals—"liberals" remained a suspect political label in the South.[33]

Hunt especially admired a former naval officer who won election as governor of Georgia in 1970. Understanding that "rustics" won elections in Georgia by portraying their opponents as excessively urbanized, James Earl Carter, Jr., described himself as a simple peanut farmer from Plains who shared the traditional values of rural Georgians. Carter portrayed his Democratic opponent, former governor Carl Sanders, as a member of the despised liberal establishment in Atlanta, a country club cocktail drinker, a fellow traveler of the late Dr. Martin Luther King, Jr., and an enemy of George Wallace. While declaring ambiguous support for racial quality, Jimmy Carter claimed that he would not be beholden to the black "bloc" vote, endorsed private schools, and insured that "local people"[34] would control education. After Carter defeated Sanders and won the general election, many of his supporters believed that he would fight to maintain segregation. In reality, Carter used racial demagoguery for political expediency to get elected governor and thereby concealed his ambition to help African Americans.[35]

As governor of Georgia, Carter developed the progressive style that Hunt later borrowed as his own. In his January 1971 inaugural speech, Carter declared that the "time for racial discrimination was over. No poor, rural, weak, or black person should ever have to bear the additional burden of being deprived of the opportunity of a job, an education, or simply justice."[36] By the end of his term, he hung the portraits of Martin Luther King, Jr., and other black Georgians in the state capital. Such symbolic efforts impressed African Americans and the national media, including *Time*, which put him on the cover in 1971 as the symbol of the "New South." Carter developed a liberal philosophy regarding race and women's issues while remaining conservative on religious and economic matters. The governor's domestic program called for altering state departments and strengthening the ethics codes. Impressed by his ability to heal racial divisions while attracting rural traditionalists and conservative businessmen, Jim Hunt applauded the governor's efforts. At a fundraising dinner in 1973, Hunt, by then the lieutenant governor, described Jimmy Carter as a man who created programs that equalized education funds between rich and poor counties, reorganized state government to make it more responsive to the citizens, initiated a thorough reform of the judicial system, and provided for more equitable taxation.[37]

Other candidates adopted the Carter approach. Even in Louisiana and Mississippi, states with terrible histories of volatile race relations, voters seemed ready for Democrats who would bring the races together. In 1971, Louisiana voters rejected Jimmie Davis, a country singer and former segregationist governor, for Congressman Edwin Edwards, a candidate who mixed his amoral personal habits with appeals to African Americans and working-class whites. In his first term, Edwards doubled the taxes on natural gas and oil, removed the sales tax, and backed a bond issue for a $54 million technical education school system. Like Hunt, he was elected to four terms as a Democrat using racial alliances and progressive education policies; unlike the Tar Heel governor, he gambled, womanized, befriended notorious persons, and got convicted of racketeering in 2000. Also in 1971, William Waller of Mississippi won a gubernatorial race using racist overtones, but he changed his style once in office. Originally considered a racial moderate for his unsuccessful efforts to prosecute Byron de la Beckwith for the murder of civil rights leader Medgar Evers, the attorney won the Democratic nomination against candidates representing the Mississippi segregationist establishment. When Medgar's brother Charles Evers became the main independent candidate to challenge Waller in the 1971 gubernatorial election, the conservative segregationists decided to rally around Waller's candidacy. Fearing the election of a black governor in Mississippi, conservative white voters gave Waller a majority and hoped that the governor-elect would continue the tradition of resistance to integration. Instead, Waller occasionally met with civil rights leaders and won praise as the first Mississippi governor to improve race relations since Reconstruction.[38]

Across the Mississippi River, Arkansas already had elected a progressive governor. To the surprise of the experts in 1970, Dale Bumpers, a relatively unknown attorney with a sense of wit and grace, defeated former governor Orval Faubus in the Democratic primary and Governor Winthrop Rockefeller in the general election. Governor Bumpers told *Time* in 1971 that he won because of the cry for new leadership in the South. Actually, he achieved victory when progressives and African Americans returned to the Democratic party because they nominated a folksy, likable candidate who rejected Faubus's racist style.[39]

Hunt certainly understood the new political trend when his neighboring state of South Carolina also elected a progressive governor in 1970. Like Jimmy Carter, John West also muted his support of civil rights during the gubernatorial campaign. Even though he had stood against the Ku Klux Klan and opposed ending compulsory school attendance as a state senator, Lieutenant Governor West, when running for governor, attacked the United States Department of Health, Education, and Welfare (HEW) for "social experimentation" regarding busing. During the gubernatorial campaign, he refused to comment on a white racist attack on a Darlington County school bus carrying African-American children. Despite West's tacit appeals to racists, South Carolina's black voters, who increased their registration by seventeen percent since 1964, backed West over the Republican party candidate supported by United States Senator Strom Thurmond, one of the first major Deep South politicians to switch to the GOP. Governor West announced at his inauguration that he was for "a government that is totally color blind,"[40] and later backed a state housing authority, the public financing of low and middle-income housing and food stamps, and affirmative action as a way to solve racial hiring problems.[41]

In 1970, Florida also elected a Democratic governor who favored progressive policies on race and politics. That year, Reubin Askew was a forty-two-year-old obscure state senator and a devout Presbyterian who worked fourteen hours a day on complex issues. Running for governor, he campaigned for complete financial disclosure for candidates, an issue that Hunt borrowed in his campaign for lieutenant governor. Askew attracted the Sunshine State's increasing urban dwellers who had grown tired of the segregationist politicians from the Panhandle. In November 1970, Florida sent Askew to Tallahassee and progressive state senator Lawton Chiles to Washington. Askew stood firm for an increase in the corporate income tax rate and supported busing as means to achieve school integration. "The South," Askew said, "is ready to adjust and become part of the nation."[42]

By 1971, Hunt understood that the political environment of the American South had changed dramatically since his college years. Despite his understanding that many southerners disdained the "liberal" label, he knew that blacks, youth, and feminists were increasing their political clout in the South. He knew of the region's large youth generation that demanded the right to participate in political decisions. He understood that African Americans, aided by the Voting Rights Act, had registered in larger numbers than ever before. He realized that American women, even in the traditional South, begun to discover their own need for political and economic fulfillment. Hunt watched as a new generation of southern politicians tried to combine these new voting groups into a new Democratic coalition. Southern governors Jimmy Carter, Dale Bumpers, Reubin Askew, and Edwin Edwards became the leaders of a regional political revolution. Keeping white rural traditionalist Democrats and the newly empowered groups within the same coalition appeared to be the ultimate struggle for the southern Democratic politician of the 1970s. As that decade began, Jim Hunt decided to take on this challenge by announcing his first bid for statewide public office.

6

"Keep Your Eye on Him": Hunt's 1972 Campaign for North Carolina Lieutenant Governor

James B. Hunt, Jr., entered the race for lieutenant governor in North Carolina with several strengths and weaknesses. He had achieved a little fame from his service as chairman of a state Democratic party commission from 1969 to 1970, but political insiders knew him better than average citizens. In 1972, Hunt faced opponents who could outspend the attorney by thousands of dollars and who faulted him for his lack of legislative and executive experience. He managed to win the lieutenant gubernatorial election because of the support of an old progressive political network and his own skills as a politician. Ironically, the breakdown of the North Carolina Democratic party in 1972 magnified Hunt's success.

After he had served as chairman of the North Carolina Democratic Study Commission in 1969, the news media wrote positively about Jim Hunt. *Greensboro Daily News* columnist Nat Walker called the attorney a rising political star who engineered from divergent views a program of sweeping change within the state Democratic party and said that a statewide race in 1972 was a possibility. "Keep Your Eye on Him!" Graham Jones wrote in a North Carolina State University alumni magazine in May 1970, congratulating Hunt for winning national acclaim for his party reforms.[1] An *Asheville Citizen* editorialist said, "Jim Hunt, Jr., seems to have his feet on the ground and his eyes trained on the future."[2]

Enthusiasm for Hunt led to speculation that he might become the party chairman when Jimmy Johnson left the job in 1969. He had a few fervent supporters in eastern North Carolina. "Jim is an enthusiastic force in our party and a true Democrat twenty-four hours of each 365 days of each year," said Wilson attorney Robert Farris.[3] A Rocky Mount businessman predicted that assistant North Carolina Democratic Party Chairman Hunt would replace the retiring chairman. Although Hunt's name indeed appeared on a list of replacements for that position, the attorney had other plans. After declaring that he had devoted "far less time to my wife, four children, and my law practice than I should," he resigned as assistant chairman.[4] Hunt, however, had not given up on a run for statewide office in 1972, even though he was not sure which office he might seek.

As early as 1968, he recruited a key lieutenant for his future statewide races. Joe Grimsley, a former acquaintance from Stantonsburg High School in Wilson County, impressed the attorney by receiving a bachelor's degree in public administration at the University of North Carolina and a master's degree in the same field at George Washington University. Grimsley, a Fulbright scholar, had also managed Peace Corps volunteers in Washington, D.C., and Tegucigalpa, Honduras. On a chance meeting in the nation's capital in 1968, Hunt had told Grimsley that it was time for him "to come back home because we can do something with the state."[5] After Grimsley had returned to North Carolina to work for the Coastal Plains Regional Commission, he and Hunt had visited YDC meetings to lay the groundwork for a future campaign.[6]

Hunt also relied heavily on former North Carolina Democratic Party Chairman Bert Bennett to help him win the state election. "With Bennett's help," political scientist Paul Luebke wrote in *Tar Heel Politics 2000*, "Hunt established a coalition based on old-fashioned county-by-county personal networks."[7] Bennett had managed the 1960 campaign of North Carolina Governor Terry Sanford, creating a base of loyal followers in all counties of the state. The former DNC chairman had won the support of sheriffs and businessmen for his candidate just by assuring them that he was the right man for the job. He and his business partners also had enough money to loan generously to a campaign.[8]

During the 1960s, many believed that Phil Carlton, not Jim Hunt, would become the young man whom Bennett's political organization would elect governor. Both Hunt and Carlton were reared in eastern farm families, served as high school presidents and officers in the Future Farmers of America, worked in the student government of North Carolina State College in the late 1950s, and volunteered for the campaign to elect Terry Sanford governor in 1960. Indeed, Carlton had a higher profile in the Sanford administration than Hunt. Reared in affluence, Carlton cultivated his family's connections with Bennett through the United Methodist Church and Shell Oil Company. After serving as a driver for Sanford in the gubernatorial campaign, Carlton had become the appointment secretary in the governor's office. In 1963, the year he had received his law degree, Carlton had prepared to run Bennett's gubernatorial campaign before he had dropped out of the race. Afterwards, Carlton had managed the campaign office of Bennett's handpicked gubernatorial candidate Richardson Preyer.[9]

Bennett insisted that he never chose between the two young men whom he called the best two volunteers of the unsuccessful 1964 effort to elect Richardson Preyer governor. After Hunt requested Bennett's help in his lieutenant gubernatorial campaign in 1971, they met at a Greenville restaurant with Carlton. Bennett told Hunt that he could throw his support to him, but his first commitment was to Carlton, who was elected district court judge in 1968. Bennett asked Carlton if he planned to run for the same office. "I'm not going to run for anything," Carlton replied.[10] The young judge got out of Hunt's way, deciding that he did not have the fire in the belly to enter the race.

Besides Bennett and his followers, Hunt had his own political contacts. Since the 1950s, he had made friends in the North Carolina Grange and the Future Farmers of America (FFA). During the 1960s, he kept in touch with his former classmates at North Carolina State College and the law school at the University of North Carolina at Chapel Hill. However, Hunt made his most important political contacts in the state's Young Democratic Club (YDC) organization. He once handed an aide a briefcase filled with YDC names. "He had signup sheets of people who came to meetings and when he was running for YDC president," former press secretary Paul Essex recalled. "He kept all that stuff and used all that stuff."[11]

In 1970, Hunt still questioned which state office he should seek. Understanding he was not prepared to become governor in 1972, he focused on the office of lieutenant governor. In the 1960s, the part-time elected job had low pay, no staff, and few responsibilities. In 1970, Governor Bob Scott introduced a government reorganization plan that called for a full-time lieutenant governor. Legislators who hungered for the position, and who did not expect Hunt to win, made the office more attractive by allowing the lieutenant governor to retain his power to appoint North Carolina Senate committee chairpersons. When North Carolinians approved the change to full-time status by ratifying state constitutional changes in a referendum, Hunt decided to run for the position.[12]

As Hunt privately planned his campaign in 1971, he understood the need to appeal to conservatives in the Democratic party who agreed with Alabama Governor George Wallace or President Richard Nixon. In one speech, Hunt strongly endorsed the free enterprise system, declaring that Nixon handled the economy well. He told a convention of police officers that a decline in traditional values undermined the nation's system of laws, education, and family life. He praised Federal Bureau of Investigation Director J. Edgar Hoover at a time when the director's use of surveillance of suspected radicals was under media criticism. He presented himself genuinely as a moral family man that wanted to revive family values and aid law enforcement.[13]

Although Hunt expressed conservative themes on morality and crime, he took a progressive view regarding the participation of African Americans, women, and young people in politics. To these groups, he cited his service on a North Carolina Democratic party commission that called for more minority and female participation at the precinct levels. He attracted established African Americans by promoting minority-owned businesses and funding for predominantly black colleges. To get the female vote, Hunt condemned gender bias in business and endorsed the Equal Rights Amendment. He attracted the young baby-boom generation with a college speaking tour, urging them to get involved in efforts for environmental protection, population control, and penal reform. Paul Dickson, a former UNC–Chapel Hill student activist known for ending the 1963 North Carolina Speaker Ban Law, served as Hunt's college director until his tragic death in a car crash in April 1972.[14]

Hunt also became attuned to the demand for a cleaner environment. A series of ecological disasters awakened citizens to the threat of industrial pollution and spawned an environmental movement that celebrated the first Earth Day in 1970. In response, President Nixon signed landmark legislation, the Environmental Protection Act and the Clean Air and Water Act. In North Carolina, factories threatened nearby lakes and forests. The state had no managed growth policy in 1971 to curtail developers from threatening state wildlife. To preserve the mountains and coasts of North Carolina, Hunt promoted effective state-managed growth.[15]

Jim Hunt mixed his environmentalism with efforts to aid rural economic growth. He understood North Carolina ranked near the bottom in per capita income and industrial wages. He endorsed the idea of "balanced growth" to protect the environment and to allow all regions of the state to develop at equal rates. Hunt said that each region would have "growth centers," or rural towns where the state government would encourage local migration, preventing huge population shifts in the largest cities. "We should be committed to guiding our growth and development to avoid both rural blight and metropolitan ugliness and congestion," he told an audience. To achieve this goal, Hunt called for the expansion of rural roads and the building of airports in rural areas. He believed so fervently in balanced growth that many considered him North Carolina's strongest advocate for state planning.[16]

Hunt also created an agenda for North Carolina public education. Realizing that the state had too many illiterates, he strongly backed a public kindergarten program for all Tar Heel children. Desiring the endorsement of the North Carolina Association of Educators (NCAE), he backed teacher salary increases, more money for holders of advanced teacher certificates, and a smaller pupil-teacher ratio. To conservatives, he promised stronger discipline in the classroom. To the community college presidents, he advocated greater flexibility in the management of their funds. Such stands made him acceptable to teachers and school administrators as the true "education" candidate for lieutenant governor.[17]

Hunt made few statements about the mandatory busing of school children for integration. In 1971, white parents in the Charlotte area sued to prevent their children from being bused to a predominantly black public school. The case reached the United States Supreme Court, where the justices ruled in the *Swann* decision that busing could be used for the purpose of public-school integration. Conservative North Carolina fumed at what they called "forced busing." Understanding that busing divided his Democratic coalition, Jim Hunt avoided the contentious issue.[18]

At the Sir Walter Raleigh Inn at the state's capital on October 4, 1971, James B. Hunt declared himself a candidate for lieutenant governor. Beside him stood his wife Carolyn, his parents Elsie and James, Sr., his four young children, campaign workers, and political allies. "I have found a desire for new and fresh leadership in North Carolina," Hunt said. He reached out to conservatives by calling for a return to patriotism and an end to the trend of increasing bureaucracy by 'solving our problems in Washington'."[19] Yet, he sought the support of progressives by praising "those who are working to strengthen us today—young people and conservationists who are dedicated to preserving our natural resources, law enforcement officers, and leaders—black and white."[20]

Jim Hunt appealed to different constituencies within the North Carolina Democratic party. The candidate's criticism of the federal bureaucracy and praise of patriotism won him support from his elderly cousin Joseph Hunt, the former North Carolina House speaker, and former Democratic National Committeeman Billy Webb, both of whom usually backed conservative Democratic candidates. Hunt's previous service to Bert Bennett's progressive candidates helped him get the backing of the oil dealer's former allies, including North Carolina Highway Commissioner Lauch Faircloth and American Federation of Labor–Congress of Industrial Organizations (AFL-CIO) leader Wilbur Hobby. Minorities and women favored Hunt because they believed that he would aid the cause of equal rights. Clarence Lightner, an African-American councilman from Raleigh who later became that city's first black mayor, lent support early in the campaign. Greensboro Democratic leader Jane Patterson and Wilson Democrat Betty McCain became prominent female supporters. He won over young idealistic college students, including future Hunt staffers Jack Cozort and Tom Taft. Hunt's campaign also attracted his former acquaintances from high school, farm organizations, and universities. Hunt's energetic personality mesmerized other people. Paul Essex, who went to North Carolina State College with Hunt and later served as a chief copy editor for the *News and Observer*, offered his help and later became the candidate's first press secretary. "I thought it was short term," he said, "but it evolved into service to Hunt for thirteen years." By cautiously defining his goals, Hunt attracted a large following.[21]

Other North Carolina politicians also sought the lieutenant gubernatorial office. At the time that Hunt made his announcement, North Carolina House Speaker Phil Godwin planned to run. Godwin had achieved notoriety in 1963 when he introduced a bill successfully outlawing communists from speaking at state universities. While his action angered academics and editorial writers, it had won him the admiration of conservative Democratic legislators who elected him to the House's top position. Hoping to be elected lieutenant governor in 1972, the conservative Democrat prevented any attempt to weaken the office. He never received the financial support that he desired or the public support of other officeholders, however. By the end of 1971, the ultraconservative Democrat decided not to run for the state's second highest executive office that he had strengthened as a legislator.[22]

The man who worried the Hunt campaign the most was Roy Sowers, the North Carolina Secretary of Natural and Economic Resources for Governor Robert Scott. Sowers appealed to older conservative voters, World War II veterans, and the influential rural county politicians who answered to Ben Roney, the former campaign manager of Governor Kerr Scott. Bennett and other Hunt supporters disdained the Roney organization for using political office primarily for the spoils of state contracts rather than for the goal of progressive government. Many businessmen considered Sowers the favored candidate and therefore co-signed a substantial campaign loan in 1971.[23]

Like Hunt, Roy Sowers varied his positions to appeal to both progressive and conservative Democrats. As the cabinet secretary in charge of protecting the state's land, he promoted environmental reform. Sowers also called for state financing of volunteer rescue squads and promoted a fund for middle-income families to borrow money to pay large medical bills. To appease conservative voters, he vowed not to back any state tax increases, condemned inflation, and promised to fight against "forced busing" to integrate the public schools. He also made his opponent an issue. Saying that he had no higher goal than to serve as lieutenant governor, Sowers accused Hunt of running for the position as part of a larger plan to grab the governor's mansion in 1976.[24]

While Hunt hoped to defeat Sowers by winning the votes of politically active Democratic women, he realized that a female opponent presented an obstacle to his plan. Margaret Harper, an insurance agent and the wife of a Southport newspaper editor, ran second in the 1968 lieutenant gubernatorial Democratic primary and hoped to finish first in 1972. She established herself as an active member of the North Carolina Democratic party while also serving as president of the North Carolina Federation of Women's Clubs and secretary-treasurer of the North Carolina Press Association. Understanding that the women's movement awakened female consciousness about their potential political power, she thought she might have a chance to become the first female lieutenant governor in North Carolina history.[25]

Although Hunt campaigners did not think that Harper could win, they took her ability to attract progressive female voters seriously, and therefore took positions favored by many feminists. Hunt opposed gender bias in the workplace, endorsed female participation in business and government, and strongly favored the Equal Rights Amendment (ERA), which declared that equality of rights under the law would not be denied or abridged by the United States or by any state on account of sex. Some of his aides worried about Hunt taking a strong pro–ERA position. "Jim might want to leave out the objective about the passage of the Equal Rights Amendment (in a speech to a woman's club) since many attorneys think what is needed is enforcement, not a new constitutional amendment," Guilford County Democratic Women Chairman Jane Patterson wrote Grimsley. "They say we have in the Constitution plenty of backing for equal rights for women."[26] However, the threat of Harper taking votes from the Wilson attorney influenced him to make a forceful stand for the amendment. On February 7, 1972, Hunt announced to the Winston-Salem Business and Professional Women's Club that he supported ERA, declaring that more than fifty percent of human talent was still shackled by attitudes, customs, and laws that discriminated against women. Such rhetoric helped Hunt undermine Harper and attract talented political women to his campaign.[27]

The Hunt campaign took less seriously the only African-American candidate in the lieutenant gubernatorial race. When Reginald Frazier, a black attorney from New Bern, announced for lieutenant governor, he hoped that his "visionary" candidacy would win a majority of blacks and white liberals. Established African Americans spurned his efforts and rising young black politicians like Chapel Hill Mayor Howard Lee refused to back his campaign because they considered Hunt a responsive candidate who would address minority concerns. African American leaders also did not believe a black candidate could win election as lieutenant governor in 1972. Upset over the lack of support from the black elite, Frazier spoke of secret deals between black leaders and Hunt. No strong proof existed of secret agreements, however.[28]

The Hunt campaign mostly focused on the well-financed campaign of Roy Sowers. Hunt heard that several anonymous wealthy people had pledged to co-sign loans worth $15,000 each to finance the cabinet secretary's campaign. Hunt wanted to take advantage of his humble financial status, highlight his ethical approach to government, and stress his main opponent's ties to millionaires. Hunt revealed his major donors at a February 1972 press conference and asked his opponents to do the same. He said that most of his expenses came from businessmen Miles Smith, Jr., and Bert Bennett, "none of whom has any business relationship with the state or makes policy decisions for the state."[29] He criticized the state campaign law that called for revealing expenditures only in the year of the election, and demanded that a new law make it mandatory to list the sources of campaign funds for an entire campaign.[30]

Sowers believed that he had no choice but to respond to the Wilson attorney's efforts to portray himself as the most ethical candidate. Despite his financial edge, Sowers understood the popularity of Hunt among Democratic insiders, eastern Democrats, urban progressives, and the politicians in Bert Bennett's informal organization. In an informal poll of seventy-seven county chairmen in February 1972, thirty-nine listed Hunt as the probable nominee. Advertisements highlighted Hunt's accomplishments, education, and youthful appearance. The day after Hunt made a campaign reform speech, Sowers revealed his major campaign financiers. That pleased the Hunt campaign. "We forced him to file [his donor lists] and showed that bad boy was getting big money," Grimsley recalled.[31] Sowers could not win by whatever action he took, since revealing the funds played into the Hunt campaign staff's efforts to portray their candidate as a man of the people and his main opponent as a candidate of the wealthy.

Hunt also increased his ethical image by backing reforms for the state senate where he would preside as lieutenant governor. In April 1972, he

called for the reduction of legislative committees, the creation of permanent professional legislative staffs, and the service of standing committees
between legislative sessions, the use of electronic voting machines, verba-
tim transcripts of all floor debates, and a strong open meeting law. While
he opposed the lieutenant governor getting extra pay for presiding over
the state senate, he rejected efforts to weaken the office by ending that
official's power to appoint committee chairpersons. Although one opponent labeled his proposals "so visionary as to defy passage,"[32] the Raleigh
News and Observer praised the candidate for advocating serious legislative
reforms.

In the spring of 1972, Terry Sanford, the candidate for whom Bennett and Hunt had worked fervently twelve years earlier, suddenly became
a distraction when he announced his bid for the United States presidency.
After completing his gubernatorial term, Sanford had served as the president of Duke University, winning praise for quelling radical campus dis-
turbances and balancing the university budget. Observing the Democratic
presidential primary, the university president expressed alarm at the failure of moderate Democratic presidential candidates like Edmund Muskie
to stop the rise of United States Senator George McGovern on the left or
Alabama Governor George Wallace on the right. Sanford especially hated
the idea of Wallace winning the first Democratic presidential primary ever
held in North Carolina. A progressive governor when Wallace demanded
segregation forever in the early 1960s, Sanford considered the Alabama
governor a demagogue who represented everything wrong with the New
South. Wanting to stop Wallace, he announced his candidacy, even though
the national party's moderately liberal faction looked to other candidates
like Senator Hubert Humphrey to stop both McGovern and Wallace from
winning the nomination.[33]

The Hunt campaign was not pleased with Terry Sanford's quixotic
presidential run. Bert Bennett said that a presidential campaign "doesn't
ring a bell with me" and focused exclusively on Hunt. Sanford gave up on
Bennett's support and relied heavily on his Duke University friends. However, the former governor often called upon his old contacts to aid his
presidential effort. Biographers Howard Covington and Marion Ellis said,
"Sanford's raid into the ranks of the old organization widened a growing
gap between Sanford and Bennett, whose political interests were on separate tracks."[34] The oil dealer got upset when the Duke president recruited
C. Woodrow Teague, a Raleigh lawyer and former campaigner of the 1960
election. Also, the Hunt campaign worried that Sanford would link Hunt
with the former governor's traditional liberalism that the Wilson attorney
had abandoned. Grimsley recalled that the campaign did not want to

defend Sanford's national positions. To the detriment of Sanford's campaign, Hunt kept his distance.[35]

The Hunt campaign did not want to alienate the supporters of George Wallace. The Alabama governor had a strong following among white eastern Tar Heels who agreed with his opposition to busing and contempt for New Left radicals. Nearly a third of North Carolina voters choose Wallace in his independent bid for the presidency in 1968. Although Hunt opposed Wallace's racial demagoguery, he found clever ways to link himself with the presidential candidate in 1972. He urged publicly that Wallace supporters be treated fairly in North Carolina and demanded that the Alabama governor be respected like any other candidate on the Democratic ticket. By remaining neutral in the presidential race, he upset Sanford supporters, but he maintained his ties among Wallace Democrats who gave their candidate a triumphant victory over Sanford in the May presidential primary. Wallace felt optimistic about his prospects after the North Carolina primary until Arthur Bremer shot and paralyzed him in a Maryland shopping center that same month.[36]

In the final weeks of the Democratic primary campaign, the Hunt workers were optimistic about the outcome. Despite a declaration by a Raleigh newspaper that Hunt, Roy Sowers, and Margaret Harper were locked in a close race, the Wilson attorney announced that he could probably win more than 50 percent of the vote, which would allow him to avoid a runoff. On May 6, 1972, Hunt finished in first place among five candidates. The Wilson attorney won 84 of 100 counties and 44 percent of the vote, ahead of Sowers with 23 percent of the vote and Harper with 20 percent. Although Hunt did not avoid the possibility of a runoff, his supporters celebrated his two-to-one margin victory over his main opponents. The Hunt team also marveled that they had defeated Sowers who spent nearly five times as much money as the Wilson lawyer. Hunt supporter David Bruton said that the election marked a decrease of influence in the "old line" traditional Democrats who backed the environmental secretary.[37]

As the second highest vote winner, Sowers had the right to call a runoff against Hunt. As he considered his decision, many of Margaret Harper's supporters opted for the Wilson attorney, including Juanita Bryant of Booneville, Harper's campaign chairperson, who announced that she would join Hunt's staff as a statewide coordinator. Although Harper did not endorse Hunt, Bryant said that various county women's organizations were ready to come "by the scores"[38] if Sowers called for a runoff. Already, Semi Mintz, a local tennis champion who worked for the Harper campaign, endorsed Hunt. The addition of Harper's supporters only added to the Hunt campaign's sense of strength. "I think it would be very foolish for Sowers to call a runoff," Henderson County Hunt-for-Lieutenant-Governor Chairman Terry Lyda said. "However, if he does, we will be ready for him."[39] Hunt's campaign staff shared the same confidence. On May 12, 1972, Roy Sowers decided not to challenge Jim Hunt in a Democratic runoff election. He announced that he would back Hunt because the state needed new blood and new energy. Concerned over divisions within the party in other state races, he said that there should be no Democratic runoffs. Sowers did not say what many Hunt campaigners believed — he could not defeat Hunt because of the Bennett organization's strength and the addition of Harper's supporters. Hunt thanked the candidate for running a "lean, issue-oriented campaign"[40] and prepared that summer for a tour of all one hundred counties in North Carolina.

Even though Sowers and Hunt displayed unity after their campaigns, the 1972 North Carolina Democratic primary actually revealed signs of its worse intra-party divisions in decades. Such tension became apparent in the United States Senate race between incumbent B. Everett Jordan and challenger Nick Galafinakis. In his seventies and ailing, Jordan made a bid for a third Senate term in 1972. His opponent, a former attorney from Durham and a three-term congressman, represented urban Democrats who opposed the Vietnam War and supported the civil rights movement. To the surprise of Democratic regulars, the congressman defeated Jordan in the primary runoff.[41]

Conservative Democrats who voted for Jordan in the primary did not wish to support the Greek-American candidate in the general election. They turned to Republican senatorial candidate Jesse Helms, a former bank executive and broadcaster for the Tobacco Radio Network and WRAL-TV in Raleigh. As a conservative Democratic newspaperman in 1950, he had involved himself in a campaign that accused North Carolina's United States Senator Frank Porter Graham of softness on segregation and communism. As a television and radio commentator in the 1960s, Helms condemned the antiwar movement, civil rights leaders, and so-called welfare cheats. Despite his differences with President Richard Nixon on several issues, including affirmative action and détente with communist nations, he switched parties in 1970 and embraced the president's opposition to "forced busing" and antiwar radicals. While his conservative rhetoric angered liberal editorialists, Helms won himself a following among rural white Democrats.[42]

The main division among North Carolina Democrats occurred in the governor's race. Greensboro businessman Hargrove "Skipper" Bowles defeated Lieutenant Governor Pat Taylor to win the Democratic nomination for governor. Not counting on Bennett's progressive network or on

Taylor's conservative supporters, Bowles attracted voters using his own wealth to finance television advertising. After the businessman won the primary runoff, he brought few Taylor supporters into his campaign. Bennett said that the Bowles campaign "rubbed their nose at the Taylor people in defeat."[43] Howard Lee, a Bowles supporter, recalled that the businessman did not work hard to get the Taylor supporters to back him. Others said that Bowles harmed himself because he used too much of his own money to win the primary. State Representative Mickey Michaux claimed that people got the notion after a while that all he was doing was just buying the governor's seat.[44]

The victory of Republican candidate Jim Holshouser over Bowles eventually allowed Hunt to claim leadership status within the state Democratic party. A few months before his victory, Holshouser knew of few political experts who predicted that he would be elected the state's first GOP governor since 1896. The Boone native was reared in the western mountains where people had supported Republican candidates since the Civil War. Elected to the General Assembly from Watauga County in 1962, he rose to the position of senate minority leader, constantly pressing the Democratic legislators for political reform. Pushed on by his friends, Holshouser decided to run for governor even though victory seemed improbable. His own party, divided between traditional Republicans and former ultra-conservative Democrats, appeared less than united after he defeated Jim Gardner to win the gubernatorial nomination. However, Democratic infighting combined with the nomination of an ultra-liberal Democratic presidential nominee gave Holshouser a small advantage.[45]

During the summer and fall of 1972, Jim Hunt did all he could to disassociate himself from Democratic presidential nominee George McGovern, whose strong antiwar stance, liberal tax program, and support for marijuana decriminalization alienated a majority of North Carolinians. Like Bowles and Galifinakis, Hunt decided not to attend the 1972 Democratic National Convention that nominated McGovern. Hunt told the press that the presidential nominee would not be an asset to the ticket in North Carolina. He told the press, "I've had a number of people tell me that they were going to vote for Skipper (Bowles) and me, but that they couldn't vote for McGovern."[46] He understood that the state's citizens could distinguish between liberal national Democrats and progressive North Carolina Democrats.

"McGovern," Bert Bennett recalled, "was a hell of a problem."[47] Hunt feared that the unpopularity of the Democratic presidential nominee could cause his Republican opponent Johnny Walker to defeat him during the expected landslide of President Nixon. At campaign rallies, Hunt called for the victories of North Carolina Democratic candidates, but he never mentioned McGovern. Although he told a woman's group in February 1972 that Nixon cared more for "bombs than for babes,"[48] he praised the president in August for backing a network of community clinics. The lack of a strong McGovern-for-President organization involving prominent Tar Heels made avoidance of the Democratic presidential nominee easy. "We (the Hunt organization) were running our own campaign," Grimsley said. "We would not deny the candidate, but we would not make him an issue in the campaign."[49]

Johnny Walker, Hunt's Republican opponent, did all he could to tie himself with Nixon. A former native of Philadelphia and a sales executive for General Electric, he became a millionaire while serving as vice president of Lowe's Homebuilders in North Wilkesboro, North Carolina. Walker announced that he would spend $600,000 of his own money to be elected the state's first Republican lieutenant governor in the twentieth century. Nevertheless, his campaign struggled to catch up to Hunt. Many political experts criticized his advertisements; Bowles supporter Howard Lee said that he had "the dumbest ads I've ever seen." Republican supporter David Flaherty recalled that Walker connected himself on television with the Johnny Walker scotch advertisement, although North Carolina conservatives strongly opposed liquor. However, Walker mainly tied himself to Nixon, carrying a Nixon flag at a Greensboro rally that the president attended. Yet, Nixon's popularity seemed of only limited help to a candidate whom the Hunt campaign believed could not communicate well politically and who did not know the role of government well.[50] Walker could not take advantage of Democratic divisions since most members of the various factions planned to back Hunt.

Once again, Hunt was battling to defeat a better-financed opponent by becoming the advocate of campaign ethics and finance reform. On the eve of the campaign, he called for laws prohibiting gifts and money for legislative votes. Saying that campaign expenditures had soared to the point of absurdity, Hunt called for spending limits on candidates for governor and lieutenant governor. After the election, he backed legislation declaring that no more than twenty percent of campaign funds come from the candidate or his immediate family, endorsed multiple financial reports for all persons running for office, and backed jail terms for violators of the campaign laws. While most of his proposals never became state law, he profited politically from the reputation as an ethical reformer.[51]

In October 1972, Bowles understood that Hunt had achieved more popularity among Democrats and unsuccessfully tried to link himself with the candidate. A few months earlier, he had rejected an offer to combine his financial resources with Hunt's. Since that time, Bowles had slipped in the polls, and hoped that he could gain popularity by appearing with the popular lieutenant gubernatorial candidate. Bennett remembered Bowles asking him if he could get on a campaign plane with Hunt. "Skipper," Bennett recalled answering, "your polls must not be looking too good to ask that."[52] Bennett refused the request since he did not want Hunt to be associated with a campaign that seemingly did everything wrong.

In November 1972, as President Nixon carried forty-nine of fifty states against George McGovern, the North Carolina Democratic party suffered its worse electoral defeat since the 1890s. Republican candidates Jesse Helms and Jim Holshouser became the first victorious GOP senatorial and gubernatorial candidates respectively in the twentieth century. Democratic leaders appeared shocked at the extent of Nixon's coattails. However, Hunt survived the debacle, easily defeating Johnny Walker. His staff cancelled an election night celebration at the Golden Eagle motel because of the gloomy mood of the main Democratic gathering at the Sir Walter Raleigh Inn.[53]

James B. Hunt, Jr., won the 1972 lieutenant gubernatorial election by creating an effective campaign organization from Bert Bennett's political network and his own friends and allies from various organizations, especially the North Carolina Young Democrats. An outstanding campaigner thanks to his long experience in state politics, he discovered effective ways to appeal to conservatives on morality and crime while retaining liberal constituencies by emphasizing race, gender, and education. Although Hunt ran against well-financed opponents, they did not have the political organization or campaign skills to defeat him. Hunt also avoided party divisions that hurt other Democratic candidates in 1972. Surviving a divisive debacle within his own party, he became at age 35 the highest-ranking Democrat in North Carolina.

7

Learning How to Lead: Hunt's First Two Years as Lieutenant Governor

James B. Hunt, Jr., learned in his first two years as North Carolina lieutenant governor how to manage effectively the affairs of the state senate and the Democratic party. A youthful appearance and a reformist mentality made Hunt appear fresh to Americans growing upset about the Watergate scandal. As the state's highest-ranking Democrat, Hunt championed campaign ethics, environmental management, utility reform, women's rights, higher education standards, and the expansion of the East Carolina University Medical School. He gradually increased his effectiveness in the legislature through his power to appoint committee chairmen. After two years of service as lieutenant governor, Hunt turned the office into a powerful position from which to run for governor in 1976.

After Hunt's election as lieutenant governor in 1972, a columnist speculated how he would get along with North Carolina Governor James Holshouser, the first Republican to win the office since 1896. News reporter Nancy Bentsen wrote shortly after the 1972 victory, "How will the two Jims work together? Neither man drinks or smokes and both express deep religious convictions."[1] She predicted that divided party leadership of state government might make Hunt "the strongest lieutenant governor in state history."[2] Bentsen added that Holshouser would need Hunt's cooperation to get his programs enacted.

Such prophecies of legislative dominance seemed inconceivable in December 1972 after Hunt's team received a weak welcome upon their arrival in the legislature. When Press Secretary Paul Essex and Legislative

Liaison Tom Taft entered the lieutenant governor's office, they discovered that the previous officeholder had removed file cabinets and plastic plants. Worse, Hunt's two staff members had no offices for themselves. "We didn't know if we might have to pitch a tent on the lawn (of the legislative building)," recalled Essex.[3] While Hunt received emergency funds to support his office until passage of the 1973 budget, he still had to resolve the office matter with legislative leaders.

Conservative Democratic legislators did not welcome Jim Hunt because they disapproved of his crusade to reform the legislature. At a January 1973 press conference, Hunt promised fewer committees and said that no state senator would chair more than one. As Senate president, he demanded the legislators work at nights when necessary. He asked lobbyists to delay all the entertainment that they traditionally provided for the legislators and to limit the number of social functions for the entire session. He briefly pondered the notion of appointing a Republican to a committee chairmanship. One legislator grumbled to a newspaper, "He never stepped foot into the Senate until January and he's telling us what to do."[4] *Charlotte Observer* columnist Larry Tarleton said that Hunt's idealistic views conflicted with the reality of legislative life. He quoted a lobbyist who said that Hunt's legislative work ethic would fail because "when it gets dark outside, these guys want to wrap their hands around a bourbon and water."[5] Tarleton said that the lobbyists and legislators often decided how they would vote during their drinking sessions; the young lieutenant governor threatened to disturb that practice. To many older legislators, Hunt seemed naïve about the ways of the assembly.

Despite such opposition, Lieutenant Governor Jim Hunt also had powerful allies in the legislature. Perhaps his most influential ally was Ralph Scott, a state senator since his brother Kerr Scott had served as governor in the late 1940s. Since 1949, Ralph Scott had become the leading legislator on education and mental health issues. A down-to-earth politician, he seemed perfect to chair the Appropriations Committee that controlled the budget, except for his habit of being so tender-hearted that he gave visitors to his office extra time to explain their dilemmas. Hunt also selected his former law partner Russell Kirby to head the Finance committee, environmentally-conscious Bill Staton to lead the Conservation and Development committee, and his old North Carolina State College friend Eddie Knox to chair the Judiciary committee. To appease the conservative Democrats, he gave chairmanships to Phil Godwin of the Banking committee and Gordon Allen of the Rules committee, although he kept Allen restrained by surrounding him with Hunt allies.[6]

The conservative Democrats challenged Hunt's efforts to manage the legislature. Senate president pro tem Gordon Allen of Roxboro represented the conservative Democrats in Person, Durham, and Orange counties. House Speaker Jim Ramsey, also of Roxboro, rose to the position after being reared by a tenant tobacco farmer, serving as a Marine officer during World War II, and winning debate championships as a young man. Both legislators considered Hunt a liberal, ambitious politician who did all that he could to make himself look good no matter whose toes that he stepped on. Godwin agreed with his colleagues. "I hope the lieutenant governor does not get involved in bills," he said. "He is the presiding officer and shouldn't get involved in anything else, or he will make enemies and kill his effectiveness."[7]

Hunt's first major confrontation with Gordon Allen came over the offices that the lieutenant governor desired for his two aides. According to Allen, Hunt summoned him to his office early in 1973. When the senator came in, he saw Hunt gathered with the Rules Committee members lined up around the office. Allen said that Ralph Scott told him to give Jim Hunt anything that he wanted. The lieutenant governor requested that the senator give the offices of the seargent-of-arms and reading clerk to Hunt's two staff members. "He wanted me to go in and throw them out," said Allen. "He was looking after himself and he was going against the strong culture in the senate. That didn't sit too well with me. Sounds like I was being ambushed."[8] Allen gave in, however, to preserve the aura of Democratic unity during the first North Carolina Republican gubernatorial administration of his lifetime.

Following that episode, Senate President Pro Tem Allen and House Speaker Ramsey continued to try to weaken Hunt's legislative powers. "We were not against him," Allen recalled later. "We were protecting our turf. We were protective as leaders of our respective houses. He was going to take our powers away from us."[9] It made no sense to Ramsey and Allen that an officer of the executive branch could wield so much power in the legislative branch. Hunt insisted that he acted more like a legislative officer as senate president, and besides, the Republican governor gave him extremely few executive duties in state government during his time as lieutenant governor.[10]

In February 1973, Allen approved efforts to strip the lieutenant governor of his power to appoint chairpersons during the interim period between legislative sessions. Hunt was surprised when a conservative house member introduced a bill calling for the legislative leaders to appoint senate chairs during the interim. Hunt argued strongly against the legislation, saying that one of the duties of a full-time lieutenant governor was to work on legislative duties between sessions. The bills decided during the interim needed day-to-day attention, Hunt said, and "I will be the only legislative officer here."[11] This anti–Hunt effort failed because the senate president's legislative allies prevented a vote. As Hunt's chances to be elected governor brightened over the next three years, he easily fought off challenges by conservative Democrats and newspaper editorialists to curtail his powers. Hunt not only ignored the criticism, but he encouraged more powers for the office, arguing that the lieutenant governor should serve on the North Carolina Agricultural Board, chair the State Board of Education, coordinate state matters with local governments, and appoint members to policymaking commissions.[12]

At times, Jim Hunt got along better with the Republican governor than he did with some members of his own party. Jim Holshouser recalled:

> We had a good relationship, and always have, despite some differences in philosophy. We both had personal respect for each other. He was the titular head of the Democratic Party. I was Republican leader. He would stand up once a month and give me hell about something. But when the chips were down, and we needed to stop some legislation that would be bad for the state, we talked about it and it [the legislation] didn't happen.[13]

The Republican governor had good reason not to annoy the senate president. With the General Assembly still in Democratic hands and with no veto power, he needed to find common ground with the lieutenant governor to get legislation passed. Both Hunt and Holshouser backed reform programs that found acceptance in other Southern states, including the creation of a statewide kindergarten program and state management of the coasts and mountains. They often met privately to discuss budget proposals before the governor introduced them to the legislature. If Hunt and Holshouser agreed on legislation, they combined their coalitions. With the help of the governor, Hunt passed the kindergarten program that he had promised to Tar Heels during his 1972 lieutenant gubernatorial campaign.[14]

During the first two years of the Holshouser administration, the governor and the lieutenant governor minimized their partisanship. At Holshouser's inaugural address in January 1973, the governor commended Hunt for moving swiftly in organizing committees. When Holshouser left the state and Hunt became acting governor, he refused to sit in the governor's office or take any executive action other than sign a ban on fires. In 1974, the governor appointed Hunt vice chairman of the State Goals and Policy Board. Hunt and Holshouser issued a joint statement endorsing industrial revenue bonds to encourage industrial growth in the areas of

Lieutenant Governor Jim Hunt, a Democrat, often tried to get along cordially with Republican Governor James Holshouser. Although Hunt sometimes gave Holshouser "hell" in public, they privately worked together on ways to benefit the state. Here, Governor Hunt presents a published version of the Holshouser Papers to the former governor. (Courtesy of the North Carolina Office of Archives and History)

North Carolina that most need growth, "thereby providing job opportunities, a higher standard of living, and a better overall quality of life."[15] Despite their bipartisan efforts, the voters defeated the proposal in a November 1974 referendum.

Holshouser and Hunt found little disagreement over the governor's first state budget in January 1973. Since North Carolina had a large budget surplus because of a tax increase passed by the General Assembly two years earlier, the Republican administration introduced a budget calling for $314 million in appropriations including the funding of a new statewide kindergarten program and state parks. Senator Ralph Scott claimed that Holshouser tried to "outliberalize" the Democrats regarding state spending. Hunt praised the funding requests, but criticized the governor for ignoring the construction of new public schools and community colleges.[16]

Holshouser and Hunt also tried to pass the Equal Rights Amendment (ERA) in early 1973, but their efforts failed. The ERA divided North

Carolina like no other issue in the 1970s. Hunt was an ardent advocate of the amendment, appointing a progressive senator to the committee that handled ERA, and participating in strategy sessions to ratify the ERA in North Carolina. As the final vote in the senate approached, Hunt counted twenty-six votes in favor of ERA and twenty-four against the amendment. The lieutenant governor prepared to cast a tie-breaking vote to ratify the ERA in North Carolina if one legislator switched his or her vote. At the last minute, Senate president pro tem Gordon Allen switched his vote against the ERA after talking to a woman who feared that she would lose her child support if the amendment passed. Two senators also decided to switch when Allen changed his vote, causing the ERA to be defeated narrowly, 23 to 27. "We had it won in 1973 and people walked," former Democratic activist Betty McCain recalled.[17] Hunt lost his opportunity to be the savior of ERA in North Carolina.

Hunt and Holshouser more successfully backed efforts to create state-funded kindergartens in North Carolina. Despite the push for better public education, the state had a high illiteracy rate. As lieutenant governor, Hunt received letters from high school students who could not put together a simple sentence or express a coherent thought on paper. Like most education professionals, he believed that a strong state-funded kindergarten program would stimulate children to start the habit of reading at an early age. Although Governor Robert Scott had initiated an experimental kindergarten program, North Carolina had few state-supported preschools when Hunt and Holshouser entered office. They backed a plan to approve funding for kindergarten for 15,000 children, or sixteen percent of those students. After the plan passed the legislature in 1973, the state phased in the program over four years so that every North Carolina child attended kindergarten by 1977.[18]

Hunt also influenced educational policy as a member of the North Carolina Board of Education. The lieutenant governor befriended Dallas Herring, a longtime board chairman known for his role in the creation of the North Carolina community college system. Herring, who favored the testing of state teachers, often conflicted with State School Superintendent Craig Phillips, a board member who opposed mandatory teacher testing and favored a large educational bureaucracy. The lieutenant governor often felt the need to choose between the two men's factions on the board. Although Hunt agreed with Herring on the testing of teachers, he favored Phillips's approach on educational bureaucracy. By muting his differences with the chairman, many observers assumed that he belonged to the pro-Herring faction.[19]

Lieutenant Governor Hunt originally backed the testing of public school teachers, but he backed off from publicly promoting the idea in the wake of the political realities. The state required public school teachers to make a minimum score on a National Teacher Examination (NTE) until late 1972, when Superintendent Craig Phillips successfully led his board faction to remove the requirement. After Hunt and Herring sought unsuccessfully to rescind that vote in 1973, the lieutenant governor persuaded his legislative allies to revive the NTE requirement by statute. Yet, support of teacher testing alienated many members of the lieutenant governor's own political coalition, including the North Carolina Association of Educators (NCAE) and civil rights leaders who believed the state used the score to keep low-scoring African Americans from teaching in integrated public schools. Even the Nixon administration claimed that the state used a racially discriminatory test score to hire teachers, and consequently sued the North Carolina Board of Education in 1973. With little fanfare and with no public criticism from Hunt, the legislature ended the requirement in the 1975 session.[20]

During his years as a board member, Hunt became concerned how personal rivalries damaged efforts to create a unified education policy in North Carolina. Hunt nominated Herring for a new term as chairman in January 1975 even though some charged that he arrogantly ran the board. The most controversial moment came two months later when Herring investigated School Superintendent Craig Phillips's optimistic statistics regarding the first months of the state kindergarten program. Phillips then angrily charged that Herring was directing a political conspiracy against him. Herring's investigation proved no foul play by the elected official's department, yet Hunt backed a constitutional amendment to have the North Carolina Board of Education appoint the state superintendent. Although the North Carolina House tabled the amendment, Hunt sought continuously to have the state have one voice in education policy.[21]

Hunt's most controversial education policy decision as lieutenant governor was his strong endorsement of a four-year medical school at East Carolina University (ECU). The controversy began in 1965, when the North Carolina General Assembly approved plans for a two-year medical school at ECU. Seven years later, the legislature approved a one-year medical school supervised by the faculty of the University of North Carolina. However, several studies indicated that the state would provide better rural medical care by expanding existing medical schools at UNC and Wake Forest University instead of creating a new school. Despite these studies, ECU president Leo Jenkins demanded that ECU have an independent four-year medical school. He received strong backing for his position from several eastern politicians including Jim Hunt.[22]

The lieutenant governor challenged arguments against the expansion of the ECU medical school. Opponents claimed that regional medical centers would provide a more efficient way to provide health to rural communities. They also believed that the Board of Governors, the governing board of the state's sixteen universities, would oppose the proposal, and did not wish the legislature to override their decision. Hunt responded to their first point by endorsing both regional medical centers and ECU expansion. To the second point, Hunt argued that the legislature could expand the medical school without the board's approval because the public health matter was "more than a matter of education per se."[23]

Jim Hunt caused controversy in April 1973 when he said that the legislature could ignore the Board of Governors if they rejected ECU expansion. For the first time, although not the last, state newspapers accused Hunt of political pandering. The *Winston-Salem Journal* charged that the lieutenant governor and other politicians decided the ECU matter because of naked political ambition. *Greensboro Daily News* columnist William D. Snider accused Hunt of succumbing to politics, arguing that the lieutenant governor and other pro–ECU backers thought more of the regional pride of eastern voters than the overall welfare of higher education in North Carolina. The *Chapel Hill Newspaper* said that he stole the pro–medical school thunder from ECU Board Chairman Robert Morgan, the North Carolina attorney general and a strong potential candidate for governor in 1976. A *News and Observer* cartoonist portrayed Lieutenant Governor Hunt as the loyal jester of ECU Chancellor Leo Jenkins.[24]

If Hunt alienated a few traditional progressive allies, he won support from North Carolina's most prominent ultraconservative. United States Senator Jesse Helms had just begun his career as a strong legislative opponent of abortion rights, busing, and détente that were to earn him the nickname of "Senator No." He practiced token loyalty to Republican Governor Holshouser, whom his allies considered too moderate on social issues. Defying the governor, Helms wrote Republican leaders that support for the medical school would broaden the party's base in the Democratic east. The newspapers subjected Helms to the same charges of irrational reasoning and political pandering as Hunt had received.[25]

The future political combatants of a bruising 1984 United States Senate election started writing cordial letters to each other. The correspondence began in early 1973 when Hunt discovered common ground with Helms on ECU expansion and the federal tobacco program. In February 1973, he urged Helms to protect a United States Department of Agriculture Research Project at North Carolina State University and successfully sought his help to preserve the federal tobacco program.

The senator thanked Hunt in 1974 for concern about his daughter who desired a state nursing position. A year later, Hunt praised Senator Helms for his opposition to President Gerald Ford's dismissal of Defense Secretary James Schlesinger. "I am deeply concerned that we are letting our guard down too much in America and I appreciate your strong position on this," Hunt said.[26] In another letter, Helms expressed his concern over Secretary of State Henry Kissinger's management of foreign policy, and worried about the health of his friend Joseph Hunt, the lieutenant governor's elder cousin and former state house speaker who suffered from an emphysema condition that would end his life in 1978. Their letters revealed cordiality between the Tar Heel politicians and an acknowledgment of mutual interests.[27]

With the support of Helms and North Carolina Attorney General Robert Morgan, Hunt and the pro–ECU legislators successfully approved $7,500,000 for the medical school in 1973, which added to the senate president's feeling that his handling of the legislative session represented a personal success. Along with the ECU medical school funding, the legislature passed other programs that Hunt desired, including a statewide kindergarten program and a $300 million dollar bond issue for public school construction. However, the lieutenant governor still failed to achieve passage of the ERA, and conservatives successfully delayed the passage of Hunt's proposals regarding political ethics, campaign finance, and state control of the coasts and mountains. The *News and Observer* challenged assertions of Hunt's success, describing a "leadership vacuum" which blocked progressive legislation caused by a Republican governor dealing with two competitive factions within the Democrats, one led by Hunt and the other by conservative leaders James Ramsey and Gordon Allen.[28]

As the 1974 session began, both pro–ECU and anti–ECU forces prepared a legislative showdown over medical school expansion. Ideological and party coalitions broke down in the face of regional rivalries. Republicans divided between Jesse Helms and Jim Holshouser; conservative Democrats either followed James Ramsey for ECU expansion or Gordon Allen for preserving autonomy for the Board of Governors, and western Democrats such as Eddie Knox differed with eastern brethren like Hunt. Fearing unnecessary political rivalries, Hunt and Speaker James Ramsey prepared to find a compromise over expansion of ECU into a four-year medical school. Hunt still hoped to convince the Board of Governors that both regional health centers and ECU expansion would benefit the state. He and Ramsey arranged a meeting between legislators, the Board of Governors, and ECU representatives to attempt one last effort at an agreement. "Nobody was in the mood to compromise," said Ralph Scott.[29] The groups abandoned the negotiations in Greensboro in mid–January 1974 when no one could come up with a solution.

For the remainder of the session, the ECU issue dominated the budget process. The lieutenant governor continued to call for a reasonable compromise that would establish a four-year medical school. On February 26, the North Carolina Senate voted narrowly to insure that ECU expansion would be part of the main appropriations bill instead of a separate matter in the legislature. Then, they approved by a larger margin a compromise engineered by Senator Ralph Scott and House Appropriations Committee Chairman Carl Stewart that added a second year to the medical school. UNC floor leader Jack Stevens realized that he did not have the votes to defeat the compromise, especially in the senate, where Hunt and Ramsey combined their coalitions, so Holshouser and the Board of Governors ended their opposition to ECU. In early April, the legislature approved the two-year medical school. The ECU backers next focused on getting two additional years added to the program so that the university would have a fully independent medical school by the end of the 1970s.[30]

Hunt urged Consolidated University President William Friday to back completely an independent four-year medical school. During the previous two years, the lieutenant governor had not discussed the matter with him, and the president had sensed that Hunt had no desire to hear arguments against expansion. "The minute the [ECU] thing got politicized, I knew what was going to happen," Friday recalled. "It was never settled on educational grounds at all."[31] During the summer of 1974, Friday dealt with a feud between ECU partisans who wanted full independence and UNC administrators who feared local control. Hunt backed ECU, writing Friday that the legislature's decision to create a second year for the medical school meant the assembly intended that the program would eventually become autonomous. "It seems to me that our General Assembly has spoken quite clearly to the question of the ECU School of Medicine on numerous occasions since legislation provided for its establishment was enacted in 1965," Hunt said.[32] Friday, faced with enormous political pressure, recommended the creation of a first-rate four-year medical school at East Carolina University, even if it cost millions of dollars. In the spring of 1975, the Board of Governors accepted Friday's recommendation for a four-year medical program.[33]

While Hunt won the loyalty of ECU partisans, he continued to face criticism from western North Carolinians who believed that he played regional politics and who condemned his support for funding ECU expansion during the 1975 recession. That year, the economic situation grew worse, forcing legislators to decide on spending priorities. Because Hunt continued to back expansion of the medical school, Charlotte educator Betty Owen grew increasingly angry. She recalled asking Hunt, "Why would you want to spend all those dollars down east for Leo Jenkins?"[34] A Charlotte man wrote that Hunt's fiscally irresponsible stand on the ECU medical school issue caused him to oppose the lieutenant governor in any future state political undertakings. A Charlotte dentist accused Hunt of taking a sectional approach that did not appeal to someone who wanted to support candidates with a broader view. Hunt tried to mend fences with potential allies, writing a "Dear Friend" letter to University of North Carolina supporters saying that he backed additional funding of medical schools at Chapel Hill, Duke, and Wake Forest and the creation of regional medical centers. He said that the state needed the new school to create doctors that would end long waits of weeks and even months by rural citizens for a routine office visit. Hunt denied that he was a provincial Eastern North Carolinian who was out to enhance his own section of the state at the expense of others.[35]

The ECU matter caused Hunt to defend himself against the charge that he followed the polls rather than led the people. Political Scientist Jack Bass's tapes of state officials reveal negative attitudes about Hunt in 1973 and 1974. "Jim Hunt, while he's a good friend of mine, I don't think displays attributes of leadership," said North Carolina Democrat Representative Mickey Michaux, an African American lawyer from Durham. "I don't think he takes the positive role that he should take."[36] Labor leader Wilbur Hobby, who had known Hunt since the 1950s, said that he did not consider the lieutenant governor a leader and was disappointed in "Jim's real faint act."[37] Despite Hunt's service as the highest-ranking Democrat in state government, a few prominent party members considered Attorney General Robert Morgan or former gubernatorial nominee Skipper Bowles the true leader of the party.[38]

Despite numerous critics, Hunt also continued to have many admirers in North Carolina. Senator Ralph Scott told interviewer Jack Bass in December 1973 that Hunt was "tops" and the undisputed frontrunner for governor. That same month, North Carolina Secretary of State Thad Eure said that he expected Hunt to win the 1976 Democratic gubernatorial nomination by the largest majority in state history. Many pro–ECU eastern Democrats backed Hunt because of his role in getting the four-year medical school. "Because of our [ECU's] strength and the outstanding leadership you have given for our cause," said ECU Chancellor Leo Jenkins, "this great achievement was made possible."[39] Western progressives that disagreed with him on the medical school issue, including Betty Owen, nevertheless remained faithful to his political future.

In 1974, Hunt dealt with other matters besides ECU, including an effort to regulate the state's coasts. Allied with Governor Holshouser, he backed a bill creating state guidelines for the coastal area, a fifteen-member coastal commission, and the adoption of a land use plan for coastal counties. The controversial bill was debated for more than a year because many coastal politicians feared the state might prevent local residents from developing their own region. Senator Julian Allsbrook of Roanoke Rapids condemned the coastal management bill, charging that "the American system of private property is under attack by forces here in Raleigh."[40] On March 26, 1974, Senate President Jim Hunt cut off debate and refused to recognize Allsbrook. Hunt instead recognized Senator William Staton, who quickly called for a final vote, which led to passage of the bill in the senate. When House Speaker James Ramsey and his allies refused to back the same legislation, Hunt and Holshouser gathered support for another version that modified the state's control of eastern lands. The revised Coastal Area Management Act (CAMA) passed on April 11, 1974 in the senate by voice vote. Hunt and Holshouser also backed an environmental management bill for the mountain areas, but the governor failed to rally his fellow western Republicans toward the legislation even though they had voted for CAMA.[41]

A Hunt initiative to cut taxes for the middle class while increasing income tax rates for the wealthy faltered in the 1974 session. Understanding the popularity of tax reduction, the lieutenant governor's progressive coalition backed an inventory tax break for businesses, a three percent reduction of the state sales tax, and an increase in income tax rates for the rich. In the previous 1973 session, the lieutenant governor had stood against all efforts to cut taxes, including Holshouser's attempt to repeal the tax on soft drinks. At that time, Jim Hunt had proclaimed that the state government had to meet the needs of the people first and then cut taxes only if money remained in the treasury. With tax reduction plans by conservative House Democrats gaining momentum in early 1974, Hunt and progressive senate Democrats created their own proposal. House Speaker Jim Ramsey and Governor Holshouser denounced the effort to raise income tax rates while cutting other people's taxes. Senator Russell Kirby, who developed the proposal, could not get the plan through his own finance committee. Faced with conservative opposition within Hunt's own party, the tax reform plan died. Troubled by his failed efforts in 1974 and needing the support of wealthy industrialists for his gubernatorial campaigns, Jim Hunt by 1976 abandoned all efforts to restructure seriously the North Carolina tax system.[42]

Despite this failure, Hunt accomplished much in the 1974 session, including a new state housing financing agency which provided low-interest funds to make mortgage loans affordable for lower income people. He also persuaded legislators to finance the ECU medical school, kindergartens, health education centers, mental health facilities, and state parks. However, the lieutenant governor failed to persuade legislators to pass tax reform or a legislative ethics code. Such failures may have had less to do with Hunt's leadership skills than with the progressive Democratic faction in the General Assembly being outnumbered by the conservatives within both parties.[43]

Hunt struggled for three years to pass effective campaign finance and ethics code legislation. He made suggestions on limiting campaign spending in late November 1972, yet nothing was passed the following year. In 1973, Hunt's staff created an ethics code that barred gifts to legislators and prevented conflicts of interest. Sponsored by Senator Bobby L. Barker, the proposals never came to a vote. Newspaper editorialists shared Hunt's dismay. "The talk on campaign spending law is turning out to be just talk," the *Raleigh Times* editorialized.[44]

The national Watergate scandal revitalized the call for campaign finance reform. In June 1972, a third-rate burglary by five men at the National Democratic Party Headquarters in the Watergate hotel initially meant little to most of the American people. By April 1973, however, Americans learned that White House aides had covered up their involvement in campaign sabotage and political burglaries. United States Senator Sam Erwin of North Carolina, who had often been at odds with Hunt's progressive faction during his years as a champion of segregation, won their praise during nationally televised hearings on the Watergate affair. The scandal revolted Americans who had considered President Richard Nixon a champion of law and order, including Hunt. "I think we can all be thankful that the whole affair was discovered before some of the men involved moved us closer to totalitarianism," he said in the summer of 1973.[45]

Hunt hoped that revulsion over Watergate would inspire the North Carolina legislature to pass campaign finance reform and ethics legislation in 1974. At a hearing in September 1973, Hunt testified that spending limits should go no higher than ten cents per eligible voter, and reporting on campaign contributions should occur at regular intervals. Spurred on by the national scandal, the legislature approved a campaign spending law in 1974 that demanded that candidates for state office file finance reports, limit media spending, and curtail contributions from a candidate and his immediate family. In 1975, the General Assembly finally passed an ethics law that required disclosure of financial interests and potential conflicts of interests for the legislators themselves. A voice in the wilderness during the 1972 lieutenant gubernatorial campaign, Hunt discovered allies for campaign finance and ethics legislation after the Watergate scandal.[46]

Watergate resulted in the resignation of President Nixon, Democratic gains in the United States Congress and the North Carolina General Assembly, the temporary demise of the state Republican Party, and an increase in Lieutenant Governor Jim Hunt's influence in the legislature. Many Americans felt little inspiration from President Gerald Ford, who dealt with the aftermath of Watergate and an approaching economic recession. Hunt also found little to admire in the new Republican president. Voters uninspired by Ford gave Democrats huge gains in the United States Congress in November 1974. A Senate newcomer included Robert Morgan, who replaced Sam Erwin after his retirement. Once a member of North Carolina Assistant Attorney General I. Beverly Lake's segregationist faction in the early 1960s, Morgan ran a "New South" campaign appealing to white moderates, African Americans, and progressive women. In North Carolina, Republican gains in the General Assembly between 1966 and 1972 vanished. Governor Holshouser, the beneficiary of the Republican surge in 1972, lost effectiveness after the voters elected more members of the opposition party to the legislature. Because many Democrats assumed that the new partisan trend might help to elect Hunt governor in 1976, they looked to the lieutenant governor for leadership on the issues.[47]

In his first two years as lieutenant governor, James B. Hunt, Jr., overcame many political struggles to achieve statewide respect. Using his power to appoint progressive state senators as committee chairpersons, he influenced legislation on various matters. However, a conservative Democratic faction, hostile to institutional reform and unhappy with someone they considered an executive usurper of legislative powers, killed several of Hunt's initiatives. Conservative opponents killed the Equal Rights Amendment, tabled a tax reduction package with an increase in income taxes for the wealthy, and delayed campaign finance legislation, all of which Hunt supported. To achieve some of his goals, Hunt allied with the Republican governor to pass the kindergarten program and the Coastal Area Management Act. He succeeded in passing campaign finance reform and ethics legislation in the wake of the Watergate scandal. The lieutenant governor's most controversial success was the creation of an East Carolina University four-year medical school deemed a waste of spending by numerous critics. Attacked as an opportunistic politician by his opponents, Hunt won the backing of easterners who applauded his zeal for the regional medical facility. Despite criticism of his leadership skills, Jim Hunt achieved enough successes during his first two years as lieutenant governor to become the undisputed frontrunner for governor in 1976.

8

The Mandate of '76:
How Hunt Became Governor

In 1976, North Carolina Lieutenant Governor James B. Hunt, Jr., finally achieved his goal of being elected the state's highest executive. All the skills that he developed from high school to state office — public speaking, parliamentary procedure, voter contact, and grassroots organizing — served him effectively in this campaign. Hunt's political organization, created from his own personal relationships and from the old political network of former Democratic party chairman Bert Bennett, strengthened between 1973 and 1976 because he gained new allies who accepted the inevitability of his triumph. The candidate selected issues which had strong resonance with the majority of Tar Heels, including education, crime, industrial recruitment, and utility regulation. Hunt's status as the front-runner scared away strong challengers and left behind candidates who either did not have the organization, political skills, or money to defeat him. To add to the North Carolinian's good fortune in 1976, he received additional votes by running on the same ticket with Jimmy Carter, the first Democratic presidential nominee from the Deep South since 1844.

Although he never admitted his intention to run for governor, Hunt gave nearly everyone the impression that he sought the state's highest executive office. By the way he acted politically, most of his aides presumed that he desired the office. Press Secretary Paul Essex understood the lieutenant governor's ambition and confronted Hunt over his physical appearance. Hunt had a pompadour haircut that some cartoonists caricatured as a large strand of hair running several inches over his forehead. "There were a lot of people concerned that he would want to look like a national leader," Essex recalled. "I thought his hair needed to be restyled."[1] After Essex told

Hunt his opinion, the lieutenant governor did not say a word. Weeks later, the press aide saw Jim Hunt with restyled hair.

Running for North Carolina's highest office meant more than cosmetics. Despite being the state's highest Democratic officeholder, the lieutenant governor understood that several party leaders believed that former gubernatorial nominee Hargrove "Skipper" Bowles should retake the nomination in 1976. Despite his unexpected defeat by Republican challenger James Holshouser in 1972, the Belk Department Store executive had many supporters, including North Carolina Democratic Party Chairman James Sugg. In early 1973, Sugg declared that both he and Jim Hunt still recognized Bowles as "the titular head of the Democratic party."[2] Two years later, Bowles sent out a mass mailing saying that he planned to run for governor the following year. The Greensboro businessman proclaimed himself dead serious about running for the office, although he refused to begin his campaign too early. He called for help against "candidates who have been seeking support for several months, one for several years." He was referring to Hunt.[3]

Understanding the need to act before Bowles created an organization, Hunt studiously courted members of the Greensboro businessman's 1972 political campaign. The Hunt loyalists identified Bowles' supporters and persuaded them to side with Hunt. When Bowles courted his allies, former Hunt aide Joseph Grimsley recalled, "they were saying to Skipper, I love you man, but I'm committed to Hunt this time."[4] Bert Bennett, who developed a political organization for Terry Sanford's gubernatorial campaign in 1960 and used his remaining contacts to help Hunt's bid for higher office, told former Bowles supporters, "Hunt's on track. You ought to stick with us this time."[5] Key advisors Joel Fleishman and Howard Lee deserted Bowles for Hunt. Lee, the mayor of Chapel Hill, claimed that he could see the handwriting on the wall regarding Hunt's future success.[6]

Bowles counted on Jim Sugg, his handpicked chairman of the North Carolina Democratic party, to help him. In late 1974, Hunt debated whether to join an effort by United States Senator-elect Robert Morgan to replace Sugg with Morgan's campaign manager Charles Winberry. The senator-elect complained that the chairman did not communicate much with elected leaders and did inept work for him during his campaign. He may have also shared North Carolina Representative Mickey Michaux's feeling that the party chairman lacked charisma and the leadership ability to run the party. Hunt refused to back Sugg's reelection, only publicly saying that he would do what was in the best interest of the Democratic party. Like Morgan, the lieutenant governor felt out of the loop at Democratic headquarters in Raleigh. Columnist Ned Cline wrote, "As the top elected Democrat, Hunt apparently feels he should be on the coaching staff even if he isn't head coach."[7]

Hunt and Morgan abandoned the attempted coup after North Carolina Democrats rallied to Sugg's defense. Attorney General–elect Rufus Edmisten, who rose to fame as United States Senator Sam Erwin's advisor during the Watergate hearings, and United States Representative Walter Jones gave the North Carolina Democratic chairman their complete support. Sugg's defenders argued that he had presided over landslide Democratic victories, allowing the party to take a 49-to-one lead in the state senate and a 100-to-ten lead in the state house in 1975. Faced with the possibility of party division, Winberry withdrew his challenge to the chairman. In January 1975, the Democratic Executive Committee easily reelected Sugg. Jim Hunt aborted attempts to take control of the state party, and instead created a strong independent political organization for his 1976 gubernatorial campaign.[8]

Hunt understood that critics would measure his performance in the 1975 General Assembly and hold him responsible for the outcome. With an enlarged Democratic majority in the General Assembly, few legislators looked to Republican Governor James B. Holshouser's recommendations for complete guidance. Even though he got along well personally with Holshouser, Hunt publicly criticized the governor on several issues. In March 1975, he rebuked Holshouser for not presenting any proposals dealing with public utility rates. "I regret the lack of leadership on the part of this administration," Hunt said. "I regret that the fine people of that General Assembly are being unjustly blamed for this lack of leadership."[9] Hunt also accused the governor of exaggerating the growth of the economy, and criticized his appointment of conservative Republicans to commissions. Holshouser understood that the criticism was part of party politics, recalling that "Hunt and I still got along."[10] Privately, Hunt prevented legislation that weakened severely the governor's powers, both for Holshouser's sake and his own ambition.

Many legislators, believing Hunt might be the next governor, turned to him in 1975 for leadership. After Holshouser introduced his budget package, Hunt promised to look over the budget with a "fine tooth comb" for items to cut. Unlike in 1973, when Hunt faced disrespectful state senators opposed to most of his proposals, the new president pro tem of the senate indicated a willingness to have Hunt's staff advise him on legislation. The Senate also paid him more respect. When Hunt remarked that members acted slowly in passing bills, numerous senators launched a wave of proposals the following week.[11]

In 1975, the General Assembly dealt with a worldwide economic recession and an energy crisis that hurt Tar Heels. While the previous two sessions had produced surpluses created by economic booms of the 1960s and 1970s, now North Carolina lost revenues from the decline in jobs, especially in the textile industry. Understanding the unpopularity of tax increases and strongly opposed to deficit financing, Hunt backed an effort to trim the fat from the state budget. He proposed a hiring freeze in state government, symbolically abandoning an earlier request to add another secretary to his busy lieutenant governor's office. While recommending budget cuts, Hunt still remained committed to a five percent raise for state employees and the expansion of both the kindergarten program and the East Carolina University medical school.[12]

Hunt tried various approaches to aid North Carolina's ailing economy. He approved the creation of a new committee exclusively dealing with North Carolina's economic woes. Headed by Senator Billy Mills of Onslow County, the committee recommended financial aid for unemployed people. To fight inflation, Hunt proposed that each senate committee proposal should require an inflation impact statement stating how the idea would affect the economy. The lieutenant governor conceded that state action would have only a limited impact on the economy, and accordingly, called for the federal government to solve the crisis. Despite the efforts of President Gerald Ford, the recession continued into 1976.[13]

The economic downturn coincided with an energy crisis that increased fuel bills dramatically. Many people complained to Hunt about their rising heating bills while utilities companies received record profits. James Taylor of Williamston wrote Hunt to say that "my wife and I are trying to use as little electricity as possible, but it seems our bill just keeps going up and up every month."[14] Lesley Allen of Selma wrote the lieutenant governor that her electric bill had doubled in a year and she was told that there were more increases ahead. In his response, Hunt said that utility rates must be as low as effective regulation can make them for the consumer.[15]

In early 1975, Hunt launched a series of proposals to reduce rates. He called for increasing the state utilities commission from five members to nine, repealing the law allowing power companies to set rates based on expectations of future expenses, and abolishing the fuel escalator clause that allowed companies to pass automatically fuel cost increases to customers. His proposals received a setback in early 1975 when Assistant Attorney General I. Beverly Lake, Jr., criticized the proposals as ineffective. Although a milder version of the bill became law, serious reform of the state utility commission did not occur until Hunt served as governor.[16]

After the 1975 session, the lieutenant governor believed that further changes were needed to make the North Carolina Utilities Commission accountable to the public. Hunt made the regulatory agency's Republican majority a prime target for criticism. In 1975 and 1976, the commission had approved several rate increases, including a 22 percent increase to Carolina Power and Light Company (CP&L). "I believe the Commission perspective is unbalanced heavily toward the companies and the stockholders," Hunt said.[17] After criticizing the commission's award of a $35 million bonus to the power companies in March 1976, he declared that the deck was stacked against the consumer since utility companies had engineers, lawyers, corporate officers and highly paid out-of-state experts to plead the companies' case. The lieutenant governor recommended a utilities commission staff that would argue on behalf of the rate-paying public.[18]

Hunt also had backed legislation in the 1975 session that dramatically changed the Democratic primaries. Two years earlier, Bert Bennett had written Hunt that a gubernatorial primary should be held "as late as humanly possible"[19] because defeated primary candidates would have less time to harbor bitterness against the party's nominees. Hunt had supported legislation to move the 1976 state primary from May to August. He also had backed the separation of the presidential primary and the gubernatorial primary, insuring that he would not be linked with liberal presidential candidate Terry Sanford. Hunt, who had abandoned the traditional Democratic liberalism of the national party, feared that might be linked to Sanford's liberal positions and the politician's antagonism toward popular Alabama Governor George Wallace. Although the legislature passed these primary bills, Hunt failed to push through a measure allowing the winner of 40 percent of a primary's vote to avoid a run-off.[20]

By the end of the 1975 session, Lieutenant Governor Jim Hunt and North Carolina House Speaker Jimmy Green were deeply divided. Born in 1921, the Washington and Lee University graduate and World War II Marine veteran owned farmland and managed tobacco warehouses in eastern North Carolina. A member of the legislature since 1961, Green believed that he was more qualified to become governor than Hunt. Although they agreed to cooperate on legislation early in the session, Hunt understood that Green might emerge as his serious rival in the 1976 gubernatorial race. As a leader of the conservative wing of the Democrats, he had loyal followers in the General Assembly who would try to help him become governor. Neither Green nor his allies had any reason to make Lieutenant Governor Hunt look good in the public's eyes.[21]

For instance, Green had no interest in helping Hunt pass the Equal Rights Amendment (ERA) in the 1975 session. The lieutenant governor, understanding the importance of winning feminist supporters in the upcoming governor's race, wanted credit for the ratification of the amendment that would guarantee women equality under the United States Constitution. "Everyone is looking to you for some leadership and favorite committee appointments (for ERA) next year," Hunt aide Joe Grimsley said in 1974. "We need this to tie up the women's politicians for 1976!"[22] Unfortunately for Hunt, ERA never came to a vote in the senate, because the North Carolina House, under the control of Speaker Green, defeated ratification. Although he opposed the amendment, Green pretended to be neutral as a way to keep the issue from damaging his expected run for state office. On the second reading of the ERA bill on April 13, 1975, Green nearly had to vote on the amendment to break a tie, yet his house allies switched their votes in favor of ERA to prevent the speaker from going on record. However, on the third and final reading of the ratification bill, the North Carolina House defeated the amendment, preventing Hunt's senate allies from ratifying ERA and leaving the matter closed until 1977.[23]

Besides ERA, Hunt and Green clashed on budget matters. The Democratic house and Democratic senate deadlocked on $6.6 million of spending bills, including Green's effort to cut funding to the Department of Public Instruction. Although Hunt opposed State Superintendent Craig Phillips's divisive attitude on the State Board of Education, he did not wish to see the elected official's research budget slashed severely, refusing to back the house-approved cuts. Senator Ralph Scott, Hunt's loyal ally, blamed the deadlock on "King James," referring to Speaker Green. House majority leader Kitchen Josey, a friend of Green, angrily responded, "Let me make a statement for King James the First [Green] and you take it back to King James the Second [Hunt]."[24] Josey blamed the gridlock on Hunt. The division between their two factions threatened to delay the session.

Finally, Hunt and Green compromised on a budget bill that restored spending for education research. "Together, we have done a great deal," the speaker announced.[25] The lieutenant governor was not so gracious. At a news conference, Hunt said that the Green made a mistake by insisting on separate legislative budget processes that created the last-minute struggle over the education cuts. He and his senate allies accepted some cutbacks, but they did not wish to see the education research programs emasculated.[26]

Hunt continued the fight to retain the superintendent's research budget in the 1976 special session. By that time, Speaker Green had decided to run for lieutenant governor instead of challenging Hunt in a race for governor. After Hunt called his demand for the funding of education research non-negotiable, Green and his allies reluctantly agreed to abandon the cuts. "We still think it is a waste of money," said Josey, but he understood that cooperation with Hunt served Green's candidacy better.[27] Yet, the feud between Hunt and Green only grew worse after they won their elections to state office in 1976.

If Hunt needed to defeat a conservative Democratic challenger like Jimmy Green to win the 1976 gubernatorial primary, he could not be perceived as soft on crime. In the 1970s, voters became alarmed at the large youth population participating in violent crime and perceived that some judges were too lenient toward felons. Hunt shared their concerns. He accepted proposals from a crime commission chaired by North Carolina Senator Eddie Knox, who endorsed the end of discretionary sentences by judges in capital cases. In a 1975 speech, Hunt talked about thirteen-year-old June Bynum of Wilson, a girl recently stabbed to death, and asked, "How many June Bynums must be killed before we decide to get serious about fighting crime in this nation and in the state of North Carolina?"[28] By 1976, he came out for an extensive crime-fighting program including a community watch program, fixed sentences for repeat offenders, forced trials after ninety days of indictment, an end to discretionary paroles, a state juvenile code study commission, and most controversially, a return to capital punishment.[29]

Besides the crime issue, Hunt wooed conservatives by opposing immorality on network television. Reared in the 1950s when his parents demanded traditional values, he did not like the influence of the 1960s counterculture upon movies and television. He enjoyed family programs like *Apple's Way*, and complained to the Columbia Broadcasting System when it cancelled the show. In public, he held a state conference on Sex and Violence on Television in March 1976 similar to the hearings that United Senator Jesse Helms conducted in Washington, D.C. At the Hunt conference, the lieutenant governor encouraged a dialogue between broadcasters and citizens as a way to encourage good television programs. Although Hunt's conference did not affect Hollywood programming, he convinced conservative North Carolina Democrats that he strongly opposed televised indecency.[30]

Hunt also focused on public education as a campaign issue. As the son of a teacher who taught illiterate farm children, Hunt believed that decent schools would create educated citizens who could work in higher-paying jobs. To end the high illiteracy rate in the state, he promised to spend fifteen million dollars on a primary reading program that called for a trained teacher aide to be used for reading instruction in every classroom. To help children know basic skills before graduation, he favored yearly standardized testing of all children in selected grade levels for reading, language arts, and mathematics. He also promoted minimum competency tests to insure that high school students had basic skills before graduation. To ensure that local areas supported education, he backed a community schools bill to turn public schools into community centers. He also promised to promote occupational education, enforce school discipline, and reduce classroom sizes. He assured North Carolinians that educational standards could be raised without increasing taxes.[31]

Hunt also wanted to improve efforts to recruit high-paying industries in North Carolina, especially after reports revealed that the state ranked as one of the last in manufacturing wages. Although previous governors emphasized the state's low wages to attract industry, Hunt wished to turn the state Department of Commerce into a recruitment agency for higher-paying industries across North Carolina. He planned to target employers of market-oriented manufacturing firms, research organizations, and development firms. When better-paying employers moved into towns, he expected the traditional industries to increase their wages to retain their employees. He hoped his education plan would create the skilled work-force needed for the new employers. When asked what his economic development program was in 1976, Jim Hunt would respond, "Education."[32]

Because many Tar Heels believed that Hunt would win the gubernatorial election in 1976, they offered to join his campaign. Political activists, conservative businessmen, and rural politicians all backed the lieutenant governor because he seemed to be a sure winner. Hunt wanted his supporters to think so, telling them about the great victory they were going to have in 1976. Many acquaintances, friends, and fans said that they would assist his efforts. Thus, Hunt had many talented people to choose to run the campaign. Former reporter Ferrel Guillory said that Jim Hunt built the 1976 campaign from "the best people of the Democratic party."[33] He attracted ordinary people, too. Hunt's hometown of Rock Ridge celebrated the first "Jim Hunt Day" a year before the gubernatorial election. An Atlantic Christian College student wrote a poem saying that Hunt was "truly sent from God above" and that he "had one more step, to be governor of our state."[34]

Hunt used this support to build one of the strongest grassroots campaign organizations in North Carolina history. He won support from the political network of Winston-Salem oil dealer Bert Bennett and from people who knew him in high school, college, farm organizations, the Young Democrats, and the state party. Hunt insured that each county had three co-chairman — one male, one female, and one African American. These chairpersons provided the literature and bumper stickers for the volunteers. They were told that they were on a crusade for better education, improved consumer protection, stronger moral standards, safer streets, and higher-paying jobs. Most of them required little convincing that Hunt was the right man and they worked hard for his election.[35]

Because of the strength of Hunt's organization, many contenders quickly dropped out of the gubernatorial contest. For a brief time, former North Carolina Senate President Pro Tem Gordon Allen and former House Speaker James Ramsey pondered a race for governor. Upset over what they considered to be Hunt's contempt for traditional senate practices, each man left the legislature in 1974 with the idea that they might run against Hunt two years later. Eventually, they rejected the idea. "What thoughts I had (were abandoned) after watching the way he could operate because he was a sure winner," Allen said.[36] Agricultural Secretary James Graham and Charlotte businessman Pat Hall briefly discussed their possible candidacies for the state's highest executive office before announcing that they would not run. North Carolina Speaker Jimmy Green, who succeeded Ramsey, decided not to take on Hunt and ran successfully for lieutenant governor in 1976. On March 25, 1976, to the relief of the Hunt campaign, Skipper Bowles decided to end his candidacy. Not mentioning the defections of his old political supporters, the Greensboro businessman said that he had developed a cardiovascular problem. With Bowles departing from the scene, Hunt briefly had no rival within the progressive wing of the North Carolina Democratic party.[37]

Conservative state senator Thomas Strickland remained in the race, despite the odds against defeating Hunt's organization. He opposed strongly the Equal Rights Amendment (ERA) and backed state aid to private colleges. A strong proponent of Alabama Governor George Wallace, Strickland hoped that he would win by linking himself with Wallace's expected North Carolina presidential primary victory in 1976. Unfortunately for the candidate, the legislature separated the gubernatorial and presidential primaries, and Wallace's popularity declined in the state. The Hunt campaign did not take the senator seriously since he had little money and organization to win a state campaign.[38]

Hunt also faced Democratic challenger Ed O'Herron, one of the wealthiest gubernatorial candidates ever to run in North Carolina. Since his youth, the Eckerd Drugs Chairman had faced and won great challenges. O'Herron's friends knew him as a Marine Corps veteran who had served at Iwo Jima, a former boxer, an expert pilot, and an outstanding golfer. An effective executive, he turned a small drug store chain into a multi-million dollar enterprise. Fiscally conservative, although moderate enough to support the ERA, O'Herron hoped to attract the business-oriented Democrats who had once voted for North Carolina Governor Dan Moore. Using the Charlotte area as his base, the former legislator planned an expensive effort against the lieutenant governor.[39]

To defeat the Eckerd Drugs chairman, Hunt strongly contested the Charlotte region. Understanding the importance of the women's vote, he demanded that Charlotte educator Betty Owen co-chair his campaign in Mecklenburg County. Still angry over Hunt's support of the East Carolina University medical school, which she considered a waste of tax dollars, she refused. Yet, he kept insisting. "Don't say no," Hunt said.[40] After receiving boxes of "Friends of Jim Hunt" material, she finally agreed to join former North Carolina Senator Eddie Knox in running the county campaign. Although Knox usually supported conservative Democratic candidates, and family members urged him to back O'Herron, the Charlotte attorney remained loyal to his old friend from North Carolina State College. He organized campaign rallies that demonstrated that Hunt had support in North Carolina's largest city and could win votes in O'Herron's base.[41]

Faced with conservative challengers, Hunt officially announced his candidacy for governor on April 5, 1976. In his Raleigh speech, he declared that he would push for no new taxes as governor of North Carolina. State government could not do all things for all people, he said, but the governor, whose office would become the nerve center of the state, could mobilize Tar Heels to solve their own problems. "We need less government, but better leadership," Hunt said.[42] As chief executive, he promised to stop the deterioration of public schools, rising crime rates, high utility rates, and the overabundance of low-wage jobs— without raising taxes.[43]

Hunt protected himself so well against charges of liberalism in his announcement speech that he angered several progressives. The *Chapel Hill Newspaper* accused Hunt of coming up with the same old political clichés and ignoring the true problems that affected North Carolina. The Raleigh *News and Observer* chided him for abandoning his 1974 tax reform proposal that called for higher taxes for the wealthy. At the same time, teachers got upset that Hunt did not forcefully back a sixteen percent pay raise in the special budget session to allow them to catch up with the rising cost of living. Because of dwindling revenues, Hunt and Speaker Green agreed to a four percent raise for teachers and state employees. Progressives unaffiliated with the Hunt campaign charged that the lieutenant governor was going too far to appease conservative Democrats.[44]

Because Hunt might be vulnerable within the state's progressive base, former state senator George Wood of Edenton suddenly joined the governor's race. Originally a candidate for lieutenant governor, the wealthy farmer and businessman believed that he could defeat Hunt in the gubernatorial primary. Political scientist Walter DeVries showed him polls demonstrating that Hunt had a strong following only among thirty percent of possible voters, leaving a large group of persons uncommitted.

While Hunt had noisy support from party activists, DeVries told Wood, he did not have the commitment of regular voters. Hunt also did not have the strong backing of the Raleigh *News and Observer*, the state's leading liberal newspaper. DeVries believed that an effective television blitz could overwhelm Hunt. In April 1976, Wood called for tax reform even if the effort increased taxes, and promised a twenty percent increase in teacher salaries over two years. He declared himself a straight shooter who belonged to no political machine. Wood received the support of Skipper Bowles and *News and Observer* editor Claude Sitton, whose editorial page declared that if Wood got his theme together and his message across, Hunt would have to work a lot harder and faster to win.[45]

Hunt's efforts to adjust his positions after Wood's entry into the race led to charges by the former state senator's political allies that the lieutenant governor "fence-straddled" the issues. When questioned in a consumer forum, Hunt said that he would accept the closing of tax loopholes for the wealthy and drop the ceiling on automobile taxes—adopting Wood's positions and shifting his stand against no tax increases. The charge of switching positions accelerated after he announced that he was open-minded to repeal of the food tax, reversing an earlier position. Most controversially, he allowed the state senate to vote to end the century-long power of lieutenant governors to appoint chairpersons—a power he had used effectively for four years—on his last day as senate president during the special budget session in early 1976. Hunt explained that he personally favored retaining the power, yet he wanted to allow senators the right to decide the matter. Such talk hardly impressed the Wood supporters, including Skipper Bowles, who said that his candidate would not ride the fence nor take two positions on one issue.[46]

Despite such criticism, the Hunt organization thrived. Bert Bennett recalled not being extremely worried about either O'Herron or Wood. Hunt received endorsements from the North Carolina Association of Educators (NCAE), the state branch of the American Federation of Labor–Congress of Industrial Organizations (AFL-CIO), and the state chapter of the predominantly black National Baptist Convention. Many voters liked this handsome, energetic young man and paid little attention to his unclear positions on some issues. Teachers forgave his stand against a large pay increase, union members forgave his backing of right-to-work laws, and African-Americans forgave his death penalty stance because the thirty-nine-year-old lieutenant governor won the support of their leaders and appeared to be the most progressive candidate.[47]

Hunt had a strong hold on the African-American vote in North Carolina. More white candidates tried to attract the growing black vote that expanded dramatically in the eleven years after the passage of the Voting Rights Act. Although many black leaders disliked Hunt's support for capital punishment and competency tests, they believed that he would treat them fairly. "Jim came across as a person that was friendly to the black community more than anyone else by far," recalled Grimsley.[48] Robert L. Davis, chairman of the Mecklenburg County Black Political Caucus, said that every time that the lieutenant governor came to town, he called black leaders to find out how he could help them. Former Raleigh Mayor Clarence Lightner said that Hunt was approachable, always keeping "the door open."[49] The African-American community also appreciated that Hunt once marched with blacks mourning the slaying of civil rights leader Martin Luther King, Jr., and that he promised to appoint a black to his state cabinet. Hunt's strong support from African Americans frustrated his opponents. A black aide for George Wood remarked in August 1976, "The only problem is that a lot of Hunt supporters would be ours, but they got committed early in the ball game and are reluctant to switch."[50]

African Americans also had reasons to be skeptical about the three candidates challenging Hunt. Strickland took so many conservative positions that black leaders refused to support him. O'Herron also left them lukewarm, since he contributed to Senator Jesse Helms's United States Senate campaign in 1972 and he failed to hire black managers at Eckerd Drugs. Despite efforts to attract African-American voters by emphasizing his opposition to capital punishment, Wood alienated blacks by using low-paid black migrant workers on his Camden County potato farm and by never clearly declaring himself a progressive candidate. African-American politician Howard Lee said that Wood's problem was that he never could decide what he wanted to be.[51]

As in the lieutenant gubernatorial campaign, Hunt faced candidates who had large amounts of money. He still had an advantage over O'Herron and Wood, however, because his campaign created a strong financial base from small individual contributions and the donations of many wealthy supporters. The millionaires also dealt with campaign finance laws (backed by Hunt in the General Assembly) that set limits on individual contributions and advertisement spending. In early 1976, Hunt released his personal financial statement, revealing his net income at $66,504 a year. O'Herron revealed that he earned $21 million annually as an executive at Eckerd Drugs, while Wood earned $1.75 million a year from his farm and businesses. Challenging his wealthy opponents at one campaign stop, Hunt said, "We've got some candidates running for governor who I suppose have so much money they don't even know how much their light bills are."[52] Hunt had the best of both worlds—the ability to run as a man of the people and the campaign chest to win the election.

Despite Hunt's lesser wealth, he spent more than any candidate in the Democratic primary. Although O'Herron and Wood used bank loans and their own personal funds, Hunt received almost $940,000 from more than 17,000 contributors ranging from the poor to the wealthy. Hunt said that his effort "shows that a campaign that depends on small amounts of money from thousands of North Carolinians can work."[53] Of course, many wealthy industrialists helped Hunt, including oil dealer Bert Bennett, chain department store owner Irwin Belk, developer Clifton Benson, banker John McNair, and manufacturer Gordon Hanes.[54]

Wood and O'Herron tried desperately to use television advertising to slow down the Hunt momentum. To attract the rural audience, Wood portrayed himself on television commercials as a hog farmer who drove a truck and a tractor. The TV ads showed images of Wood's attendance at University of North Carolina (UNC) Board of Governors meetings and his conversation with former North Carolina State University (NCSU) Chancellor John Caldwell, who served as his campaign chairman. Using a different strategy, O'Herron presented himself on television as a mature, successful businessman who would stop inflation by bringing industries with better-paying jobs to North Carolina. During the final weeks before the primary, O'Herron's television commercials attacked Hunt personally. The businessman described Hunt as a hack politician who desired higher office at any price. He said that Hunt was "still complaining about the teaching of reading in the public schools"[55] even though he had the opportunity to solve those problems as a member of the North Carolina Board of Education. O'Herron also argued that a vote for him would be an alternative to Hunt's "political machine" and an "opportunity to say no to the hack politicians who had their chance and failed."[56] The candidate's televised attack was a desperate attempt to win votes, and the effort failed dismally.

Lieutenant Governor Hunt also focused on television advertising as a way of attracting voters. One commercial showed him talking to an audience of whites and African Americans. He said that they should be as "mad as fire" about a 14-year-old North Carolinian whom he met who could not read, adding "I think people had a right to get mad when our schools don't teach children to read."[57] In another commercial, he slammed a jail cell door and promised to get tough on crime. He also ran advertisements in tobacco regions where he pledged to defend the federal tobacco program.[58]

Hunt's leading opponents expected to lose the first primary and rally all those who wanted to defeat the lieutenant governor in the run-off. They were sorely disappointed when Hunt won 53 percent of the vote in the Democratic primary, becoming the first gubernatorial candidate in twenty years to avoid a run-off. Without the help of either the North Carolina Democratic party organization or the Raleigh *News and Observer* (which endorsed George Wood), Hunt won the election by a commanding margin. The gubernatorial nominee then replaced party chairman Jim Sugg, whom he tried unsuccessfully to oust in 1974, with Betty McCain, a fervent Hunt loyalist and the first women to chair a major state party in North Carolina. Finally, the North Carolina Democratic party and the Hunt campaign merged to help the lieutenant governor win in the fall.[59]

Hunt challenged former Human Resources Secretary David Flaherty in the general election. The son of a Democratic unionized mailman of urban Boston, Flaherty recalled living through poverty in the Great Depression. Often rebellious as a young man, he had abandoned his parent's traditions of Roman Catholicism and Democratic voting for Methodism and Republicanism. "I just didn't like being told what to do," Flaherty remembered.[60] After serving in the United States Army, he had attended Boston University, winning the student body presidency and graduating with a degree in business administration. Looking for new challenges, he had moved his family to Lenoir, North Carolina, and had accepted a job as assistant sales manager for Broyhill Furniture. Since company owner J. E. Broyhill had served as a prominent leader in the state Republican party, Flaherty had decided to get involved in North Carolina GOP politics.[61]

As the party increased in strength, David Flaherty rose in prominence. Serving as a Young Republican leader in 1960, Flaherty had worked hard for the unsuccessful effort of Republican gubernatorial candidate John Gavin. He had sent letters across the state asking voters to dump Democratic gubernatorial candidate Terry Sanford, and had organized a large Gavin rally in a Democratic county. Although Gavin lost by a narrow margin, Flaherty believed that his efforts had signaled future success for the state GOP. In the 1960s, he had become chairman of the North Carolina Young Republicans and had won election to the state house of representatives. In a legislative minority that had included his friend James B. Holshouser of Boone, he had achieved few victories because Democratic house leaders often declared opposition to a bill because the sponsor was "nothing but a Republican."[62] Yet, Flaherty still felt confident about the state GOP, and helped his friend Holshouser win the gubernatorial election in 1972. The governor had appointed him Secretary of Human Resources, where he managed social welfare programs.[63]

By the time Flaherty won the state GOP gubernatorial nomination, the North Carolina Republican party was weakened because of factionalism. United States Senator Jesse Helms never seemed content with Holshouser's mild conservatism and turned his fundraising organization into

a rival of the state Republican Party. In 1976, Helms strongly backed Ronald
Reagan for the GOP presidential nomination against President Gerald
Ford, who depended on Holshouser to help him win the North Carolina
primary. Surprisingly, Reagan defeated Ford in North Carolina, revitaliz-
ing his sagging campaign. The Helms forces wanted to help Reagan win
so badly that they denied the North Carolina governor a delegate seat at
the 1976 Republican National Convention. The Holshouser-Helms duel
occurred at the same time that Flaherty, a former member of Holshouser's
administration, sought the GOP gubernatorial nomination against North
Carolina Baptist Association President Coy Privette, a social conservative
with views similar to those of Helms.[64]

Although Flaherty defeated Privette in the run-off, he entered the
general election with few resources. Already having spent $240,000 in the
primaries, he had only $51,000 for the general election. Although Jesse
Helms endorsed his candidacy, Flaherty believed that the senator campaigned for him with limited enthusiasm. Even his friend James Holshouser seemed to devote more time to President Gerald Ford's presidential
campaign than to Flaherty's gubernatorial race. The utility companies,
demonized by Hunt earlier in the year, did not give money to Flaherty and
instead funded the Democrat. The Republican candidate accused Hunt of
being a mere politician, but the charges failed to stick. Defeating Jim Hunt
seemed a hopeless task.[65]

A year earlier, Flaherty had hoped to link his Democratic challenger
with a liberal presidential candidate. When he had considered a race for
governor in 1975, he never expected that former Georgia Governor Jimmy
Carter, a fiscal conservative, would lead the national Democratic ticket.
Neither did Jim Hunt. At that time, many political experts thought George
Wallace would win the state primary as he did in 1972. Although once
associated with progressive candidates, Hunt did all he could to make
himself compatible to Wallace voters. In 1973, he had lent his support to
a resolution honoring Wallace's courage during an assassination attempt.
In February 1974, Hunt had greeted Wallace at the airport and had praised
the Democrat at a Raleigh rally. He had met Wallace at the airport again
in 1975, when the Alabama politician had arrived to testify at a legislative
hearing about the state presidential primary. The lieutenant governor had
served as Wallace's escort during his visit to insure that conservative
Democrats would not link him with liberal presidential hopeful Terry Sanford.[66]

Hunt's appeasement of Wallace ended in 1976 after Jimmy Carter
defeated the Alabama governor in the North Carolina presidential primary. Hunt modeled himself more after Carter than Wallace or even

Sanford, who dropped out of the presidential race in January 1976. Since 1971, Hunt had admired the Georgia governor for embracing civil rights for African Americans and women while rejecting traditional liberal approaches to the economy. Each man looked toward their Protestant faith as the basis for moral decisions. They had met several times, including at a 1973 North Carolina fundraising dinner where Hunt lavishly praised Carter's efforts at improving education, reorganizing Georgia government, reforming the judicial system, and launching an early childhood development program. Less than two years later, the virtually unknown former governor shocked political experts by winning the New Hampshire presidential primary and defeating Wallace in Southern primaries, including North Carolina. After Carter won the Democratic presidential nomination, he appeared with the lieutenant governor at a political rally in Charlotte where someone took a photo of the two men that Hunt later used to connect himself with the nominee. The gubernatorial candidate linked himself with Jimmy Carter because even the state's conservative white Democrats embraced the Southern Baptist politician.[67]

Hunt ignored his Republican challenger and ran a campaign promoting his favorite issues. He called upon North Carolina to "move forward again to improve reading skills, restore faith in government, fight crime, and support economic development."[68] Bluegrass musicians played their banjos at well-attended rallies, where young volunteers passed hand fans that stated "I'm a Jim Hunt fan." As the general election approached, the Hunt campaign organizers appeared optimistic. They knew that their candidate had the advantage in finances, political organization, name recognition among voters, and identification with the principal issues.[69]

In November 1976, Hunt won sixty-five percent of the vote against the Republican candidate, receiving wide backing from all sections of North Carolina. David Flaherty conceded the election after hearing the early returns and congratulated Hunt for achieving the "mandate from the people he asked for."[70] Looking back, former campaign manager Joe Grimsley said that they did not expect such a landslide, and he believed that Jimmy Carter helped Hunt by carrying fifty-six percent of the vote against President Gerald Ford in North Carolina. "We thought we would win by several percentage points, but in the end, Carter became much stronger, and it threw our numbers even higher," he recalled.[71] The national ticket helped Jim Hunt win by a landslide and establish a mandate for his programs.

At the North Raleigh Hilton, James B. Hunt, Jr., celebrated his victory. "My friends, happy days are here again," he said as sweat ran down his neck. He promised "a new beginning for North Carolina."[72] At age 39, he

Jim Hunt was elected as governor in 1976, the bicentennial year of the United States. In this photo, the recently elected politician reveals bicentennial symbols at a January 1977 press conference. (Courtesy of the North Carolina Office of Archives and History)

had reached a goal that some people claimed he had desired since childhood. From 1973 to 1976, he had used the office of the lieutenant governor as a base to run for the state's highest office. Building upon his earlier organization, he attracted all factions of North Carolina Democrats who perceived him as a moral champion of the people who would inevitably win the 1976 race. Hunt ignored the state Democratic party and organized an independent political organization that attracted support in every county. Understanding the concern about illiteracy, crime, rising utility rates, declining ethics, and low-paying jobs, he developed proposals that put him out in front of these popular issues. Refusing to be trapped by ideology, he blended conservative themes of low taxes and crime, populist themes of fair utility rates, and liberal themes of race and gender equality to forge a popular message. At times, he straddled issues and distanced himself from other candidates to insure that he would not appear either too conservative or too liberal. Such behavior frustrated his opponents and even some of his friends, but his most loyal followers ignored his political maneuvering. Hunt organized his campaign so well and attracted so many contributors that he easily defeated an extremely wealthy candidate from Charlotte, a progressive challenger who had the support of the state's leading Democratic newspaper, and a Republican opponent weakened by internal party squabbles. With a mandate from the state's citizens, Jim Hunt prepared an active agenda for North Carolina in 1977.

9

The New Beginning:
Jim Hunt and the 1977 Agenda

Treating his 1976 landslide victory as a mandate, North Carolina Governor James B. Hunt, Jr., advocated a "new beginning" for law enforcement, consumerism, education, and industrial expansion. Demonstrating strong leadership, he brought loyal supporters to all levels of state government, took control of the parole system, expanded his power over boards and commissions, and successfully lobbied for a state constitutional amendment that allowed him to run for a second consecutive term. Despite the defeat of the Equal Rights Amendment (ERA) and the efforts of the lieutenant governor to interfere with his agenda, Hunt successfully influenced the state legislature to pass most of his proposed legislation in 1977. Although a minority complained that the governor created a powerful political machine dedicated to Hunt's perpetual rule, most North Carolinians admired the activist leader for improving education, getting tough on crime, dealing with the energy crisis, and restructuring government without raising taxes.

Those Tar Heels who already knew Hunt as one of the hardest working politicians seemed amazed at his intensity during his first year as governor. "The energy of the governor is extraordinary, the way he moves all around the state raising public concern about issues," Hunt aide Joel Fleishman said.[1] Special Assistant Joe Pell said that a deep, inner fire that burned with extraordinary intensity drove the governor. "This man can't wait to get up in the morning," Pell said. "After we get his schedule set, he started adding more (items) himself. People around him beg him to stop, but he doesn't hear a word of it."[2]

The active governor had the loyal support of his wife and children.

Governor Hunt is pictured here sitting for the first time at the governor's desk in the State Capitol as his family looks on. His critics debate how long Hunt had desired to be in the governor's chair; some insist that he had wanted the job since he was six. Hunt claims that he didn't think about a life in public service until he attended college, but his cousin Carl Henley claims that Jimmy Hunt had said, as a teenager, that he would someday be governor of North Carolina. (Courtesy of the North Carolina Office of Archives and History)

Since her marriage to the Wilson County native in 1958, Carolyn Leonard Hunt had understood her husband's desire to attend political functions, committee meetings, out-of-state conferences, and late-night work sessions. "Being a political wife takes understanding and trust," she said. "You have to believe what he's doing, especially when he's away so much."[3] Mrs. Hunt shared many of his goals, including the improvement of education in North Carolina and the passage of ERA. Despite her feminist views, she quit her teaching job to take care of their four kids during the 1976 gubernatorial campaign and became a fulltime first lady. The following year, their four children — Rebecca, 16, Baxter, 13, Rachel, 11, and Elizabeth, 6 — moved away from the tobacco farm to urban Raleigh, becoming symbols of the youth and energy of the new administration.[4]

    On January 8, 1977, Jim Hunt's family watched as he took the oath as governor of North Carolina for the first of four times. The previous

Carolyn Hunt, the wife of Governor Jim Hunt and former teacher, served as a strong advocate of education and women's rights. He met her at an agricultural convention while they were still teenagers, and he married her in 1958. Their marriage has lasted for more than forty years because, Carolyn has said, they understand each other well. In this photo, North Carolina's first lady volunteers as a reader at Wiley School. (Courtesy of the North Carolina Office of Archives and History)

evening, he had attended an inauguration festival hosted by Andy Griffith, the Tar Heel–born actor whose 1960s television show pictured community values that Hunt wanted the state to emulate in real life. At a freezing inaugural, the governor announced his goals to the crowd:

> I want to declare here, today, to all those who seek a better life — to the child struggling to learn at school, to the working parents planning their future and their children's future, to the young people trying to find a place in society, to the farmer in his fields, to the mill worker, to the elderly, to the sick, to the disabled, to the handicapped — that you have a friend in the Governor's Office.... Let us commit ourselves— here, today — to a new beginning in North Carolina.[5]

A new beginning meant a change from the administration of James B. Holshouser, the first Republican governor in seventy-one years. Hunt's

Here, Jim Hunt, his wife Carolyn, and family members pledge allegiance at Hunt's January 1977 gubernatorial inauguration. A year earlier, Hunt defeated wealthy opponents in the Democratic primary and easily defeated Republican candidate David Flaherty in the general election. Hunt believed that he had a mandate from a majority of Tar Heels to pass his legislative agenda in 1977. (Courtesy of the North Carolina Office of Archives and History)

cabinet included important supporters, two women, and one African American. Joseph Grimsley, an old Wilson County acquaintance and former campaign manager, took charge of the Department of Administration with help from Deputy Secretary Jane Patterson, a former civil rights activist. Lauch Faircloth, the wealthy hog farmer who had worked for Democratic candidates since the 1940s, presided over the restructured Department of Commerce. Hunt appointed Chapel Hill Mayor Howard Lee to head the Department of Community Development and Natural Resources (NRCD), making Lee the first African-American cabinet member in North Carolina history. Former Raleigh Mayor Tom Bradshaw took control of the Department of Transportation. Hunt also named women to fill two positions— Sarah Morrow over Human Resources and Sara Hodgkins over Cultural Resources. To address the overcrowding of prisons, he selected Amos Reed of Florida to head the Department of Corrections.[6]

In front of the governor's mansion, the Hunt family once again pledged allegiance to the American flag. Pictured above from left to right are his daughter Rebecca, his son Baxter, his daughters Rachel and Elizabeth, his wife Carolyn, and Jim Hunt. The governor won praise for being a strong family man. His children symbolized the youth and vitality of the new administration. (Courtesy of the North Carolina Office of Archives and History)

Hunt relied on a strong team in his governor's office as much as he relied on his cabinet secretaries. Press Secretary Gary Pearce, a former Raleigh *News and Observer* reporter whose uncombed, long hair earned him the name "Hairy Gary" and whose drinking habits differed from Hunt's abstinence so much that staffers called them the "Odd Couple,"[7] nevertheless turned the press office into an effective tool for promoting the governor. Special Assistant Joe Pell took over the patronage duties, defending the right to appoint loyal campaign workers. Hunt also strongly depended on Budget Director John Williams, a businessman who had served as the finance chairman to Robert Scott's successful campaign for governor in 1968. The tough aide did Hunt's bidding in unpleasant situations. Hunt used these men to control most state policy decisions from the governor's office.[8]

Hunt micro-managed the state government. He did so because, according to Grimsley, "he personally feels accountable for everything."[9]

The governor selected loyal lieutenants and gubernatorial aides to monitor state departments to insure that cabinet secretaries did not make serious policy mistakes. Grimsley recalled getting into several disputes with the governor's special assistant, Banks Talley, over management of the Department of Administration. Although Talley left office in 1978, Grimsley ended up losing his department's budget bureau to the governor's office because of Hunt's emphasis on centralization. While Grimsley resisted control briefly, other cabinet officials less close to Hunt simply accepted rule by the governor's office. Hunt recruited Sarah Morrow to serve over Human Resources by giving her a higher salary than any other cabinet member. In 1977, she received negative publicity as the result of a mishandled firing of an administrator and the discovery of abuses at a state mental hospital. To insure Hunt had control over that department, and with Morrow's blessing, the governor approved his old college friend Tom Gilmore as her deputy secretary in 1978. Hunt also appointed a loyal deputy at the Department of Natural Resources and Community Development to insure that Secretary Howard Lee managed his employees effectively. The governor scrutinized the departments to make them more effective and to ensure that staffers followed the governor's agenda.[10]

To insure loyalty in all departments and to hire the numerous supporters from his 1976 campaign, Hunt urged the replacement of all major staffers in state government. In what his rivals called "Jim Hunt's Christmas Massacre," the governor-elect had asked for the resignations of 169 state policymakers in December 1976. After receiving resignations from most of Governor Holshouser's appointees, the incoming administration fired the few Republicans who refused to quit. To make matters worse for the weakened GOP, the 1977 Democratic-dominated General Assembly approved restructuring legislation that forced Republicans off of boards and committees. The legislature also passed a law that allowed the governor to fire all employees hired in the last five years— or in other words, anyone hired by the previous Republican administration. The matter drew criticism even from liberal newspapers when state Democratic Party Chairwoman Betty McCain called for the hiring of hardworking Democrats and the ouster of Republican "culprits."[11] Senate Minority Leader Donald Kincaid claimed that Hunt reorganized the government to depose Republicans. Special Assistant Joe Pell defended the governor's spoils system, saying "the game of politics, as far as I know, is still played on the basis of 'to the victor belong the spoils.' That's not considered illegal."[12] Republican lower-level staffers kept their jobs once the courts ruled that the statute was unconstitutional.

Hunt also attempted to exert strong leadership in his handling of the

Even before Governor James Holshouser prepared to be replaced by the lieutenant governor at the 1977 inauguration (pictured here), Hunt planned to
replace several Holshouser appointees in the administration even in the lower
levels of state government. Hunt wished to reward those who helped him in the
1976 campaign and he also desired loyal employees to implement his reforms.
(Courtesy of the North Carolina Office of Archives and History)

energy crisis. Because severe winter weather in February 1977 coincided
with a national energy crisis that drained natural gas supplies, Governor
Hunt declared a state of emergency in North Carolina, ordering a ten-
hour, four-day work week for state employees, the lowering of thermostats
in public buildings, and voluntary limits on store hours. President Jimmy
Carter asked the nation to stop wasting energy, and Hunt reiterated the
request to Tar Heel citizens. "We must conserve more," the governor
demanded. "Not just in the short run, but for years to come. We must learn
to stop being a wasteful people."[13]

A firm believer in economic voluntarism, Hunt tried to convince
businesses to support voluntary guidelines on store hours and heating levels, but his efforts produced mixed results. When retail stores complained
that they could not profit on a 48-hour week, the governor raised the limit
to fifty-four hours. Hunt's concession failed to persuade the convenience
store owners, who threatened to ignore the guidelines. The governor then

ordered businesses to heat their establishments no higher than sixty-two degrees for forty-eight hours and mandated fifty-five degrees for the remainder of all open store hours. As more heating oil arrived in the state in March 1977, Hunt ended the emergency office hours and heating mandates. The governor still took the energy crisis seriously by successfully pushing legislation that gave tax credits to Tar Heels who insulated their houses.[14]

Governor Hunt, who pledged to reduce high utility rates, succeeded in 1977 in restructuring the North Carolina Utilities Commission to favor consumers. Worrying that wealthy attorneys of the power companies influenced the commission to increase electric rates dramatically during the energy crisis, he urged the creation of a public staff to argue on the behalf of the people in utility rate cases. Several political leaders opposed the bill. North Carolina House Speaker Carl Stewart considered the restructuring too expensive, and Attorney General Rufus Edmisten wanted the state justice department to defend consumers. Despite their opposition, Hunt used his popularity to lobby successfully to pass the most important pro-consumer bill on his agenda.[15]

Nothing, however, divided North Carolinians in the 1977 session like the Equal Rights Amendment (ERA). That year, the legislature debated the ERA for the third time in six years. The women's rights amendment was the main goal of the women's movement in the 1970s. Femi-

Jim Hunt is pictured here circa 1977 with Julie Grimsley, the daughter of Administration Secretary Joseph Grimsley and the sister of the author. In the 1990s, Julie Grimsley Perry served as an auditor on the Utilities Commission's Public Staff, which represents the public in utility rate matters. Hunt urged the legislature to create the public staff in 1977 after people complained about high utility rates. (Courtesy of Julie Grimsley Perry)

nists argued that the current laws exploited women and made them second-class citizens, and only the ERA could destroy the barriers of sexism and inequality. Opponents feared that ERA would destroy special legislation protecting women and threaten the family structure.[16]

In 1977, ERA proponents hoped that the sympathies of Governor Jim Hunt and United States President James Earl Carter would assure passage in North Carolina and create momentum for two more states to ratify the amendment into the United States Constitution. North Carolina United for ERA (NCUERA) activists counted on Hunt's strong leadership to win, hoping that the governor would use his appointive power, grassroots support, and political organization to influence the legislature to pass ERA. Hunt also received pro–ERA pressure from native Tar Heels like Nancy Snowden, who claimed, "I have silently watched discrimination for twenty-six years— in my paycheck, on job applications, on the street; in short, in all aspects of my life as a woman."[17] His wife Carolyn also urged her husband to strongly back ERA.

Many conservative North Carolinians took an opposite view of the amendment. They wrote the governor that ERA would destroy the family, create unisex bathrooms, draft young women, legalize homosexual marriages, forge a socialist dictatorship, and destroy the natural relationship between men and women. One wife wrote Hunt that "men and women don't want to be equal. I don't want to be."[18] Another housewife, Mrs. Allie Phillips, said, "I am honored to be a wife, mother, and I do not want to see some things change."[19] A Christian Church preacher from Raleigh stated that the ERA originated in Communist Russia under Karl Marx. Mrs. Ola Johnson of Selma would not have disagreed, asserting that many women wanted no part of "this Jew and Communist movement."[20] Even though some Tar Heels condemned ERA with ludicrous arguments, the governor could clearly see that many of his constituents opposed the amendment.

Several Tar Heels criticized Jim Hunt personally for supporting ERA. Mrs. Deborah Waller wrote that she was ashamed that Hunt supported ERA since "any Christian person would not be for such an ungodly act."[21] The Reverend Charles E. Keith said that he could not understand how a man of Hunt's religious and cultural standing could lend his influence to such a dangerous piece of legislation. Other ERA opponents demanded his neutrality. Ossie D. Fredericks of Salisbury said that Hunt should not use his office to influence state legislators. Even the governor's wealthy friend Gordon Hanes said that there was no point in "destroying yourself on an issue which basically is not of earth-shaking importance."[22] Hunt, however, believed that the ERA issue was important enough to offend social conservatives who had supported him in his earlier campaigns.

The anti–ERA movement turned to other notable Tar Heels to stop the amendment. Former United States Senator Sam Erwin called ERA a dangerous measure and condemned Hunt for his support of the amendment. North Carolina Supreme Court Chief Justice Susie Sharp, a classmate of the governor's mother and the woman who swore Hunt in as governor, urged senators to vote against ratification. She told one senator, "I sure hope you won't let the young governor twist your arm."[23] Most importantly, the anti–ERA opponents included Lieutenant Governor Jimmy Green, president of the state senate.

After the ERA passed the North Carolina House, Hunt prepared a major lobbying effort in the senate to sway four undecided senators. He invited these men to the governor's mansion for tea and conversation leading one Hunt aide to later say, "We damn near gave away the state."[24] President Jimmy Carter and his wife Rosalynn joined the effort to influence the undecided senators. Hunt also tried to prevent defections, literally looking for Charlotte legislator James McDuffie in motels in Raleigh to insure that anti–ERA opponents did not change his mind. The governor did all he could to insure that the amendment would pass the senate.[25]

Despite the lobbying of the governor and of the president, the ERA opponents defeated the measure, 24 to 26. Wavering senators paid more attention to conservatives in their home districts and to traditional women in their own families than to the governor or the president. According to Grimsley, Senator John Henley's wife told him before they went to church on Sunday, "You better not vote for that."[26] Hunt lost another legislator's vote after his mother told him to oppose the amendment. Newspaper columnists Robert Novak and Rowland Evans said that Hunt's efforts produced more votes than the president, "but not by much. He feels (that) any pro–ERA voters he secured in the Senate were matched by anti–ERA votes won over by the revered retired Senator Sam Erwin."[27] The combination of prominent opponents, grassroots conservatives, and family pressure doomed the ERA in 1977.

Few Tar Heel feminists blamed Hunt for lack of zeal. Ruth Mary Meyers, president of the North Carolina chapter of the League of Women Voters, wrote Hunt that "you did not disappoint us.... You worked until the bitter end to try to win back the votes that slipped away."[28] ERA supporter H. Gayle Ward of Raleigh said that she was grateful that the governor took great risks by coming out strongly for the amendment. Hunt recalled, "We got every vote we could have possibly got. We played it as hard as we could play it. We played it as close as you could get."[29] Hunt lobbied unsuccessfully for ERA two more times in 1979 and 1982, but he never seemed as close to victory and as frustrated by defeat as in 1977.

After watching Hunt get defeated on ERA, Lieutenant Governor Jimmy Green struggled with the governor to control the North Carolina Board of Education. Early in April 1977, Hunt decided not to reappoint Board Chairman Dallas Herring, whose 22-year service had won praise from educators for keeping the public schools open during the integration crisis and for helping Governor Terry Sanford create the state community college system in the 1960s. Although Hunt personally liked Herring, he wanted to end the chairman's divisive clashes with State School Superintendent Craig Phillips, an elected official. He also wanted a chairman who would be more loyal to him and more supportive of educational bureaucracy. He announced his intention to appoint David Bruton, a 42-year-old doctor and a Hunt supporter from Southern Pines. While Herring said that he had no bitterness toward the governor, his angry supporters on the board retaliated by approving Jimmy Green as interim chairman. It soon became apparent that the lieutenant governor did not intend to leave his new position. Green delayed the senate appointment of Hunt's four new nominees on the board and backed legislation making himself permanent chairman.[30]

By May 1977, the tensions between the governor and the lieutenant governor reached new heights after Green's allies on the North Carolina Senate Government Committee overwhelmingly recommended the chairmanship bill. At first, Hunt decided not to fight in the senate, hoping that he could win the battle in the house. After discussing the matter with his aides, he decided that he needed to wage a senate fight, since Green's chairmanship would endanger the success of Hunt's education reforms. The following week, the governor lobbied North Carolina senators to vote against the bill. The senate was divided. "You either go with Hunt or go with Green," said Senator Ralph Scott.[31] Despite efforts by state senators loyal to Hunt, Green's allies passed the bill, 31–18. To encourage the other legislative body to back his proposal, Green created a subcommittee of his loyal allies to determine the merits of bills coming from the North Carolina House. Gubernatorial aides called it a "Get Hunt" committee determined to blackmail the other body into approving the legislation by denying pet projects to members of the house. Hunt, who wanted to reform state education policy, faced the possibility of having his main political rival in a position that could sabotage his reforms.[32]

To make matters worse, Green acted in other ways that widened the rift with the governor. When House Speaker Carl Stewart offered a compromise that allowed Green to chair a new board in charge of only the community colleges, the lieutenant governor rejected the proposal. Without informing Hunt, Green introduced legislation making the inventory taxes of businesses deductible on state income tax returns, a proposal that the governor considered fiscally unsound. Even the lieutenant governor's remarks to newspapers caused tensions. In an interview with a *News and Observer* reporter, Green said that Jim Hunt had little knowledge of business or the legislature. Later, Green announced that he might run for governor in 1980, even against Hunt if "there's a groundswell out there."[33] Editorial pages condemned the bickering between the two elected officials, mostly blaming Green. North Carolina Senator Melvin R. Daniels lamented, "The state cannot stand four years of this."[34]

The relationship improved in June 1977 after Green failed in his effort to become permanent chairman of the state Board of Education. A house committee rejected the chairmanship bill, and the North Carolina Senate approved Hunt's four new nominees, thus giving the

Governor Jim Hunt had a turbulent relationship with Lieutenant Governor Jimmy Green, pictured here smoking a cigar at the 1981 inauguration. In 1977, Green unsuccessfully tried to control the North Carolina Board of Education against the wishes of the governor. Green considered running against Hunt in 1979, abandoning the idea when it seemed that the governor might be unbeatable. However, Hunt sometimes appeased Green to insure that the governor's programs passed the legislature. (Courtesy of the North Carolina Office of Archives and History)

governor a majority of allies on the board. Green stepped aside for Hunt appointee David Bruton, who pledged to back the governor's education programs. To insure peace for the remainder of the session, Hunt offered Green some concessions, including approval of the lieutenant governor's chairmanship of the Government Operations Committee and the appointment of a Green ally on the Board of Education's finance committee. The governor also remained neutral on several measures backed by Green's conservative allies, including the removal of the state insurance commissioner's power to prevent rate hikes. At the same time, Green did not interfere with Hunt's efforts to increase his patronage powers. Green and Hunt compromised to maintain harmony and to achieve political benefits for each other.[35]

The resolution of the chairmanship fight allowed Hunt to concentrate on the implementation of his education agenda. In his 1977 state of the state address, he proposed to invest $15 million to put special reading aides and instructional materials in the first three grades of public schools in North Carolina. He backed the testing of students in early grades to improve their reading and math skills. He also called for a minimum competency test to insure that students had basic skills before they graduated from high school. In addition, he endorsed a community schools act that

Jim Hunt desired strongly to improve North Carolina education and pushed for mandatory competency tests and reading aides during his first term. Here, Hunt volunteers at Broughton High School in Raleigh. (Courtesy of the North Carolina Office of Archives and History)

would turn educational facilities into places of public use. The legislature passed these bills by June.[36]

The bill calling for a competency test for high school students caused mild controversy before the General Assembly passed it. The North Carolina Association of Educators (NCAE) and African American civil rights groups both opposed this bill for different reasons. The NCAE feared that poor scores would unfairly reflect on public school teachers, and black leaders said that the tests contained cultural biases that discriminated unfairly against African Americans. Hunt assured both groups, which strongly backed him in the 1976 gubernatorial campaign, that the tests would be used to improve the skills of all Tar Heel students, including blacks. Because of these assurances by the governor and his support of a pay increase for teachers, the NCAE and civil rights organizations did little to defeat the minimum competency bill.[37]

University of North Carolina graduate student Marc Sosne wrote a study of the passage of the minimum competency bill and concluded that Governor Hunt played the most important part in determining the successful outcome. "Hunt proposed the legislation, chose the representatives who would introduce and sponsor the bill, and shepherded the bill through the political process until its passage into law," Sosne said.[38] He concluded that Hunt used a cross section of liberals and conservatives, ex-educators and non-educators, Democrats and Republicans, and legislators from all parts of the state to sponsor the bill. With the aid of legislative liaison Charles Winberry, a Rocky Mount lawyer with uncanny political skills, Hunt persuaded the legislature to reject unnecessary amendments and pass the minimum competency bill by an overwhelming margin.[39]

During the rest of his first term, Hunt defended his education program against charges that his proposals failed the students in North Carolina. After Tar Heel students performed poorly on a trial run of the minimum competency test in April 1978, Hunt approved a state Competency Test Commission that eased testing standards. As a result, only fifteen percent of North Carolina students failed the revised minimum competency test later that year. If the easier examination received criticism from newspapers, including the *News and Observer*, the dropout rate in North Carolina did not increase dramatically as a result of the test, defying the predictions of several critics. The minimum competency test, in addition to the reading aide program and the grade-school examinations, increased Hunt's reputation as a leading education governor.[40]

The Community Schools Act proved to be a less successful initiative. Arguing that the citizens owned the libraries, gyms, shops, laboratories, meeting rooms, and equipment in the public schools, the governor urged the people to use educational facilities as community centers. He wanted community life to center around a public school, just as his family had focused on Rock Ridge High School activities in the early 1950s. Not everyone shared the governor's views. Education advisor Betty Owen recalled the fears of the principals who worried about the end of their public school "fiefdoms," forgetting that the taxpayers paid for the schools. "What if a group of women use our sewing machines and break them?" Owen recalled one principal asking.[41] In addition to these concerns, most Tar Heels never got accustomed to attending night activities at public schools, and therefore, the act did not seriously affect North Carolina.[42]

Hunt also backed a new approach to crime. He urged the legislature to enact a community watch program, fix sentences for repeat offenders, force trials after ninety days of a person's indictment, and end discretionary paroles. He called for the creation of the North Carolina Department of Crime Control and Public Safety to create comprehensive planning and coordination of the state criminal justice system. After the legislature approved this department, Hunt appointed his old North Carolina State College friend Phil Carlton as the secretary. Although Carlton managed the highway patrol, he could not centralize crime prevention efforts effectively because the North Carolina Attorney General still controlled the State Bureau of Investigation (SBI) and the local sheriffs handled law enforcement in their own counties. Because crime control officials could only make recommendations regarding crime prevention, several conservative politicians called for its abolition, yet Hunt continued to defend the department as a useful aide to local law enforcement.[43]

As part of Hunt's crime program, the governor strongly favored a bill reviving the death penalty in 1977. Twenty years earlier, as a student at North Carolina State College, Hunt had opposed capital punishment. "But in later years," he said, "after I read a lot of theology, I came to realize that human beings have an awesome responsibility to maximize love and to minimize hurt and especially death."[44] To minimize hurt and death, he argued, the state had the right to put murderers to death. As a lieutenant gubernatorial candidate in 1972, he had avoided the death penalty issue following the *Furman vs. Georgia* decision that suspended capital punishment because it discriminated unfairly against minorities. Three years later, however, with crime becoming a major issue in North Carolina, Hunt had told audiences that a revived death penalty was a humane instrument since it saved lives by deterring murder. After a philosophy professor denounced Hunt for his alleged sadistic approach to capital punishment, the lieutenant governor had responded:

My position in favor of capital punishment for certain crimes is based on two things. First, a personal belief that this is a deterrent to those who would commit these crimes and second, recent studies in penology and in criminal behavior that tend to substantiate that point of view. I am not suggesting that we, in any way, permit this punishment only to the poor, or to those who cannot, for one reason or another, obtain adequate legal aid. I suggest what we must make sure, as a state, that people accused of a capital crime receive the finest defense available to them, no matter what their status in life.[45]

Hunt maintained his support for the death penalty as a gubernatorial candidate and as governor. At times during the 1976 gubernatorial campaign, especially among African American audiences who opposed capital punishment, he qualified his support by advocating the death penalty for only the most heinous of murders, such as the killing of children. He also promised that all persons accused of capital crimes would get a good defense, and asked friends like former law partner John Webb about the best way that indigent defendants could receive a fair trial. By soft-pedaling the issue, he won the votes of death-penalty opponents who agreed with him on progressive issues. The majority of North Carolinians backed the death penalty, however, and he stood by them. After the legislature passed a new death-penalty statute in 1977, he declared that he would resist efforts to block executions. Hunt's position did not seriously alienate the anti-capital punishment minority in North Carolina until 1984, when, during a close United States Senate race against Jesse Helms, he refused to prevent the executions of two convicted murders. Those advocates who tried to get Hunt to change his mind on capital punishment discovered that their efforts were futile.[46]

Hunt only had a few failures in the 1977 session. He failed to pass a mandatory sentencing law because many legislators feared that the United States Supreme Court might overturn the statute. His proposal to eliminate the $120 sales tax limit on luxury vehicles went nowhere, partially because Hunt and his lobbyists did not put much priority on a bill that he promised to support in the 1976 gubernatorial campaign only after his opponent George Wood made tax reform an issue. He also remained the only governor in the United States without veto power. His staffers acknowledged that Hunt strengthened the executive branch so much and won so many legislative victories in 1977 that a strong fight for the veto would have only increased charges that he had too much power.[47]

Hunt still fought for the right of governors to run for two consecutive four-year terms. House member Tom Gilmore, an old Hunt friend from North Carolina State College, introduced a bill that called for a referendum on gubernatorial succession. "We still rank last in average industrial wages, low in per capita income, high in infant mortality, high in illiteracy, and the same time North Carolina is last in return on federal tax dollars in so many areas," said Gilmore.[48] Gubernatorial succession, he argued, would translate plans of progress into reality. In May 1977, the house and the senate passed a referendum that would allow the voters to change the state constitution in November.[49]

By the fall, the battle lines were drawn between supporters and opponents of gubernatorial succession. Former Governor James Holshouser co-chaired the succession campaign, arguing that the change might benefit the Republicans in the future. Most backers of the referendum, however, wanted Hunt to seek and to win reelection. They included organizations such as the North Carolina Association of Educators (NCAE) and the state branch of the American Federation of Labor–Congress of Industrial Organizations (AFL-CIO). Many feminists and African American leaders also endorsed gubernatorial succession.[50]

Several conservatives rallied against the succession amendment. They accused the governor of accumulating too much power at the expense of the legislative branch. Former United States Senator Sam Erwin said that gubernatorial succession would lead to governors spending all their time creating political machines to insure a second term. Lieutenant Governor Jimmy Green, who wished to run for governor in 1980, also strongly opposed the amendment. Green's friend C. Kitchen Josey served as treasurer for "Carolinians Against Succession," financed by anonymous donors. Wake County District Attorney Burley Mitchell, a good friend of Governor Hunt, sued in state court to force the group to reveal their financiers. Although this effort failed, the Hunt people realized that the secret donors were Green's conservative friends.[51]

Although Governor Hunt insisted that he had not yet made plans to run for reelection, he strongly backed the movement for succession. A brief controversy occurred when Secretary of Administration Joseph Grimsley sent out a memo that planned the strategy to win the referendum, leading Hunt to spurn any personal involvement in the struggle and turn leadership over to Hugh Morton, chairman of the Committee to Reject or Reelect. In private letters, the governor still told political supporters that North Carolina needed gubernatorial succession so that the chief executive would be more responsive to the people. He wrote friends like Joe Zaytoun to "get out there and let's put every muscle we have on the succession vote."[52] He also told supporters that a defeat at the polls would make him a lame-duck governor earlier than previous governors.[53]

In November 1977, the succession amendment passed narrowly. While almost fifty-three percent of North Carolinians backed the idea, nearly forty-eight percent opposed the amendment. Carter Wrenn, former director of the National Congressional Club, speculated that if the conservative fundraising organization of United States Senator Jesse Helms had used its financial resources against the amendment, they could have prevented succession and a second term for Governor Hunt. Former Congressional Club Chairman Tom Ellis wondered what would have happened had a printing machine error not delayed submitting the organization's letters against the succession amendment. Despite the complaints of conservatives, Hunt won the day. Even though the governor had not yet announced for reelection, his followers celebrated the victory by wearing "Hunt Again" buttons. "This is the day when the people of this state made a step to go forward, and be a progressive state," Hunt announced.[54] To the governor, progress meant the ability of an active executive to run for a second consecutive term.

The year 1977 proved extraordinary for North Carolina Governor James B. Hunt, Jr. Using his 1976 landslide victory as a mandate for action, he reorganized state government, centralized power in the governor's office, and wielded enormous patronage clout. Hunt also successfully pushed through a comprehensive program of legislation dealing with education, crime, utilities, and industrial recruitment. He suffered setbacks: the defeat of the Equal Rights Amendment made him vulnerable to the conservative wing of the Democratic party, allowing Lieutenant Governor Jimmy Green to engage in a personal confrontation over control of the North Carolina Board of Education. Hunt, however, defeated Green over control of education policy and the right of the governor to succeed himself. Because Jim Hunt accumulated so much executive power and achieved so many of his legislative goals in 1977, he had, at age forty, become one of the most powerful governors in North Carolina history.

10

Jim Hunt's "Political Prisoners": The Wilmington Ten and the Charlotte Three

Governor Jim Hunt faced the greatest controversy of his first term when he decided on the sentences of African Americans charged by North Carolina authorities with political terrorism during the Vietnam War era. He spent days debating the fate of the Wilmington Ten, nine black men and one white woman convicted of conspiring to burn a grocery store and shooting at policemen and firemen in 1971. The case received worldwide publicity as human rights organizations described the defendants as political prisoners jailed for civil rights activities. The same organizations made a similar claim for the Charlotte Three, the nickname for three African American men convicted of burning a stable in 1968. In each case, Amnesty International and civil rights groups demanded a pardon for the defendants. Both times, the governor refused to condemn law enforcement for any mistakes or to accept the innocence of the convicted defendants, but he commuted the severe sentences of the remaining prisoners. The absence of a pardon, especially in the case of the Wilmington Ten, angered the defendants' advocates and embarrassed the Carter administration, whose spokespersons declared that the case undermined the president's human rights campaign. Despite international criticism of the governor's decisions, Hunt remained popular in North Carolina. Conservative whites hailed his refusal to give in to outside pressure, and most African Americans lost interest in the cases by the time that the governor released the last so-called political prisoner from jail in December 1979.

The Wilmington Ten case that attracted international attention originated during the era of rising black militancy in the late 1960s and early 1970s. Disgusted with the nonviolent philosophy of Martin Luther King, Jr., because they believed it to be an ineffective tool for black empowerment, many young African Americans accepted the idea that whites only respected force and therefore violence could be used to achieve political ends. Tired of being told to assimilate into white society peacefully, they embraced their dark skin and African heritage. Unhappy with seeing the majority of their race in low-paying jobs, they denounced the entire economic and political system as perpetuating racism; some embraced socialism. Instead of "We Shall Overcome," the young African Americans chanted "Black Power" and "Black Pride."

Such ideas found their way to high schools in Wilmington, North Carolina. In 1971, a Wilmington principal suspended students for attempting a sit-in to protest the refusal of school officials to permit a commemorative program for civil rights leader Martin Luther King, Jr. After fights broke out between blacks and whites at three recently integrated high schools, white policemen broke up disputes. Many black students met at Gregory Congregational United Church of Christ (UCC) to plan a boycott to protest the closing of all-black Williston High School, the lack of a black studies program, and the absence of a day celebrating King's life. The Reverend Leon White, head of the UCC's North Carolina–Virginia Commission for Racial Justice, attended the students' second meeting at Gregory Congregational Church. He invited Ben Chavis, a twenty-four-year-old minister and former resident of Oxford, North Carolina, to organize the protest. A descendant of prominent nineteenth-century free black North Carolina minister John Chavis, the UCC minister mobilized Wilmington's black community behind the students.[1]

The week that the Reverend Chavis arrived, the violence grew worse in Wilmington and claimed two lives. Racial strife spread from the schools and besieged the community as shooting, rock throwing, and bombing occurred in the black section of the city. Two cranes were dynamited in downtown Wilmington, and anonymous persons phoned bomb threats to two predominantly white high schools. The city government imposed a curfew in Wilmington and temporarily closed the schools. On Friday night, February 6, arsonists burned Lum's Restaurant and Mike's Grocery.

Arriving at the burning store, policemen and fire fighters encountered sniper fire. One policeman was shot in the leg, while another officer shot and killed Stevenson Gibbs Mitchell, a nineteen-year-old black Wilmington high school student who, according to police reports, carried a shotgun. On Saturday morning, the police discovered Harvey Edward Cumber, a 57-year-old white man, shot to death. Found near a barricade beside Gregory Congregational Church, he had been armed. The violence led city authorities to claim that they could not control the city, prompting Governor Robert Scott to order the National Guard into Wilmington.[2]

Law enforcement focused on Gregory Congregational Church, finding evidence that violent persons used the building as a base for their activities. Looking in the basement, officers found shotgun shells, .22 caliber bullets, blasting caps, and dynamite. Chavis, who returned to Oxford that weekend, claimed that student activists used the weapons for self-defense against Ku Klux Klan members and racist whites who rampaged through the streets during the riot. He blamed city officials for spreading misinformation, including lies about the death of Stevenson Gibbs Mitchell, who Chavis said actually died unarmed. Chavis also accused Wilmington officials of threatening the civil rights activists, ignoring evidence of racist attacks, and "setting up the black community for annihilation."[3] The Reverend Gene Templeton, the white minister of the black congregational church, said that snipers fired into his building. However, the police claimed that they found no evidence of any such gunfire.[4]

Law enforcement officers waited another year before charging Chavis and nine other suspects with arson during the Wilmington riot. In May 1971, Allen Hall, a rotund teenaged high school dropout arrested for assaulting a teacher during the protests, told officers that he burned Mike's Grocery Store on orders from the Reverend Ben Chavis. Jerome Mitchell, a black student charged with robbery and murder, corroborated Hall's account. The two men then identified ten suspects involved in the arson from photographs of the February 1971 student demonstrations. Wilmington officials also discovered thirteen-year-old Eric Junious, who agreed to verify the other young men's accounts.[5]

As the Wilmington prosecutor gathered evidence, Reverend Chavis faced another charge resulting from a violent incident in his hometown of Oxford. According to African-American ex-convicts Theodore Alfred Hood and Walter D. Washington, Chavis and Charlotte antiwar activist James E. Grant asked them to kill two white Oxford men exonerated by a white jury after being charged with killing a black Vietnam War veteran. Washington and Hood never committed those murders because the police caught them with illegal explosives in their car and charged them with violations of federal law. According to Washington and Hood, Chavis and Grant feared that they might tell investigators about the Oxford plot and offered them some money to violate their bail and flee the country. Using the testimony of the two ex-convicts, the federal authorities indicted Chavis and Grant on charges of helping fugitives escape from justice. A United States Bureau of Alcohol, Tobacco, and Firearms (ATF) official wrote in a memo, "Because of the degree of terrorism attributed to Chavis and Grant, it is in the federal interest that they be brought to justice, whether through state or federal prosecution."[6] Although a jury found Grant guilty of the fugitive-abetting charges in April 1972, they did not convict Chavis because of insufficient evidence.

In 1972, Wilmington prosecutor Jay Stroud finally brought "The Wilmington Ten" to trial. In March, police arrested Ben Chavis after he attended the Black Political Convention, indicting him and nine defendants for arson and the shooting of city workers. He and eight other black defendants hired James Ferguson, a respected Charlotte civil rights lawyer, while Anne Shepard, the only white defendant, hired a personal counsel. During jury selection, the prosecution and defense agreed on ten blacks and two whites. However, prosecutor Jay Stroud conveniently missed court for what he claimed were stomach pains. Stroud's absence prompted the judge to rule a mistrial and led to convening a second jury comprised primarily of whites.[7]

The new jury heard the testimony of Anne Shepard for the defense and three black witnesses for the prosecution. Shepard, the only defendant to testify, said that she never urged violence and did not see the other defendants handle any firearms. Eric Junious rebutted her testimony by claiming that Shepard told the heavily armed defendants, "Let's show these crackers what we mean" after hearing Chavis urge arson and shooting. Then, witness Jerome Mitchell testified that the minister ordered several young men to burn down the grocery store. The most damaging witness against the defendants, however, was Allen Hall, who portrayed Chavis as the violent leader of the Wilmington Ten. Hall described the Gregory Congregational Church as full of young blacks armed with shotguns, rifles, and pistols. He called the UCC minister "the imperial wolf"[8] who walked around with a .45 automatic in a side holster. According to Hall, Chavis told them that the owner of Mike's Grocery had cussed out a black girl and that they should go down there and burn down the store. He said that the minister described the "Chicago strategy," a technique used by Windy City rioters in April 1968 who set fires and waited for police and firemen to arrive so that they could shoot at them. Hall next described Chavis watching as the teenagers burned Mike's Grocery. Based on the testimony of the prosecution witnesses, the jury convicted all ten defendants, and the state judge approved sentences for them that totaled 232 years in prison.[9]

Although Ferguson challenged the jury verdict, he could not prevent his clients from going to prison. In the North Carolina Court of Appeals, the attorney argued that the prosecutor used deceptive tactics to prevent a majority black jury, and that the judge refused to remove jurors who belonged to the Ku Klux Klan. Despite these claims, the state appellate court upheld the convictions in 1974. When the United States Supreme Court decided not to intervene in 1976, the Wilmington Ten began serving their sentences. At Caledonia Prison Farm, the Reverend Chavis preached about prison rights to African American inmates. Fearing his ability to cause a prison riot, the state transferred the minister to the more heavily guarded Central Prison in Raleigh. By late 1976, Chavis developed a strong following among African Americans, both inside and outside of prison, who believed that racist Wilmington officials framed him for leading civil rights demonstrations.[10]

African Americans had little trouble believing that racist North Carolina law enforcement targeted blacks, especially after the case of Jo Ann Little. In 1975, the state charged the female African-American prisoner with murdering a white jailer in Washington, North Carolina. Little testified in court that the jailer tried to rape her and that she retaliated by stabbing him several times with an ice pick. Because Little insisted that she was an innocent victim of small-town North Carolina racism and sexism, hundreds rallied to her defense and the jury acquitted her. In 1978, Little escaped to New York after being sentenced for another charge. Captured by New York law enforcement, she told them not to return her to North Carolina since she feared for her life in the Tar Heel prisons. Hunt briefly considered letting her serve her prison time in the northern state since she claimed to like New York so much. He abandoned the idea because he did not wish to support the charge that most North Carolina prison officials mistreated African Americans. Many blacks, however, accepted her judgment of the state. They believed that Jo Ann Little, like Ben Chavis, was a black martyr to North Carolina's racist justice system.[11]

Events in 1976 eventually brought the Wilmington Ten issue to Governor Hunt. That year, three prosecution trial witnesses recanted their testimony. In October, Allen Hall said that he agreed to lie for the state in return for District Attorney Jay Stroud dropping several years off his prison sentence. Hall claimed that the district attorney then showed him photographs and told him which African American protestors to implicate. Then, Jerome Mitchell said that he also lied for the prosecution, and Eric Junious confessed that Stroud offered him a mini-bike in exchange for his false testimony. In addition, the Reverend Templeton, the white minister of the UCC church that served as a base for black protestors, and his wife claimed that five of the Wilmington Ten stayed with them at their home at the time of the bombing of Mike's Grocery. The recantations of three witnesses and the Templetons' revelations led many people to believe more

fervently that North Carolina law officials had falsified a case against innocent black defendants. By 1977, the human rights group Amnesty International listed the Wilmington Ten as political prisoners.[12]

When Hunt became governor, he received several pleas to do something about the ten prisoners. Imani Kazana, National Coordinator for the
Wilmington Ten Defense Committee, urged the governor to act boldly in
the first weeks of his administration and free the convicted group. "The
entire world is watching to see whether your administration will in fact
right the wrongs of the past," he said.[13] In January 1977, Congressman Parren Mitchell, chairman of the Congressional Black Caucus, urged Hunt to
direct an immediate investigation of the Wilmington Ten. Charles E. Cobb,
director of the New York-based Commission for Racial Justice, demanded
the release of the defendants. Hunt even received letters from France for
"la liberation de Monsieur le Reverend Ben Chavis."[14]

A report on the Columbia Broadcasting System (CBS) television program "60 Minutes" in early 1977 cast doubt on the guilt of the Wilmington Ten. Television journalist Morley Safer's report stressed the attacks of
white racists on Gregory Congregational Church, the reluctance of city
officials to protect the civil rights activists, and Allen Hall's claim that he
burned the store without orders from Chavis. After watching the broadcast, Mrs. Olivia Behlen of Florida wrote Hunt, "Are you satisfied, if not
proud, to be the governor of the most racist state in the union?"[15] Samuel
Hirsh of New York City wrote the governor that after he viewed the program, he was convinced that the charges of frame-up seemed to be well
founded. These letter writers concluded that state officials framed the
Wilmington Ten and they wondered why the Tar Heel governor did not
act abruptly in freeing the prisoners. Hunt replied that he wanted to wait
until the courts finished with the case.[16]

At the same time that letters, mailgrams, and telegrams poured into
the governor's office from around the world that demanded justice for the
Wilmington Ten, President Jimmy Carter introduced his campaign to ele-
vate the nation's concern for human rights around the world. Many people wrote Hunt saying that the incarceration of the defendants undermined
the president's efforts to free political prisoners. A Miami resident said
that human rights talk from Washington reeked of hypocrisy while the
"Wilmington Ten continue to rot in the jails of North Carolina."[17] A New
York City woman concluded that the United States could not be concerned
about human rights all over the world when the nation had such a situation in the United States. A president of a Wisconsin college wrote Hunt
that Carter's efforts to champion human rights "becomes empty and hyp-
ocritical rhetoric if we violate the rights of our fellow Americans at

home."[18] Although many people in the Carter administration shared the same conclusion, they hoped that state officials would take care of the problem.

The hope that the state judicial system would free the Wilmington Ten eroded following evidence that the three witnesses possibly lied about their recantations. Prosecutor Jay Stroud claimed that Allen Hall, Jerome Mitchell, and Eric Junious misled people because they desperately sought acceptance from the black community which condemned them for their actions against the Wilmington Ten. He told Governor Hunt that Mitchell wrote letters in prison about how he was abused, harassed, hit, and cut because he testified against the defendants. Like Mitchell, Hall was "excluded from effective participation with other young black people, both in and out of prison,"[19] because of his testimony. After Stroud confronted Hall about his recantation, the witness admitted in a tape-recorded conservation that he had recanted his testimony falsely in order to win favoritism in the black community. Stroud also denied giving a motorbike to Junious in exchange for testimony, claiming that the prosecutor gave him the vehicle as a Christmas present.[20]

North Carolina Superior Court Judge George M. Fountain accepted Stroud's arguments in May 1977 and rejected the Wilmington Ten's request for a new trial. The judge concluded that the witnesses had told the truth during the trial and that pressure from the black community had led to the recantations. He discovered no evidence of deals in exchange for false testimony and said that a state official's aid to Junious did not represent a bribe in exchange for untruthful comments in court. He also knew that Junious testified against the Wilmington Ten again to a grand jury in March 1977. "The retractions of Allen Hall, Jerome Mitchell, and Eric Junious are not true and they did not perjure themselves at the trial," concluded Judge Fountain.[21] He rejected the request for a new trial. Defense attorney James Ferguson, who wanted to know why Hall and the other two witnesses received credibility in 1972 that they lacked five years later, appealed the matter of a new trial to the North Carolina Court of Appeals.

Throughout 1977, Hunt abstained from making comments about the Wilmington Ten, waiting for the state courts to decide whether to give them a new trial. In the summer, he met with Ben Chavis's mother Elizabeth, a retired schoolteacher, who asked the governor to free her son. He also received letters from Democratic congressmen and Amnesty International asking him to pardon the defendants. Not all contact with Wilmington Ten advocates went smoothly, however. When Congressional Black Caucus members tried to visit Hunt on a Sunday in December 1977, the governor said that he usually spent that day with his family, not an untruthful statement, and declined to meet with them. Although the congressmen met with Hunt's attorney, Jack Cozort, they clearly did not appreciate the snub. They still hoped that Hunt would pardon the defendants if the North Carolina courts did not release them.[22]

In January 1978, the North Carolina Court of Appeals denied a request for a retrial, which finally forced Hunt to deal with the Wilmington Ten. "We were surprised," Press Secretary Gary Pearce said. "It came earlier than we thought."[23] Hunt spent several days examining the case. As he privately deliberated on the fate of the Wilmington Ten, he received pressure from many more people to free them. United States Attorney Mickey Michaux, who had endorsed Hunt in 1976, told the governor that "if you are worried about your political neck, I think you would get this situation behind you. This is a problem that casts a stone at the state."[24] Letters came from prominent individuals and concerned citizens demanding justice. Even the niece of Governor Hunt's handpicked Democratic party chairperson, Betty McCain, argued in behalf of Amnesty International for the defendants.[25]

On January 23, 1978, the governor, addressing a statewide television audience, announced his decision on the Wilmington Ten. Hunt said that he had spent hundreds of hours of study on the case, reviewed each defendant's record, and directed his legal counsel to talk with several of the defendants. He briefly described the course of events from the 1971 riot in Wilmington to the legal process that ended earlier that month. He proclaimed:

> From all that I have learned in reviewing this case, I have concluded that there was a fair trial, the jury made the right decision, and the appellate courts reviewed it properly and correctly. I have confidence in what our courts and judges have done. Accordingly, I cannot and I will not pardon these defendants.[26]

The governor then discussed the sentencing of the defendants. He said the lack of fair-sentencing guidelines in North Carolina allowed the penalties for destroying a building to exceed the penalty for firing on policemen and firemen. He concluded:

> As governor, I considered several factors in looking at these sentences. I had to take into account the atmosphere and tension in Wilmington seven years ago. Those were troubled times in North Carolina. I also considered the defendants' ages—they were young, several of them high school students. Also, this was the first offense for most of them. I have given long and prayerful consideration to all these

Jim Hunt said that the toughest decision of his first term was to decide on the fates of the Wilmington Ten, a group of mostly African American activists charged with arson and the shooting of city officials in a 1971 Wilmington riot. In this photo, Hunt points to Wilmington Ten documents which he had studied for hours. On a live television broadcast, he told North Carolinians that the defendants deserved commutation of their sentences, but not pardons. The decision angered the national media, human rights groups, and African Americans, but most white Tar Heels accepted his decision as the proper one. (Courtesy of the *News and Observer*)

> factors. I have concluded that the sentences of these men in prison, which range from a minimum imprisonment of twenty to twenty-five years, are too long. I will *not* reduce their sentences for conspiring to shoot at policemen and firemen. I believe, however, that a reduction in the sentences imposed for firebombing an unoccupied building is in order.[27]

Hunt's decision to commute the sentences, and not to pardon the defendants, immediately drew criticism from the Wilmington Ten's advocates in North Carolina. Defense attorney James Ferguson said that Hunt made a "crass political appeal to the basest instincts of the people of this state."[28] Elizabeth Chavis called Hunt "a prejudiced one-sided God-forsaken leader"[29] who would never serve as governor again. At a press conference at Central Prison, her son Ben Chavis denounced Hunt for his decision not to pardon the Wilmington Ten. The prisoner claimed that the governor sought to cover up the state's involvement in the frame-up and compared Jim Hunt to Pontius Pilate, the Roman magistrate who ordered the death sentence of Jesus Christ.[30]

Many observers wondered if the governor had permanently damaged his relationship with the state's African-American voters after several black Hunt supporters criticized his decision. Harvey Gantt, a black city councilman from Charlotte, said he thought that the governor should have been more lenient. Reverend Joy Johnson, a prominent black minister from Robeson County, said that Hunt missed an opportunity to do a great humanitarian act for the state, the nation, and the world. Ralph Campbell, a black leader from Raleigh, said that Hunt hurt himself badly with the black community. A black activist told the *News and Observer* that the action undermined all the things the governor had done for African Americans in his first year as governor. However, black leaders hesitated to endorse more extreme measures than simply criticizing the governor's decision. For example, after the UCC Racial Justice Commission director asked for blacks to withdraw from the Hunt administration, no prominent African American heeded his call. Natural Resources and Community Development (NRCD) Secretary Howard Lee refused to resign, despite the black cabinet member's disapproval of the decision, saying "it would be unfortunate and unfair if Jim Hunt and his administration were judged solely on the Wilmington Ten."[31] Other African American politicians refused to condemn Hunt strongly because he had a good hiring record regarding blacks, supported civil rights and affirmative action, and formed a Democratic coalition that challenged white racist traditionalists.[32]

Hunt received criticism for his decision from across the country and from around the world. "I have heard excellent comments about your enlightened leadership," wrote William A. Draves of Kansas. "Thus, it was with shock and dismay that we learned of your decision not to pardon the Wilmington 10."[33] Congressman Robert Drinan of Massachusetts, a white Jesuit priest and a Democrat, said that the governor had not learned much from the thousands of hours that he allegedly spent studying the case. Representative Parren Mitchell of the Congressional Black Caucus said that he would oppose all human rights commitments that arose in Congress, even if the president proposed them, because the nation could no longer support human rights abroad and deny it at home. *Washington Post* Columnist Mary McGrory criticized the young governor, claiming that Hunt did the worse possible thing by yielding to local prejudice while under international pressure. She said that Hunt viewed himself as a progressive New South leader who could go all the way to the presidency, yet he "trampled his national dreams into the dust as he showed a profile in timidity on the Wilmington 10."[34] The Soviet Union declared in its news agency *Tass* that the decision of Governor Hunt was a "new arbitrary act by the racist authorities against victims of political repression."[35]

Despite the outcry from various critics, Hunt received praise for his decision from most whites in North Carolina. Supporters of conservative Lieutenant Governor Jimmy Green, Hunt's main political rival, approved of the governor's decision. The exception was North Carolina Senator I. Beverly Lake, Jr., who rebuked Hunt for responding to outside pressure. Yet, Wilmington prosecutor Jay Stroud said that he concurred with what the governor had said in his January 23rd speech. White progressive allies, including State Senator McNeill Smith and businessman Bert Bennett, also praised Hunt. Other Tar Heels applauded the decision. "I was in a meeting this morning early with local businessman, and your decision met the approval of everyone there," said a Rocky Mount auto dealer.[36] Virginia Warren of Lillington wrote the governor, "Be assured that if you decide to run again, you will have the five votes in this household."[37] A Charlotte man said that he represented the large, silent majority in North Carolina who seldom made a public spectacle of their opinions, and he was proud of the decision. Several Republicans wrote that they had not voted for Hunt in 1976, but they would support him the next time.[38]

The Carter Administration reacted with mixed signals to Hunt's decision. At a press conference, President Carter said that the federal government would not intervene "as far as I know. This is a state case."[39] United States Attorney General Griffin Bell reiterated the president's refusal to intervene, saying that the issue was in fact a state matter. At a meeting with Governor Hunt regarding tobacco policy in February 1978, Carter never mentioned the defendants. It appeared that the president did not wish to offend his extremely loyal supporter during a time when Health, Education and Welfare (HEW) Secretary Joseph Califano was expanding his campaign against tobacco, North Carolina's most profitable crop, and demanding the desegregation of the state university system.[40]

Despite his respect for Hunt's loyalty, President Carter shifted toward private support for the Wilmington Ten because of demands from his national black constituency. A large demonstration by thousands of African Americans for the Wilmington Ten in March 1978 and a letter by prominent national liberal Democrats on behalf of the defendants in September of that year put tremendous pressure on the president to act. Although President Carter demonstrated no desire to challenge Hunt's decision publicly, he tolerated the statements by other federal officials on behalf of the defendants. Within the White House, a Carter domestic staff member wrote the director of the National Conference of Black Lawyers to express that her "sincere best wishes and moral support are with you and the family of Reverend Benjamin Chavis, Jr."[41] Pat Derian, an administrator of Carter's human rights policy, publicly declared her sympathy for the Wilmington Ten on a Sunday television news program. More controversial, United Nations Ambassador Andrew Young said in an interview with a French newspaper that he believed in the innocence of the Wilmington Ten, who were among "hundreds, perhaps thousands"[42] of political prisoners in the United States. Young's foolish remarks damaged his relations with the president, but clearly Carter began to believe that the Wilmington Ten convictions undermined his human rights policy more than any other domestic event in the United States. Therefore, the president allowed the United States Justice Department to seek quietly the reversal of their convictions in federal court.

As Federal Judge Franklin Dupree debated whether to give the Wilmington Ten a new trial, the president's cautious approach toward the defendants angered his black congressional allies. In July 1978, after two months of deliberation, the attorney general filed an amicus brief in federal court on behalf of the Wilmington Ten at the request of nearly sixty members of Congress. Liberal Democratic congressmen demanded a stronger response. Representative John Conyers of Michigan wrote the president that "the governor of North Carolina has abdicated his responsibility in the matter,"[43] and chided the president himself because he too did very little to support the human rights of Ben Chavis and the other defendants. "We ask you to speak out for the human rights of the Wilmington Ten as you have done for those you have felt were persecuted in other lands," Conyers said. The criticism occurred at the same time that many African-American leaders charged that the Carter administration ignored their concerns regarding worsening economic conditions in the black community.[44]

The president also received pressure from a high level African American White House aide. The president had hired Louis Martin, who had served both John F. Kennedy and Lyndon Johnson, in August 1978 to deflect criticism of insensitivity to blacks. A month later, Martin wrote to Carter that "the agitation over the Wilmington Ten at home and abroad is expected to intensify in the weeks ahead. It is an issue that we do not need."[45] Martin hoped that Governor Hunt, not Carter, would settle the issue. Although North Carolina parole boards had released nine of the ten defendants by late 1978, the Wilmington Ten's advocates still wanted the

Reverend Ben Chavis out of prison. Martin suggested that Carter should persuade Governor Hunt to further reduce Chavis's sentence so that the minister might be paroled by the end of the year. Although a new trial would appease many African Americans, Martin wrote Carter, the second best deal would be for Hunt to reduce the sentences further. Carter rejected the advice of both Conyers and Martin, refusing to support publicly the Wilmington Ten or to pressure Governor Hunt to free Chavis. Instead, he allowed the United States Justice Department to challenge the Wilmington Ten convictions in the federal courts.[46]

On November 15, 1978, the United States Justice Department filed a court brief arguing that the Wilmington Ten had not received a fair trial and cited the prosecution's failure to give the defense a revised statement of Allen Hall's testimony. Drew Drays, assistant attorney general for civil rights, helped write the brief to Federal Judge Franklin T. Dupree arguing that the Wilmington Ten had been denied due process of law at their trial. The decision left Hunt stunned, since the president had never expressed any negative feeling about the governor's decision to commute the sentences. Governor Hunt later felt vindicated when in June 1979 Dupree denied the motion for a mistrial. However, the attorneys for the Wilmington Ten challenged the decision in a federal appellate court, still relying on assistance from the United States Justice Department to reverse the convictions.[47]

Although the Wilmington Ten received tremendous international publicity, the Charlotte Three affair also attracted the support of human rights activists and civil rights groups. This episode involved three African Americans strongly opposed to the Vietnam War. One defendant, James Grant, was a Penn State University Ph.D. who had volunteered for medical work in South Vietnam. Coming back disillusioned with the war, he had participated in the antiwar movement, burned his draft card in a demonstration in New York City, embraced Marxism, and counseled young people against the war. In Charlotte, he had met T. J. Reddy, a poet and playwright dedicated to "black consciousness," and Charles Parker, an honor student at the University of North Carolina at Charlotte (UNCC). Their antiwar activism had made them controversial figures in the Charlotte community.[48]

According to federal prosecutors, the three men had asked black felons David Washington and Alfred Hood to burn the Lazy B Stables in September 1968 after the owner denied Reddy and his white wife permission to ride horses there. The same two witnesses had also accused Grant of helping them flee from justice after urging the murders of two white racists in Oxford, North Carolina. In January 1972, a grand jury had indicted

Reddy, Parker, and Grant on charges of burning the stables. Convicted of the crime, the three defendants had appealed the verdict. The Charlotte Three's attorneys had argued that Hood and Washington had been convicted criminals who sought less prison time because of their testimony. They also had claimed that North Carolina Judge Frank Snepp proved his bias against the defendants by calling them over-educated revolutionaries, and by imposing the longest prison sentences for arson in Charlotte's history — ten years for Parker, twenty for Reddy, and twenty-five for Grant. Unfortunately for the Charlotte Three, the North Carolina Court of Appeals had refused to reverse their convictions.[49]

New information had led to demands by concerned citizens that Governor Hunt decide on the fate of the three defendants. The federal government had revealed in 1974 that it had paid witnesses Washington and Hood $4,000 each for their testimony, approved by Assistant Attorney General Robert Mardian, who would later be convicted of illegal activities in the Watergate scandal. In June 1976, Federal Judge James McMillan had granted bond to the remaining two prisoners, Reddy and Grant, since Parker had already left prison because his milder sentence allowed for an early parole. James Ferguson, who had also represented the Wilmington Ten, had attempted to reverse the convictions. As with the Wilmington Ten, Governor Hunt had stayed out of the matter until the courts had made a final decision. In October 1978, the United States Supreme Court had decided not to hear the case, forcing Grant and Reddy to begin serving their sentences. With court challenges for the Charlotte Three exhausted, Governor James B. Hunt, Jr., decided once again on the sentences of suspected black militants involved in a controversial arson case during the Vietnam War era.[50]

Many artists who knew T. J. Reddy wrote letters to Hunt defending the imprisoned black poet. Sandra Beck of Charlotte said, "I have known T. J. for a couple of years, and I've encountered few people so creatively and constructively oriented. He gave encouragement and support to a number of young writers and artists, myself being one of them."[51] The executive director of the North Carolina Cultural Arts Coalition said that the black poet had been an asset to several art organizations because of his expertise, commitment, and dedication. Others urged Hunt to read Reddy's poems to discover the humanity of the prisoner. Chapel Hill publisher Judy Hogan said, "I am completely convinced of his innocence, as are the people I know in the literary and artistic community."[52] Hunt realized that the state's art community strongly backed the black poet.

Others urged the governor to pardon Charlotte activist James Grant. Hunt received these requests from several residents of Connecticut, where

Grant had attended undergraduate college, including a phone call from Governor Ella Grasso. Political activists also pressured the governor on Grant's behalf. Southern prisoner-rights advocate L. C. Dorsey said that Grant was paying dearly for the freedom to disagree with "a senseless war, racial oppression at home, and the plight of those who had taxation without representation."[53] Community activist Nicholas Garrin wrote that Grant deserved a pardon because of his fight against unfair utility bills and rat-infested slums that affected the poorest citizens of Raleigh.[54]

Demands to free the defendants mainly came from Charlotte, the city where the stable burning had taken place. In November 1978, the city council passed a resolution applauding Hunt's willingness to review collectively and individually the cases of T. J. Reddy, James E. Grant, and Charles Parker. Charlotte Councilman Harvey Gantt, who had failed to persuade Hunt to pardon the Wilmington Ten, said that "the central question before you, Jim, is whether any real purpose would be served by further imprisonment of these men."[55] The future Charlotte black mayor urged Hunt to commute their sentences.

Only a few letter writers warned Hunt against pardoning the Charlotte Three. They reminded him that the fire had caused tremendous pain to the horses that were burned alive. William Perry Whitlow of Charlotte, a stable owner, said, "I am nauseated by all the protests of unfair treatment and denial of rights of these felons."[56] Linda Bishop of Charlotte urged the governor not to respond to racial or political pressure. However, those citizens hostile toward Reddy and Grant were less vocal than the Queen City residents who wanted to move beyond previous racial struggles. Racial animosity indeed had subsided; Historian J. Christopher Schultz said that Charlotte was "decidedly quiet" by 1979.[57]

That year, Hunt aides and North Carolina Democratic party officials worried over the impact of T. J. Reddy, James Grant, and Ben Chavis in prison as the governor began his campaign for re-election. Herbert N. Lape, a vice chairman of the state Democratic party, wrote Hunt in December 1978, "Many of the good people in this precinct view both the Wilmington Ten and the Charlotte Three cases as primarily white witch hunts that involved racial bigotry. Governor, you have an opportunity of helping to heal wounds of distrust that are a legacy of this period of our state's history and a legacy of these two trials."[58] Administration Secretary Joseph Grimsley wrote a memo to Hunt claiming that "the state's repressive image is beginning to spill over in this administration to yourself personally."[59] Grimsley, who would serve as Hunt's campaign manager in 1980, urged the governor to turn over the cases to a parole commission or to commute the sentences.

In July 1979, Hunt announced his decision on the Charlotte Three. After the governor and his legal counsel conducted a painstaking examination of the record of their case, Hunt concluded that the defendants had received a fair trial "presided by one of our state's most capable judges."[60] The governor defended the federal payments to witnesses Hood and Washington as part of an established program by the United States Justice Department to provide for the protection and relocation of witnesses in federal cases. Although state prosecutors did not know about the money, Hunt said, the courts ruled correctly that the federal payments had not prevented a fair trial. The governor nevertheless decided to reduce the sentences of the two remaining defendants in jail because they had made progress toward rehabilitation. Hunt said that Grant's record in prison had been spotless, while Reddy deserved his outstanding conduct record by participating in several community projects while free on bond. Therefore, Hunt reduced the defendants' sentences to time already served so that they could be released immediately.[61]

Hunt's commutation did not completely satisfy all supporters of the Charlotte Three. Although Reddy was disappointed that he had received no pardon, he said that he was glad to get out of prison. James Ferguson, attorney for both the Wilmington Ten and the Charlotte Three, once again criticized Hunt for not granting a pardon. However, other Charlotte Three supporters praised the governor. Attorney Barry Nakell of Chapel Hill expressed his appreciation, while UNC–Charlotte Professor Loy H. Witherspoon thanked Hunt "for reassuring us that our trust [in you] was not misplaced."[62] Without tremendous publicity, he disposed of a potentially troubling legal matter.

Although the governor handled the Charlotte Three commutations quietly, he encountered protests because of the imprisonment of civil rights leader Ben Chavis, leading him to commute the minister's sentence at the end of 1979. For months, protestors followed the governor on his visits to other states and demanded pardons for the Wilmington Ten. At the same time, Hunt received letters from professors describing the Reverend Ben Chavis's progress at Duke University, where he was allowed to study religion on a educational release program. Finally, in December 1979, Hunt agreed to release Chavis. "I am acting on his parole two weeks early because of his excellent record in prison, including achieving straight As in ministerial school at Duke University, and to permit him to be at home with family on Christmas," the governor announced.[63] By Christmas Eve, Hunt released the last of the so-called political prisoners.

With no more African-American activists in jail, Hunt discovered that the issue waned considerably in North Carolina's black communities by the time that he faced challengers in his campaign for re-election in 1980. In Wake County, the Wake Black Democratic Caucus and Black Women's Caucus ignored the controversy and endorsed Hunt in the Democratic primary. In a few black precincts, Hunt received bare majorities as protestors carried "Remember the Wilmington Ten" signs near the polling places, yet he still won more African-American votes than Democratic challenger Robert Scott. Angry over Hunt's victory, UCC minister Leon White promised to launch a black gubernatorial challenge in the general election after criticizing black leaders for backing the governor for "a few crumbs from Jim Hunt's table — some high-paying jobs and government grants."[64] However, the black challenge to Hunt in the general election went nowhere. Former cabinet officer Howard Lee said that the African Americans who opposed Hunt did not have a significant voice in the large black communities, while respected black leaders who opposed his Wilmington Ten decision put the matter behind them. They focused more on public schools, black appointments, and affirmative action where the governor had a favorable record. During the general election in November 1980, an overwhelming majority of African Americans backed Governor Hunt against conservative Republican gubernatorial candidate I. Beverly Lake, Jr.[65]

A year after his release, Ben Chavis won exoneration from a federal appellate court. In December 1980, the federal appeals court in Washington reversed the Wilmington Ten convictions, arguing that the defense had not received key evidence when they had not obtained an altered version of Allen Hall's testimony at the original trial. North Carolina Attorney General Rufus Edmisten shared the sentiments of those Tar Heels who wanted to put the matter behind them and decided not to challenge the decision. Feeling exonerated by a federal court and by the civil rights community, Chavis served for more than a decade as director of the UCC Commission for Racial Justice. He reached the height of his success by becoming executive director of the National Association for the Advancement of Colored People (NAACP) in 1993.[66]

Governor James B. Hunt, Jr., made reasonable decisions when he decided to commute the sentences of the Wilmington Ten and the Charlotte Three. He studied both cases seriously and concluded that Benjamin Chavis and Jim Grant used their followers to wage a terrorist campaign against white racists in a way strongly deviating from the Reverend Martin Luther King's ethic of civil disobedience and nonviolent protest. Well-meaning Americans ignored the evidence against the two men and their followers, perceiving them as innocent victims of state and federal conspiracies similar to the efforts used by the Nixon Administration to prosecute antiwar critics. If the defendants' advocates never looked too closely to examine their guilt, Governor Hunt can be faulted for never seriously condemning the mistakes of law enforcement, including the error that caused a federal appeals court to throw out the conviction of the Wilmington Ten. Yet, Hunt made up for his lack of criticism against the prosecutors by commuting the sentences on property crimes given by judges unsympathetic to black militancy. The governor's commutations can be compared with President Carter's pardons of draft resisters and commutations for Watergate schemer G. Gordon Liddy and New Left radical Patty Hearst as a way to heal the bitter divisions of the Vietnam War era. Hunt's actions balanced the defendants' responsibility for their crimes with the need for racial healing. The Wilmington Ten and the Charlotte Three were not political prisoners, but arsonists and terrorists who fought racists by any means necessary, and Hunt handled these cases reasonably well.

11

The Califano Controversies: Jim Hunt's Conflicts with the United States Department of Health, Education, and Welfare (HEW)

The Wilmington Ten Affair revealed differences between North Carolina Governor Jim Hunt and the Carter administration, but nothing divided the state's chief executive and the federal government more than two crusades waged by United States Health, Education, and Welfare (HEW) Secretary Joseph Califano. The former White House aide alienated the North Carolina governor after he demanded the immediate integration of the state university system and introduced an extensive campaign against tobacco smoking. Both HEW efforts received strong condemnation in North Carolina, especially among white conservatives, and therefore Hunt found little political ground on which to compromise. The impasse led President Jimmy Carter to choose between his contentious HEW secretary and his loyal supporters in North Carolina. Because of this problem and numerous other reasons, Carter fired Califano, weakening both of the HEW secretary's initiatives. Despite support for these efforts by Califano's successor, Patricia Harris, the desegregation matter was resolved in North Carolina's favor during the Reagan administration, and the anti-tobacco campaign received little support from the White House until President Bill Clinton challenged the tobacco industry in 1995.

Jim Hunt, who had spent his youth working on his family's tobacco farm and later studied how to improve the federal tobacco program, realized that there was a threat to the product in January 1964 when the United States Surgeon General linked cigarette smoking to lung cancer and heart disease. That year, Hunt had worked on the gubernatorial campaign of Judge Richardson Preyer, who like all North Carolina politicians, no matter how progressive, defended the profitable crop. A large majority of Tar Heels had argued that the state's economy needed tobacco sales, expressed doubt about the Surgeon General's findings, and proclaimed that adults should have a right to choose whether to smoke. By the 1970s, North Carolina politicians had accepted the fact that federal health officials challenged smoking and that the Federal Communications Commission (FCC) had prevented cigarette advertisements on radio and television. Despite the federal government's anti-tobacco campaign, however, Tar Heel officials had remained content as long as presidents distanced themselves from the Surgeon General and backed federal tobacco subsidies.[1]

As lieutenant governor, Hunt had feared that the Nixon and Ford administrations desired to weaken seriously the federal tobacco program. In late 1973, Agriculture Secretary Earl Butz had said that he might kill controls on tobacco production for a year as a way to help reduce inflation. Immediately, Lieutenant Governor Hunt had condemned Butz's efforts to cancel the results of elections by tobacco farmers who voted for a three-year extension of the allotment program. He had also unsuccessfully tried to invite the secretary to meet with North Carolina farmers to hear their concerns. Hunt also wrote to the state's congressmen to complain about the United States Department of Agriculture. United States Senator Jesse Helms had told the lieutenant governor that Butz assured him that nothing drastic had been done about the tobacco program, yet Hunt still remained concerned about the direction of federal agricultural policy.[2]

The lieutenant governor continued to raise concerns about Republican efforts to gut the federal tobacco program. After Agricultural Secretary Butz had announced ten percent increases in flue-cured tobacco production in 1973 and 1974, Hunt had feared that the decisions would dramatically lower prices and force farmers out of business. "It is vitally important that we realize our tobacco program can be ruined by gradual production increases just as effectively as it can be ruined by terminating it all at one time," Hunt had announced. "Instead of just killing the program outright, Secretary Butz appears determined to '10 per cent' us to death."[3] The following year, President Gerald Ford vetoed a bill that extended federal tobacco price supports. Hunt had said that these actions demonstrated that the Ford administration had no concern for the tobacco farmer.[4]

In 1976, Hunt strongly backed Democratic presidential candidate Jimmy Carter partly because the former Georgia governor favored federal price supports. Further, Hunt had never considered any serious threat to tobacco when the victor nominated Joseph Califano for Secretary of Health, Education, and Welfare (HEW) in December 1976. Like Hunt, Califano had been an attorney with strong connections to the national Democratic party. Unlike the Tar Heel politician, Califano was reared in an Italian American neighborhood in Brooklyn, received a degree from Harvard University Law School, and had not witnessed Jim Crow laws in action until he moved to Virginia as a young man in the late 1950s. While serving there as an attorney for the Pentagon, Califano had observed racially segregated movie theaters and restaurants. In 1962, as a special assistant to Secretary of the Army Cyrus Vance, Califano visited the University of Mississippi to examine the federal troops that President John F. Kennedy ordered there to insure the registration of African-American student James Meredith. While there, whites heckled him, as a "nigger lover." After Kennedy's assassination, Califano worked as a special assistant to President Lyndon Johnson, where he helped the president turn HEW into an effective agency devoted to fighting poverty and racial injustice. From 1969 to 1976, he served as a private attorney for clients that included the *Washington Post* during the Watergate affair. As the HEW department's new secretary in early 1977, Califano wanted to prove that Johnson's Great Society programs that aided the poor and minorities could work successfully after the previous two Republican administrations had weakened them. He focused originally on improving welfare programs and paid less attention to the health issues regarding tobacco, although he had quit smoking cigarettes two years earlier.[5]

In the first months of 1977, relations between the North Carolina governor and the HEW secretary went smoothly as they discussed the president's plans to restructure the welfare system. The governor offered his suggestions on welfare reform, and Califano urged the participation of North Carolina welfare officials in evaluating federal proposals to change the programs. In one letter, Hunt addressed Califano as "Joe." Neither man expected that their relationship would fray in the following years because of controversial matters like university desegregation or a federal crusade against tobacco.[6]

By the end of 1977, Califano decided to initiate a campaign to end cigarette smoking in the United States. Although he had never intended in January 1977 to criticize the use of tobacco, he talked with several health professionals who urged such a campaign. They told him that cigarettes killed 320,000 Americans a year mainly from heart disease and lung cancer, and said that teenage smoking had increased during the 1970s as tobacco companies singled out young people in their advertising campaigns. Califano also learned that the Nixon and Ford administrations had slashed the budgets of the anti-smoking campaign to appease the tobacco lobby. Alarmed by these reports, the HEW secretary decided to launch a crusade against smoking. On January 11, 1978, he instituted a broad public education program that called for more television commercials against the use of cigarettes, an increase in the federal tobacco tax, and letters to school superintendents urging anti-smoking campaigns targeted at students. Califano said that society had a responsibility to tell young people that smoking was unhealthy, dangerous, socially unacceptable, and a leading cause of premature death. With that press conference, Califano initiated the most serious federal assault on tobacco use ever waged up to that date.[7]

Alarmed at the attack on the crop, Hunt criticized Califano's anti-tobacco campaign that President Carter mildly supported. As early as November 1977, Hunt had condemned HEW for suggesting the replacement of the tobacco price-support program with welfare payments to small farmers. After the announcement of the anti-smoking campaign, the governor said that Califano had gone too far, since "you can't make people stop smoking."[8] He urged the HEW secretary to meet with North Carolina tobacco farmers and find out how his efforts would hurt them. He proclaimed that farmers netted $1,073 an acre on tobacco while peanuts, the second most profitable Tar Heel crop, only earned them $172 an acre. Carter indicated support for Califano, however, saying at a press conference in January 1978 that the initiative did not differ from that of all the other HEW secretaries since 1964. The president said that they all supported the effort to reduce the consumption of tobacco, "certainly smoking, which is the most potentially harmful."[9] The president still stood strongly for federal tobacco supports, finding no contradiction in his positions.

The anti-smoking campaign galvanized Tar Heels against HEW and made Califano the number-one enemy of tobacco farmers. Bumper stickers appeared in North Carolina proclaiming "Califano is Dangerous to My Health" and "Califano Blows Smoke." After communicating with Hunt, United States Commerce Secretary Juanita Kreps, a Tar Heel native, told President Carter at a cabinet meeting that the anti-smoking campaign was hurting the administration's image in her state. United States Senator Jesse Helms of North Carolina put riders on appropriation bills that tried unsuccessfully to take away HEW funds for any anti-smoking effort. Tar Heel Democrats distanced themselves from the unpopular cabinet official.[10]

Governor Hunt and United States Senator Robert Morgan, a Democrat from North Carolina, met with President Carter on February 28, 1978, to express personally their concerns about the HEW secretary. Before the meeting, White House aide Jack Watson told the president that Hunt did not expect to change Carter's mind on the anti-tobacco campaign, but wanted to demonstrate to Tar Heels that he was fighting for tobacco and relieve him of the "heavy pressure he is receiving in North Carolina."[11] At the meeting, Hunt and Senator Morgan told Carter that the president suffered politically in North Carolina because of Califano's anti-smoking campaign and the effort to desegregate the state's higher education system. They urged the president to cool the rhetoric on the anti-smoking campaign, and to get the HEW secretary to stop referring to smoking as slow-motion suicide. The Tar Heel politicians said that Califano's crusade would kill any chance of defeating Senator Jesse Helms, running for reelection in 1978. Carter made no promises to end the anti-smoking campaign, but he clearly realized that the initiative hurt him in North Carolina, a state within his political base.[12]

Neither Califano nor Hunt could be certain whom Carter truly supported. In a February 6, 1978, meeting with Califano, Carter had reportedly told the HEW secretary that he approved of the efforts against tobacco. In Califano's book, *Governing in America*, Califano claimed that the president told him in March 1978 that he approved of the anti-smoking program because his own father smoked "four or five packs a day and he died of lung cancer, perhaps because of cigarette smoking."[13] (Califano's statement challenges the fact that the president's father actually died of pancreatic cancer.) Despite Carter's reassurances, the HEW secretary believed that the president wanted him to ease off the anti-tobacco campaign. Carter expressed concern to Califano about offending Hunt at the same time that the governor faced controversy over his decision to commute sentences for the Wilmington Ten. Also, Vice President Walter Mondale asked Califano to ease off North Carolina, which the HEW secretary refused to do. During this time, presidential health advisor Peter Bourne criticized publicly efforts by HEW to turn smokers into second-class citizens. These events led Califano to believe that he did not have Carter's full support.[14]

President Carter's statements in North Carolina also undermined the HEW secretary's efforts. When the president visited Winston-Salem, North Carolina, the home of R. J. Reynolds Tobacco Company, on March 17, 1978, he made a speech declaring that it was an honor to be in the "greatest tobacco state in the world."[15] Addressing an audience of farmers during an August 1978 visit to Governor Hunt's hometown of Wilson, Carter reiterated his support for tobacco price supports and talked about his own family producing "the two greatest crops in my life — peanuts and tobacco."[16] He described HEW's tobacco campaign as an enlightened education and research program that attempted to make smoking safer — a false statement that infuriated Surgeon General Julius Richardson. Through contradictory language, the president tried to appease anti-tobacco liberals and Tar Heel tobacco farmers at the same time.[17]

As Califano struggled with Governor Hunt over tobacco, President Carter continued to support the governor of North Carolina. When Carter visited the state, he stressed his friendship and admiration for his loyal backer. "I first met him [Jim Hunt] before he was governor and before I was president," said the president on his March 1978 Winston-Salem trip. "We formed an instant personal friendship, and his leadership of your state has brought credit to you and the admiration of the rest of the nation."[18] Hunt loyally supported Carter's energy program, presidential vetoes, and anti-inflation strategies. At a Democratic mini-convention in 1978, Hunt aided Carter against United States Senator Ted Kennedy's allies who fought against the president's plank endorsing a balanced federal budget. In turn, the president lauded the "superb, young leadership exemplified by Jim Hunt,"[19] especially praising the governor's anti-crime legislation. Such praise of Hunt, a pro-tobacco governor, added to Califano's concern over the president's support of his anti-smoking campaign.

At the same time that the HEW secretary was waging a crusade against cigarettes, Senator Jesse Helms was campaigning for reelection against state Insurance Commissioner John Ingram. The Republican senator had two advantages— Califano belonged to the other major party, and many Democrats could not unite behind their nominee. Although Hunt and Ingram belonged to the same party, they did not have a very close relationship. Ingram had resented Hunt for allowing the legislature to weaken his office in 1977, while many Hunt insiders had considered some of the commissioner's crusades against the insurance companies as irresponsible. Privately, Hunt's team supported senate candidate Luther Hodges, Jr., against the insurance commissioner in the Democratic primary. After Ingram won, he asked North Carolina Democratic Party Chairperson Betty McCain, a Hunt appointee, to use the state party's funds to run his campaign. Although she allowed the party to pay the rent for his campaign headquarters, she refused to allow him to control the party's finances. Hunt campaigned for Ingram, yet said nothing critical about Helms. The senator, who had corresponded with Hunt since their first elections to public office in 1972, told a reporter that Hunt would support his reelection if Helms were a Democrat. "We've had a good working relationship," said the senator,[20] who also remarked that the governor had never made a

critical remark about him. *Charlotte Observer* columnist Ned Cline speculated that some Hunt staffers wanted the governor to run against Helms
in 1984 after he served two four-year terms, and therefore, the governor
did not try hard to help Ingram. Hunt dismissed such talk, insisting that
he favored the insurance commissioner, and criticized Helms for creating
false impressions among the electorate. Hunt still did not change the minds
of a small majority of Tar Heel voters who believed that Helms had done
a fine job fighting for North Carolina interests in Washington, especially
against Joe Califano.[21]

Despite the anti-smoking campaign of Califano and his successor
Patricia Harris, Hunt continued to promote tobacco. In August 1979, the
same month that the president forced the resignation of Califano, Hunt
stood beside a pile of tobacco and started the auction bidding at a warehouse in Greenville, North Carolina. He mainly helped tobacco farmers
by aiding the product's sales in other nations. In November 1979, Governor Hunt went on the first tobacco trade mission in thirty years traveling
to China to promote the sale of North Carolina cigarettes. Accompanied
by several representatives of the tobacco industry, he met with Communist officials who desired most-favored-nation trading status to reduce
tariffs on Chinese goods entering the United States. Discussing trade with
Vice Premier Kang Shi-en, the governor said, "Tobacco farmers can be a
strong force supporting most-favored nation status for the People's Republic of China."[22] With Califano removed from HEW, the Carter administration appeared to be less of a hindrance against the governor's plans to
aid tobacco farmers. Although Patricia Harris continued the anti-smoking campaign as HEW secretary and later as head of the newly created
Health and Human Services (HHS) Department, Hunt ignored her efforts.
He worried more about a United States Treasury Department plan to
increase federal tobacco taxes to balance the budget. White House aides
agreed that the plan called for too expensive a political price to achieve
new revenue and shelved the proposal.[23]

As governor of North Carolina, Jim Hunt did what was expected to
promote the state's most profitable crop. The chief executive, who owned
a tobacco farm and also sold the crop, understood that tobacco was the
backbone of the agrarian economy. Therefore, he ignored the health risks
by declaring smoking a matter of adult choice, reacting to Califano's anti-
tobacco campaign as negatively as anyone who expected to survive in
North Carolina politics. Hunt also opposed any effort to weaken the federal tobacco program. Only in the governor's recruitment of new industries did he reveal an inclination to move beyond the tobacco economy.
"If you listened to Hunt's speeches on farming, it's protect the tobacco

program," said UNC Southern Studies Professor Ferrel Guillory. "He's got the right pitch. Yet, his governing emphasis was on diversifying the state's economy."[24] If he looked to the day that North Carolina did not rely so heavily on tobacco, the governor disguised such an effort by becoming the crop's number-one cheerleader.

In addition to struggling with Califano over tobacco, he tangled with the HEW secretary over the thorny issue of university desegregation. In the summer of 1977, Secretary Califano had alienated Governor Hunt by issuing strong criteria for the desegregation of the North Carolina University system. The university desegregation matter had begun in 1970 when HEW demanded ten states, including North Carolina, eliminate dual black-white university systems. A year later, the National Association for the Advancement of Colored People's (NAACP) Legal Defense Fund (LDF) sued the Nixon administration for not enforcing the law. In February 1973, Federal Judge John Pratt, ruling for the LDF, ordered HEW to force the ten states to implement desegregation plans. Although the federal government had accepted ten plans, including North Carolina's proposal in 1974, the LDF sued again, arguing that the proposals did not sufficiently end segregated universities. A week before Califano was sworn in as HEW secretary, Judge Pratt had ruled that six of the ten state plans did not sufficiently integrate the university systems and ordered HEW to demand that these states, including North Carolina, create new desegregation plans to remedy the problem.[25]

By the middle of 1977, the HEW secretary had discovered information that made him passionate about integrating North Carolina's university system. That year, ninety-four percent of the students at traditionally white universities in North Carolina were white, while ninety-six percent of the students at traditionally black universities were black. Just as revealing, the legislature had provided most new degree programs and new buildings to traditionally white universities in the 1970s, including the East Carolina University medical school and the North Carolina State University veterinarian school. The state's white bias had upset University of North Carolina Board of Governors member Julius Chambers so much that the black attorney had resigned from the board in the summer of 1977. To remedy the matter, Califano sought the assistance of Office of Civil Rights (OCR) Director David Tatel, a blind attorney well liked by the civil rights community. In July 1977, Califano introduced stringent new criteria that demanded an end to the duplication of non-curriculum courses taught at black and white universities within the same region.[26]

Tatel sent the new criteria on July 2, 1977, to Governor Hunt, who responded by designating Bill Friday, president of the state university system, as North Carolina's principal negotiator with HEW. "He (Hunt) never did interfere (with negotiations)," Friday recalled. "I would keep him informed every time I went to Washington, talked with him, told him when Joe (Califano) would call him, told him what the next move would be."[27] Hunt trusted the UNC president to do the right thing. Friday favored the gradual integration of the dual university system, but he feared that the elimination of program duplication at traditionally black and white universities would be unrealistic and subsequently undermine control by college administrators. He knew that the state university system, mostly created during the Jim Crow era, could not be integrated quickly. Friday also worried about the federal government running the universities just as the North Carolina legislature had tried to control UNC policy in 1963 with the Speaker Ban Law.[28]

Friday and the UNC Board of Governors addressed Califano's concerns in the *Revised North Carolina State Plan ... Phase II*, which promoted gradual integration without ending program duplication. Board Chairman William Johnson, a conservative judge from Lillington, told the governor that the plan was a positive response by the board to eliminate racial dual systems. On September 2, 1977, Hunt sent *Phase II* to HEW's Office of Civil Rights, accompanied by a letter urging Califano to modify his demands. In the letter, Hunt denied the accusation that the state ran a racist higher education system. "No one has for two decades been prevented by reasons of race from attending any other institutions now constituting the University of North Carolina," he wrote.[29] He also said that de facto segregation at North Carolina universities could not be eliminated quickly. Despite the governor's support of Phase II, Califano rejected the plan for not dealing with program duplication, and negotiations between the two camps continued.

The HEW secretary did not anticipate that the anti-smoking campaign would make it harder for him to negotiate university desegregation with North Carolina officials. On January 20, 1978, Hunt met Califano at a Democratic fundraiser in Atlanta and urged the governor to get personally involved in resolving the desegregation of the university system. Hunt agreed to talk with UNC President Bill Friday, but according to Califano, he did not want to become personally involved. Hunt, Califano said, was more concerned about the anti-smoking campaign. "In Virginia," Califano told historian William Link, "I was dealing with [Governor] Miles Godwin, [who was] much more conservative than Friday or Hunt, but in two or three phone conversations, we had a deal."[30] Califano concluded that North Carolina's financial and business community's anger over the anti-smoking campaign made it difficult for Hunt, "a responsible person and a good governor,"[31] to negotiate with HEW.

Hunt presented his differences with Califano at the meeting with Senator Morgan and President Carter in January 1978. Discussing the desegregation controversy, Hunt said that HEW had unfairly rejected a plan dedicated to achieving integration of North Carolina's universities. The governor proclaimed that a federal suit against the university system would cost Carter the state in the 1980 presidential election. Although Carter did not promise Hunt that he would rein in Califano, he later privately encouraged the HEW secretary to reach a settlement. Understanding the importance of North Carolina to his reelection plans, the president had hoped for a successful compromise.[32]

Negotiations appeared fruitful in the spring of 1978 when both sides reached a tentative settlement. In May, Secretary Califano and UNC approved a plan that called for unspecific promises to eliminate unnecessary program duplication at the colleges. Governor Hunt proclaimed the compromise "welcome news to all North Carolinians."[33] Yet, the agreement broke down after HEW bureaucrats and UNC administrators failed to agree on the specifics of ending program duplication. For example, no Tar Heel official wanted to decide whether to end the nursing program at UNC–Greensboro, a traditionally white university, or at the North Carolina Agricultural and Technology State University, a traditionally black institution, both located in the same city. After the victories of conservative politicians in the November 1978 elections encouraged UNC board members resistance, negotiations reached a complete stalemate. In early 1979, HEW rejected the Tar Heel studies that claimed that there had been no unnecessary duplication of programs, announced the failure of the May 1978 agreement, and said that the department planned to cut federal funds to the UNC system. Neither conservative board members nor liberal bureaucrats had wished to compromise.[34]

Hunt had hoped to ease HEW off its stringent demands by demonstrating black opposition to the proposals. He understood that North Carolina's black chancellors feared that HEW's plans might destroy the identity of traditionally African-American universities. Realizing this fact, Hunt arranged a meeting between the HEW Office of Civil Rights Director David Tatel and the black chancellors in Washington, D.C., in February 1979. At this meeting, Tatel told the chancellors that HEW truly wanted to strengthen the black colleges and accomplish significant integration without completely destroying the racial identity of the institutions. Some of the African-American administrators accepted the HEW viewpoint, which meant that Hunt's efforts to demonstrate black opposition had backfired.[35]

Califano also attempted a public relations campaign to win support for university desegregation in North Carolina. "If I can get television to bring those sorry black colleges into [the nation's] living rooms, Hunt and Friday will have to move," the HEW secretary told a White House aide.[36] He believed that if North Carolina citizens witnessed the poor quality of the institutions, embarrassed Tar Heel officials would support the federal position. Califano announced that he would send Tatel with a photographer to visit the traditionally black universities. Tatel's visit revealed images of unclean swimming pools, leaky roofs, and inadequate laboratories at traditionally black universities. Hunt said of the images, "My heart just aches when I see some of those buildings these children have to go to school in. We have a long way to go in providing adequate facilities at these traditionally black institutions."[37] Privately, however, Hunt was upset about the visit and complained to administration officials about unwarranted federal interference.[38]

Despite unfavorable feelings about HEW, Hunt wanted UNC to continue negotiations with the federal government. Historian William Link wrote,

> Hunt, for his part, was desperately seeking to avoid litigation. Because he was a strong supporter of the Carter administration, his inability to settle the case favorably could be easily portrayed as a political failure. As [OCR Director David] Tatel subsequently observed, the governor faced a difficult dilemma. Hunt wanted to be helpful and had his heart "really in the right place"; Tatel left with a "very, very positive reaction of him, as someone who wanted to see this resolved and wanted to see it resolved in the right way." At the same time, Tatel maintained that Hunt "wasn't willing to take on the people in North Carolina whose view was that nobody should touch the UNC system." To Tatel, Hunt faced the same problem that confronted a university president who was forced to fire "a very successful football coach": He couldn't touch it.[39]

Link declared that Hunt had straddled the issue as a way to reach an agreement between HEW and the UNC Board of Governors. Both sides believed that the North Carolina governor sympathized with their position. By using his adept political skills, Hunt had hoped to create a deal and avoid litigation.[40]

Such efforts had seemed nearly hopeless on March 26, 1979, when HEW announced a partial cutoff of federal funds to the University of North Carolina, effective in thirty-four days. Governor Hunt promised to make up for the loss of federal revenue by using funds provided by the North Carolina General Assembly. At the White House, domestic policy advisors Jack Watson and Stu Eizenstat, a UNC graduate with friendly ties to Tar Heel officials, asked President Carter to enter the matter by talking to Hunt, despite Califano's opposition. "Although we tentatively defer to Joe's judgement on the matter because he is so much closer to the negotiations than we are," they wrote the president, "we are both concerned about waiting too late for you to ask Jim Hunt for his help in resolving this dispute."[41] Concerned over the political outcome, White House staffers anxiously wanted to stop a university lawsuit against the federal government and feared that the abrasive HEW secretary would destroy any chances of a settlement. Califano, however, had requested that the president not personally negotiate the university desegregation matter with the governor because he feared the president would settle for too little and face embarrassment if the federal court rejected the settlement. With the Carter administration divided, a deal with North Carolina seemed remote.[42]

With time running out, Hunt introduced a compromise proposal. He told Califano that he would abandon a proposed $40 million tax cut and use that money to upgrade North Carolina's black universities if HEW would ease off its demand to end program duplication immediately. Califano told Hunt that his proposal was a major step forward, but he wanted a stronger way to deal with course duplication or the court would throw out the settlement. In a firm voice Hunt replied, "This is as far as we can go."[43] Friday backed the compromise, further telling the governor that he wanted to express his appreciation for the courage and leadership that he had shown in the matter. Link described Hunt's offer as the most ambitious commitment ever made by a North Carolina political leader to rectify past ills in public higher education. The historian credited Hunt with abandoning a popular tax relief measure and committing himself to major expenditures toward the enhancement of traditionally black institutions.[44]

HEW rejected Hunt's initial compromise, but the department still negotiated with the governor to create a more acceptable proposal. On April 14, 1979, Califano called Hunt at his Rock Ridge farm and asked if the governor could meet with his executive assistant Richard Beattie. This meeting produced no breakthroughs. Califano then decided to negotiate personally with the governor. In his 1981 memoirs, Califano recalled that he and Hunt had talked on the telephone and agreed to a compromise on April 19, 1979. Califano claimed that the governor agreed to give $40 million to the traditionally black institutions, create twenty new programs at black campuses, end new programs at white campuses that impeded desegregation, and stop program duplication by 1983 if these measures failed to desegregate universities. Califano said that UNC officials had planned to introduce this compromise to the North Carolina Board of Governors on April 20. Yet, Hunt later denied Califano's account, saying that he had agreed to no specific plan, while UNC officials declared that President Friday only planned to present a plan that would further aid negotiations with HEW. Perhaps Califano was confused about what Hunt and UNC had agreed to.[45]

Negotiations collapsed, however, because a majority of the UNC Board of Governors, led by Chairman Johnson, rejected negotiations and approved a court battle against HEW. At the April 20 meeting, Friday told the board about new proposals to settle the HEW matter that included Hunt's offer to spend $40 million for traditionally black institutions, yet he admitted that "we have no agreement, no end to this ordeal, to bring to you today."[46] The board declined even to consider Friday's proposals. Instead, Johnson focused the entire meeting on whether to file a federal lawsuit. After the board's attorneys had argued that court action would force HEW to back down, the board's majority approved litigation. These members felt even better about their decision a few days later after Federal Court Judge Franklin Dupree, Jr., prevented a cutoff of federal funds to the UNC system until HEW resolved the matter in court. Although Hunt said that he had regretted the use of litigation instead of negotiation, he announced that he would support the decision.[47]

The failure of the negotiations led White House aides to renew efforts for President Carter's intervention. On May 12, Watson and Eizenstat urged President Carter to call Governor Hunt and revive negotiations. However, Califano still feared that the president would be soft with the governor regarding the end of program duplication. He had told Carter that in the event he talked to Hunt, he should be aware that the North Carolina legislature had awarded most new degree programs and construction projects to traditionally white universities. Carter did telephone Hunt on May 14, only to discover that the governor could not move the board from its position. Despite the president's best efforts, UNC continued its suit against HEW.[48]

Califano's dilemma with North Carolina over university desegregation and tobacco did not help his relationship with President Carter. Several aides advised the president to fire the HEW secretary. Carter said in his memoir, "Most of my advisors, including Fritz [Walter Mondale], told me that if I was determined to reassess my administration, then I also had to prepare to make some major changes in my cabinet. I was told that [Energy Secretary James] Schlesinger, Califano and [Treasury Secretary Sidney] Blumenthal needed to be replaced."[49] Carter's Georgian aides Hamilton Jordan and Jody Powell had perceived Califano as too close to the traditionally liberal Washington establishment, including *The*

Washington Post editors, who disdained the southern president. Others had declared that the cabinet secretary had an abrasive personality. Of course, Califano's presence in the cabinet had hurt the president's popularity in North Carolina, although former state party chairperson Betty McCain later insisted that Hunt and the Tar Heel Democrats played no role in his forced resignation. Hunt did not recall that he had said anything to President Carter at the 1979 summer summit that led to Califano's removal. However, Hunt added, he "might well have."[50] Mainly, Califano had alienated the White House because he did not represent the economically conservative approach that President Carter had desired to bring to Washington.

President Carter used a boost of popularity after a 1979 Camp David summit meeting to get rid of Califano. During a summer of gas lines and high fuel prices, Carter received a lower public approval rating than had President Richard Nixon during the Watergate crisis. Despondent over the inability of the public and Congress to accept his energy proposals, he held meetings with prominent Americans at Camp David to discover solutions to the nation's problems. One visitor included Governor Hunt, whose jog with the president was photographed by *Newsweek*. On July 15, 1979, President Carter talked to the nation about a crisis of the American spirit and urged a return to sacrifice in the struggle to conserve energy. Although critics later dubbed the address "the malaise speech" which condemned Americans for the nation's problems, analysts that week had called the speech the best that Carter had ever given. Using the television address as a new beginning, he then asked each cabinet member to write a resignation letter. Stunned, Califano had submitted the letter, not expecting to lose his job.[51]

Later that month, Carter accepted the resignation of Secretary Califano. According to the former HEW secretary, the president had praised his performance as outstanding, called him "the best secretary of HEW," and declared that the reason for his dismissal was "friction on the White House staff."[52] According to Califano, though later disputed by White House aides, Carter had said that he needed to get the cabinet ready for the 1980 election, which the HEW secretary interpreted to mean that he had been fired to help Carter win North Carolina. After his forced resignation, Califano received a phone call from Arkansas Governor Bill Clinton. "If you go into elective politics," Clinton had told him, "I'll help."[53] The young governor had disapproved of the firing of the HEW secretary. As president, Clinton enthusiastically supported an anti-tobacco campaign even stronger than Califano's crusade.

Tar Heel politicians received the news of Califano's forced resignation with glee, although they had known that the Carter administration would not change the HEW secretary's policies. "You don't see me crying," Hunt had remarked.[54] Carter replaced Califano with Housing and Urban Development (HUD) Secretary Patricia Harris, a black woman who had promised to be open-minded about smoking and integration issues. Several civil rights organizations feared that she might not press hard enough on university desegregation. Attorney Joe Rauh wrote to Harris that "North Carolina's defiance of HEW has been egregious,"[55] citing statistics proving that the state's universities had remained substantially segregated. Seeking to prove herself as a supporter of civil rights, Harris used a meeting with President Friday and UNC board members on October 3, 1979 to define her position. Emphasizing her opposition to the dual system of higher education in North Carolina, she demanded immediate compliance and then ended the meeting abruptly before the UNC president could finish his presentation. Friday reported the extremely bitter conference to the governor, who then became angry at the way a federal official had treated his own Tar Heel representative. According to Friday, Governor Hunt told Carter advisors privately that he could not possibly support the president if HEW did not settle the UNC case satisfactorily. President Carter later called Governor Hunt on October 19, apologizing for the rude attitude of the HEW secretary.[56]

Despite this incident, Governor Hunt remained loyal to President Carter. He later insisted that he never had a strained personal relationship with the president. Even the desegregation matter had not adversely affected their relationship. "As much as Califano was a lightning rod and vilified here by a lot of people," Hunt recalled, "my relationship with Carter stayed very good. I can recall going to governors' conferences and I would be his number one supporter of all governors of either party. Many Democrats were very lukewarm about him. Our relationship remained strong."[57] When Ted Kennedy decided to challenge President Carter in the Democratic primary, Hunt endorsed the president and remained a loyal supporter during the general election campaign. Despite Hunt's endorsement, President Carter, hurt by declining economic indicators and unresolved foreign crises, lost the state as well as the election to Ronald Reagan.[58]

In 1981, the North Carolina university system and the Reagan administration resolved the desegregation matter. A year earlier, Congress had replaced HEW with two new departments, HHS and the United States Department of Education, which received responsibility over the controversial suit. When Terrence Bell became Reagan's Secretary of Education, he was determined to reduce the burden of the federal government on all state education systems, including North Carolina's. Bell and the UNC system agreed on a consent decree that set non-binding goals of ten percent black enrollment in traditionally white universities, the same percentage of whites at traditionally black institutions, and the enhancement of the state's five traditionally black universities. Although some civil rights organizations called the agreement a sellout of civil rights, Governor Hunt and President Friday were content over what William Link called an acceptable plan that enhanced university integration while still preventing federal control of the higher education system.[59]

If Hunt did what was expected of a North Carolina politician during Califano's anti-tobacco campaign, he sometimes exceeded expectations during the desegregation controversy. When HEW proved recalcitrant and threatened to remove funds from the universities, Hunt proposed an expensive effort to revitalize the state's decaying traditionally black institutions. He successfully pushed for $40 million of improvements for the black universities even after the negotiations failed. Throughout the HEW crisis, he alienated few African Americans, arguing that the struggle was over the means, not the ends, of achieving integrated institutions. Hunt's opposition to HEW never seriously damaged his relationship with his black constituency. In other words, blacks and whites accepted a predominantly segregated university system as long as there were no legal obstacles to prevent attendance at the institutions.

Although North Carolina Governor James B. Hunt, Jr., supported business diversification and black college enhancement, he risked little of his popularity with conservative whites in North Carolina during the struggles against HEW. A political professional, Hunt sought to reach compromises without alienating his constituencies, unlike Joseph Califano. Forced into action by the federal courts, Califano tried his best to improve traditionally black universities. Genuinely concerned about the effects of tobacco, the HEW secretary unleashed the most aggressive anti-tobacco campaign until the Clinton efforts of the 1990s. If White House aides objected to Califano's abrasive personality, they also strongly opposed the anti-tobacco crusade in North Carolina as politically dangerous to Carter's reelection campaign. In this case, the president did not show political courage. Especially for his role in launching the first aggressive anti-tobacco campaign in American history, Califano deserves to be called what President Carter had allegedly told him in July 1979 — he was one of the best welfare department secretaries in American history.

12

The Selling of North Carolina, 1977–1980: Jim Hunt and the Economic Expansion of the Tar Heel State

In 1977, North Carolina Governor James Hunt began an intensive campaign to bring new businesses into the state. Understanding that North Carolina relied traditionally on low-wage industries, he developed an economic strategy to attract companies that paid high salaries. He promoted education as a tool to create the work force needed for the new industrial economy and approved the construction of highways to make sure that no town in North Carolina remained isolated from economic growth. From Israel to Japan, Hunt promoted tourism and recruited businesses, including machine manufacturers, microelectronics firms, and Hollywood filmmakers. In the early years of his industrial recruitment campaign, the governor received criticism from a state labor commissioner who called his efforts ineffective, conservatives who feared that the new jobs undermined the state's traditional low-wage industries, and radical unionists who complained that Hunt ignored the workers. Although the Tar Heel State would have expanded economically without Governor Jim Hunt, his salesmanship certainly accelerated the process that turned North Carolina into one of the fastest growing states in the nation.

North Carolina made industrial progress in the decades after World War II, but wages remained low in the 1970s. In the previous three decades, many of the state's citizens had moved from the farms to the cities in large numbers, changing the farm population from forty percent in 1945 to eight percent in 1974. In the 1950s, the state had ranked first nationally in the production of cigarettes, textiles, and furniture. Two decades later, companies producing fabricated metal, chemicals, and electronic machinery provided the most jobs in North Carolina. Despite this change, most Tar Heels remained in low-wage occupations. In 1976, North Carolina ranked at the bottom in the United States regarding industrial wages, even below Alabama and Mississippi. This alarming statistic led to a debate between Tar Heel traditionalists, who desired to keep low wages to attract businesses, and "New South" progressives, including Jim Hunt, who wanted to create high wage jobs by improving education, race relations, and the state's infrastructure.[1]

Hunt's corporate pragmatism had evolved from his agrarian beliefs in high school. Reared in the tobacco community of Wilson County, young Jimmy Hunt had strongly defended the agricultural sector against politicians who cared only for urban interests. Majoring in economics at North Carolina State College, he had accepted the inevitability of southern urbanization and had favored Keynesian economics, or the use of government as an engine to promote industrial wealth, as advocated by his economics professor, Quentin Lindsey. As an economic advisor with Lindsey in Nepal, Hunt had criticized Marxism and applauded the Nepalese king's efforts to transform the economy from feudalism to capitalism. Although a supporter of President Lyndon Johnson and Vice President Hubert Humphrey, he had abandoned their Great Society liberalism when running for office in the early 1970s. Like other New South politicians, he argued that the focus of economic policy should be industrial growth, not government programs. Favoring liberal policies granting equal rights to women and African Americans, he usually opposed liberal economic policies that aimed at sharing the wealth.[2]

As a thirty-five-year-old candidate running for lieutenant governor in 1972, Hunt had talked about raising industrial wages in North Carolina. Speaking to textile manufacturers, he had told them that he knew the difficulties that the industry faced from foreign competition. "Given the choice of low-paying jobs or no jobs at all," Hunt had said, "we must opt for the jobs."[3] Yet, he later added, the state must set its goals higher and begin the job of raising per capita income. Hunt's moderate position had set him apart from conservatives within the North Carolina Democratic party as well as conservative Republicans in the General Assembly and the United States Senate.[4]

In 1976, gubernatorial candidate Jim Hunt, whose pollster had told him that Tar Heels desired high wage jobs, found a base among North Carolina businessmen who profited from the building of roads or who depended on well-educated employees. According to political scientist Paul Luebke in *Tar Heel Politics 2000*,

> Hunt's support from big business came disproportionately from growth-oriented sectors: bankers, real estate developers, truckers, and executives of multinational corporations. Such capitalists have an unambiguous interest in economic growth and recognize the importance of politicians who believe in government-financed infrastructure such as highways, public schools, and water/sewer lines.[5]

Luebke even gave these businessmen a name, calling them "modernizers." He labeled their opponents "traditionalists" who feared the demise of low-wage industries. Conservative political advisor Carter Wrenn said that Luebke exaggerated the modernizer-traditionalist emphasis, since many Tar Heel businessmen looked at other factors when selecting candidates, such as who would win the election and who the businessmen liked personally. Hunt's success depended on a blend of these factors. Because of his energetic personality, his policies and the inevitability of his victory, Jim Hunt received the endorsement of growth-oriented businessmen for governor in 1976.[6]

In 1977, newly elected Governor Jim Hunt introduced a strategy to encourage long term economic growth by improving education and infrastructure. The governor successfully promoted education reform, including minimum competency exams and reading aides in the public schools, to end high illiteracy rates among the young and prepare them for the industrial economy. He convinced the General Assembly to pass a $300 million highway construction bond referendum to insure that no rural town remained isolated from economic growth. He also favored a water and sewer bond referendum that year to improve the infrastructure of rural towns and make them more attractive to industries. A majority of voters approved both bond issues in November 1977.[7]

To recruit industries, Hunt appointed Lauch Faircloth as Secretary of Commerce. Faircloth, a successful farmer and businessman from Sampson County, had served progressive Democratic candidates since the 1940s, when he had driven gubernatorial candidate Kerr Scott to campaign rallies across the state. Governor Terry Sanford, who had once called Faircloth the only man who "chewed tobacco and wore a Brooks Brothers suit,"[8] had appointed the businessman to the North Carolina Highway Commission. A few years later, Governor Bob Scott appointed him the commission's chairman. Faircloth had used this position to support the building of roads across the state, including highways in his home county, an action that alienated both Republicans and the Raleigh *News and*

Observer, whose editorialists declared that the millionaire did not have the vision of economic justice for the post. Hunt dismissed such talk about a man who had aided his campaigns as early as 1971. Remembering his crucial support, Hunt forgave Faircloth for his salty language and assertive behavior at cabinet meetings. Although the Commerce Secretary worked hard to recruit industries, Hunt loyalists Betty McCain and Joseph Grimsley claimed that the governor did more to recruit industries than did Faircloth.[9]

In 1977, Hunt restructured the North Carolina Department of Commerce to promote industrial recruitment and tourism. In September of that year, he announced a reorganization of the state's economic development efforts to provide more innovative and aggressive ways of bringing in better-paying jobs. The restructuring of the department included the creation of a Business Assistance Division that provided each industry in the state with a personal government contact, and an International Development Division that explored the ignored markets of the Middle East, Africa, South America, and the Far East. Also, Hunt's reorganization created a tourist division that promoted advertising messages about North Carolina to 200 million English-speaking North Americans. Because of the governor's efforts, both tourism and industry increased in North Carolina.[10]

Hunt constantly sought the feedback of local officials during his industrial recruitment efforts. In October 1977, he introduced a series of county conferences where people discussed local economic problems, addressed statewide economic development issues, and shared their ideas about developing a better quality of life. Hunt declared, "I think this will be the first time in our history that every county has had the opportunity to discuss a major issue during the same period of time."[11] He also created local development advisory councils to address the concerns of small towns. Sometimes, rural mayors called the governor directly with a problem resolving most local matters themselves. The councils then dealt with less important issues. Former Hunt advisor Paul Essex called the councils "the biggest waste of time,"[12] because Hunt discovered other ways to communicate effectively with local governments.

Hunt hoped that his ambitious efforts at industrial recruitment would attract those North Carolina businessmen still skeptical about a progressive Democrat in the governor's mansion. Despite the governor's vows of economic conservatism, several businessmen still viewed him as an economic liberal. As governor, Hunt tried his best to change this perception. In January 1978, at the first of a series of economic development conferences, he told the audience that "we must have in North Carolina a business climate that is receptive to growth and encourages confidence among business leaders."[13] Hunt announced support for a $10 million reduction of the manufacturer's inventory tax to bring in big payrolls to the state. In the next two years, the governor went further to destroy false images of being an economic liberal when he promoted a cut in income taxes and state budget cuts. After he helped enact these proposals into law, businessmen contributed generously to his reelection campaign.[14]

To promote economic development in rural regions, Hunt endorsed "balanced growth," an effort to insure growth in all areas of North Carolina. Even before his election as lieutenant governor, he had attended meetings that dealt with the gap between urban and rural regions of the Tar Heel State. As governor, Hunt had promoted a hundred conferences in 1977 in preparation for a White House conference on balanced growth. In 1979, Hunt encouraged the legislature to pass the North Carolina Balanced Growth Policy Act that committed the state to encourage diversified job growth in all its different regions. The act focused particular attention on those groups that had suffered from high rates of unemployment or underemployment in isolated communities. He tried to convince large companies that small North Carolina cities were a new frontier for urbanization in America. Despite Hunt's efforts, rural communities lagged behind the large cities because the towns lacked educated employees, highways, airports, and a strong infrastructure. The governor succeeded better at urging high wage companies to move to large urban regions with universities, such as the Raleigh-Durham area and Charlotte.[15]

To aid economic growth in North Carolina, Governor Hunt turned to the administration of Jimmy Carter, whom he loyally supported. At times, President Carter aided the governor in his campaign to attract more industry into North Carolina. Although the president ignored Hunt's request to subsidize the state's industrial recruitment strategies, he approved the creation of free trade zones in the Charlotte area to allow foreign industries to manufacture goods free of American tariff duties. The Carter administration also supported development policies that aided small cities and rural areas, which benefited Governor Hunt's balanced growth approach to state industrial growth. President Carter believed that he had aided the Tar Heel State, telling an interviewer in October 1978 that "we have focused our attention more on North Carolina because of Hunt's interest."[16] Despite Carter's efforts to help the state's economy, a majority of Tar Heels rejected his bid for reelection, partially because they blamed him for the weak national economic situation while praising their own governor for North Carolina's industrial growth.

During his first term, Hunt had sought energetically to recruit businesses from across the nation. The governor had brought the North Carolina Symphony to Chicago to show business leaders that they would invest in a region of culture. If a company debated whether to locate a factory in the state, Hunt worked hard to sell the state. For instance, when Cummings Diesel debated whether to locate a plant in Nash County in September 1980, Hunt told their officials that he would help meet the company's needs on training, road access, and education. "We will provide whatever training needs you have, to prepare our workers to perform the very high skilled tasks that will be involved in your manufacturing processes," the governor wrote Cummings executives.[17] He bragged about the local community college's ability to train workers and promised to have the state study road facilities for the incoming factory. This incident highlights the claim that the governor devoted one-fourth of his working time as governor to recruiting new businesses.[18]

Governor Hunt also recruited companies from Europe. Preparing for his first trip to West Germany as governor in 1979, he requested meetings with businessmen there. Occasionally, a German businessman wrote back and told him not to come to their offices because such a visit would waste the governor's time. Despite these responses, Hunt went to Europe twice during his

Jim Hunt, pictured here arriving from Europe in August 1978, tried hard to recruit North Carolina industry more than any governor in the twentieth century. The governor's travels took him to the American Midwest and West Coast, the Middle East, Japan, China, and Europe. Hunt's efforts brought new jobs to North Carolina and helped to create the microelectronics and location-filming industries. (Courtesy of the *News and Observer*)

first term to recruit businesses and to promote tourism in North Carolina. By February 1980, he had won the commitment of fifteen European companies to establish Tar Heel plants. "Those fifteen companies will invest over $120 million and employ over 1,300 people in North Carolina," Hunt had said. "That's not a bad return on two trips which cost the state a total of approximately $40,000."[19] He had clearly understood that wealthy European corporations could create hundreds of Tar Heel jobs.

Hunt also sought business from the Middle East and Asia. In 1978, he and Lieutenant Governor Jimmy Green visited Arab countries and Israel to attract business. More than a year later, the governor and other North Carolina officials traveled to the People's Republic of China, where they had tried to sell Tar Heel tobacco, and to affluent Japan, whose investment Hunt had declared might be three times more important that that of Europe. Although some Japanese business leaders questioned the productivity of North Carolina workers, Hunt received the commitments of Saito Wood and two other Japanese companies to build plants in the state. Because of these commitments by Japanese industrialists, Hunt won funding from the General Assembly to create two liaison offices in Tokyo and Osaka to recruit industry.[20]

In his search for new businesses, Hunt discovered that the motion picture industry in California could also bring revenue to North Carolina. The governor desired a share of Hollywood's major-studio profits from location filming. He understood that Georgia, the first southern state to have a film commission, was receiving big dividends from this decision. Hunt understood that "the typical film cost $5 or $6 million, and about $4 million of that will be spent in the state in which the film is shot."[21] Since the state had different seasonal weather and scenery for just about any film, the governor encouraged the legislature to create an office of motion picture development to recruit location filming. By 1980, Governor Hunt's film commission had achieved some successes. Tri-Star Pictures had decided to use the Biltmore House, the former Asheville mansion of the Vanderbilt railroad tycoon family, for the comedy *Private Eyes* starring Don Knotts and Tim Conway. Another studio had brought British actor Peter Sellers to the Biltmore House to film the black comedy *Being There*. Hunt had ordered all cabinet members to cooperate in every way with motion picture companies filming in the state and approved the creation of a short film to recruit the industry using James Taylor's song "Carolina on My Mind." In November 1980, he met with Los Angeles studio executives to sell location filming in North Carolina, telling them that "we are eager to work very hard to make it easy and economical for filmmakers to work in our state."[22] At the end of his Los Angeles trip, Hunt announced that a major studio would film *Brainstorm*, the largest motion picture to be shot in North Carolina up to that date. Hunt's efforts launched the construction of a motion picture studio in Wilmington, first owned by Dino De Laurentiis in the 1980s, and later bought by Screen Gems Studios to film movies and the television programs *Matlock* and *Dawson's Creek*.[23]

Films only provided short-term employment for North Carolina citizens, so Hunt concentrated on the microelectronics industry as an avenue for permanent high-paying jobs. The governor was convinced that he could create better jobs by attracting the new and expanded high-technology industry. Influenced by his science advisor, Quentin Lindsey, Hunt had hoped to attract computer and software companies to the state. He realized, however, that the state had several weaknesses. In 1980, the Massachusetts Department of Manpower Development had rated North Carolina twenty-first of twenty-five states in high tech industry manufacturing employment—more than ten percent below the national level, with Florida's high tech employment rate nearly three times greater. Hunt still desired to have the Research Triangle Park challenge Silicon Valley in California. Political scientist Randall Rothenburg said of the governor in his study of innovative Democratic politicians, "A fully converted Atari Democrat early in his first term, Jim Hunt envisioned a way to make the Research Triangle even more attractive to business by improving its research and development capabilities."[24] Hunt decided to proceed with the challenge of turning a low-wage manufacturing state into a region of high technology.

Late in his first term, he encouraged several state policy initiatives designed to make North Carolina a center of the microelectronics industry. He backed the creation of a high school devoted solely to science and mathematics to create engineers and scientists for the emerging industries. In the spring of 1980, Hunt formed a blue-ribbon committee with the heads of Duke University, the University of North Carolina, and the state's community colleges to explore how to launch a statewide microelectronics boom. The committee suggested that the state form a nonprofit corporation that would sponsor research and development efforts and train students in technology and applications. In June 1980, Hunt accepted these recommendations and committed almost one million dollars to finance the Microelectronics Center of North Carolina. In November, he made a publicized trip to Silicon Valley with plans to sell the state to microelectronics firms. He argued that the Research Triangle Park had plenty of industrial development sites, cheap land, cheap housing, a relaxed quality of life, and a new microelectronics research center within a short distance of three major universities. By the end of 1980, the state had invested $24 million in the recruitment of high-tech businesses, hoping to create a Tar Heel Silicon Valley.[25]

Governor Hunt's efforts at recruiting microelectronic industries increased in his second term. In 1980, General Electric announced that it would locate a new microelectronics research, development, and production plant in North Carolina. Within the next two years, Hewlett Packard and Texas Instruments purchased land parcels in Wake County to build microelectronics factories. Because of Governor Hunt's success, the General Assembly approved the Microelectronics Research Center in early 1981 without even a committee vote. North Carolina legislators accepted the governor's verdict that "the microelectronics industry is our chance — perhaps the only chance that will come in our lifetime — to make a dramatic breakthrough in elevating the wages and per capita income of the people of this state."[26] Although the Research Triangle Park did not rival Seattle or Silicon Valley in the 1990s, it still became a leading producer of computers and technology in the South.

Although most of Governor Jim Hunt's industrial recruitment campaign focused on long-term successes, he realized that he needed victories in the short term. He often made speeches declaring excellent news about new factories coming to North Carolina. "In the first six months of this year, our state attracted over $1 billion in investment in new and expanded industries," he declared in the summer of 1978. "That is as much as we attracted in all of 1976, which was a record year at the time. And it's far ahead of 1977's record pace; we attracted a total of $1.45 billion in new investment that year."[27] In 1980, North Carolina ranked eighth in the nation in spending on industrial recruitment with its $500,000 budget.

A few people criticized the governor's industrial recruitment campaign. Labor Commissioner John Brooks, an independently elected Democratic official, claimed that the governor still brought the same low-wage jobs as his predecessors had because he attracted corporations that mainly offered unskilled employment. Indeed, statistics had proved that no economic miracle had occurred. In 1979, the United States Department of Commerce listed North Carolina as having the lowest manufacturing wages in the nation, still below Alabama and Mississippi. The governor admitted during his first term that the high wage jobs he had promised had not yet arrived.[28]

Because of a national recession beginning in 1978, the Hunt administration had conceded the need to attract low-wage industries in rural regions, leading his industrial recruiters to stress the state's predominantly non-unionized status in order to attract businesses. The governor had pledged not to sell the state as a source of cheap labor, but he had realized the need for jobs of any wage, and therefore had focused on highlighting worker productivity. Two hundred and eighty-seven North Carolina manufacturing plants closed permanently between 1978 and 1982 with the loss of 27,131 jobs, and another 244 plants closed temporarily, causing 36,000 workers to go on the unemployment rolls. The need for jobs had caused the state to advertise to West German firms in 1979 that North Carolina had low work stoppages, high rates of vocational training, and the lowest unionized employment in the fifty states. The effort proved highly effective. With help from the state Department of Commerce, North Carolina produced 7.8 billion dollars worth of new and expanded plants and 120,000 new jobs between 1977 and 1984. The governor regretted that he could not raise the state's per capita income and industrial wages faster, but he believed that his efforts would pay off in the future. In a 1981 interview, Hunt declared that the impact of a governor on industrial recruitment was not realized until long after the governor's effort had begun.[29]

Hunt got along well with organized labor during the industrial recruitment campaign even as he advertised North Carolina's lack of unions as a method to recruit businesses. In 1976, he had sought the endorsement of the state American Federation of Labor–Congress of Industrial Organizations by attending their conventions. He had received the early support of state AFL-CIO leader Wilbur Hobby because he promised not to call the National Guard to suppress a labor strike and favored a North Carolina labor education center. As governor, Hunt spent more time with corporation executives than with labor representatives. Although the Hunt administration had never suppressed a strike and had further appeased Hobby with generous contracts to his printing business, Hobby and other labor leaders remained on the sidelines during gubernatorial decisions.[30]

Governor Hunt's promise to create a labor education and research center at a North Carolina university remained unfulfilled. In 1977, Chancellor Albert Whiting of North Carolina Central University, a predominantly black institution, had agreed to house the center at his campus in Durham. The curriculum would include courses in collective bargaining, grievance procedures, labor history, and occupational safety. The charter had stated that the center would help meet the continuing education and research needs of persons concerned with labor education and provide for the continuing education of labor leaders. Governor Hunt's office approved a temporary staff for the center with federal funds and expected routine approval from the University of North Carolina Board of Governors. However, the board had little sympathy for unions. "As you might expect, there

is not much enthusiasm for this," UNC Administrator Walton Jones wrote
the governor. "President Friday puts his full support behind it. With his
continued support, I feel sure we will get it pass the board."[31] The labor
center's opponents had been frustrated in October 1977 when the UNC
planning committee approved the proposal. Afterwards, traditional conservatives called attention to a private AFL-CIO eight-year organizing plan
to increase their power in the state and had argued that an active labor
movement endangered the low-wage textile, furniture, and apparel industries in North Carolina. Despite support for the labor center by Consolidated University President William Friday and the state's major
newspapers, the conservative majority on the board killed the proposal.
Political scientist Paul Luebke of Duke University argued that Hunt could
have pushed more strongly for the center, but he chose not to act. The AFL-
CIO had planned to persuade the governor to push for the proposal, but
the labor organization backed off because they feared their action would
encourage traditionalists to fight harder.[32]

In 1977, Hunt had pleased the union leaders by recruiting a unionized company in Person County, North Carolina, despite the protests of
local officials. After the state had announced that the Brockwork Glass
Company, a Pennsylvania company with unionized plants, would start a
factory in Person County, local officials passed a resolution discouraging
the move because they feared that the new company would force wage
increases upon the local businesses. "I think before the state starts inter-
vening, it [at] least ought to check with us to see what our position is,"
Person County Industrial Development Commission Chairman Michael
Carden said. "We have a history of non-union industry around here and
our labor force doesn't think union."[33] Faced with hostile local officials,
the company decided not to locate in that county. In a similar incident in
Cabarrus County, Cannon Mills, the region's predominant textile company,
had attempted to organize the community in December 1977 to oppose
the arrival of a cigarette-manufacturing company which planned to pay
unionized wages well above the county average. Cannon Mills' efforts to
challenge the new Philip Morris factory failed because of community support for the new company and Governor Hunt's call to the Philip Morris
chairman not to withdraw from the county. Yet, the governor had felt
uncomfortable rejecting the advice of local officials and local businessmen, and most companies that his administration recruited for rural
regions had no desire to pay wages higher than the county average. Because
the governor avoided friction with local officials, there were no further
reported incidents of the North Carolina Commerce Department being at
odds with rural communities.[34]

The only time that Hunt interfered in a labor dispute was during the nationwide independent trucker strike in 1979. He ordered the National Guard to protect fuel terminals after picketers blocked two terminals in Greensboro and Charlotte in their efforts to oppose high costs and confusing federal regulations. According to former Press Secretary Gary Pearce, the governor "stood on a truck at a gasoline terminal in Greensboro and quieted an angry crowd of striking, independent truckers," adding that his "willingness to hear them out and speak up for needed changes brought North Carolina through without violence or serious disruption."[35] With adept political skill, Hunt announced his sympathy for the strikers while enforcing the law.

Usually, Hunt expressed his neutrality on labor matters, especially during the struggle between J. P. Stevens Company and the textile workers union in the 1970s. During the decade, the Amalgamated Clothing and Textile Workers (ACTWU) organized a boycott against the company because of its resistance to the unionization of the Roanoke Rapids plant despite a union election victory there in 1974. The ACTWU won its case in 1980 after persuading sympathetic institutional stockholders and other pro-union advocacy groups to demand that the directors allow the factory to unionize. As the battle between the forces of capital and labor raged during Hunt's first term, the governor stayed out of the conflict. He had expressed his neutral philosophy toward unions in remarks at a ceremony welcoming a Belgian factory in Wilmington on September 21, 1977. The governor declared that he favored the right-to-work law preventing closed union shops in North Carolina, had sought the best-paying industries, and would neither encourage nor discourage unions. For a progressive governor in a state that traditionally disdained unionization, neutrality was the wisest policy to take politically.[36]

Even in the case of textile mill workers stricken by a cotton dust disease, the governor approached the matter cautiously. Lacy Wright, a retired textile worker with severe lung problems, had united with young activists to form the Carolina Brown Lung Association (CBLA). Although the American Textile Manufacturers Institute had challenged their evidence, the industry found it difficult to fight white, sickly, elderly and nonunion workers who had not been associated with the Communist fringe of the union movement. After the CBLA had brought their concerns to Governor Hunt, he appointed a group in 1979 to investigate the way that the North Carolina Industrial Commission delayed claims for textile workers who could no longer work after breathing cotton dust. This decision had failed to appease the CBLA, which wanted an investigation of the industry, and the textile industrialists, who had wanted the matter dropped. By the end of his second term, Hunt had eliminated regulations that restricted mill workers' eligibility for workers' compensation. Cautious regarding struggles between employers and employees, the governor had tried to balance the needs of ailing textile workers with the desires of the industrialists to remain competitive.[37]

Hunt's neutrality successfully pacified the AFL-CIO, leaving many supporters of worker's rights with no place to turn to but the governor. A small minority of Tar Heel economic liberals, including Dr. Paul Luebke, criticized Hunt's tax breaks for businesses, state budget cuts, and unwavering support for the highway lobby. However, they understood that no economic liberal could possibly launch a strong challenge against the popular governor. Hunt's roots went so deep into North Carolina progressivism, which differs dramatically from economic liberalism because the philosophy emphasizes the modernization of business instead of the redistribution of wealth. Also, Tar Heel economic liberals could not rely on a coalition of African Americans and white women against the governor. Leubke explained,

> Jim Hunt immeasurably strengthened the corporate pragmatist perspective within the North Carolina Democratic Party. He placed conservative business-oriented Democrats on the defensive and through political appointments of blacks and women, protected his left from urban liberals and populists who saw him as too friendly with the politically moderate corporate establishment.[38]

Hunt judged his economic policies to be a success because North Carolina's economy boomed in the two decades following his first term. According to *The State of the South 2000*, North Carolina had job growth of more than fifty-seven percent and population growth of nearly thirty percent between 1978 and 1997, which was well above the national and southern rates. Most of the growth came to Raleigh-Durham, which produced 401,782 jobs in that period to become the third fastest growing southern region in the late twentieth century, behind only Orlando, Florida, and Austin, Texas. The Raleigh-Durham area matched Austin in the creation of professional, scientific, and technical positions. The same study revealed that Charlotte produced 381,503 jobs between 1978 and 1997 to become the eleventh fasting growing southern city of that period. Within these years, North Carolina tied Virginia by producing 1.3 million new urban jobs, surpassed only by Texas with 4 million, Florida with 3.6 million, and Georgia with 1.5 million. The rural areas still relied on the traditional factories, and therefore lagged behind, yet the Tar Heel State matched Texas in the 1978–1997 period by producing 330,000 rural jobs, second in the South only to Georgia with 350,000. Although rural jobs in textiles, apparel, and tobacco processing declined by one-third in North Carolina from the late 1970s to the late 1990s, positions grew in business and health services in the Tar Heel State at nearly double the national rates. If Governor Hunt failed to achieve balanced growth, he gets credit for creating thousands of rural jobs and for perpetuating the economic boom in the Tar Heel cities.[39]

Statistics indicate that Governor James B. Hunt's policies to recruit industries succeeded dramatically. He successfully promoted education to create the new industrial workforce, favored transportation projects to unify the state economy, and endorsed the building of rural infrastructure as a way to promote small towns to businesses. Hunt restructured the Department of Commerce to attract new high-wage businesses in North Carolina that included microelectronics firms and biotechnology producers. He also promoted good race and gender relations as a way to create statewide business stability. All these policies, which fit within the North Carolina progressive tradition, helped the state to grow. Hunt helped North Carolina to compete with Texas, Florida, and Georgia, and to become one of the fastest growing southern states in the late twentieth century.[40]

13

Jim Hunt and Howard Lee:
The Governor and the State's
First Black Cabinet Secretary

Howard Lee discovered unexpected challenges after North Carolina Governor Jim Hunt appointed him the first African-American cabinet secretary in the state's history. Before he took over the Department of Natural Resources and Community Development (NRCD), he had already won the respect of African Americans and white progressives by becoming the first black mayor of Chapel Hill and the first serious black candidate for lieutenant governor. These earlier triumphs sometimes did not help him in dealing with a huge bureaucracy that staffed thousands of employees and handled millions of dollars. Dissatisfied employees and gubernatorial aides caused Lee trouble. He suffered most when the news media reported that his department granted federal funds to embezzlers. Hunt's political enemies used the black secretary's difficulties to highlight possible corruption in the administration. Although the governor defended Lee publicly, he sought privately another role for his embattled secretary and eventually gave him little reason to remain in the position. Howard Lee's struggle revealed the difficulty of a governor's efforts in dealing with a cabinet appointee from his black constituency whose errors became more of a focus of the media than his accomplishments.

Although Jim Hunt and Howard Lee were reared in southern agricultural communities during the Great Depression, their differing races and economic circumstances made each boy's experiences extremely dissimilar. While Jimmy Hunt lived with college-educated parents in Rock Ridge, North Carolina, a black sharecropper reared Howard Lee in Lithonia,

Georgia. As Rock Ridge whites respected Hunt's father James, Lee recalled watching his black father get ordered out of a store for "getting smart"[1] with the white owner. While young Jimmy Hunt believed that segregation was better for both races, Howard Lee violated segregation ordinances at public restrooms. As Jimmy became the highest awarded student at a white high school, Howard dropped out of a black high school twice to take odd jobs before finally graduating in 1953. Clearly, the two youths developed from distinctly different backgrounds.[2]

Despite these differences, Hunt and Lee had much in common by the 1960s. Each man married at a young age and received undergraduate degrees in 1959. They both entered the University of North Carolina in the early 1960s with the goal of improving other people's lives, although Hunt chose to study law and Lee directed his energies toward a masters degree in social work. Hunt and Lee remained sympathetic with the civil rights movement, but they also equally understood the importance of working within the existing political system to achieve lasting goals. Most importantly, each man participated in the Young Democratic clubs of North Carolina, where they met, became friends, and pursued their dreams of future political office.[3]

Even in the early 1960s, one could observe a great difference in political styles between Jim Hunt and Howard Lee. Hunt restrained himself from making unpopular statements, and he refrained from taking unnecessary risks that might lead to political defeat. In contrast, Lee took great risks in his early political career and was not afraid of speaking his mind. While Hunt remained neutral in the Democratic primaries as YDC president in 1968, Lee ran the Orange County campaign of Reginald Hawkins, a black gubernatorial candidate who had no chance to defeat Robert Scott, the eventual nominee and governor. As Hunt allied with Governor Scott and won the position of assistant party chairman, Lee criticized the governor for not doing enough for African Americans. While Hunt delayed making a run for office, despite his increasing political contacts, Lee decided in 1969 to run for mayor of Chapel Hill, a university town with an eleven percent black population, against a Democratic white incumbent. Although the political experts dismissed his chances as hopeless, Lee created an alliance of blacks, students, and professors and became the first black mayor of a biracial town in North Carolina. As mayor, Lee made inroads among Democrats, and Governor Robert Scott made Lee vice chairman of the state Democratic party. Even though Hunt and Lee had contrasting political styles, they seemed to have promising political futures.[4]

The year 1972 proved to be elevating for Jim Hunt and upsetting for

Howard Lee. As Hunt sought to become lieutenant governor, Lee tried to become a United States congressman. Both candidates hoped to win African Americans voters without alienating too many whites. Hunt succeeded, winning the lieutenant gubernatorial primary, but Lee failed to defeat the white Democratic incumbent in the Second District of North Carolina. As Hunt ran for lieutenant governor in the general election, Lee campaigned for Democratic gubernatorial nominee Hargrove "Skipper" Bowles, who promised him a cabinet office if he won. Unfortunately for Lee, Bowles lost the election to Jim Holshouser, the first Republican gubernatorial victor in North Carolina since 1896. When Bowles sought the 1976 gubernatorial nomination, Lee could see the momentum gathering around Lieutenant Governor Hunt for that office. He refused to back Bowles against Hunt, and after announcing for lieutenant governor in 1976, sought a closer relationship with the Hunt campaign.[5]

In 1976, Hunt announced for governor as Lee ran for lieutenant governor, hoping that Hunt progressives would help him defeat his conservative challengers. Once again, political experts gave Lee little chance of victory. Despite the doubters, Lee finished first in the Democratic primary against eight contenders in August 1976. He ended in a September runoff against white conservative Democratic candidate Jimmy Green, speaker of the North Carolina House. Hunt silently supported Lee, even though he proclaimed his neutrality publicly. Many Hunt supporters, including former Democratic party chairman Bert Bennett and North Carolina Senator Ralph Scott, also wanted Lee to win. "The Hunt people gave as much support to me as they reasonably could without getting in trouble," Lee said.[6] Although the Hunt campaign managers never endorsed Lee, they reassured the candidate privately of their support.

During the second primary, Lee felt his momentum undercut by Green because of subtle racial appeals. "Green did everything to keep race in front of the majority of the voters," Lee recalled.[7] His opponent's advertisements showed the white candidate and the black candidate side by side, declaring, "unless the people come out and vote on September 14, the election will be decided by a relatively small segment of the population"[8]— meaning that the black population would select the Democratic nominee. Lee tried to convince white voters that he had moderated his economic populism and accepted Hunt's proposals on education and economic development. Despite these appeals, he lost momentum. Even the rumor that blacks planned to hire an assassin to kill the governor if Lee was elected lieutenant governor was taken seriously by the Lee campaign. The black candidate also could not motivate lower-income African Americans to return to the polls in large numbers. In September 1976, Lee lost the

second primary to Jimmy Green. Despite the state's progress in race relations, subtle racism undermined Lee's campaign.[9]

After the primaries, Lee and Hunt made commitments to each other
for the fall campaign. The lieutenant governor asked Lee to be first vice-
chairman of the state party. Lee accepted, and then asked if Hunt would
give him serious consideration after the election for a cabinet post. The
lieutenant governor, who had already promised black leaders that he would
select an African American for his cabinet, assured Lee that he absolutely
would. In the fall campaign, Lee worked on Operation Big Vote, helping
the gubernatorial candidate to keep in frequent contact with local black
leaders and to attract black voters in North Carolina for Hunt's successful effort that November.[10]

In late 1976, Governor-elect Jim Hunt appointed Howard Lee as Secretary of Natural and Economic Resources, which was renamed the Department of Natural Resources and Community Development (NRCD) in
1977. Hunt understood the political symbolism of picking the most popular African American candidate in North Carolina who had also worked
hard to attract the black vote for his general election campaign. He also
selected Lee because they shared the same goals of attracting industrial
growth to rural communities and balancing environmental regulation with
community development. Further, Hunt secured Lee's promise that the
mayor would put his political ambitions aside. These factors aside, Lee
understood that the governor took a chance on appointing a small-town
mayor to run a large government department.[11]

As a cabinet official, Lee did not want to be perceived as the black
representative of the Hunt administration. The black leaders wanted Lee
to become spokesman for the black community of North Carolina, a role
that he declined. "Many blacks were looking to me to accomplish goals
that in many instances were impossible for me to accomplish," he
recalled.[12] When there were racial problems in Wilmington and Greensboro, he refused to be called in as a mediator. As NRCD secretary, he tried
to serve all citizens without regard to color. For example, he met with a
group of white fishermen not known for their racial enlightenment. When
a staff member warned him that most of them disliked blacks, Lee replied,
"I am as much a secretary of the bigots as I am of everybody else."[13] When
he arrived at the meeting, the white fishermen gave him suspicious looks.
Lee addressed the white crowd for twenty minutes, and then, to his surprise, he received a standing ovation.[14]

Although Lee aimed at racial neutrality, he fought discrimination
against blacks when it fell within his responsibilities as NRCD secretary.
For example, he discovered that a water company requesting state grants

stopped their pipelines at the entrance to a black community. After Lee asked company officials why this occurred, they replied that the residents could not afford to pay for water. Lee refused to accept this answer, telling the company that he would not award state funds until they served all people equally. The company relented and agreed to continue the pipeline.[15]

Although he helped blacks in this matter, Lee faced the public wrath of many African Americans angry over his moderate stand regarding the Wilmington Ten. The NRCD secretary desired a pardon for the defendants, but the governor decided to commute the sentences. Lee recalled,

> I had more pressure on that issue than any other issue that I can recall being in office. I thought it would be reasonable to put it behind us by giving a pardon, but I understood the politics of it.... Besides, he [Hunt]believed in their guilt. I told the governor, "It would be easier on me if you pardoned them, but I can defend commutation. At least, they're getting something, and they probably don't deserve anything."[16]

Secretary Lee's refusal to criticize Governor Hunt strongly and resign his position angered many African Americans. He told black supporters, "It would be unfair and unfortunate if Jim Hunt and his administration were judged solely on the Wilmington Ten."[17] Shortly after Hunt's decision, Lee went to a human relations banquet at McKimmons Center in Raleigh. On his way, blacks heckled him and a woman hit his wife. Lee publicly lost his cool and chased the assailant until his friends grabbed him and calmed him down. This was only one of many incidents that caused stress between himself and other African Americans. "I was called an Uncle Tom, I was called an Oreo," Lee remembered.[18] Black activists who believed that he would support the Wilmington Ten unquestionably did not remember his earlier record of fighting violent black crime as Chapel Hill mayor when he had called for the prosecution of black radicals who had burned down a public school administration building. Many blacks misperceived Lee as Hunt's loyal pawn.[19]

After weeks of being called Jim Hunt's "Uncle Tom," Lee happily observed as the governor took actions that appeased the black community. In the early months of 1978, the governor appointed Richard Erwin, the first black appellate judge in North Carolina, and made a rare primary endorsement that year to help Erwin remain in that position. Also that year, Hunt named Ben Ruffin as the first special assistant for minority affairs in the governor's office. In December 1979, the governor finally released the Reverend Ben Chavis, the last member of the Wilmington Ten remaining in a prison. Shortly after the minister's release, Lee and Chavis

Governor Jim Hunt tried to break racial barriers while serving as governor. Here, the governor welcomes South African visitors in the North Carolina Senate Chamber in the State Capitol on March 24, 1979. (Courtesy of the North Carolina Office of Archives and History)

met each other at a black event. The former convict shook Lee's hand and said, "No matter what people say about you, I think that you are a very first class individual, I have a lot of respect for you, and I respect the positions you had to take."[20] Unlike many of his admirers, Chavis understood that as a black official, Lee had to tread carefully once he had achieved power.

African Americans who disagreed with the NRCD secretary on the Wilmington Ten applauded his choice of a prominent, politically active black woman for deputy secretary of Lee's department. Eva Clayton had created strong ties in the eastern black community by running symbolically for Congress in 1966 and directing the Soul City Foundation, a black economic development project. She also served as the chairperson of the Warren County Democratic party and as a coordinator for the Hunt campaign in eastern North Carolina. She joined NRCD because she shared Hunt's desire to end the rural migration to the cities. To accomplish this goal, she backed the use of federal funds to train poor people in small towns for better jobs, especially in the east. Clayton's concern for this troubled area helped her maintain a political base that allowed her to win United States congressional races in that region in the 1990s.[21]

With the aid of Clayton, Lee accomplished many important projects at NRCD. He finished the first phase of the North Carolina zoo before the scheduled deadline. He urged successfully the creation of a Mountain to Sea trail across the state. Lee expanded the coastal area management program to protect natural resources near North Carolina islands and sounds. The NRCD secretary also initiated a Housing Finance Agency to help community development, developed a plan to save the Chowan River, and strengthened the marine fisheries program [22]

Although Lee trusted Clayton as a loyal advisor, he distrusted others in his department who felt a need to tell the governor's office about activities within NRCD. As Lee took office, he believed that he had the confidence of the governor, who told North Carolina mayors in March 1977 that the NRCD secretary "understands your problems, and he is a strong supporter of programs that are oriented to local governments."[23] Even as he praised cabinet officials like Lee, Hunt centralized decision making in the governor's office by communicating with lower level officials about departmental issues. After Lee discovered that Hunt had sent directions to a deputy secretary without his knowledge, the NRCD secretary confronted the governor on the matter and received an apology. Despite the governor's expression of regret, the incident increased Lee's concern that the governor did not trust him to run his own department.[24]

Betsy Warren Harrison, former special assistant to Secretary Lee at NRCD, blamed the troubles between Lee and Hunt on a group of staffers who were not too comfortable about an African American running their department. Harrison recalled that "many never worked for a black man"[25] and were not comfortable about that situation. According to Harrison, some of these employees would report NRCD problems directly to the governor's office instead of to the secretary. A few employees even alerted newspaper reporters about problems in the department that later became sensationalized scandals. Such an atmosphere made it hard for Lee to trust both his own employees and the governor's staff. [26]

Lee's firing of an NRCD official caused tension between the cabinet secretary and the governor's staff. In August 1978, Lee announced that he had fired Harvey M. Lincoln, the director of the state jobs program, because he failed to keep track of local spending of federal Comprehensive Employment and Training Administration (CETA) funds. After the firing, the NRCD secretary told Raleigh *News and Observer* reporter Ted Vaden that he could not tell the governor whether or not the state made any difference in training citizens for better jobs because his employees had allowed audits to pile up in Raleigh. "I can't tell you why it wasn't done," he said. "I've never gotten a satisfactory answer myself."[27] To improve the auditing, Lee moved the CETA program into his own office, where the NRCD secretary took a greater responsibility for monitoring the programs. Lee's public remarks about NRCD incompetence, his firing of a senior official, and reports of low morale among jobs program employees undercut Hunt's efforts to portray his administration as getting things done effectively.[28]

The lack of support in Lee's decision to fire Lincoln seemed apparent after the governor's top aide immediately hired the former NRCD official to work at another department. John Williams, head of the North Carolina Budget Division and Hunt's most influential advisor, hired Lincoln two days after Lee fired him. Williams even paid Lincoln a higher salary. "I was surprised," Lee told the press. "I didn't consider it a slap in the face. I was surprised."[29] Lee, however, truly did consider the hiring as a rebuke, and concluded that the governor and his top aides had lost trust in him.

Nothing proved this conclusion more than Governor Hunt's handling of the polychlorinated biphenyl (PCB) crisis. In the summer of 1978, tanker trucks dumped PCBs secretly on the side of two hundred miles of eastern state roads. Many residents became extremely concerned about possible lethal effects from the oily brown toxic waste near the highways. One observer said that "the wind could be blowing it to you and your eyes would sting, your nose would burn, and you'd be sick to your stomach."[30] When Secretary Lee learned about the spill, he called the governor's office while Hunt was on vacation. A gubernatorial aide told Lee, "You're Secretary of Natural Resources. That's why the governor put you there. It's your job to keep this away from him. Deal with it!"[31] That night, Lee discussed his plans to dispose of the PCBs on national television. After the governor watched the broadcast, he raced back to Raleigh, held a series of meetings and discussions about the matter, and eventually took the PCB matter away from the NRCD secretary. Hunt claimed that he made this decision to demonstrate his leadership during a public health crisis and motivate a stronger response from the state's public health agencies. The governor never criticized publicly Lee's management of the crisis. However, Hunt's decision further reinforced the secretary's belief that he did not have the governor's complete trust.[32]

After Hunt removed Lee from his responsibilities of PCB disposal, the secretary was alarmed to discover that the governor's office had selected a majority black county in which to dump the toxic soil. In the first week of the crisis, the governor announced plans to cover the affected areas with charcoal, remove grass and soil near the highways, and find a place to bury the toxic soil. He soon discovered, however, that it was difficult to find

Howard Lee, pictured here at a press conference on the 1978 PCB spill, tried very hard to be an effective secretary of Natural Resources and Community Development (NRCD). Lee's status as the first black cabinet secretary in North Carolina history gave him added media attention that may have hurt him at times. State auditors and reporters discovered wrongdoing by employees in his department and blamed Lee's mismanagement as the cause of the scandals. Lee stayed on as NRCD secretary into Hunt's second term despite an effort by the governor to put him into other positions. Feeling a lack of support by Hunt, Lee finally resigned in July 1981. (Courtesy of the *News and Observer*)

a location. After months went by with no removal, a Johnson County citizen put up signs on the roads saying, "PCB Cleanup — Hunt's Folly." The governor appealed to President Jimmy Carter for help, but the administration refused to declare the toxic waste location a disaster area. Hunt tried to find a waste site in another state and debated whether to treat the PCBs on the roadside. Finally, he decided on a 142-acre site that the Environmental Protection Agency approved in Warren County, a majority black population area. Angry black county officials tried to stop the removal with court injunctions, but the dumping of PCBs in Warren County finally occurred in the early 1980s. Although the Hunt administration denied any intention to harm black citizens, Lee claimed that his lack of participation in this decision only increased African American belief that Hunt had chosen the county so that he would not offend whites.[33]

The PCB matter caused Lee little public embarrassment. However, Lee received public criticism for granting Comprehensive Employment Training Administration funds to an eastern North Carolina job-training program that embezzled the money. In 1978 and 1979, NCRD auditors raised concerns about serious bookkeeping problems at the Eastern North Carolina Opportunities Center (ENC-OIC) in Roper, North Carolina. NRCD Internal Audit Division Director Benjamin Carroway demanded that Lee terminate CETA funds to the Roper Center. When Lee learned that the job-training center had replaced its top employees, however, he continued the federal funding. Eva Clayton concurred in his decisions, telling an NRCD official that it would be premature to judge the Roper Center incapable of rectifying a past management error.[34]

In the summer of 1979, a newspaper described the misuse of CETA funds by the Roper Center. *News and Observer* reporter Pat Stith wrote that the job-training program suffered from delinquent billings, infrequent budget control, no documentation for expenditures, and a lack of equipment. After reading these reports, Hunt appointed a special investigator to study the matter, which led to the indictments of three former employees, including its former executive director. The governor defended Lee's error by saying that he was under great pressure to spend the federal funds to retrain unemployed people during a national recession. Yet, the CETA scandal still embarrassed Hunt. Although the embezzled funds remained a fraction of all NRCD expenditures, the spending looked bad to an administration that tried constantly to promote the positive public image of the governor.[35]

Lee received further criticism when auditors and the media revealed the misuse of CETA funds by North Carolina American Federation of Labor–Congress of Industrial Organizations President Wilbur Hobby, a political ally of Hunt and Lee. Since the 1940s, Hobby had helped progressive Democratic politicians while serving as a member of the Durham chapter of the Tobacco Workers International Union. As head of Voters for Better Government in the 1950s, he had united Durham's blacks, Duke University academics, and union members into a progressive urban coalition. He had supported civil rights in the 1950s despite being called a "nigger lover" by white union men, and briefly lost his union position because he had stood up for blacks. When racism in the state union had subsided in 1969, he had won election as president of the state's AFL-CIO chapter.[36]

Even before becoming the chapter's president, Hobby had served as a powerful ally to many progressive Democrats, including Jim Hunt, who repaid the favor by giving state government contracts to his printing company. According to Howard Lee, Hobby had made a career out of receiving grants from various state departments before he ever received money from NRCD in 1977. Thirteen years earlier, Bert Bennett had written a memo to a gubernatorial campaign headquarters declaring that Hobby wanted some printing work, and he had been "a good friend of ours and we might want to pay a little attention there."[37] Hobby had continued his profitable alliance with the Democrats into the 1970s, serving as the second vice president to the Durham County Democratic Executive Committee in 1968 and writing a strong pro-labor platform for the North Carolina Democratic Convention in 1972. Four years later, Hobby had developed strong ties to candidates Jim Hunt and Howard Lee. Before the Democratic primary, the state AFL-CIO had endorsed Hunt for governor and Lee for lieutenant governor. After Hunt had won the election and Lee had become NRCD secretary, Hobby expected a portion of the CETA money from his old friends.[38]

By August 1979, Hobby came under scrutiny from several people and organizations. That month, Pat Stith began a newspaper series questioning irregularities in CETA expenditures from Hobby's printing company, Precision Graphics. Also, State Auditor Henry Bridges charged that the company had misspent eighty percent of a $130,833 CETA contract to train keypunch operators. When NRCD auditor Ben Carroway visited Precision Graphics on August 29 to discuss the missing funds, Job-Training Director Morton Levi called him a liar and nearly hit him. Carroway left that meeting convinced that Hobby had misused the money. The labor leader claimed that an investigation would exonerate him of any wrongdoing. Federal investigators believed otherwise, charging Hobby and Levi in February 1981 with using false schemes to steal CETA funds.[39]

Despite continuing reports that embarrassed NRCD in the fall of 1979, Hunt refused to fire his embattled NRCD secretary. In September, ten NRCD officials said that they had resigned from the department to protest Lee's failure to push for strict air pollution standards for utilities companies. Although Hunt desired to have good relations with environmentalists, he shared the secretary's emphasis on industrial growth. Besides similar ideological beliefs, the governor retained Lee for political reasons. Hunt did not wish to alienate African Americans at a time when he ended his role in the Wilmington Ten Affair by commuting the sentence of Ben Chavis. He also realized that Lee had powerful progressive allies, including North Carolina Senator Ralph Scott, who told the governor that he was glad to see Hunt stand up for the cabinet official. Scott added, "I have the feeling that someone is out to get him, and I hope you will give him all the help you can. Howard has a very difficult job, and I really believe his honesty and integrity are above reproach."[40] In 1979 and 1980, the governor defended the NRCD secretary because of their old friendship, his belief in Lee's honesty, and his usefulness as a political supporter during his campaign for reelection.

In 1980, Lee tried to contain the political damage from the NRCD scandals. Hunt's Republican opponent I. Beverly Lake, Jr., ran advertisements portraying the CETA embezzlement as a political payback arranged by the untrustworthy quartet of Lee, Hunt, Clayton, and Hobby. Lake demanded that the governor fire Lee for implementing an unsavory scheme. During the televised gubernatorial debate in September, Lake launched an attack on Hunt's use of federal job-training funds to finance a political machine. That same week, a jury found the former director of the Roper Center guilty after the prosecutor described how embezzlers swindled federal funds because of the apathetic attitude of NRCD managers. Following the trial, Lee apologized for his department's sloppy work regarding the contracts and campaigned vigorously for Hunt's reelection. He worked hard in the latter effort because, he recalled, "I felt that I let him down."[41] Since Lee recognized that he had made mistakes at NRCD that embarrassed the governor, he wanted to help Hunt win as many votes as possible.

Yet, even as he tried to help Hunt politically, the investigation of Wilbur Hobby caused Lee to embarrass Hunt once again. In the fall of 1980, both the governor and the NRCD secretary turned against Wilbur Hobby, their former political ally, who refused to say what had happened to the missing funds. "Our people have gone through his records carefully and they are convinced much is owed by his firms," said the governor,[42] insisting that the state would subpoena all of Hobby's records to find out where the money went. As Governor Hunt presented the appearance of an impartial investigator, Lee requested that the United States Department of Labor review the matter instead of State Auditor Henry Bridges, who embarrassed NRCD every time that he audited the department. At first, the governor agreed to Lee's request, but when this decision appeared to be a way to avoid a state investigation, the governor changed his mind and allowed Bridges to handle the matter. Lee apologized to the governor for directing him the wrong way. Lee's decision added to the reasons why Hunt decided to ask his NRCD secretary to accept a different cabinet position in the second term.[43]

Shortly after Hunt's reelection, he met Lee at the governor's mansion and said, "Howard, it's time for us to make a change in NRCD. We need to find where we can use you."[44] Jim Hunt suggested that Lee become secretary of the Department of Correction, but Lee feared that the predominantly black prison population would look upon him as a friend, and therefore riot for better treatment. Rejecting that offer, Lee declared that he would remain at NRCD or he would leave the Hunt administration. He debated whether to resign like Eva Clayton, who left the department in

December 1980 because she also received negative publicity. Lee finally decided to fight for his job, calling friends, both black and white, to ask Hunt to retain him. Loyal allies from the black community phoned the governor and urged him to keep Lee in his position. Faced with the political need to appease his black constituency, Hunt reluctantly allowed Lee to stay at NRCD.[45]

Despite reappointment as secretary in January 1981, Lee decided to leave NRCD a few months later. He understood what happened to two other cabinet secretaries in whom the governor had lost confidence. That same January, Hunt had not reappointed Correction Secretary Amos Reed because he had made too many independent decisions. A few months later, the governor accepted the resignation of Tom Bradshaw, secretary of the Department of Transportation (DOT) and a loyal ally of Hunt, because of a scandal. In 1980, state investigators charged that DOT officials, without Bradshaw's knowledge, colluded with highway contractors to rig state bids. This embarrassing news came when the governor wanted to increase taxes to improve the state highway system. In early 1981, a few legislators told Hunt that they would not approve a tax increase unless the governor reorganized DOT and possibly removed the secretary. Realizing that his absence would aid the governor's tax plans, the DOT secretary resigned in May. If a loyal Hunt supporter like Bradshaw could be pressured to leave, Lee wandered how long he could survive in the cabinet.[46]

Lee suspected that several people wanted him out. In March 1981, Administration Secretary Joseph Grimsley, a loyal Hunt aide who had served as his campaign manager for three consecutive elections, told a reporter that he regretted that the governor had not appointed him as head of NRCD in the second term. Meanwhile, Democratic legislators announced plans to transfer important programs out of Lee's department. The NRCD secretary suspected that the governor's intention to run against United States Senator Jesse Helms in 1984 made him want to remove a controversial black member from his cabinet. "I began to feel, rightly or wrongly, that a strong message was being sent that I needed to get out, or I was going to end up so emasculated that I never had a prayer in politics," Lee recalled. "I knew if I stayed there, I would be scarred for the rest of my life."[47] He also believed that without the governor's confidence, he could no longer give effective leadership to NRCD. Frustrated, he wrote a letter of resignation to the governor and put it on his desk. When Lee read in the newspaper about his resignation, he knew that the governor had accepted it.[48]

Publicly, the governor expressed his regret about Lee's exit at a dinner honoring the secretary in July 1981. He told the predominantly black crowd that his critics tried to get at the governor by attacking Lee, and declared that "he has never let me down, and he has never given up the good fight."[49] He praised Lee's efforts for developing the plan to save the Chowan River, strengthening the marine fisheries program, and completing the African phase of the state zoo. Actually, Hunt believed that changes needed to be made to improve the morale at NRCD and he appointed Grimsley as secretary after Lee's departure. Asked about the resignations of Lee and Bradshaw, Hunt said in 1999, "Sometimes, they are inheriting the problems of the past, but you have to get them cleaned up. You have to find a way to get a new start. As I recall, that's what happened there."[50] As an ardent supporter of civil rights, he received no joy in removing the only African American from his cabinet, and tried to make it up to the black community two years later by appointing Henry Frye as the first black on the North Carolina Supreme Court, as well as making other black appointments.

Howard Lee struggled in the months following his exit from NRCD. He had no immediate job offers and he nearly declared bankruptcy. The federal trial of Wilbur Hobby in December 1981, which revealed NRCD failures, certainly did not help his employment prospects. It gave Lee no pleasure to learn that Hobby, who lost the state AFL-CIO presidency, faced health problems, and served jail time, suffered more in 1981 than he did. Despite revelations of NRCD mismanagement, Lee found jobs at the UNC School of Social Work, the National Child Welfare Leadership Center, and private business. Although Lee lost a Democratic primary race for United States Congress in 1984, he succeeded politically in the 1990s by winning elections to the North Carolina Senate. In his new role, Lee repaired his battered reputation from the NRCD experience by promoting the education and economic development agenda of Governor Hunt, then serving his third and fourth terms. The senator said that he harbored no personal bitterness at the man who once sought his removal; he understood the political motivation behind that decision.[51]

Howard Nathaniel Lee faced many challenges during his tenure as Governor James Baxter Hunt's secretary of Natural Resources and Community Development. Hunt certainly wanted the black official to succeed, since his success at NRCD would reflect well on his own administration and make it easy to appreciate a key member of his African American constituency. Indeed, Lee accomplished some favorable goals, including the completion of the African phase of the North Carolina zoo, developing the Mountain to Sea trail and the Housing Finance Agency, challenging racism in water projects, and expanding the coastal area management program. Lee accomplished these goals as head of a department that included a few

employees who did not like to be run by a black person and who sometimes undermined their own boss by describing NRCD troubles to the
governor's staff or to the press. There were whites, within NRCD and out
side the department, who wanted him to fail. Hunt, however, wanted Lee
to succeed. When the NRCD's problems became too embarrassing for the
administration, the governor tried to find another role for the secretary.
Faced with resistance to this idea by Lee's allies, Hunt retained Lee as
NRCD secretary in the second term. Yet, Lee quit anyway a few months
after reappointment when he understood that the governor had lost
confidence in him. Governor Jim Hunt made history by appointing
Howard Lee as the first black cabinet secretary of North Carolina, but then
he discovered that the harder job for a progressive governor with a black
constituency was to remove him.

14

The Reelection of Jim Hunt, 1980: A Progressive Wins in a Conservative Year

North Carolina Governor Jim Hunt won reelection in 1980 despite serious efforts by the state's social conservatives to defeat him. Besides his progressive constituency, he attracted economic conservatives because of his tax cut and industrial recruitment, and won anti-crime conservatives because of his support of the death penalty. Strongly moral conservatives in the state also admired his adherence to faith and family values. Despite these qualities, Hunt still did not satisfy the increasing number of social conservatives and fundamentalists who believed that the young governor, because of his association with the national Democratic party, was a closet liberal who favored feminism, gay rights, abortion, and secular education. The rising conservative tide even influenced Robert Scott, Hunt's challenger in the 1980 Democratic gubernatorial primary, to back away from a progressive assault on the governor's policies and instead rely on the difficult strategy of appealing to both liberals and the governor's conservative opponents. Hunt easily defeated Scott and then faced Republican gubernatorial candidate I. Beverly Lake, Jr., in the general election. Financed by United States Senator Jesse Helms's powerful campaign organization and backed by fundamentalist ministers, Lake nevertheless lost the election because of Hunt's popularity among mainstream Democrats, his powerful status as an incumbent, and by the financing provided by a business community which favored the governor's economic policies.

Most observers believed that Jim Hunt would run for reelection following the passage of the constitutional amendment allowing gubernatorial

James Baxter Hunt, Jr., had high popularity ratings when Hugh Morton took this photo of him in 1979. Always trying to take a middle position between the ideological approaches of ardent progressives and ultraconservatives, he constantly defended himself against charges that he straddled the fence on the issues. In his first term, most Tar Heels accepted his efforts on crime prevention, education, and industrial recruitment. (Courtesy of the North Carolina Office of Archives and History)

succession in 1977. After the General Assembly enacted most of his programs that year, the governor won a high approval rating that reached sixty-four percent in November 1978. The majority of voters perceived Hunt as strong on crime, dedicated to education, and devoted to industrial recruitment. They praised the governor as a Christian family man dedicated to the highest personal values. Even Jesse Helms, the leader of conservative Tar Heel Republicans, did not dare to criticize the popular governor. By the end of 1978, Hunt was the most popular politician in the state.[1]

The governor, who usually took centrist positions, discovered that the political ground had shifted toward economic conservatism in the 1978 elections. Two years earlier, as a gubernatorial candidate, Hunt had promised not to raise taxes, and then proceeded to implement his 1977 reforms without increasing new revenues. In January 1978, he had told a reporter that he felt boxed in by that promise because he could not reform the state tax system without raising taxes. Such informal talk ended after North Carolina legislators caught "tax cut fever" and demanded the reductions of state revenues. At first, the governor refused to cut taxes, but he promised to introduce a tax rebate plan in the next legislative session. After the November 1978 elections brought more conservatives into the legislature that applauded Proposition 13, an initiative that cut public spending drastically in California, the ambitious governor accepted public opinion and backed a tax cut.[2]

In addition to this measure, Hunt trimmed state services and announced a hiring freeze in state government proving himself attuned to the "Proposition 13" mood. The governor's proposed $78.2 million revenue reduction package included a decrease of the business inventory tax and an increase in personal income tax exemptions. Hunt said that his budget provided a "reasonable amount of tax relief for our hard-pressed citizens without taking money out of one of the public's pockets to put it in another."[3] Even after the governor provided $40 million of spending for African American universities to appease the United States Department of Health, Education and Welfare (HEW), the final budget still contained a significant tax cut.[4]

If Hunt acted conservatively in tax matters, he still promoted a progressive education agenda. In his 1979 State of the State Address, he called

Governor Jim Hunt in November 1978. Although his Democratic coalition lost seats in the 1978 congressional elections, Hunt remained popular throughout North Carolina. (Courtesy of the North Carolina Office of Archives and History)

for expanding remedial education of needy students, adding vocational education positions, raising substitute teacher pay, and funding the community colleges and the university system adequately. He proposed the creation of the North Carolina School of Science and Mathematics, a residential high school dedicated to creating future engineers and scientists for the emerging information economy. Hunt successfully passed his educational priorities that session.[5]

Also, Governor Hunt introduced successfully a child care initiative in 1979. Believing that the raising of children determined their future success, he proposed a childhood nurturing program called "Raising a New Generation." The plan established a statewide committee that coordinated existing health care and education services to young children. A state pamphlet lauding the program declared that Hunt wanted to "coordinate resources to literally raise up new generations, human beings free of physical, mental, social, and economic handicaps."[6] The governor hoped that the public would view the program as a way to improve children's health so that they could be well enough to read and write. Instead, religious fundamentalists criticized the act as an attempt to replace families with government, and Hunt spent much time defending the program from unwarranted charges.[7]

Also in the 1979 session, Hunt once again tried to pass the Equal Rights Amendment, which declared that equality of rights under the law would not be denied or abridged by the United States or by any state on account of sex. Two years earlier, the governor had failed to pass ERA despite strenuous lobbying. Following that failure, North Carolina feminists tried to defeat anti–ERA legislators in 1978, arguing that they needed to approach the governor from a "position of strength."[8] Despite help from Carter White House aide Sarah Weddington, the efforts of the North Carolinians United for ERA (NCUERA) failed miserably and three new anti–ERA legislators joined the state senate. The conservative trend caused ERA supporters to worry that Hunt would retreat from his strong commitment to the amendment. Weddington urged that President Carter pressure the governor to fight hard for the ERA to help the president ratify the amendment and win the women's vote in 1980. "The situation in North Carolina has reached a critical point," she said. "Governor Hunt does not understand that the ERA can be helpful to you. Without North Carolina, we will have a much more difficult time with Florida and Oklahoma."[9] Another White House aide, Rosalina Whelon, said that a strong fight for ERA would aid the governor's national ambition by presenting him in a vocal, visible role as a spokesman for the progressive South.[10]

Despite the pressure from the feminists, Hunt understood the slim chances of ERA passage in a conservative General Assembly. In early 1979, he worked with former North Carolina First Lady Jessie Rae Scott and Senate President Pro-tem Craig Lawing to produce swing votes for the amendment. After the pro–ERA leaders decided to introduce a ratification bill in the Senate, Hunt urged NCUERA to flood the mails with popular support for ERA. However, the anti–ERA opposition brought rural conservatives wearing STOP ERA buttons and carrying Bibles to Raleigh on chilly February mornings. These anti–ERA crowds encouraged many legislators not to ratify the amendment. Governor Hunt feared that the ERA battle would polarize the senate so badly that the contest would affect other legislation, and therefore accepted the decision by pro–ERA senators to kill a ratification bill in committee.[11]

The retreat of Hunt on ERA angered feminists who accused him of not delivering the amendment for political reasons. They claimed that the governor failed to understand the importance of ERA and accused Hunt's female appointees of doing nothing to help them. Despite threats to withdraw support from Hunt, the NCUERA remained loyal to the governor because the anti–ERA forces had grown stronger, and the organization needed Hunt's help to pass the amendment in his expected second term. Unfortunately for the feminists, the final attempt to pass ERA in North Carolina failed in 1982 despite the governor's support.[12]

Hunt created more controversy in the 1979 legislative session by limiting a pay raise to state employees and teachers. A loyal supporter of President Carter, the governor endorsed the administration's austerity plan that mandated no wage increases over 5.5 per cent as a way to reduce inflation. Although the legislature approved Hunt's requested five per cent pay raise, they added an extra $200 bonus to each teacher and state employee. The governor condemned this effort endorsed by Senate President Jimmy Green and House Speaker Carl Stewart, who both sought votes for their lieutenant gubernatorial campaigns in 1980. North Carolina teachers, opposing the governor's resistance to a higher pay increase, marched on the legislature in July 1979 with signs saying "Dump Hunt." The governor held his ground until President Carter discontinued his own austerity plan by endorsing a seven per cent raise for federal employees in November 1979. Although Hunt said that the president "should have stuck by his fight against inflation,"[13] the governor proposed his own increase in salaries for North Carolina teachers and employees. Because the legislature accepted his proposal, Hunt entered the reelection campaign of 1980 with the backing of these interest groups.[14]

In 1979, Governor Hunt prepared privately to run for reelection. If he seemed preoccupied with education, industrial recruitment, or his oldest daughter Rebecca's wedding that summer, he still planned a campaign. In August, he told 1,500 people at his hometown's "Jim Hunt Appreciation Day" that he was still debating whether to run for governor again. Three months later, Hunt announced his decision. He created an exploratory committee of loyal followers to decide the merits of a second term that, to no one's surprise, recommended that he run for the top office. By the end of 1979, the governor raised $600,000, selected David Sawyer as his television consultant, and rehired Administration Secretary Joseph Grimsley as his campaign manager. The Hunt campaign then selected county chairpersons that had the responsibility of raising money from all one hundred counties of North Carolina. To get the campaign funds, the chairpersons blended grassroots campaigning techniques, such as picnics and concerts, with the solicitations of loyal business contributors. By early 1980, Hunt prepared his reelection team for a victorious run in the spring and fall.[15]

Before the campaign began, Governor Hunt dealt with a violent incident between radical groups that marred the state's reputation. In early November 1979, a group of Nazis and Ku Klux Klan fired upon a Communist rally in Greensboro and killed five people. The victims belonged to the Workers Viewpoint Organization, a small militant Communist sect that had scheduled a "Death to the Klan" rally in a low income black neighborhood. Angry Klansman and Nazis from nearby rural areas decided to challenge them violently. At the time of the shooting, the governor was in Asia on an industrial recruitment trip. Feeling no need to rush home, Jim Hunt allowed Crime Control and Public Safety Secretary Burley Mitchell to protect a funeral march for the murdered activists with five hundred National Guardsmen and four hundred policemen.[16]

The governor returned to the state and discovered that people were divided over their attitudes toward the murdered Communists. He heard from a few conservatives like a Columbus man who said that "Jew Marxist groups" had "aggravated the Klan to take the action that they did."[17] A few Tar Heels argued for the abolition of the Communist party in the United States, leading Hunt to reply that even these radicals had freedoms under the Constitution. Mainly, he heard from critics who said that the incident once again proved the falsity of North Carolina's progressive image. One man declared that the governor's failure to pardon the Wilmington Ten had motivated racists to freely attack blacks and leftist whites. Ramon Leganeche of Seattle said that Jim Hunt left the enforcement of civil rights in the state to rightwing crackpots. On the eve of his reelection campaign, the governor once again dealt with a troubling racial affair that damaged the state's reputation.[18]

Hunt defended the state's progressive record, blamed the Greensboro tragedy on the failure of law enforcement to infiltrate radical groups, and asked the State Bureau of Investigation (SBI) to spy on subversive organizations. Hunt's tough rhetoric appeased many voters, even if he displeased the North Carolina Attorney General, the American Civil Liberties Union (ACLU), the Ku Klux Klan, and the Communists. Although the Ku Klux Klan disliked Hunt because of his racial liberalism, the Communists despised the governor because of the absurd belief that he allied secretly with the racist Klan and the Federal Bureau of Investigation (FBI) to execute the leadership of their party. They launched an unsuccessful civil suit against eighty-eight defendants, including Governor Hunt. In the summer of 1980, the Communists ransacked Hunt's reelection headquarters in Raleigh. At the 1980 Democratic National Convention in New York City, the North Carolina governor received extra security because of the leftist threat. The most dramatic incident occurred at a press conference on July 23 when party member Nelson N. Johnson heckled the governor with spirited epithets. "You're nothing but a murderer," Johnson shouted at Hunt. "You're nothing but a conspirator. You're a nothing but a sham and a liar."[19] After the governor asked repeatedly for the Communist to sit down, and told Johnson that he fortunately lived in a country with freedom of speech, the secret service escorted the heckler out of the press conference. The governor took abuse from the Communists stoically. "Please covenant with me to pray for these persons," he wrote to a minister. "I do want them to be a positive part of this great democracy which grants so much privileges to its citizens."[20] Of course, the display of Tar Heel extremist groups hatred did not hurt him politically.

As Jim Hunt considered a campaign for reelection, he worried about a challenge from Lieutenant Governor Jimmy Green. For three years, many political observers wandered if the conservative politician would act upon his animosity toward Hunt and run against him in 1980. Following struggles over policy and appointments in the 1977 session, the two politicians tried awkwardly to work together. Hunt broke the tension by inviting Green on foreign trips to recruit industry and by granting favors to Green's political allies. Despite these overtures, some of Green's friends, including Archie Johnson, liked his chances of defeating Hunt. Johnson argued that the lieutenant governor could defeat the governor since "Jimmy Green is a conservative and the country is turning conservative."[21] In early 1979, Green criticized Hunt for achieving too much power and for trying to establish a political dynasty in North Carolina. Briefly flirting with a conservative Republican candidacy for governor aided by Jesse Helms's political organization, Green retreated from that idea after the polls revealed that Hunt would defeat him no matter what party he belonged to. Instead, he ran successfully for reelection as lieutenant governor in 1980.[22]

Other possible Democratic contenders also considered Hunt's popularity and dropped out of the race. Attorney General Rufus Edmisten, ambitious for higher office since he had served as an aide to United States Senator Sam Erwin in the Watergate hearings, pondered a candidacy for governor. He criticized Hunt for transferring power from the state Justice Department to the newly created Department of Crime Control and Public Safety, and accused Hunt of prioritizing education and health over the prevention of rape and murder. Like the lieutenant governor, Edmisten decided eventually not to challenge Hunt's powerful organization and waited until 1984 to run for governor. Insurance Commissioner John Ingram also disliked Hunt, believing that the governor cooperated with conservative legislators in 1977 to remove his power to challenge insurance companies. He also believed that Hunt could have helped him more effectively with his unsuccessful 1978 candidacy against Jesse Helms. After brief consideration for the position, Ingram realized that he could not defeat Hunt and decided not to run against the governor.[23]

One prominent North Carolina Democrat decided to take on the challenge in 1979, even though a year earlier, former Governor Robert Scott seemed to be the unlikeliest candidate to run against Governor Hunt. Their relatives had personal connections dating back to the 1910s, when Bob's father Kerr had roomed with Jim Hunt's maternal uncle, Clarence Brame, at North Carolina State College. Thirty years later, the Hunts had helped North Carolina Agricultural Secretary Kerr Scott win the 1948 Democratic gubernatorial primary as well as the general election. After Governor Scott had appointed Jimmy's mother Elsie to the state health commission, and his state employees had paved a gravel road near the Hunt tobacco farm as part of the rural road construction program, the family bonds strengthened. The Scotts and Hunts had attended gatherings where Robert met young Jimmy. The Hunts had backed Kerr Scott's successful campaign for United States Senator in 1954, mourned his death at a Haw River funeral in 1958, and supported his son Robert's successful campaigns for lieutenant governor in 1964 and governor in 1968. To return the favor for his support, Governor Scott had appointed Hunt as chairman of a North Carolina Democratic Party Study Commission, giving the young Wilson attorney his first statewide publicity. In 1971, Robert's uncle, North Carolina Senator Ralph Scott, had backed Jim Hunt's successful campaign for lieutenant governor. In that position, Hunt had appointed Ralph Scott as chairman of the powerful Senate Appropriations Committee. Four years later, Ralph Scott had served in the 1976 Jim Hunt for Governor campaign while his nephew Robert had stayed out of the race. He had announced, "I will not run against Jim Hunt. His background and philosophy coincide with mine and I think he's done a great job. I wouldn't have any reason to run against Jim."[24] In 1976, Robert Scott had thought of Hunt as carrying on his family's progressive legacy.

Events in early 1979 strained the relationship between Bob Scott and the governor. Three years earlier, Hunt had helped Scott obtain a policy-making position in the Carter administration. After Hunt had lobbied President-elect Carter for a federal position for Robert Scott, the president had selected the former governor as co-chairman of the Appalachian Regional Commission (ARC) in May 1977. After getting this position, Scott had discovered that he did not like the work in Washington and hated the long weekly commute to his farm in North Carolina. By early 1979, he desired the vacant presidency of the North Carolina community college system. However, the North Carolina Board of Education, chaired by Hunt's political ally David Bruton, wanted to hire Larry Blake, a college president of a Canadian university. Although Hunt asked Bruton to consider Scott for the position, the board voted 10 to 2 to approve Blake. Scott complained that the governor failed him by not forcefully demanding his appointment, adding, "If you're going to be governor, then govern."[25] Although Hunt declared that the board had acted independently, Scott suspected that former Democratic Chairman Bert Bennett, Hunt's powerful political ally, had urged that the governor keep the former governor out of that post. Scott and Bennett had disliked each other since the Winston-Salem businessman had refused to use the political organization of Governor Terry Sanford to support the young man for governor in 1964. Scott feared that the governor might be serving as Bennett's instrument to end his political career.[26]

By the spring of 1979, Hunt realized that the Scotts had turned against him. During the legislative session, Robert Scott criticized Hunt for practicing the politics of retrenchment instead of backing more funds for education and highways. The former governor feared that Hunt abandoned his progressive base to win conservative votes. His uncle Ralph Scott agreed, declaring, "I've about decided that Hunt's not as progressive as I used to think."[27] Fearing loss of political support by the Scotts, the Hunt administration gave Robert's wife Jessie Rae a job in the Department of Human Resources. Although the governor's aides insisted that she got the job because of merit, Hunt apparently desired that the hiring would repair the rift between the governor and the state's most prominent political family.[28]

Although the Hunt administration gave Scott's wife a job, he still considered a race for governor. He left a $52,000-a-year position as ARC Chairman in July 1979 and started a campaign office three months later. Although Scott later claimed that he ran for governor to test the power of incumbency, he clearly missed being the state's top elected official. He also knew that he could find supporters among those Democrats who did not get choice appointments from Hunt, including the governor's former law partner, Russell Kirby. He also realized that several groups, including teachers and state employees, had gripes against the governor. With mild confidence, Scott announced his candidacy in October 1979. He understood that Jim Hunt led him by forty percent in state polls, yet he planned to get his vote "off the streets and back at the branch heads like my father did. It's going to be uphill all the way."[29] Despite losing several of his former aides to Governor Hunt, Scott hoped to imitate his father's 1948 upset.[30]

Faced with an uphill challenge, he ruled out strategies that worked well for the Scotts in the past. He could no longer count solely on the state's decreasing agrarian population. The candidate also realized that progressive blacks and whites still followed Governor Hunt despite his economic retrenchment and his controversial decision not to pardon the Wilmington Ten. "We'll match our progressive record against Scott's any day," said a Hunt Democrat.[31] Scott then sought to appeal to nearly everyone who disliked the governor. To the fundamentalists, he declared that Hunt's "New Generation" plan gave too much power over raising families to the state government. To anti-nuclear activists upset by the 1979 accident at Three Mile Island, he promised not to build dangerous nuclear power plants in North Carolina. To the less affluent, he criticized the "Jimmy Hunt School for Science and Math" as an elitist center that pulled the best students from North Carolina classrooms. To economic conservatives, he described Hunt's hiring of reading aides as a mere jobs program. Because Scott appealed to a mixed constituency, the *News and Observer* declared that he did not voice a clear, compelling justification to defeat the governor.[32]

A series of scandals in late 1979 and 1980 encouraged Scott to criticize Jim Hunt for running a large political machine concerned only with money and power. In the fall of 1979, investigations revealed that the Department of Natural Resources and Community Development awarded federal funds to a company run by Hunt's loyal union ally Wilbur Hobby that embezzled the money. In February 1980, reports surfaced that Alcoholic Law Enforcement agent Mather H. Slaughter compiled political profiles of county sheriffs and submitted them to the governor's office as a way of examining the loyalty of these officials toward the administration. Slaughter also criticized the political loyalty of a civil preparedness division director who later got fired from that position. Hunt apologized for Slaughter's activity, but insisted that no one in his administration was removed for political reasons. Later that year, investigators revealed that contractors and employees of the Department of Transportation rigged state bids on highway contracts. These events encouraged Scott to charge that the governor operated a political machine that often practiced corruption. He even claimed that Hunt's involvement in the Slaughter matter "could contain the seeds of impeachment."[33]

Once a loyal advocate, Scott accused Hunt in 1980 of the worse of political crimes. Most voters ignored the charges, refusing to connect the morally abstentious Presbyterian governor with sordid political practices. Hunt's refusal to respond negatively also added to his allure among Democrats. In May 1980, the governor defeated Robert Scott in every county in the state. Bert Bennett, who had assisted Hunt's reelection efforts, recalled that "we couldn't have found a weaker candidate if we had to get one."[34] Scott later said that he ran in 1980 to test the power of an incumbent governor, and "I sure found out!"[35] Afterwards, Scott congratulated Hunt and said that he would work to re-elect the governor. In his second term, Hunt forgave Scott for the bitter campaign and healed the wounds with the prominent political family by finally appointing him president of the North Carolina community college system in 1984.[36]

After the primaries, Hunt faced his first strong challenge from the National Congressional Club, a conservative organization that had increased its political influence since the mid-1970s. Created to pay off the campaign debt of Jesse Helms in 1973, the organization, led by conservative activists Thomas Ellis and Carter Wrenn, discovered the effectiveness of direct-mail fundraising techniques. The Congressional Club's letters raised millions from Americans who learned that Senator Helms needed their help against Ted Kennedy, George McGovern, radical feminists, militant blacks, homosexuals, isolationists, and liberals devoted to forced busing, abortion on demand, socialistic government, the "give-away" of the Panama Canal, and a weak military. Believing themselves more conservative than Republican, the organization's leaders briefly considered the creation of a third party in 1975 until their favorite presidential candidate, Ronald Reagan, refused to leave the GOP. In 1976, the Congressional Club achieved a great victory by helping Reagan win the North Carolina Republican primary against President Gerald Ford. The victory revived Reagan's sagging political fortunes, began the decline of Governor Jim Holshouser's control of the state GOP, and gave the Congressional Club more influence over the North Carolina Republican party. After Helms won reelection in 1978, Wrenn and Ellis sensed an approaching conservative revolution that would reverse the liberal trend of previous decades. In the 1980 elections, they concentrated on three targets— President Jimmy Carter, United States Senator Robert Morgan of North Carolina, and Governor Jim Hunt.[37]

The National Congressional Club allied with fundamentalist ministers who considered Governor Hunt an enemy of social conservatism. They did not appreciate the governor's support of ERA, a measure that they believed would destroy the family. Although they respected Hunt's strong personal moral behavior, they worried about his alliances with Democrats who favored gay rights and state-funded abortions. They especially condemned Hunt's New Generation Act as an attempt to replace the family with state government, criticizing a statement in the "Raising a New Generation" blue book which said, "Sex education and contraceptives should be available to all sexually active persons regardless of age."[38] Although the governor said that he did not agree with the statement, the fundamentalists decided to take more aggressive steps to oppose him. The Reverend Daniel D. Carr said that he smelled a "humanist in the woodpile"[39] because the governor backed the New Generation plan. In November 1979, television evangelist Jerry Falwell of Lynchburg, Virginia, came to the Raleigh capital for a "freedom rally" and called on Christians to support the campaigns of conservative candidates, including I. Beverly Lake, Jr., Hunt's Republican opponent for governor. Kent Kelly of the Church for Life and Liberty went even further in opposing Hunt, claiming that the governor lied about his stands on abortion, the death penalty, liberalization of divorce, drugs, and liquor legislation. Hunt, who had won over religious conservatives in 1976 because of his moral demeanor, discovered that many fundamentalists had turned against him.[40]

Despite the support of politically active fundamentalist ministers, the National Congressional Club realized that they would have a difficult time defeating Hunt. Even Senator Helms, who maintained cordial relations with Hunt through letters and aid to the state Commerce Department, refused to criticize the governor during his senate reelection campaign in 1978. Carter Wrenn realized that only an alliance of conservative Democrats and Republicans could defeat the popular governor in 1980. The National Congressional Club needed a candidate who could unite the conservative Democrats of eastern North Carolina with traditional Republicans in the western part of the state. Lieutenant Governor Jimmy Green appeared to be the perfect candidate, but he refused to run against Hunt. However, they soon discovered Democratic State Senator I. Beverly Lake, Jr., who agreed in 1979 to switch parties and run for governor on the Republican ticket.[41]

As the son of the prominent eastern North Carolina judge, Lake belonged to the conservative Democratic faction that young Jim Hunt had challenged in the 1960s. A graduate of Wake Forest law school, Lake had helped his father, Assistant Attorney General I. Beverly Lake, Sr., manage a 1960 gubernatorial campaign dedicated to keeping segregation in the public schools. At the same time, young Jimmy Hunt had backed progressive candidate Terry Sanford in a bitter contest where each candidate had accused the other of extremism. Sanford had defeated Lake, who had remained bitter for four years. In 1964, with the help of his son, Lake Sr., had challenged the Sanford organization's gubernatorial candidate, Richardson Preyer, whom Hunt had campaigned for. Lake Sr., had finished third and failed to make the Democratic primary runoff, but he had endorsed Dan Moore, Preyer's opponent, who had influenced his followers to oppose the progressive candidate. After Moore had defeated Preyer in the runoff and won election as governor, he appointed Lake, Sr., chief justice of the North Carolina Supreme Court. This time, Hunt had felt embittered, and he did not applaud this political payoff.[42]

However, in the early 1970s, as Hunt expanded his political coalition, he had become friendly to the Lakes, including the son who had followed his father's career path by becoming an assistant attorney general investigating utility rate increases. The only public display of tension between the two men before 1979 occurred four years earlier, when Lake had criticized Lieutenant Governor Jim Hunt's Utility Commission reforms, causing Senator Wesley Webster to accuse the assistant attorney general of sabotaging Hunt politically. Despite this event, the two Democrats had campaigned together in 1976 to help Hunt become governor and Lake become a state senator. The next year, Senator Lake had sponsored some of Governor Hunt's anti-crime proposals. Despite opposition to Hunt's support for several progressive measures, Lake backed the governor's bills to revive the death penalty and to impose mandatory sentences. "We agreed on some things and disagreed amicably," Lake recalled years later.[43]

By 1979, Lake no longer could loyally support the governor. The North Carolina senator opposed the two-term amendment that allowed Hunt to run for a second term. The senator also opposed the ERA, which Hunt supported, because he believed that women's rights would occur naturally without an amendment that might create unintended consequences. Lake also rejected the governor's initiatives on education, opposing the secular approach of teaching children and the excessive administration of schools by bureaucracies in Raleigh.[44]

Prompted by the National Congressional Club's promises of funds in late 1979, Lake switched to the Republican party and announced his candidacy for governor. To improve his image, he shaved his mustache, causing Hunt to remark that the senator did not want to look like Thomas Dewey, the Republican whom President Harry Truman defeated in 1948. Lake made sure that he had the support of Senator Helms and former Governor Holshouser, who represented the moderate faction of the state GOP. He even had the silent approval of Lieutenant Governor Jimmy Green, who allowed Lake to remain chairman of the Senate Judiciary Committee in the Democratic legislature despite Hunt's demands for his ouster. The day of his announcement, Lake said that Governor Hunt "has courted and followed ultra-liberal leadership in Washington" and walked "down the path of swelling bureaucracy, burdensome regulations, and even higher spending."[45] The Republican candidate promised to bring true conservative leadership to Raleigh.

Despite the support of Republican politicians, Lake discovered that the National Congressional Club's fundraising apparatus could not overwhelm Jim Hunt easily in 1980. The Republican candidate believed that the Congressional Club would provide the funds to win as it had done with Jesse Helms in two United States Senate elections. He did not believe the Democratic accusation that the Helms organization used Lake simply to distract Hunt from aiding President Carter against Reagan in the national election. The National Congressional Club clearly wanted to defeat Hunt, a possible future rival of Senator Helms, but they had difficulty raising funds through direct mail because Helms's national constituency did not find much urgency in removing a North Carolina governor. Unlike President Carter or Senator Morgan, Hunt shared little blame for an alleged weakened military or national malaise. The Lake campaign also could not rely on conservative businessmen who planned to back Hunt because he was perceived as the certain winner.[46]

While Lake struggled to attract voters, Hunt appeared likely to win the general election. Voters accepted the image of a hardworking governor who had improved public education through reading aides and competency tests, successfully recruited higher-paying industries, and strengthened the state's efforts against criminals. As Hunt's county chairpersons solicited thousands of dollars for the governor's campaign, his media advisor, David Sawyer, waged a $300,000 television advertising blitz that stressed the candidate's family life, support for tobacco, opposition to crime, education program, and efforts to attract high-paying jobs to North Carolina. In one commercial, Hunt walked through a room of sophisticated gadgets. "Look closely at this silicon chip," said the governor, revealing an object in his hand. "I want to continue to take this future kind of technology and turn it into a future full of jobs in North Carolina."[47] Hunt presented himself as a successful governor who would improve the state further if given another four-year term.

The governor usually refrained from mentioning Lake, and tried to run a positive campaign without any personal attacks. If he mentioned his opposition, he declared that he ran against people who wanted to turn the clock back on reform. Only in one instance did his campaign turn personally negative. To attract African-American and progressive voters, Campaign Manager Joseph Grimsley decided to connect Lake Sr.'s, prosegregationist views of the 1960s with his son's conservative candidacy. He also wanted to challenge the charge made by religious fundamentalists that Lake represented the true moral choice. In August 1980, he offered information on Lake Sr.'s earlier segregationist views and the Republican candidate's divorce. Grimsley said that he put out this information because he did not want to be caught napping against further nasty attacks by the Congressional Club. Lake had already criticized Hunt for covert liberalism and political corruption. Yet, Hunt disapproved of Grimsley's action, and prevented further release of the information. For the remainder of the campaign, Hunt did not criticize his Republican opponent personally.[48]

By October, Lake believed the chance of victory against the incumbent North Carolina governor was nearly hopeless. Hunt had raised $2.4 million to Lake's $179,770, and he had hardly enough money for television advertisements. The National Congressional Club never raised enough money to help him. The state's major newspaper editors endorsed the governor and criticized Lake's campaign. "Governor Hunt was the sitting governor," Lake recalled. "He controlled the appointments. He had a vast political organization in place. He had contacts throughout in the business community. There was just no way anybody could raise any significant amount of money to run against him (successfully)."[49] Even the moderator of the televised debate between Lake and Hunt took the Democrat's side by rejecting the GOP candidate's cardboard pictures.

At that debate at Meredith College in Raleigh on September 8, 1980, Lake launched into negative attacks against Hunt. He accused the governor of running a "Soviet Union–like child care system,"[50] adding unnecessary bureaucracy by creating the Department of Crime Control and Public Safety, and using federal job training funds to finance his political machine. Hunt mostly ignored the barbs. "I'm really disappointed that Senator Lake is using these kinds of tactics," Hunt said. "I think it is better to talk about the real issues, such as jobs, education, reducing crime, and moving forward."[51] The debate provided little help for Lake's campaign after newspaper editorialists criticized his negative style and applauded Hunt's upbeat approach.

Lake realized that he could only win by attaching himself to the coattails of Republican presidential candidate Ronald Reagan. In the 1980 campaign, Hunt provided the assistance that the White House desired in the Tar Heel State, even declaring at a Democratic rally that Jimmy Carter was one of the greatest presidents in history. Lake believed that a majority of Tar Heels did not share that view, witnessed Carter slipping in North Carolina polls, and hoped for a miraculous victory that came from Reagan's coattails. No such miracle occurred. To be sure, North Carolina Republican successes were big. They carried the state for Reagan, won a congressional seat held by Hunt's former political mentor Richardson Preyer, ousted Hunt's former ally Ralph Scott from the North Carolina

Senate, and upset United States Senator Robert Morgan. Yet, they failed to defeat Hunt, a major goal. Carter Wrenn speculated that Reagan added about four percent of the vote to Lake, which was not enough to win, but enough to change the outcome for John East, the Republican candidate who defeated Morgan. Apparently, Tar Heel voters separated Carter's performance as president from Hunt's efforts as governor.[52]

On election night, Hunt achieved a landslide victory in North Carolina. The governor won sixty three percent of the voters and carried eighty seven of the state's one hundred counties. Hunt declared, "There is no question that the people of North Carolina have responded to positive appeals."[53] Lake won only thirty eight percent of the vote despite the success of Reagan and East. Political scientist Paul Luebke later wrote, "Hunt's crucial asset in the 1980 race was the breadth of his coalition, which made him invulnerable to serious attack in either the May gubernatorial primary or the November election."[54] The Raleigh *News and Observer* declared:

> Hunt got a remarkable vote of confidence from Tar Heels, who showed their interest in personal competency and demonstrated results in the governor's race. The governor made some beginnings on difficult problems in his first four years. He committed himself to improving reading and general educational quality in the public schools. He talked about the problems of low per capita income and poor distribution of income by economic development and diversification of jobs. He set about to give the impoverished, the sickly, and the neglected children in North Carolina a better chance at the good life with clear attention to their needs. Despite some miscues in his administration in handling things like the CETA [Comprehensive Employment Training Act] job training programs and some concern about the use of political patronage in state government, Hunt emerged from his first term virtually unblemished.[55]

News analysts wrote that the victory would give Governor Hunt a powerful platform for a possible 1984 challenge to Jesse Helms. The governor responded, "I have no thoughts at all regarding the future except to be the best governor I can be."[56] Yet, Hunt's supporters immediately talked about a "battle of the titans" between Helms and Hunt in 1984, and some even predicted that Governor Hunt would eventually be elected president of the United States.

Despite a rising conservative tide that peaked nationally in 1980, Governor James B. Hunt, Jr., won reelection by blending a North Carolina progressive agenda with some conservative measures. Sensing the political trend in 1978, Hunt adapted to the new national mood that condemned big government and demanded tax cuts. Hunt's conservatism alienated a

In this photo, Hunt addresses a crowd at his 1981 inauguration that began his second term. Hunt seemed to be the certain frontrunner for reelection in 1980 after pushing for a change in the North Carolina constitution to allow governors to run for a second term. However, former Governor Robert Scott challenged him in the Democratic primaries, despite his family's long connection with the Hunts. Hunt easily defeated Scott, and won another easy triumph in the general election against Republican candidate I. Beverly Lake, Jr. (Courtesy of the North Carolina Office of Archives and History)

few progressives, including former North Carolina Governor Robert Scott, who decided to run against the governor in 1980. However, Scott discovered that he could not win votes among the governor's solid constituency of African Americans, females, teachers, and state employees. Although each progressive group was never satisfied with the entirety of Hunt's decisions, they believed that supporting an incumbent governor who backed most of their positions was better than risking defeat by endorsing a new candidate. Without the Hunt progressives, Scott searched for votes among conservative Democrats, and thus gave his losing campaign a lack of focus.

The greatest threat to Governor Jim Hunt's victory was the social conservatives who had proven their electoral strength by electing Jesse Helms to two terms as United States Senator. Despite Hunt's fiscal conservatism, the social conservatives disapproved of the governor's support of the Equal

Rights Amendment, the right to abortion, and a state-managed child care system. Using the National Congressional Club as a financial base and supporting a former Democrat for governor, they discovered that the governor's political organization was too powerful to defeat. By citing his record on education, crime, utility reform, and industrial recruitment, the governor gained support from both middle-class Democrats and wealthy businessmen. An effective politician, Hunt could be conservative on fiscal and crime issues while still holding on to the progressives who favored civil rights, education bureaucracy, and high-wage jobs. Using his great political skills, the progressive governor was able to win reelection in 1980 despite the national conservative trend.

15

James B. Hunt, Jr., and the Evolution of North Carolina Progressivism, 1937–1980

James B. Hunt, Jr., clearly fits within the progressive tradition of North Carolina. Tar Heel progressivism emphasizes public education and improved transportation routes to recruit modern industries and to insure equal opportunity to its citizens. During Hunt's early political career in the 1970s, the Tar Heel progressive tradition evolved to accept the social equality of women and African Americans.

Hunt certainly fulfilled the traditions of the first North Carolina progressive generation of the 1830s and 1840s. Just as antebellum reformers sought to increase the electorate by enfranchising poor white men in the early nineteenth century, Hunt supported the vote for African Americans and college students in the 1960s and the 1970s. More than a century after Governor John Motley Morehead backed the creation of better roads, canals, and railroads, Hunt urged the development of more highways to unify the state's economy. The antebellum progressives had approved the first funds for public schools; in the 1970s, Hunt endorsed the creation of the first statewide kindergarten program, improved the salaries of teachers, and raised the standards of students.

Hunt also continued the traditions of the post–Civil War progressives. Like many of the Reconstruction-era Tar Heel Republicans, he accepted an agenda of public school education and measures aiding African Americans. Like the first generation of "New South" Democrats, Hunt favored efforts to recruit businesses into the state. Like the North Carolina Populists, he walked to achieve a state government supportive of the farmers.

Hunt, the Radical Republicans, and the populists shared the identical goal of black participation in government. However, Hunt lived during a time when this ideal was accepted by a majority of white North Carolinians.

Hunt also followed the example of progressive governors of the early twentieth century. He devoted himself to the public school system just like one of his predecessors, Charles Aycock, governor from 1901 to 1905. He expanded a state highway system that began during the administration of Governor Cameron Morrison in the 1920s, and reorganized state government to boost efficiency just like Governor O. Max Gardner did during the Great Depression. During his childhood in the 1940s and early 1950s, Jimmy Hunt accepted the agrarian progressivism of North Carolina Governor Kerr Scott, who backed paved roads and electricity in rural towns. Hunt never forgot Scott's deeds, emulating the "Squire of Haw River" during his own efforts to expand rural transportation routes in the 1970s.

Hunt also accepted many goals of North Carolina Governor Luther Hodges, a former businessman who emphasized industrial recruitment in the 1950s. Hodges pushed for the creation of the Research Triangle Park that led to the first computer firms locating in the state. After the 1954 *Brown vs. Board of Education of Topeka, Kansas* decision, Hodges maintained the state's progressive image by tolerating token integration in a few urban schools. Hunt became more racially liberal than Hodges during his college years, and he continued Hodges's effort to attract high-wage industries to the Research Triangle.

Hunt admired Hodges's predecessor, North Carolina Governor Terry Sanford, for improving education and race relations in the early 1960s. Sanford clearly fitted the progressive tradition since he backed better public schools and the improvement of the community college system. As a Tar Heel progressive, Sanford did not want to alienate the business community, and therefore, he financed education programs with a food tax that fell mostly upon the poor. Understanding the need for better race relations to attract businesses, Sanford spoke strongly for the improved treatment of African Americans. Thus, he began the evolution of the Tar Heel progressive tradition that Hunt continued as governor.

In 1964, Jim Hunt learned the limits of the progressive tradition in North Carolina. Sanford's organization backed Richardson Preyer for governor, and Hunt campaigned enthusiastically for the candidate. However, an alliance of businessmen and rural segregationists, disliking Sanford's connections with liberal Democratic presidential administrations, defeated the progressive candidate in a Democratic primary runoff. Disgusted over Preyer's defeat, Hunt spent two years in Nepal before returning to Young

Democratic Club politics in North Carolina in 1966. He learned that association with liberals in the national Democratic party cost a progressive candidate votes in a socially conservative southern state like North Carolina. Understanding this important lesson, Jim Hunt avoided the perception of being a liberal.

As Hunt planned to enter North Carolina politics, the state Democratic party revealed signs of serious divisions between its progressive and conservative factions. By 1968, conservative white Democrats either drifted toward the Republicans or toward such white supremacist independents as former Alabama Governor George Wallace. At the same time, the Democratic party accepted an increasing number of African Americans, feminists, and young people between the ages of 18 and 21. Hunt desired to unite conservative Democrats with the newly empowered groups, and he studied politicians like Georgia Governor Jimmy Carter to discover how to build a unified political coalition that focused on industrial progress.

By revising the Tar Heel progressive agenda, Hunt created a victorious statewide coalition to win the lieutenant governor's race in 1972. Like earlier progressives, he campaigned for better education and improved economic growth. He favored racial and gender equality, backed college-age voting, and campaign finance reform. Yet, he also lauded strong law enforcement, accepted George Wallace as a fellow Democrat despite his racist rhetoric, and rejected higher taxes on the wealthy as a method to achieve state revenue. To win the election, Hunt avoided unpopular social matters such as public school busing to integrate the races or foreign policy issues such as the Vietnam War. Using this strategy, Hunt created a winning coalition of voters who shared the idea that the state must progress even if its people differed on specific ideological beliefs.

As lieutenant governor from 1973 to 1977, Hunt fulfilled the Tar Heel progressive tradition. He worked with Republican Governor James Holshouser to create the first statewide public kindergarten system and the first state management of the North Carolina coasts. He promoted a medical school at East Carolina University, which increased opportunities in medical education and appeased his eastern political base. The lieutenant governor favored an educational bureaucracy in Raleigh instead of letting local school boards control the policies. Hunt endorsed reform of the utility commission when electric rates skyrocketed in 1975 and 1976. He also successfully called for campaign finance reform and legislative ethics legislation in the wake of the Watergate scandals.

In 1976, Lieutenant Governor Jim Hunt practiced a pragmatic version of progressivism as he sought the state's highest executive office. He supported reading aides and competency tests, better regulation of the

utilities companies, civil rights for blacks and women, and the recruitment of higher-paying industries. Yet, he appeased the conservatives by
rejecting a tax increase, supporting capital punishment, and promoting
family values. Hunt's pragmatic progressivism helped him to avoid a
Democratic runoff and win a landslide victory in the general election.
Without abandoning the main ideals of Tar Heel progressivism, he used
his political skills and personal popularity to expand his political base.

By the end of Governor Jim Hunt's first year in office in 1977, he
fulfilled many promises to his progressive constituencies. The state General Assembly backed Hunt's efforts to establish reading aides, create tests
for grade school and high school students to evaluate their progress, and
raise the pay of teachers. Hunt also won their backing for the restructuring of the state commerce department so that the agency could recruit
higher-paying industries and encourage more tourism. The governor also
persuaded the legislature to create a public staff that argued on behalf of
the public in utility rate cases, and a new department to combat crime.
Hunt supported successful referenda that improved rural infrastructure
and increased North Carolina highways. The Tar Heel progressives
applauded his efforts. Therefore, they accepted Hunt's centralization of
state government, use of patronage for political supporters, and a constitutional amendment allowing the governor to run for a second term.

Jim Hunt alienated liberals during the Wilmington Ten Affair. Many
North Carolina blacks and white liberals urged him to pardon the mostly
African-American defendants, calling them political prisoners jailed
because of provincial racism. Instead, Hunt commuted the sentences of
the prisoners and praised the state officers who convicted them. He
repeated this act with the Charlotte Three in 1979. The supporters of the
so-called political prisoners condemned the governor as a mere politician
who simply wanted to attract white conservative voters. Actually, Hunt
made his decision because he accepted the guilt of the defendants, but he
believed that their sentences were too harsh. As a Tar Heel progressive,
Hunt desired to promote racial harmony to insure a stable business environment, and practiced this belief mildly by commuting the sentences of
the black defendants. Yet, the governor believed that his higher duty was
to make sure that the state punished the guilty, and therefore, he never par-
doned the African-American prisoners.

Governor Hunt revealed the differences between Tar Heel progressivism and modern liberalism in the struggle with United States Department of Health, Education, and Welfare Secretary Joseph Califano over
tobacco issues. Although traditional liberals helped to create the federal
tobacco program in the 1930s, a rising faction of modern liberals heeded

the 1964 United States Surgeon General's report linking cigarette use and lung cancer, and approved of a campaign warning about the health threat from tobacco smoking. In 1978 and 1979, Tar Heel progressives, sympathetic to the state's farmers, condemned Califano's aggressive anti-smoking program as an effort to destroy North Carolina's economy. Hunt, a tobacco farmer, led the charge against Califano to insure that the eastern tobacco farmers would not abandon the state's progressives for more conservative candidates like United States Senator Jesse Helms. Distancing himself from anti-tobacco liberals, the governor continued the strong alliance between North Carolina progressives and tobacco farmers that had lasted for more than a century.

Hunt and other Tar Heel progressives also challenged Califano's efforts to end the remaining vestiges of segregation in the North Carolina university system. A symbol of pride to white Tar Heel progressives, the universities became the subject of controversy because federal judges and federal bureaucrats in the 1970s brought attention to the de facto segregation that still existed within these institutions. Embarrassingly, white Tar Heel progressives admitted that traditionally white universities gained most from the state's spending on higher education. In 1979, Hunt proposed to end disparities by giving $40 million to traditionally black universities. Many Tar Heel blacks accepted Hunt's successful proposal since they wanted to preserve the racial identify of the previously all-black universities more than they desired to create a completely integrated system of higher education.

Governor James B. Hunt also revealed his North Carolina progressivism during his industrial recruitment campaign. He successfully promoted education to create the new industrial workforce, favored transportation projects to unify the state economy, and endorsed the building of rural infrastructure as a way to get businesses to invest in small towns. Hunt restructured the North Carolina Department of Commerce to attract new high-wage businesses that included microelectronics and biotechnology producers. He traveled to Chicago, Los Angeles, Beijing, Tel Aviv, Bonn, and Tokyo to bring factories and plants into the state. During this effort, he appeased most modern industrialists. Hence, in true Tar Heel progressive fashion, Hunt remained neutral on unionization and never pushed for higher taxes on the wealthy.

Despite his support for economic policies that appeased some conservatives, Governor Hunt sided with liberals by endorsing the inclusion of African Americans and women in top government positions. As a North Carolina progressive, Hunt believed that affirmative action provided stability among the races and the sexes, and encouraged a stable environment for business investment. In his first two terms, Governor Hunt appointed the first black cabinet secretary in North Carolina history, the first black state court of appeals justice, and the first black justice on the state supreme court. He also appointed women to lead the departments of Cultural Resources, Human Resources, and Administration. Fulfilling affirmative action guidelines, he appointed many blacks and women to lower levels of government as well. In the 1970s, high-level black and female appointees became progressive symbols of the Hunt administration, yet these officials became burdens when they made mistakes. For example, Human Resources Secretary Sarah Morrow and Natural Resources and Community Development Secretary Howard Lee received bad publicity from the press from mistakes made by subordinates and some critics faulted their management styles. Understanding the symbolism of high level racial and gender appointees, Jim Hunt was simply reluctant to remove them.

In 1980, Hunt used pragmatic progressivism again to win reelection as governor despite the southern trend toward the Republican party. The governor acknowledged a political climate of economic conservatism in 1979; therefore, he endorsed successfully a tax cut for North Carolina citizens and a job freeze in state government. Although many economic conservatives approved of Hunt's efforts, most social conservatives disdained the governor. They rejected Hunt's approval of the Equal Rights Amendment, a state-sponsored child care plan, and the state financing of abortions. Yet, Governor Hunt won so much support from the economically conservative business community that the social conservatives failed to recruit many followers for the governor's Republican opponent, I. Beverly Lake, Jr. This candidate failed to convince the public that the governor was a closet liberal at the same time that Ronald Reagan, a conservative GOP presidential nominee, carried the Tar Heel State and the nation.

Following his victory, Jim Hunt once again discovered the limits of North Carolina progressivism. In 1981, the governor, understanding the need for a tax increase to improve the state's crumbling highway system, encouraged the General Assembly to approve the only tax increase passed during one of his four terms as governor. Many businessmen who profited from the building of roads to aid their industries favored the tax increase. Despite this fact, the social conservatives used the tax increase to claim falsely that the governor was an economic liberal. Recognizing that the public had little understanding of the difference between Tar Heel progressivism and traditional liberalism, the National Congressional Club, an association linked with Senator Helms, began a media campaign placing Hunt in the same ideological spectrum as United States Senator Edward Kennedy and civil rights leader Jesse Jackson. Hunt, unconcerned about the personal attacks, announced his intention to run against Helms in 1984. To combat Hunt, Helms ran advertisements questioning the governor's stands on a variety of social and foreign policy issues, including the Martin Luther King holiday. The commercials usually ended with the question, "Where do you stand, Jim?" Hunt, who had won three consecutive elections as governor practicing pragmatic progressivism, discovered that Helms had successfully portrayed him as a fence-straddling politician and a covert liberal. In the general election, Helms ran commercials describing Governor Hunt as a "Mondale liberal," associating him with the 1984 Democratic presidential candidate, Walter Mondale, who was unpopular in North Carolina. Hunt defended himself eventually against the false charges, but he had fought back too late, discovered that Reagan's popularity in the state added to Helms's political strength, and consequently, he lost the election. Despite practicing caution in 1984, Hunt discovered even that moderate ties to liberals in the national Democratic party had cost him a victory.[1]

Hunt prospered as a corporate attorney for the eight years that Republican Governor Jim Martin ran the state government. The second GOP gubernatorial candidate to win election in the twentieth century, Martin opposed tax increases and urged the legislature to eliminate the inventory tax on businesses. Meanwhile, Hunt refrained from politics, refusing to run for the senate again. He watched quietly as progressives suffered further defeats. Martin won reelection in 1988, the North Carolina House removed progressive Speaker Liston Ramsey and replaced him with a conservative Democrat in 1989, and Harvey Gantt, a popular African-American candidate from Charlotte, lost to Jesse Helms in 1990. More disillusioning to Hunt that year, his wife Carolyn lost a school board election in Wilson County.

Jim Hunt returned to politics in 1992 with the backing of most of his old coalition, and began the first of two new terms with a mildly progressive agenda. He promoted successfully a "Smart Start" initiative that included the state's first child health screenings, day care subsidies, and parental education programs. He encouraged the legislature to pass high salary increases for teachers and state employees, environmental legislation against polluting hog farmers, and relief for easterners devastated by Hurricane Floyd in 1999. At the same time, he appeased Tar Heel conservatives by refraining from tax increases, supporting an expensive prison-building program, and working cordially with a Republican house of representatives that served from 1995 to 1999. Hunt continued to have support from African Americans, feminists, educators, and forward-looking industrialists because he supported a modest version of their progressive agenda.[2]

The combination of low taxation and high spending eventually led to budget problems by Hunt's final year as governor. A few months after he left office in 2001, the state's economy slid into a recession that troubled his predecessor, Mike Easley, and the North Carolina legislature during 2001 and 2002. Some commentators blamed Jim Hunt for the recession; others longed for his leadership during the economic crisis. This matter awaits a historian who can study the 1990s from a timely distance.

James B. Hunt, Jr., certainly fulfilled the Tar Heel progressive tradition. North Carolina conservatives often believed that he borrowed their ideas to win elections, yet he never accepted their calls for low-wage industries, rejection of statewide educational bureaucracy, and opposition to measures promoting racial and gender equality. Many of these conservatives called him a Tar Heel liberal, but he clearly was not one of the few North Carolinians who promoted organized labor, attacked tobacco use, opposed the death penalty, and favored higher taxes on the wealthy. As an elected official, Jim Hunt stood up for the North Carolina progressive tradition, which evolved in the 1960s and 1970s to accept new concepts of equality, but which continued to emphasize its traditional support for education, transportation, and industry.

Notes

Chapter 1

1. Herbert Snipes Turner, *The Dreamer: Archibald DeBow Murphey, 1777–1832* (Verona, Va.: McClure Printing Company, 1971), 12, 61.

2. *Ibid.*, 12–43.

3. Charles Sydnor, *Development of Southern Sectionalism, 1819–1848* (Baton Rouge: Louisiana State University Press, 1948), 82, 278.

4. *Ibid.*, 285–87.

5. Sydnor, *Sectionalism*, 835; Eugene D. Genovese, *The Slaveholders Dilemma: Freedom and Progress in Southern Conservative Thought, 1820–1860* (Columbia, SC: University of South Carolina Press, 1992), 20–21.

6. Donald G. Mathews and Jane Sherron De Hart, *Sex, Gender and the Politics of ERA* (New York: Oxford University Press, 1990), 4; Albert Coates, Testimony to ERA Committee in Raleigh, February 21, 1977, ERA File, State Archives, Division of Archives and History, Raleigh, North Carolina (hereinafter cited as NCDAH).

7. Burton Alva Konkle, *John Motley Morehead and The Development of North Carolina* (Philadelphia, PA: William J. Campbell, 1927), ii, 153–54, 187.

8. Thomas Jeffrey, "Internal Improvements and Political Parties in Antebellum North Carolina, 1836–1860," *North Carolina Historical Review* 55 (Spring 1978), 138.

9. Horace Raper, *William W. Holden: North Carolina's Political Enigma* (Chapel Hill, NC: University of North Carolina Press, 1985), 9–10, 16, 17.

10. Raper, *Holden*, 45–57; Glenn Tucker, *Zeb Vance: A Champion of Personal Freedom* (Indianapolis, IN: Bobbs-Merrill Company, 1965), 320–400.

11. V. O. Key, Jr., *Southern Politics in State and Nation* (Knoxville: University of Tennessee Press, 1949, reprinted 1984), 207–08.

12. Otto Olsen, "Albion Tourgee, Carpetbagger," *North Carolina Historical Review* 40 (Autumn 1963), 452–54.

13. Raper, *Holden*, 199–226.

14. Tucker, *Vance*, 461–62.

15. Elgiva D. Watson, "The Election Campaign of Governor Jarvis, 1880: A Study of the Issues," *North Carolina Historical Review* 48 (Summer 1971), 299.

16. Charles Sellers, "Walter Hines Page and the Spirit of the New South," *North Carolina Historical Review* 24 (October 1952), 487, 488; Alice Reagan, *North Carolina State University* (Ann Arbor, MI: Edwards Brothers, 1987), 14.

17. Melton McLaurin, "The Knights of Labor in North Carolina Politics," *North Carolina Historical Review* 49 (Summer 1972), 304–11.

18. Stuart Noblin, *Leonidas Polk: Agricultural Crusader* (Chapel Hill: University of North Carolina Press, 1951), xv–xviii.

19. Clement Eaton, "Edwin A. Alderman: Liberal of the New South," *North Carolina Historical Review* 23 (April 1946), 211–12; Frenise Logan, "The Movement in North Carolina to Establish a State Supported College for Negroes," *North Carolina Historical Review* 35 (July 1958), 169–70.

20. James L. Hunt, "The Making of a Populist: Marion Butler, Part One," *North Carolina Historical Review* 62 (Spring 1985), 69; James L. Hunt, "The Making of a Populist: Marion Butler, Part Two," *North Carolina Historical Review* 62 (Summer 1985), 201.

21. Allen W. Trelease, "The Fusion Legislatures of 1895 and 1897: A Roll Call Analysis of the North Carolina House of Representatives," *North Carolina Historical Review* 57 (July 1980), 280.

22. *Ibid.*

23. David S. Cecelski and Timonty Tysons, eds., *Democracy Betrayed: The Wilmington Riot of 1898 and Its Legacy* (Chapel Hill: University of North Carolina Press, 1998), 74–76; Oliver H. Orr, Jr., *Charles Brantley Aycock* (Chapel Hill: University of North Carolina Press, 1961), 137–38.

24. Jeffrey Crow, *A History of African Americans in North Carolina* (Raleigh: North Carolina Department of Archives and History, 1992), 119.

25. *Ibid.*

26. Orr, *Aycock*, 137–50; Edwin Alderman, "Charles Brantley Aycock: An Appreciation," *North Carolina History Review* 1 (July 1924), 249.

27. Mary Jo Jackson Bratton, "Cradled in Conflict: Origins of East Carolina University," *North Carolina History Review* 63 (January 1986), 82–83; Joseph F. Steelman, "Edward J. Justice: Profile of a Progressive Legislator, 1899–1913," *North Carolina History Review* 48 (April 1971), 151–52.

28. Bratton, "Cradled in Conflict," 90.

29. Arthur S. Link, "The Wilson Movement in North Carolina," *North Carolina Historical Review* 23 (October 1946), 488; Joseph F. Steelman, "The Progressive Democratic Convention of 1914 in North Carolina," *North Carolina History Review* 46 (Spring 1969), 99–101.

30. Mathews and De Hart, *ERA*, 9, 10; Elma C. Green, "Those Opposed: The Anti-Suffragists in North Carolina, 1900–1920," *North Carolina Historical Review* 67 (July 1990), 328; Kathryn L. Nosstrom, "'More Was Expected Of Us': The North Carolina League of Women's Voters and the Feminist Movement in the 1920s," *North Carolina Historical Review* 68 (July 1991), 319.

31. Robert E. Ireland, "Prison Reform, Road Building, and Southern Pro-

gressivism: Joseph Hyde Pratt and the Campaign for 'Good Roads and Good Men,'" *North Carolina Historical Review* 68 (April 1991), 136.

32. Douglas C. Adams, "A Progressive-Conservative Duel: The 1920 Democratic Gubernatorial Primaries in North Carolina," *North Carolina Historical Review* 55 (Winter 1978), 437.

33. Heriot Clarkson, "A Biographical Sketch of Cameron Morrison," *Letters and Papers of Cameron Morrison, Governor of North Carolina, 1921–25* (Raleigh: North Carolina Printers, 1927), xl–xlii; William Richardson, "Angus Wilton McLean," *Papers and Letters of Governor Angus Wilton McLean, 1925–29* (Raleigh: North Carolina Printers, 1931), xv.

34. Crow, *African Americans*, 134.

35. Suzanne Cameron Linder, "William Louis Poteat and the Evolution Controversy," *North Carolina Historical Review* 40 (Spring 1963), 143, 153.

36. Paul R. Clancy, *Just A Country Lawyer* (Bloomington, IN: Indiana University Press, 1974), 91–95.

37. Richard Watson, "Southern Democratic Primary: Simmons vs. Bailey in 1930," *North Carolina Historical Review* 42 (Spring 1965), 21–46.

38. Joseph Morrison, *Governor O. Max Gardner* (Chapel Hill: University of North Carolina Press, 1971), 58.

39. *Ibid.*, 61.

40. Jack Bass and Walter DeVries, *The Transformation of Southern Politics: Social Change and Political Consequences* (Athens: University of Georgia Press, 1995), 219.

Chapter 2

1. Betty Baker, *Henry Hunt: Family and Descendants of Virginia and North Carolina* (Raleigh: Betty Baker, March 1994), 1–2.

2. *Ibid.*, 2–5.

3. *Ibid.*, 33.

4. *Ibid.*, 49–52.

5. *Ibid.*, 38–40, 52–54.

6. *Ibid.*, 38–39, 54; James Baxter Hunt, Sr., interview by author, December 27, 1999.

7. Ruth J. Davis, *History of the County of Wilson* (Wilson: Published by author, 1985), 154; James B. Hunt, Jr., interview by author, December 14, 1999.

8. *Ibid.*, 339.

9. *Ibid.*, 258, 339.

10. Davis, *Wilson*, 94, 258; Interview with Five North Carolina Governors, WUNC-TV, April 1993, North Carolina Collection, Wilson Library, University of North Carolina at Chapel Hill (hereinafter cited as NCC-UNC).

11. Robert Hunt, interview by author, September 26, 1999; James B. Hunt, Jr., *North Carolina People*, interview by William Friday, December 31, 1999, WUNC-TV; 1934 *Agromeck*, 73, 310, North Carolina State University Archives, Raleigh (hereinafter cited as NCSU).

12. Hunt, Sr., interview by author; Anthony Badger, *Prosperity Road:*

Tobacco and the New Deal (Chapel Hill: University of North Carolina Press, 1980), 235.

13. "Jim Hunt: Man in Politics with a Longtime Ambition," *Durham Morning Herald*, December 5, 1974, NCC-UNC; Robert Hunt, interview by author, October 26, 1999.

14. Robert Hunt, interview by author; *Addresses and Public Papers of Jim Hunt, Governor of North Carolina, 1977–1981* (Raleigh, NC: North Carolina Department of Archives and History, 1982), 127.

15. "Rock Ridge Set Pattern for Wilson County School System," *Wilson Daily Times*, History Supplement, May 6, 1955, 5a; Ava Gardner, *Ava: My Story* (New York: Bantam Books, 1990), 25; Hunt, Jr., interview by author.

16. "Jim Hunt ... Our Man in Raleigh," *New East* 5 (November 12, 1973), 12, NCC-UNC.

17. Davis, *Wilson*, 155, 165; William D. Snider, *Helms and Hunt: The 1984 North Carolina Senate Race* (Chapel Hill: UNC Press, 1985), 11; Robert Hunt, interview by author.

18. Robert Hunt, James B. Hunt, Jr., and James B. Hunt, Sr., interviews by author; Davis, *Wilson*, 259; "Saratoga Grange Studies Wage Scales," *Wilson Daily Times,* January 13, 1949; "Grange Installs Its New Officers," *Wilson Daily Times*, January 22, 1949, 3; Randall Rothenberg, *The Neoliberals: The New American Politics* (New York: Simon & Schuster, 1984), 181.

19. "100 Most Influential North Carolinians," (Raleigh) *News and Observer*, August 22, 1999, 12i; Hunt, Jr. and Robert Hunt, interviews by author; Snider, *Hunt*, 11.

20. Robert Hunt and Hunt, Jr., interviews by author; Linda Barnes, "Rock Ridge Yearbook is Finished," *Wilson Daily Times,* March 4, 1955, 2.

21. Snider, *Hunt*, 12; Hunt, interview by Friday; Pearl Johnson Hunt, interview by author, December 27, 1999; Interview with Five North Carolina Governors, NCC-UNC.

22. Snider, *Hunt*, 12.

23. "Man in Politics," NCC-UNC.

24. James B. Hunt, Jr., "An Economic Analysis of Optimum Flue-Cured Tobacco Production Practices Under Acreage Control and Poundage Control" (M.A. thesis, Agricultural Economics, North Carolina State College, 1962), 20–25; Carl Henley, interview by author, January 25, 2000.

25. Robert Hunt and James B. Hunt, Sr., interviews by author; Snider, *Hunt*, 13.

26. Pearl Johnson Hunt, interview by author.

27. Rothenberg, *Neoliberals*, 181.

28. Robert Hunt, interview by author.

29. *Ibid.*

30. Henley, interview by author.

31. Hunt, Sr., interview by author.

32. V. O. Key, Jr., *Southern Politics in State and Nation* (Knoxville: University of Tennessee Press, 1949), 211.

33. Davis, *Wilson,* 235; Introduction, *Address and Papers of W. Kerr Scott, Governor of North Carolina, 1949–1953* (Raleigh: North Carolina Archives,

1955), xvi; Jimmy Hunt, "From Your Editor," *The Agriculturalist* (May 1988), 5.

34. Hunt, Jr., interview by author; Art Eisenstadt, "Hunt Hopes His Roads Lead to Washington," Newspaper Clippings, NCC-UNC.

35. "Wilsonians Join Road Delegation," *Wilson Daily Times*, Feb. 10, 1949, 1; Hunt, "From Your Editor," 5.

36. Hunt, "From Your Editor," 5.

37. Interview with Five North Carolina Governors, NCC-UNC.

38. Hunt, Jr., interview by author.

39. Lesley Wayne, "He's Been Looking Up For This For A Long Time," *News and Observer,* December 17, 1972, Newspaper Clippings, NCC-UNC; Hunt, Jr., interview by author.

40. "Man in Politics," NCC-UNC; Robert Scott, Haw River, to the author, Raleigh, January 13, 2000; "Mrs. J. B. Hunt Named To State Health Board," *Wilson Daily Times*, May 7, 1949, 1.

41. Dr. Hamilton W. Stevens, Wilson, to Governor Kerr Scott, Raleigh, May 20, 1949, 1949 Health Board File, North Carolina Governor Kerr Scott Papers, State Archives, Division of Archives and History, Raleigh (hereinafter cited as NCDAH).

42. Julian M. Pleasants and Augustus M. Burns, *Frank Porter Graham and the 1950 Senate Race in North Carolina* (Chapel Hill: UNC Press, 1990), 51–144, Snider, *Hunt*, 13.

43. Hunt, interview by Friday, WUNC-TV.

44. "Man in Politics," NCC-UNC.

45. Robert Hunt, interview by author.

46. "Man in Politics," NCC-UNC.

47. Ginny Carroll, "Politics Taught Hunt 'What Government Can Do For People,'" *News and Observer*, Newspaper Clippings, NCC-UNC.

48. "Man in Politics," NCC-UNC.

49. Davis, *Wilson*, 356–57; Hunt, Jr. and Hunt, Sr., interviews by author.

50. Davis, *Wilson*, 357; Hunt, Jr., interview by author; "Governor's Ag Teacher Dead at 82," *Wilson Daily Times*, March 9, 1982, 2a.

51. "Teacher," 2a; Carl Henley, interview by author.

52. "Rock Ridge Band Presents Concert," *Wilson Daily Times*, May 8, 1955, 3; Linda Barnes, "Only Three Weeks Until Vacations," *Wilson Daily Times*, May 13, 1955, 3; Linda Barnes, "Rock Ridge Beta Club Members Elect New President, Secretary," *Wilson Daily Tiimes*, April 18, 1955, 3; Snider, *Hunt*, 14.

53. Snider, *Hunt*, 13; "James B. Hunt Jr. Becomes First North Carolina Governor From Wilson County," *Wilson County Times*, January 8, 1977, 1; Carroll, "Politics Taught Hunt," and J. A. C. Denn, "When Will Jim Hunt's Veil Drop?" *Chapel Hill Newspaper*, NCC-UNC, Hunt to Electric Membership Association, February 8, 1972, Speech File, Lieutenant Governor James B. Hunt, Jr., Papers, NCDAH.

54. Hunt, Jr., interview by author.

55. *Ibid.*

56. "Black Creek To Stay Unbeaten," *Wilson Daily Times*, January 26, 1955, 7; "Elm City Girls Defeat Rock Ridge," *Wilson Daily Times*, January 29, 1955, 3;

"1955 All-Wilson County Boys' Basketball Team," *Wilson Daily Times*, March 12, 1955, 6; Linda Barnes, "Rock Ridge High Students Travel to Wilson," *Wilson Daily Tiimes*, March 10, 1955, 10; "Man in Politics," NCC-UNC.

57. Eisenstadt, "Washington," NCC-UNC.

58. "73 Seniors Awarded Diplomas at Rock Ridge School," *Wilson Daily Times,* June 1, 1955, 7.

59. *Ibid.*

Chapter 3

1. Terry Carter, "In the Good Old Days," *Technician*, November 20, 1981, 4, James B. Hunt Jr. File, University Archives, North Carolina State University Libraries, Raleigh (hereinafter cited as NCSU).

2. James B. Hunt, Jr., interview by author, December 14, 1999.

3. Alice E. Reagan, *North Carolina State University: A Narrative History* (Ann Arbor, MI: Edward Brothers, 1987), 152–153; William Friday, interview by author, December 29, 1999.

4. "Mrs. Hunt Talks About Her Son And His Aims," Jim Hunt for Lieutenant Governor Advertisement, James B. Hunt, Jr., File, Wilson County Library, Wilson, North Carolina; James B. Hunt, Sr., interview by author, December 27, 1999.

5. Elizabeth Dowling, "Unwanted Spotlight Shines on First Lady," (Raleigh) *News and Observer*, December 26, 1982, 1C.

6. *Ibid.*, 1C; Robert Hunt, interview by author, October 26, 1999; Hunt, Sr., interview by author; Carl Henley, interview by author, January 25, 2000.

7. Gary Pierce, "Governor James Baxter Hunt, Jr.," *Addresses and Papers of James B. Hunt, Jr., Governor of North Carolina, 1977–1981* (Raleigh: North Carolina Department of Archives and History, 1982), xxiv.

8. Art Eisenstadt, "Hunt Hopes His Road Leads to Washington," Newspaper Clippings, North Carolina Collection, Louis Wilson Library, University of North Carolina at Chapel Hill (hereinafter cited as NCC-UNC); Dowling, "Spotlight," C1; Peggy Payne, "Jim Hunt: Ag Grad to Governor," *North Carolina State Alumni* 49 (November/December 1976), 7, University Archives, NCSU.

9. Reagan, *State*, 164, 165; Ned Cline, "Hunt Marched to Different Beat," Clippings, NCC-UNC; Hunt, Jr., interview by author.

10. Debbi Sykes, "Jim Hunt: Determination Carries Over Into His Politics," *Daily Tar Heel*, February 11, 1983, Clippings, NCC-UNC; Hunt, Jr., interview by author.

11. Robert Hunt, interview by author.

12. Quoted in William Chafe, *The Unfinished Journey: America Since World War II, Second Edition* (New York: Oxford University Press, 1991), 159, 161.

13. Numan Bartley, *The New South, 1945–1980* (Baton Rouge: Louisiana State University Press, 1995), 217.

14. Payne, "Grad," 6.

15. *Ibid.*, 7; Ginny Carroll, "Politics Taught Hunt 'What Government Can Do For People,'" (Raleigh) *News and Observer*, Clippings, NCC-UNC; James B.

Hunt, Jr., speech, "State City Partnership: Some Ideas on Urban Policy," September 18, 1972, Speech File, Lieutenant Governor James B. Hunt, Jr., Papers, State Archives, Division of Archives and History, Raleigh (hereinafter cited as NCDAH); Phil Carlton, interview by author, September 8, 2000.

16. Jimmy Hunt, "From Your Editor," *Agriculturalist*, March 1958, 5–6.

17. *Ibid.*, 10.

18. Carroll, "Politics Taught Hunt," NCC-UNC.

19. Carl Henley, interview by author; 1959 *Agromeck Yearbook*, 138, University Archives, NCSU.

20. Jimmy Hunt, "Together We Stand," *Agriculturalist*, October 1956, 10; Jimmy Hunt, "A Student Grange for State College," *Agriculturalist*, April 1957, 16.

21. Jimmy Hunt, "From Your Editor," *Agriculturalist*, April 1958, 5; Jimmy Hunt, "From Your Editor," *Agriculturalist*, October 1957, 5; Jimmy Hunt, "Is There Any Future in Farming?" *Agriculturalist*, December 1957, 5.

22. Jimmy Hunt, "Together We Stand," *Agriculturalist*, October 1956, 6.

23. Henley and Hunt, interviews by author; 1959 *Agromeck*, 138, University Archives, NCSU.

24. Minutes, North Carolina State College Student Senate, February 7, 1957 and May 7, 1957, both in North Carolina State College Student Senate File, and "Hunt is Candidate For S. G. Veep," *Technician*, March 25, 1957, 1, University Archives, NCSU.

25. "Jim Hunt is New President of State Student Government," *Technician*, September 23, 1957, 1, University Archives, NCSU.

26. Carroll, "Politics Taught Hunt," NCC-UNC; Hunt, Jr., interview by author.

27. David Barnhardt, "Representative Did Not Truly Represent," *Technician*, October 14, 1957, 1; Minutes, NCSC Senate, September 18, 1958, University Archives, NCSU.

28. Eddie Knox, interview by author, September 12, 2000; "Eddie Knox Announces Candidacy for SG Presidency," and "Letter to the Editor," *Technician*, April 6, 1959, 1, 4, University Archives, NCSU.

29. Phil Carlton, interview by author, September 8, 2000; "Carlton Elected SG Secretary," *Technician*, November 17, 1958, 1, University Archives, NCSU.

30. Thomas Gilmore, interview by author, December 10, 2000; 1959 North Carolina State College *Agromeck Yearbook*, 129, 131, 155, and "Gilmore is Seeking Senior Vice Presidency," *Technician*, April 17, 1958, 5, University Archives, NCSU.

31. Abraham Holtzman, interview by author, December 9, 1999.

32. Minutes, NCSC Student Senate, October 16, 1958, NCSC Senate File, University Archives, NCSU; William Friday, interview by author, December 29, 1999.

33. Hunt, Jr., interview by author; "SG President Race to Be Between Hunt and Thomason," *Technician*, April 14, 1958, 1; "Presidential Candidates Give Platforms," *Technician*, April 17, 1958, 10; "Letter to the Editor," *Technician*, April 21, 1958, 2, University Archives, NCSU.

34. Jimmy Hunt, "From Your Editor," *Agriculturalist*, May 1958, 5, 6, University Archives, NCSU.

35. "Jim Hunt Reelected President," *Technician*, April 24, 1958, 1; "Hunt

Makes Post-Election Statement," April 24, 1958, *Technician*, 1, University Archives, NCSU.

36. "Constitutional Changes Given Final Approval by Student Government," *Technician*, May 8, 1958, 1, University Archives, NCSU; Reagan, *State*, 166.

37. "Miss Leonard Marries James Baxter Hunt Jr.," *Wilson Daily Times*, August 22, 1958, 3; Robert Hunt and Carl Henley, interviews by author; Dowling, "Spotlight," C2.

38. Aaron Capel, "Diploma Story Explained," *Technician*, October 9, 1958, 1; Jim Hunt, "Diploma — Second View," *Technician*, October 16, 1958, 1, University Archives, NCSU.

39. Payne, "Ag Grad," 7.

40. Reagan, *State*, 148–49; William C. Friday and Carl Henley, interviews by author; "27 Arrested During Campus Riot," *Technician*, March 11, 1957, NCSU Archives.

41. "SG President Hunt Discusses Sportsmanship," *Technician*, September 18, 1958, 1; Jimmy Hunt, "An Open Letter to the Student Body," *Technician*, February 10, 1958, 2, NCSU, "SG Head Urges Good Sportsmanship," *Technician*, January 12, 1959, 1, University Archives, NCSU.

42. Roger Faulkner, "Campus Personalities: President of SG," *Technician*, January 15, 1959, 3; Terry Carter, "In the Good Old Days: Governor James B. Hunt, Jr., Alumnus at Large," *Technician*, November 20, 1981, 4, James B. Hunt, Jr., File, University Archives, NCSU; William D. Snider, *Helms and Hunt: The North Carolina Senate Race, 1984* (Chapel Hill: UNC Press, 1985), 14.

43. Vance Roberts, "Committee Appointed to Study Fee Allocation," *Technician*, Nov. 24, 1958, "CU, *Technician* Fees to Be Studied," *Technician*, December 8, 1958, 1, University Archives, NCSU; Reagan, *State*, 165.

44. Dawn M. Clayton, "Issues Explored In Student Forum," *News and Observer*, Newspaper Clippings, Governor James B. Hunt Papers, NCDAH; Abraham Holtzman, interview by author, December 9, 1999; James B. Hunt, Jr., interview by William Friday, *North Carolina People*, WUNC-TV, December 31, 1999; Carter, "Alumnus," *Technician*, Hunt File, University Archives, NCSU.

45. Holtzman, interview by author.

46. Payne, "Ag Grad," 6; Carlton, interview by author.

47. "University Defends Budget Requests," *Technician*, February 26, 1959, 1, University Archives, NCSU; Snider, *Hunt*, 15.

48. Holtzman, interview by author; Payne, "Ag Grad," 7, University Archives, NCSU.

49. Friday, interview by author.

50. "Hunt: Top Senior," *Technician*, April 13, 1959, 1; Carter, "Alumnus," University Archives, NCSU.

51. Faulkner, "Personalities," *Technician*, January 15, 1959, 3, University Archives, NCSU.

52. "Mrs. Hunt Talks About Her Son and His Aims," Jim Hunt for Lieutenant Governor Advertisement, James B. Hunt, Jr., File, Wilson County Library, Wilson; Hunt, Jr., interview by author; Interview with Five North Carolina Governors, April 1993, WUNC-TV, NCC-UNC.

53. Quentin Lindsey, interview by author, October 7, 1999.

54. Howard E. Covington Jr. and Marion Ellis, *Terry Sanford: Politics, Progress and Outrageous Ambitions* (Durham: Duke University Press, 1999), xviii; "Former YDC President to Speak at SG Banquet," *Technician*, May 2, 1959, 1, University Archives, NCSU; Terry Sanford to James B. Hunt, Lucama, January 5, 1960, Wilson County Sanford for Governor File, Terry Sanford Papers, Southern Historical Collection, Louis Wilson Library, University of North Carolina (hereinafter cited as SHC-UNC).

55. James B. Hunt, Jr., "Acreage Controls and Poundage Controls; Their Effects on Most Profitable Production Practices for Flue Cured Tobacco" (M. A. Thesis, Agricultural Economics, North Carolina State College, 1962), 1.

56. *Ibid.*

Chapter 4

1. Bert Bennett, interview by author, October 12, 1999.

2. Bennett, interview by author; Marjorie Hunter, "Bennett Gets Party Post," *Winston-Salem Journal*, August 10, 1960,"Tar Heel of the Week: Bert Bennett," (Raleigh) *News and Observer*, August 3, 1960; Bert Bennett to Clint Newton, May 22, 1964, Bert Bennett File, Terry Sanford Papers, Southern Historical Collection, Louis Wilson Library, University of North Carolina at Chapel Hill (hereinafter cited as SHC-UNC); Ginny Carroll, "Politics Taught Hunt 'What Government Can Do for the People,'" *News and Observer*, October 7, 1984, James B. Hunt, Jr., Newspaper Clippings, North Carolina Collection, University of North Carolina (hereinafter cited as NCC-UNC).

3. "A Talk with Bert Bennett: Strategy of a Tough Campaign," David Cooper, *Winston-Salem Journal*, 1964, Bennett File, Sanford Papers, SHC-UNC.

4. Howard E. Covington and Marion A. Ellis, *Terry Sanford: Politics, Progress, and Outrageous Ambitions* (Durham, NC: Duke University Press, 1999), 226–28.

5. James B. Hunt, Jr., interview by author, December 14, 1999; William Chafe, *Never Stop Running: Allard Lowenstein and The Struggle to Save American Liberalism* (New York: Basic Books, 1993), 95, 177–78.

6. Hunt, interview by author.

7. Covington and Ellis, *Sanford*, 228.

8. *Ibid.*, 228–29, 235; John Drescher, *The Triumph of Good Will* (Jackson, MS: University Press of Mississippi, 2000), 182.

9. Covington and Ellis, *Sanford*, 240, 268; Terry Carter "In the Good Old Days—Gov. James B. Hunt, Jr., Alumnus at Large," *Technician*, November 4, 1981, 4, University Archives, North Carolina State University Libraries, Raleigh, North Carolina (hereinafter cited as NCSU).

10. Drescher, *Good Will*, 126–27.

11. Numan V. Bartley, *The New South, 1945–1980* (Baton Rouge: Louisiana State University Press, 1995), 258.

12. Interview of Five North Carolina Governors, WUNC-TV, April 1993, NCC-UNC.

13. James B. Hunt, Jr., "Dedication of Joseph M. Hunt, Jr. Expressway,"

Addresses and Papers of James Baxter Hunt, Jr., Governor of North Carolina, Volume 1, 1977–1981 (Raleigh: North Carolina Department of Cultural Resources, 1983), 321; Covington and Ellis, *Sanford*, 291; "Clarence Brame Funeral Rites Held Sunday," *Wilson Daily Times*, October 23, 1961, 6.

14. Joseph Wayne Grimsley, Jr., "Challenges to the North Carolina Speaker Ban Law, 1963–1968" (M. A. thesis, North Carolina State University, 1994), 2–108.

15. Covington and Ellis, *Sanford*, 45.

16. *Ibid.*, 45–46, 53; James B. Hunt, "Albert Coates Center Groundbreaking," March 3, 1978, *Addresses and Papers*, 256.

17. Debbi Sykes, "Jim Hunt: Determination Carries Over Into His Politics," *Daily Tar Heel*, February 11, 1983, NCC-UNC; Democratic National Committee News Release, 1962, Jim Hunt File, University Archives, NCSU; Joseph Lieberman, *The Power Broker: A Biography of John M. Bailey* (Boston: Houghton-Mifflin Co., 1966), 3–5.

18. John Webb, interview by author, December 7, 1999; James B. Hunt, Jr., "Lyndon Johnson," January 1973, Speech File, Lieutenant Governor James B. Hunt, Jr., Papers, State Archives, Division of Archives and History (hereinafter cited as NCDAH), Raleigh.

19. Hunt, Jr., interview by author.

20. *Ibid.*

21. Sikes, "Politics," NCC-UNC; Bert Bennett to Jim Hunt, Chapel Hill, August 23, 1963, Bennett File, Sanford Papers, SHC-UNC; Covington and Ellis, *Sanford*, 337.

22. Bert Bennett to Mr. J. L. Atkins, Jr., Durham, August 28, 1963; Bennett to Dr. Ralph Brinkley, Durham, September 17, 1963; Bennett to Phil Carlton, December 1963, Bennett File, Sanford Papers, SHC-UNC.

23. Bennett to Phil Ellis, April 21, 1964, Bennett File, Sanford Papers, SHC-UNC.

24. Bert Bennett to Ted Cramer, November 19, 1963, Bennett File, Sanford Papers, SHC-UNC; Bennett, interview by author.

25. Covington and Ellis, *Sanford*, 334; Bennett to Robert Cox, December 2, 1963, Bennett File, Sanford Papers, SHC-UNC.

26. Bennett to Phil Carlton, January 28, 1964; Bennett to Ted Cramer, February 3, 1964, Bennett File, Sanford Papers, SHC-UNC.

27. Bert Bennett to Jim Hunt, February 4, 1964, Bennett File, Sanford Papers, SHC-UNC.

28. Bennett to Conner Vick, March 6, 1964, and Bennett to Carlton, March 2, 1964, both in Bennett File, Sanford Papers, SHC-UNC.

29. Bennett to Atkins, March 23, 1964, Bennett File, Sanford Papers, SHC-UNC.

30. Bennett to Hunt, April 20, 1964, and Bennett to Vick, March 6, 1964, both in Bennett File, Sanford Papers, SHC-UNC.

31. Bert Bennett to Red Lackey, March 11, 1964, Bennett File, Sanford Papers, SHC-UNC; Bennett, interview by author; Covington and Ellis, *Sanford*, 339.

32. Bennett to Henry Hall Wilson, White House, Washington, D.C., April 22, 1964, Bennett File, Sanford Papers, SHC-UNC.

33. Webb, interview by author; David Cooper, "Bennett Says Organization

Not Dead," *Winston-Salem Journal,* July 11, 1964, Bennett File, Sanford Papers, SHC-UNC.

34. William D. Snider, *Helms and Hunt: The North Carolina Senate Race, 1984* (Chapel Hill: UNC Press, 1985), 16.

35. A. L. May, "Bert Bennett, Power Behind the Candidate," *News and Observer,* Newspaper Clippings, Hunt Papers, NCDAH; Bennett, interview by author.

36. J. A. C. Dunn, "When Will Jim Hunt's Veil Drop?" *Chapel Hill Newspaper,* and Ferrell Guillory, "Nobody Dissuades Hunt," *News and Observer,* Clippings, NCC-UNC.

37. "Jim Hunt: Man in Politics with a Longtime Ambition," *Durham Morning Herald,* December 5, 1974, and Carroll, "Politics," Clippings, NCC-UNC; Hunt, Jr., interview by author; Graham Jones, "Keep Your Eye on Him: A Nuts and Bolts Man," *North Carolina State Alumni News,* May/June 1970, 8, University Archives, NCSU.

38. Leo Bhuwan Lal Joshi, *Democratic Innovations in Nepal: A Case Study of Political Acculturation* (Berkeley: University of California Press, 1966), 466–73; Ranjee Parajulee, *The Democratic Transition in Nepal* (New York: Rowman and Littlefield Publishers, Inc., 2000), 11, 28, 36–39, 49, 51.

39. James B. Hunt, Jr., "Nepal: A Test Ground for Economic Theories," *North Carolina State Alumni News 38* (September–October 1965), 4–5, University Archives, NCSU; Joshi, *Innovations,* 473; Parajulee, *Transition,* 51, 222.

40. Quentin Lindsey, interview by author, October 7, 1999; Hunt, Jr., interview by author; Snider, *Hunt,* 16; Interview of Five North Carolina Governors, WUNC-TV, NCC-UNC.

41. Lindsey, interview; Hunt, "Theories," 5, University Archives, NCSU; Carroll, "Politics," and Guillory, "Dissuades," both in Clippings, NCC-UNC.

42. Hunt, "Theories," 7.

43. *Ibid.*

44. Jenneale Coulter Moore and Grace Rutledge Hamrick, *The First Ladies of North Carolina* (Charlotte: Heritage Printers, Inc., 1981), 85; Interview of Five North Carolina Governors, NCC-UNC.

45. Elizabeth Dowling, "Unwanted Spotlight Shines on First Lady," *News and Observer,* December 26, 1982, C1, Carolyn Hunt File, Wilson County Library, Wilson, North Carolina; "A New Energy From Within," *Wachovia* 65 (Spring 1978), 19, NCC-UNC; Hunt, "Theories," 7.

46. Hunt, interview by author; Sykes, "Determination," NCC-UNC.

47. Lindsey, interview by author.

48. Bennett and Hunt, interviews by author; Snider, *Helms,* 16.

49. Webb, interview by author.

50. *Ibid.*

51. "Man in Politics," NCC-UNC.

52. Webb, interview by author.

53. *Ibid.*

54. Carroll, "Politics Taught Hunt," NCC-UNC: Robert Scott, Haw River, North Carolina, to the author, Raleigh, received January 2000; North Carolina Democratic Executive Committee 1969 news release and "800 Attend YDC Meet-

ings," *Tar Heel Democrat* 4 (Winter 1968), 3, both in North Carolina Democratic Executive Committee File, North Carolina Governor Robert Scott Papers, NCDAH.

Chapter 5

1. Numan Bartley, *The New South, 1945–1980* (Baton Rouge: Louisiana State University Press, 1995), 395–99; John Webb, interview by author, December 9, 1999.

2. Elizabeth Dowling, "Unwanted Spotlight Shines on First Lady," (Raleigh) *News and Observer*, December 26, 1982, C1, Carolyn Hunt File, Wilson County Library, Wilson, North Carolina; Ned Cline, "Hunt Marched to Different Beat," Clippings, North Carolina Collection, Louis Wilson Library, UNC-Chapel Hill (hereinafter cited as NCC-UNC); Robert Hunt, interview by author, October 26, 1999; "Lucama Woman Hurt in Two-Car Accident," *Wilson Daily Times*, April 4, 1968, 2A.

3. Jim Hunt, "YDC Program for Victory in 1968," *Tar Heel Democrat* 4 (Winter 1968), 1, 1968 North Carolina Executive Democratic Committee File, Governor Robert Scott Papers, State Archives, Division of Archives and History, Raleigh, North Carolina (hereinafter cited as NCDAH).

4. Jim Hunt for Lieutenant Governor Advertisement, James B. Hunt, Jr., File, Wilson County Library; Webb, interview by author.

5. "Violence Hits Some NC Cities After King Death," *Wilson Daily Times*, April 5, 1968, 1.

6. "Memorial Service Set for King," *Wilson Daily Times*, April 5, 1968, 1; Craig Dearhardt, "Quiet Group Honors King," *Wilson Daily Times*, April 8, 1968, 1; Craig Dearhardt, "Vandals Strike 30 Firms; Police Arrest 30 Persons," *Wilson Daily Times*, April 8, 1968, 1.

7. Dearhardt, "Group," 1; Betty McCain, interview by author, October 6, 1999.

8. William D. Snider, *Helms & Hunt: The North Carolina Senate Race, 1984* (Chapel Hill: University of North Carolina Press, 1985), 17.

9. Joseph Grimsley, Sr., interview by author, October 3, 1999; Jim Hunt, statement, July 1976, Speech File, Lieutenant Governor James B. Hunt, Jr., Papers, NCDAH.

10. Ruth J. Davis, *History of the County of Wilson* (Wilson, NC: self-published by Ruth J. Davis, 1985), 88.

11. Jim Hunt, Jr., statement to National Democratic Commission on Party Structure and Delegate Selection, June 16, 1969, 1969 National Democratic Executive Committee File, and memo, 1968 Democratic National Convention File, Robert Scott Papers, NCDAH.

12. James Ferguson II, Charlotte, to Democratic Chairman John Bailey, August 10, 1968; George R. Ragsdale to Billy Webb, August 15, 1968; George Ragsdale, memo to Dan Moore, June 5, 1968, and James V. Johnson to Dan Moore, September 20, 1968, 1968 Democratic National Convention File, Scott Papers, NCDAH.

13. Webb, interview by author.

14. *Ibid.*

15. Bartley, *New South*, 399.

16. Nat Walker, "Jim Hunt's Political Star on Rise," *Greensboro Daily News*, January 18, 1970, 12A, James B. Hunt, Jr., File, University Archives, North Carolina State University Libraries, Raleigh, North Carolina (hereinafter cited as NCSU).

17. 1969 news release, North Carolina Democratic Party, and Charlie Rose, "YDC Report," *North Carolina Democratic Executive Committee Progress*, May 9, 1969, 3, both in 1969 Democratic Executive Committee File, Scott Papers, NCDAH.

18. James B. Hunt, Jr., to North Carolina Democratic Executive Committee Director Charles Barbour, August 29, 1969, and Hunt, testimony to National Democratic Commission on Party Structure and Delegate Selection, Atlanta, June 16, 1969, both in 1969 North Carolina Democratic Executive Committee File, Scott Papers, NCDAH.

19. Hunt to National Democratic Commission, 1969 North Carolina Democratic Executive Committee File, Scott Papers, NCDAH.

20. James B. Hunt, Jr., "Hunt Offers Plan for Reorganization of Democratic Party," North Carolina Democratic Executive Committee *Progress*, May 9, 1969, 1969 North Carolina Democratic Executive Committee File, Scott Papers, NCDAH.

21. Memory F. Mitchell, ed., *Addresses and Papers of Robert Scott, Governor of North Carolina, 1969–1973* (Raleigh: North Carolina Department of Cultural Resources, 1978), 210–11; Robert Scott, Haw River, to the author, Raleigh, received January 2000.

22. Press release, North Carolina Democratic Executive Committee, October 17, 1969, Executive Committee File, Scott Papers, NCDAH; Snider, *Hunt*, 17.

23. Jim Hunt to Robert Scott, October 17, 1969; Minutes of Regional Hearing of Democratic Party Study Commission; Hunt to Fellow Democrats, December 29, 1969, 1969 North Carolina Democratic Party File, Scott Papers, NCDAH.

24. Statement by Governor Bob Scott, January 10, 1970, 1970 North Carolina Democratic Executive Committee File, Scott Papers, NCDAH; Graham Jones, "Keep Your Eye on Him! A Nuts and Bolts Man," *North Carolina Alumni News*, May/June 1970, 8, University Archives, NCSU.

25. Jack Bass and Walter DeVries, *The Transformation of Southern Politics: Social Change and Political Consequences* (Athens: University of Georgia Press, 1995), 6.

26. Stephen Ambrose, *Nixon: The Triumph of a Politician, 1962–1972* (New York: Simon and Schuster, 1989), 365.

27. *Ibid.*, 360; Earl and Merle Black, *How Presidents Are Elected* (Cambridge; Harvard University Press, 1992), 304–305.

28. Bartley, *New South*, 211, 382, 393–97.

29. Bass and DeVries, *Politics*, 64; Dan T. Carter, *The Politics of Race: George Wallace, The Origins of the New Conservatism, and the Transformation of American Politics* (Baton Rouge: Louisiana State University, 1995), 371–99.

30. Bass and DeVries, *Politics*, 290; Bob Zelnick, *Gore: A Political Life* (Washington, D.C.: Regnery Publishing, Inc., 1999), 63.

31. Bass and DeVries, *Politics*, 307; George Bush, *All the Best, George Bush: My Life in Letters and Other Writings* (New York: Scribners, 1999), 128.

32. Bass and DeVries, *Politics*, 39, 358; "New Day A'Coming in the South," *Time*, May 31, 1971, 17.

33. Bass and DeVries, *Politics*, 12, 47.

34. V. O. Key, Jr., *Southern Politics in State and Nation* (Knoxville: University of Tennessee Press, 1949), 106; Betty Glad, *Jimmy Carter: In Search of the Great White House* (New York: W. W. Norton and Company, 1980), 127–37.

35. Glad, *Carter*, 141.

36. *Ibid.*

37. *Ibid.*, 141–52; James B. Hunt, Jr., introduction to Jimmy Carter at Vance–Aycock Dinner, October 20, 1973, Speech File, Lieutenant Governor James B. Hunt, Jr., Papers, NCDAH.

38. Bass and DeVries, *Politics*, 159, 171–75, 211; Ferrel Guillory, interview by author, December 15, 1999; Charles Evers, *Have No Fear: The Charles Evers Story* (John Wiley and Sons, Inc., 1998), 265–72.

39. Bass and DeVries, *Politics*, 101; Randall Bennett Woods, *Fulbright: A Biography* (New York: Cambridge University Press, 1999), 654; "Day A'Coming," 19.

40. Bass and DeVries, *Politics*, 262, 263; "Four Men for the New Season," *Time*, May 31, 1971, 18; Nadine Cohadas, *Strom Thurmond and the Politics of Southern Change* (New York: Simon & Schuster, 1993), 411–12. When West became governor, he hailed the conviction of the whites charged with the attack on the bus.

41. Bass and DeVries, *Politics*, 264.

42. Bass and DeVries, *Politics*, 164, 264, "Four Men," 19.

Chapter 6

1. Nat Walker, "Jim Hunt's Political Star on Rise," *Greensboro Daily News*, January 18, 1970, 12A; Graham Jones, "Keep Your Eye on Him! A Nuts and Bolts Man," *North Carolina Alumni News*, May/June 1970, 8, University Archives, North Carolina State University Libraries, Raleigh, North Carolina (hereinafter cited as NCSU).

2. Jones, "Eye," 8.

3. Robert Farris, Wilson, to Governor Robert Scott, Raleigh, October 18, 1969, 1970 North Carolina Democratic Executive Committee File, North Carolina Governor Robert Scott Papers, State Archives, Division of Archives and History (hereinafter cited as NCDAH), Raleigh, North Carolina.

4. Mitchell Farris, Thomas Farris Motors, Rocky Mount, to North Carolina Governor Robert Scott, October 23, 1969, and James B. Hunt, Jr., press release, North Carolina Democratic Party Headquarters, December 22, 1969, both in 1969 North Carolina Democratic Executive Committee File, Scott Papers, NCDAH.

5. Joseph Grimsley, interview by author, September 26, 1999.

6. *Ibid.*

7. Paul Leubke, *Tar Heel Politics 2000* (Chapel Hill: University of North Carolina Press, 1998), 33.

8. Joseph Grimsley, interview by author, June 17, 2000.

9. Howard E. Covington and Marion A. Ellis, *Terry Sanford: Politics, Progress, and Outrageous Ambitions* (Durham, NC: Duke University Press, 1999), 216, 337; Phil Carlton, interview by author, September 8, 2000.

10. Bert Bennett, interview by author, October 12, 1999; Carlton, interview by author; Betty McCain, interview by author, October 7, 1999; William D. Snider, *Hunt and Helms: The North Carolina Senate Race, 1984* (Chapel Hill: UNC Press, 1985), 16–17; Ginny Carroll, "Politics Taught Hunt 'What Government Can Do For The People,'"(Raleigh) *News and Observer*, Clippings, North Carolina Collection, Louis Wilson Library, University of North Carolina at Chapel Hill (hereinafter cited as NCC-UNC).

11. Paul Essex, interview by author, December 7, 1999.

12. Grimsley, interview by author; Gordon Allen, interview by author, July 12, 2000.

13. Jim Hunt, "Citizen Responsibility in Support of Law Enforcement," North Carolina and South Carolina Law Enforcement Officers Association, July 20, 1971, Speech File, Lieutenant Governor James B. Hunt, Jr., Papers, NCDAH; Snider, *Helms*, 33.

14. James B. Hunt, Jr., speech, Winston-Salem Business and Professional Women's Club, February 7, 1972, and James B. Hunt, Jr., "Paul Dickson Dies," April 29, 1972, both in Speech File, Lieutenant Governor Hunt Papers, NCDAH; "Wilson Lawyer Jim Hunt in Race for No. 2 Post," *News and Observer*, October 5, 1971, 3; "Hunt Schedules Five Campus Stops Today," *News and Observer*, April 12, 1972, 7.

15. Grimsley, interview by author.

16. James B. Hunt, Jr., untitled speech, Pembroke State University, January 10, 1972, Speech File, Lieutenant Governor Hunt Papers, NCDAH; "Hunt Likes Road Phase of Policy," *News and Observer*, October 11, 1972, 14.

17. James B. Hunt, Jr., "Education: The Key to Progress," Greenville chapter of the North Carolina Association of Educators, April 25, 1972, and Hunt, untitled speech to the Association of Community College Presidents, April 27, 1972, both in Speech File, Lieutenant Governor Hunt Papers, NCDAH.

18. Grimsley, interview by author.

19. "Wilson Lawyer Jim Hunt in Race for No. 2 Post," *News and Observer*, October 5, 1971, 5; Announcement of Candidacy, Speech File, Hunt Papers, NCDAH.

20. Hunt, Announcement of Candidacy, Speech File, Hunt Papers, NCDAH.

21. "Wilson Lawyer," 1, "Hunt Names Campaign Co-Chairmen," *News and Observer*, October 25, 1971, 2; Essex, interview by author; "Under the Dome," *News and Observer*, October 20, 1971, 1.

22. Grimsley, interview by author.

23. *Ibid.*; J. Hoye Stultz, Rockingham County, to James B. Hunt, Jr., May 10, 1972, Election File, Lieutenant Governor Hunt Papers, NCDAH.

24. "Sowers Deplores High Food Costs," *News and Observer*, April 4, 1972, 5; "Sowers Supports Tax Study," *News and Observer*, April 20, 1972, 12; "Rescuer Funds Asked By Sowers," *News and Observer*, April 23, 1972, 9; "Loan Fund is Sowers's Plan," *News and Observer*, April 25, 1972, 6B; "Hunt Said After Governor's Job," *News and Observer*, April 27, 1977, 8.

25. "Mrs. Harper to Run for Number 2 Post," *News and Observer*, February 9, 1972, 1.

26. Jane Patterson, Greensboro, to Joseph "Swag" Grimsley, Raleigh, January 8, 1972, ERA File, Lieutenant Governor Hunt Papers, NCDAH.

27. James B. Hunt, Jr., speech to Winston-Salem Business and Professional Women's Club, February 7, 1972, ERA File, Hunt Papers, NCDAH.

28. "Black Unity Cited," *News and Observer*, April 15, 1972, 9; "Barbee Chides Hunt on Legislative Ideas," *News and Observer*, April 8, 1972, 7.

29. "Under the Dome," *News and Observer*, October 20, 1971, 7; Campaign Financing Reform and a Truth-in-Campaign Reporting Statement, December 14, 1971; Jim Hunt, "Statement on State Board of Elections," February 8, 1972, Speech File, Lieutenant Governor Hunt Papers, NCDAH.

30. Hunt, "Statement," Speech File, Hunt Papers, NCDAH.

31. "Under the Dome," *News and Observer*, February 23, 1972, 1; Jim Hunt for Lieutenant Governor Advertisement, James B. Hunt, Jr., File, Wilson County Library; Steve Berg, "Sowers Names Supporters Who Aided Campaign Loan," *News and Observer*, February 11, 1972, 6; Grimsley, interview by author.

32. "Legislative Reforms Proposed By Hunt," *News and Observer*, April 5, 1972, 7; "Hunt Right About the Legislature," *News and Observer*, April 8, 1972, 4, "Pay Change Urged for Lt. Governor," *News and Observer*, October 12, 1971, 7.

33. Howard E. Covington, Jr., and Marion Ellis, *Terry Sanford: Politics, Progress, and Outrageous Ambitions* (Durham: Duke University Press, 1999), 398.

34. *Ibid.*, 398 — 406.

35. *Ibid.*, 403; Grimsley, interview by author.

36. Grimsley, interview by author; "Hunt Requests Fair Treatment of Wallace," *News and Observer*, April 14, 1972, 7.

37. David Bruton, Southern Pines, to James B. Hunt, Raleigh, May 8, 1972, and Terry Lyda, Henderson, to Jim Hunt, May 9, 1972, both in Election File, Hunt Papers, NCDAH; "Taylor Deciding on Runoff," *News and Observer*, May 8, 1972, 9B; "Finances Dictate People for Sowers," *News and Observer*, May 5, 1972, 10.

38. Jim Hunt, statement, May 9, 1972, Election File, Hunt Papers, NCDAH; "Opponent's Aides Back Hunt," *News and Observer*, May 10, 1972, 7.

39. "Under the Dome," *News and Observer*, May 12, 1972, 6; Terry Lyda to Jim Hunt, May 9, 1972, Election File, Hunt Papers, NCDAH.

40. Bob Wilson, "Sowers Decides Against Runoff," *News and Observer*, May 13, 1972, 1.

41. Snider, *Hunt*, 30–31.

42. *Ibid.*, 25 — 40.

43. Bennett, interview by author.

44. Howard Lee, interview by author, October 26, 1999; James B. Holshouser, interview by author, October 20, 1999; H. M. Michaux, interview by Jack Bass, November 20, 1974, Southern Oral History Collection, Wilson Library, UNC (hereinafter cited as SOHC-UNC).

45. Holshouser, interview; David Flaherty, interview by author, October 13, 1999.

46. "Under the Dome," *News and Observer*, June 11, 1972, 1; Bob Joyce, "N. C. McGovern Aid Thin," *News and Observer*, July 15, 1972, 1, 2.

47. Bennett, interview by author.

48. James B. Hunt, Jr., "Equal Rights for Women," February 7, 1972, Winston-Salem Business and Professional Women's Club, Speech File, Hunt Papers, NCDAH.

49. James B. Hunt, Jr., "100-County Tour Conclusion," August 17, 1972, Speech File, Hunt Papers, NCDAH; Grimsley, interview by author.

50. Bob Wilson, "Walker is Driving to Catch Hunt Lead," *News and Observer*, November 5, 1972, 6; Lee, interview by author.

51. Ferrel Guillory, "Nixon Stops at Greensboro," *News and Observer*, November 5, 1972, 2; Grimsley, interview by author.

52. Bennett, interview by author; "Hunt Proposes New Ethics Laws," *News and Observer*, November 1, 1972, 6; Ferrel Guillory, "Spending Limit Plan Spelled Out By Hunt," *News and Observer*, November 21, 1972, 2D.

53. Grimsley, interview by author.

Chapter 7

1. Nancy Bentsen, "Hunt: A New Relationship," (Raleigh) *News and Observer*, November 11, 1972, 6.

2. *Ibid.*

3. Paul Essex, interview by author, December 7, 1999; Joseph Grimsley, interview by author, June 17, 2000.

4. "Lt. Gov. Hunt on Appointments," January 10, 1973, Speech File, Lieutenant Governor James B. Hunt, Jr., Papers, State Archives, Division of Archives and History, Raleigh, North Carolina (hereinafter cited as NCDAH); Leslie Wayne, "Hunt Appoints Scott, Kirby to Head Key Committees," *News and Observer*, January 11, 1973, 5; Leslie Wayne, "Hunt's Relationship With Assembly Unusual," *News and Observer*, March 4, 1973, 43.

5. Larry Tarleton, "Hunt's Idealistic Views Will Conflict with Reality," *Charlotte Observer*, January 14,1973, 6.

6. Gayle Lane Fitzgerald. *Remembering a Champion* (Raleigh: Edwards & Broughton, Inc., 1988), 147–49; Wayne, "Appoints," 5; Wayne, "Relationship," 41.

7. Gordon Allen, interview by author, July 12, 2000; Ferrel Guillory, "He's Never Been a Man to Let Opportunity Pass Him," *News and Observer*, April 4, 1973, 3D; Wayne, "Relationship," 41.

8. Allen, interview by author.

9. *Ibid.*

10. Joseph Grimsley, interview by author, June 17, 2000.

11. Leslie Wayne, "Hunt Pledges to Oppose Committee Guidance Bill," *News and Observer*, February 27, 1973, 6.

12. Gary Pearce, "The Lieutenant Governor Post: The Struggle To Define It," *News and Observer*, February 23, 1975, 2; "Lieutenant Governor Needs Limits," *News and Observer*, February 26, 1973, 4.

13. James Holshouser, interview by author, October 20, 1999.

14. Grimsley, interview by author.

15. Memory Mitchell, *Addresses and Public Papers of James Eubert Holshouser,*

Governor of North Carolina, 1973–1977, ed. (Raleigh: North Carolina Department of Cultural Resources, 1978), 11; Holshouser, interview by author.

16. Ferry Guillory, "Governor Boosts Services," *News and Observer*, January 18, 1973, 1; Leslie Wayne, "Democratic Lawmakers Between Rock, Hard Place," *News and Observer*, January 29, 1973, 1.

17. Leslie Wayne, "Senate Panel Votes Approval of ERA," *News and Observer*, February 23, 1973, 6; "Under the Dome," *News and Observer*, February 28, 1973, 1; Gordon Allen, interview by author, July 12, 2000; Leslie Wayne, "Senate Defeats ERA," *News and Observer*, March 1, 1973, 1; Donald G. Mathews and Jane Sherron De Hart, *Sex, Gender and Politics of ERA* (New York: Oxford University Press, 1990), 68; Betty McCain, interview by author, October 6, 1999.

18. Jim Hunt, speech at Ninth Annual Reading Symposium, Boone, North Carolina, October 11, 1974; "Kindergartens," *Charlotte Observer*, March 16, 1973, 24A; "Kindergarten Bill Enacted," *News and Observer*, Education File, Lieutenant Governor Hunt Papers, NCDAH; Fitzgerald, *Champion*, 149.

19. Minutes, Board of Education meeting, April 5, 1973, 190, North Carolina Board of Education Papers, NCDAH; William Link, *William Friday: Power, Purpose & American Higher Education* (Chapel Hill: University of North Carolina Press, 1995), 161; Angela Davis, "Career Education Endorsed," *News and Observer*, April 6, 1973, 8.

20. "New Teacher Test Stands," *News and Observer*, February 2, 1973; complaint, United States vs. North Carolina Board of Education, Education File, Lieutenant Governor Hunt Papers, NCDAH; Steve Adams, "Law to Phase Out Teachers Test," *News and Observer*, June 20, 1975, 26.

21. Steve Adams, "Phillips Says Panel Tried to Discredit Him," *News and Observer*, March 7, 1975, 1; Steve Adams, "Herring Reelected School Board Chief," *News and Observer*, January 10, 1975, 1.

22. Link, *Friday*, 222–23; Leo Jenkins, Greenville, to Jim Hunt, Attorney at Law, Wilson, North Carolina, January 20, 1972, Education File, Lieutenant Governor Hunt Papers, NCDAH.

23. James Holshouser, "Message to Delivery of Medical Care to Rural Centers," *Papers*, 22; Lesley Wayne, "ECU Medical Plan Back, Seen," *News and Observer*, April 17, 1973, 7; William Friday, interview by author, December 29, 1999.

24. Editorial, *Winston-Salem Journal*, August 27, 1973; William D. Snider, "The Trouble with the ECU Dispute," *Greensboro Daily News*, February 1974; "Jim Hunt Still Running According to Program," *Chapel Hill Newspaper*, April 18, 1973, 4; "N & O Scolded about Cartoon," Education File, Lieutenant Governor Hunt Papers, NCDAH.

25. "Helms Exploits Medical School Issue," *News and Observer*, April 26, 1973; editorial, *Winston-Salem Journal*, August 27, 1973, Education File, Hunt Papers, NCDAH.

26. Jim Hunt, Raleigh, to Jesse Helms, Washington, D. C., February 12, 1973, Agriculture File, Lieutenant Governor Hunt Papers, NCDAH; Jim Hunt to Jesse Helms, December 9, 1974; Jim Hunt to Jesse Helms, November 21, 1975, unprocessed 1973–1974 Files, Lieutenant Governor Hunt Papers, NCDAH.

27. Jesse Helms to Jim Hunt, December 1, 1975, unprocessed 1975–1976 Files, Lieutenant Governor Hunt Papers, NCDAH.

28. James B. Hunt, Jr., "Legislature Praised," (Kannapolis, NC) *Daily Independent*, May 24, 1973, Education File, Lieutenant Governor Hunt Papers, NCDAH; Claude Sitton, "Much Ado About Very Little," *News and Observer*, April 8, 1973, 4D; Ferrel Guillory, "'1974 Effect' and 'New Situation' Have Slowed Legislative Effects,'" *News and Observer*, April 15, 1973, 2D.

29. Leslie Wayne, "ECU Referendum Stymied By Panel," *News and Observer*, February 8, 1974, 1; Link, *Friday*, 235–36; Leslie Wayne, "ECU Compromise Effort Abandoned," *News and Observer*, January 15, 1974, 1.

30. Link, *Friday*, 236–38.

31. Friday, interview by author.

32. Jim Hunt, Raleigh, to William Friday, Chapel Hill, August 2, 1974, Education File, Lieutenant Governor Hunt Papers, NCDAH; Link, *Friday*, 238–41.

33. Friday, interview by author; Link, *Friday*, 243.

34. Betty Owen, interview by author, October 7, 1999.

35. Tom Ashcroft, Charlotte, to Jim Hunt, June 20, 1975; Dr. Thomas Nisbett, Charlotte, to Hunt, July 9, 1975; Hunt to "Dear Friend," June 19, 1975, Education File, Lieutenant Governor Hunt Papers, NCDAH.

36. H. M. Michaux, interview by Jack Bass, November 20, 1974, transcript, Southern Historical Collection, Louis Wilson Library, UNC (hereinafter cited as SHC-UNC).

37. Wilbur Hobby, interview by Bass, December 1973, transcript, SHC-UNC.

38. *Ibid.*

39. Ralph Scott, interview by Jack Bass, December 20, 1973, and Thad Eure, interview by Bass, December 12, 1973, both in SHC-UNC; Leo Jenkins, Greenville, to Jim Hunt, Raleigh, July 11, 1975, Education File, Lieutenant Governor Hunt Papers, NCDAH.

40. James E. Harrington to Jim Holshouser, June 30, 1974, Environment File, Lieutenant Governor Hunt Papers, NCDAH; Thomas J. Schoenbaum, *Islands, Capes, and Sounds* (Winston-Salem: John F. Blair, 1982), 264.

41. Schoenbaum, *Islands*, 265–66; Holshouser, interview by author.

42. Ferrel Guillory, "Holshouser: Repeal Drink Tax," *News and Observer*, April 1, 1973, 1; Ferrel Guillory, "House Sets Debate on Tax Reductions," *News and Observer*, February 17, 1974, 1; Ferrel Guillory, "NC Senator OKs Tax Package," *News and Observer*, April 4, 1974, 5; Ferrel Guillory, "Holshouser, Ramsey Shun Hunt's Tax Bill," *News and Observer*, April 6, 1974, 1; Ferrel Guillory, "Legislature Rules Out Tax Relief," *News and Observer*, April 10, 1974, 1.

43. Ferrel Guillory, "Hunt Endorses Housing Unit," *News and Observer*, March 20, 1974, 8; Ferrel Guillory, "A Session of Struggles," *News and Observer*, April 14, 1974, 1; Robert B. Cullen, "'74 Session's Record Indicates a Divided Leadership," *News and Observer*, April 15, 1974, 6.

44. "Senate Gets an Ethics Bill," *News and Observer*, January 11, 1973, 5; "Talk on Campaign Spending Law is Turning Out to Be Just Talk," *Raleigh Times*, May 16, 1973, Politics File, Lieutenant Governor Hunt Papers, NCDAH.

45. Jim Hunt, "Lessons from Watergate," July 23, 1973, Speech File, Lieutenant Governor Hunt Papers, NCDAH.

46. Daniel Hoover, "Campaign Spending Bill Enacted," *News and Observer*,

April 11, 1974, 1; "Ethics Law Enacted for N. C. Legislators," *News and Observer*, June 12, 1975, 1.

47. President Gerald Ford, Washington, to Senator (sic) Jim Hunt, Raleigh, December 4, 1974, Economics File, Lieutenant Governor Hunt papers, NCDAH.

Chapter 8

1. Joseph Grimsley, interview by author, June 16, 2000; Paul Essex, interview by author, December 7, 2000.

2. "Bowles Swing Opens," (Raleigh) *News and Observer*, March 1, 1973, 15; Mary Day Mordecai, "Sugg Addresses Wake County Democratic Women," *News and Observer*, June 15, 1975, 12.

3. "Under the Dome," *News and Observer*, June 15, 1975, 1; "Under the Dome," *News and Observer*, October 13, 1975, 1.

4. Joseph Grimsley, interview by author, September 26, 1999.

5. Bert Bennett, interview by author, October 12, 1999.

6. Howard Lee, interview by author, October 26, 1999.

7. Daniel Hoover, "Democratic Chorus Mostly in Harmony," *News and Observer*, January 5, 1975, 6; Mickey Michaux, interview by Jack Bass, transcript, November 20, 1974, Southern Historical Collection, Louis Wilson Library, University of North Carolina, Chapel Hill, North Carolina (hereinafter cited as SHC-UNC); James B. Hunt, Jr., statement, December 12, 1974; Ned Cline, "Disputatious Democrats Brighten GOP Prospects," *Greensboro Daily News*, Elections File, Lieutenant Governor James B. Hunt, Jr., Papers, State Archives, Division of Archives and History, Raleigh, North Carolina (hereinafter cited as NCDAH).

8. Walter Jones, Washington, D.C., to Jim Hunt, Raleigh, January 3, 1975; "Winberry Not to Seek Party Post," *Greensboro Daily News*, December 15, 1974, Elections File, Lieutenant Governor Hunt Papers, NCDAH; "Sugg Reelected: Tar Heel Democrats Organize," *News and Observer*, January 5, 1975, 4.

9. James B. Hunt, Jr., untitled speech, March 19, 1975, Speech File, Lieutenant Governor Hunt Papers, NCDAH.

10. Ferrel Guillory, "Hunt Issues Warning on Tax Revenue," *News and Observer*, October 29, 1975, 21; Jim Hunt, Raleigh, to Lloyd Childers, unprocessed Hunt Papers, NCDAH; James B. Holshouser, interview by author, November 5, 1999.

11. Ferrel Guillory, "N. C. Budget Cuts Are Pledged," *News and Observer*, February 15, 1975, 1; "Under the Dome," *News and Observer*, January 30, 1975, 6; "Under the Dome," *News and Observer*, February 8, 1975, 1.

12. Gary Pearce, "Assembly Faces Tough Budget Cutting Job," *News and Observer*, March 30, 1975, 1; "Under the Dome," *News and Observer*, January 21, 1975, 1.

13. "Committee to Study Solutions to NC Economic Woes," *News and Observer*, January 16, 1975, 1; "Under the Dome," *News and Observer*, January 22, 1973, 1.

14. James Taylor, Williamston, NC, to Jim Hunt, Raleigh, February 8, 1975, Energy File, Lieutenant Governor Hunt Papers, NCDAH.

15. Lesley Allen, Selma, NC, to Jim Hunt, Raleigh, January 10, 1975; Jim Hunt, Raleigh, to Mrs. Nancy Holmes, Belmont, NC, March 3, 1976; Mrs. A. F. Klein, Greensboro, to Jim Hunt, Raleigh, March 3, 1976, Energy File, Hunt Papers, NCDAH.

16. Ferrel Guillory, "Soaring Utility Rates," *News and Observer*, February 9, 1975, 2D; "Utility Bill Survives Lake's Attack," *News and Observer*, March 16, 1975, 4D; Gary Pearce, "Criticism Outrages Utility Bill Sponsor," *News and Observer*, March 13, 1975, 1.

17. Jim Hunt, Raleigh, to George Norman, Greensboro, April 21, 1976, Utilities File, Lieutenant Governor Hunt Papers, NCDAH.

18. "Hunt Raps Bonus to Utilities," *News and Observer*, March 16, 1976, 17; Robert Davis, Brevard, NC, to Jim Hunt, Raleigh, April 11, 1975, Utilities File, Lieutenant Governor Hunt Papers, NCDAH; Ferrel Guillory, "Pro-Consumer Utilities Staff Part of Hunt's Plan for Panel," *News and Observer*, June 24, 1976, 1.

19. Bert Bennett, Winston-Salem, to Jim Hunt, Raleigh, August 14, 1973, Elections File, Lieutenant Governor Hunt Papers, NCDAH.

20. Grimsley, interview by author; Daniel C. Hoover, "Bills to Move N. C. Primary Approved," *News and Observer*, May 22, 1975, 1, 8; "Keep Majority Rule for Primaries," *News and Observer*, May 16, 1975, 4.

21. Memory Mitchell, *Addresses and Papers of James Baxter Hunt, Jr., Governor of North Carolina 1977–1981*, ed. (Raleigh: Division of Archives and History, 1982), 167.

22. Joe Grimsley to Jim Hunt, memo, April 30, 1974, ERA File, Lieutenant Governor Hunt Papers, NCDAH.

23. Ferrel Guillory, "N. C. House Defeats ERA, 62–57 as Three Legislators Switch Votes," *News and Observer*, April 17, 1975, 1; Gary Pearce, "Vote Switch Saves ERA," *News and Observer*, April 14, 1975.

24. Ferrel Guillory, "Assembly Negotiations Fail," *News and Observer*, June 25, 1975, 1.

25. Ferrel Guillory, "Budget Cuts Defended as Assembly Adjourns," *News and Observer*, June 27, 1975, 1.

26. Ferrel Guillory, "Hunt Praises Assembly, Hits Budget Process," *News and Observer*, June 28, 1975, 19.

27. Ferrel Guillory, "Conferees Agree on State Budget," *News and Observer*, May 8, 1976, 1.

28. Eddie Knox, interview by author, September 12, 2000; James B. Hunt, Jr., "Crime," speech to Charlotte Kiwanis Club, August 14, 1975, and Hunt, news release, August 21, 1976, both in Speech File, Lieutenant Governor Hunt Papers, NCDAH.

29. Ferrel Guillory, "Governor Hopefuls Give Views on Major Issues," *News and Observer*, August 8, 1976, 1, 10.

30. John Cowden, CBS-TV, to Jim Hunt, Raleigh, December 19, 1974; Jim Hunt, speech to North Carolina Conference on Programming, March 3, 1976, Speech File, Lieutenant Governor Hunt Papers, NCDAH.

31. James B. Hunt, Jr., "Public Schools and the Community: Strengthening Quality Education in the 1970s: A Position Statement," July 10, 1976, Clippings, North Carolina Collection, Louis Wilson Library, UNC (hereinafter cited as

NCC-UNC); Daniel Hoover, "Hunt Wants to Expand Reading Pilot," *News and Observer*, August 4, 1976, 5.

32. Ferrel Guillory, "Hunt's Plan Would Woo Higher Pay Firms," *News and Observer*, June 15, 1976, 7; Betty Owen, interview by author, October 7, 1999.

33. Dixon Hall, Kenansville, NC, to Jim Hunt, Raleigh, June 7, 1974; Preston Hill, Raleigh, to Jim Hunt, Raleigh, June 13, 1974; Jim Hunt, Raleigh, to Burley Mitchell, Raleigh, September 23, 1974, unprocessed Lieutenant Governor Hunt Papers, NCDAH; Ferrel Guillory, interview by Joseph Meisner, April 29, 1996, SHC-UNC.

34. "Under the Dome," *News and Observer*, October 25, 1999, 1; Mary Beth Edwards, "The Ballad of Jim Hunt," April 28, 1976, unprocessed Lieutenant Governor Hunt Papers, NCDAH.

35. Martin Donsky, "Hunt Works Hard for Every Vote," *News and Observer*, June 22, 1976, 1, 12.

36. Gordon Allen, interview by author, July 12, 2000.

37. "Under the Dome," *News and Observer*, September 13, 1975, 9; Daniel Hoover, "Democratic Chorus Mostly in Harmony," *News and Observer*, May 5, 1975, 1; Martin Donsky, "Bowles Pulls Out of Governor's Race," *News and Observer*, March 25, 1976, 1.

38. "Keep Majority Rule for Primaries," *News and Observer*, May 16, 1975, 4; Martin Donsky, "Strickland Engineers a Low-Key Campaign," *News and Observer*, June 28, 1976, 1, 2.

39. Ferrel Guillory, "Eckerd Chairman is Ready to Join Governor's Race," *News and Observer*, May 25, 1975, 8.

40. Owen, interview by author.

41. Knox, interview by author.

42. Ferrel Guillory, "Hunt Vows Candidacy, No Tax Rise," *News and Observer*, April 6, 1976, 1.

43. *Ibid.*

44. "Hunt Delivers Political Clichés," *Chapel Hill Newspaper*, April 7, 1976, 6; "Hunt Drifts into a Campaign Issue," *News and Observer*, April 8, 1976, 4; Ferrel Guillory, "Teachers, Business Hit Pay Hike Plan," *News and Observer*, April 9, 1976, 1.

45. Daniel Hoover, "Wood Pondering Governor's Race," *News and Observer*, April 28, 1976, 8; Martin Donsky, "Bowles Endorses Wood for Governor," *News and Observer*, June 13, 1976, 1; "Wood Sets Himself Apart from the Field," *News and Observer*, June 21, 1976, 1.

46. Martin Donsky, "Lt. Governor's Power Cut; Assembly OKs Budget," *News and Observer*, May 15, 1976, 1, 6; "Hunt Explains his Stand on Appointive Powers," *News and Observer*, May 17, 1976, 6; Donsky, "Endorses," 6.

47. "Educators Back Hunt, Flaherty," *News and Observer*, May 23, 1976, 1; Daniel Hoover, "NC Labor Gives Hunt the Nod," *News and Observer*, July 15, 1976, 13; "Black Baptists Pick Candidates," *News and Observer*, August 6, 1976, 13.

48. Grimsley, interview by author.

49. Martin Donsky, "Black NC Appointee Pledged," *News and Observer*, August 3, 1976, 1; Martin Donsky, "Hunt Bid Backed By Key Black Leaders," *News and Observer*, August 3, 1976, 6.

50. Donsky, "Leaders," 1.

51. Lee, interview by author; Donsky, "Appointee," 1.

52. Martin Donsky, "O'Herron Worth $21 Million," *News and Observer*, April 28, 1976, 1; Martin Donsky, "Hunt Blasts Two on Wealth," *News and Observer*, August 6, 1976, 15.

53. Martin Donsky, "Hunt's Funding Base Broader Than Others," *News and Observer*, August 11, 1976, 15B.

54. Jim Hunt, "Business Leaders for Hunt," July 3, 1976, Speech File, Lieutenant Governor Hunt Papers, NCDAH.

55. Ferrel Guillory, "Advertising Costs in Primary to Top $1 Million For Trio," *News and Observer*, August 2, 1976, 1, 6; Ferrel Guillory, "O'Herron To Increase His Attacks on Hunt," *News and Observer*, August 10, 1976, 5B.

56. Guillory, "O'Herron," 5B.

57. Guillory, "Advertising," 1.

58. *Ibid.*

59. Jim Hunt, statement on Betty McCain, August 27, 1976, Speech File, Lieutenant Governor Hunt Papers, NCDAH; William Snider, *Helms and Hunt: The North Carolina Senate Race, 1984* (Chapel Hill: University of North Carolina Press, 1985), 35.

60. David Flaherty, interview by author, October 13, 1999.

61. *Ibid.*

62. Flaherty, interview by author.

63. *Ibid.*

64. *Ibid.*; Jules Witcover, *Marathon: Pursuit of the Presidency, 1972–1976* (New York: Viking Press, 1977), 410–21.

65. Flaherty, interview by author; Daniel Hoover, "Hunt, Flaherty Tour State," *News and Observer*, November 2, 1976, 1; Ferrel Guillory, "Flaherty Quits After Hearing Early Returns," *News and Observer*, November 3, 1976, 1.

66. "Under the Dome," *News and Observer*, May 22, 1973, 1; Daniel Hoover, "Thin Crowd Hears Wallace," *News and Observer*, January 17, 1974, 1; Ferrel Guillory, "Politicians Hope Wallace Aura will Rub Off On Them," *News and Observer*, April 13, 1975, 2D.

67. Jim Hunt, introduction to Jimmy Carter at Vance-Aycock Dinner, October 20, 1973, and Hunt, speech at North State Caucus Meeting, July 24, 1976, Speech File, Lieutenant Governor Hunt Papers, NCDAH; Grimsley, interview by author.

68. Hoover, "Tour," 1.

69. Guillory, "Returns," 1.

70. Guillory, "Returns," 1.

71. Grimsley, interview by author.

72. Dennis Rogers, "Exuberant Hunt Sees Happy Days," *News and Observer*, November 3, 1976, 6.

Chapter 9

1. Martin Donsky, "Hunt's First Year — An Active Governor," (Raleigh) *News and Observer*, January 8, 1978, 1D.

2. *Ibid.*

3. Elizabeth Dowling, "Unwanted Spotlight Shines on First Lady," *News and Observer*, December 26, 1982, 2C.

4. Stephanie Stallings, "Lively Hunt Family Set For Governor's Mansion," *News and Observer*, November 4, 1976, 13A.

5. Ann Feetham, "Festive Prelude to Inauguration," *Wilson Daily Times*, January 8, 1977, James B. Hunt file, Wilson County Library, Wilson, North Carolina; James B. Hunt, Jr., "Inaugural Address," *Addresses and Papers of James B. Hunt, Jr., Governor of North Carolina, 1977–1981* (Raleigh: North Carolina Department of Cultural Resources, 1982), 2.

6. Hunt, *Papers*, 25, 189.

7. "The Odd Couple," *Charlotte Observer*, March 12, 1978, Clippings, Governor James B. Hunt, Jr., Papers, State Archives, Division of Archives and History, Raleigh (hereinafter cited as NCDAH).

8. "Hunt Assistant Defends State Patronage," *Hickory Record*, November 11, 1977, Press Secretary's File, and A. L. May, "Grandfatherly Williams's Hunt Tough Bad Guy," *News and Observer*, January 29, 1979, Clippings; both in Hunt Papers, NCDAH.

9. Martin Donsky, "Grimsley's Style Making Waves for Hunt," *News and Observer*, November 1977, press secretary's file, Hunt Papers, NCDAH.

10. Joseph Grimsley, interview by author, October 12, 2000; Bill Gilkeson, "'Swag' Has His Turf Cropped," *Durham Morning Herald*, October 15, 1978, 1D; Ted Vaden, "Rep. Gilmore Accepts Human Resource Post," *News and Observer*, January 4, 1978, 21; Howard Lee, interview by author, October 26, 1999.

11. Martin Donsky, "Behind Hunt's Plan to 'Control the Bureaucracy,'" *News and Observer*, January 3, 1977, 2; Daniel Hoover, "Hunt Forces Moving Into State Posts," *News and Observer*, January 11, 1977, 1; "Hunt: Employees Won't Lose Jobs," *Greensboro Daily News*, June 23, 1977, Press Secretary's File, Hunt Papers, NCDAH.

12. "Hunt 'Purging Parole Board,'" *News and Observer*, June 3, 1977, "Assistant," *Record*, Press Secretary's File, Hunt Papers, NCDAH.

13. Steve Adams, "Hunt Orders Heating Limit," *News and Observer*, February 15, 1977, 1.

14. Steve Adams, "Hunt Ponders 54-Hour Week," *News and Observer*, February 12, 1977, 1; Cole Campbell, "Convenience Shops Spurn Hunt's Plan," *News and Observer*, February 16, 1977, 1; Adams, "Hunt Drops Hours Limits for Stores," *News and Observer*, February 1, 1977, 1; Ken Freidlin, "50-Day Workweek Returns Monday," *Winston-Salem Journal*, March 3, 1977; Ken Friedlin, "Actions by '77 Assembly Had a Distinct Hunt Flavor," *Winston-Salem Journal*, December 1977, Press Secretary's File, Hunt Papers, NCDAH.

15. "Edmisten Threatens Fight Over Hunt's Utility Proposal," *Greensboro Daily News*, April 7, 1977; "House Speaker Attacks Plan to Reshuffle Utilities Plan," *Durham Morning Herald*, April 1, 1977, Press Secretary's File, Hunt Papers, NCDAH.

16. Donald G. Mathews and Jane Sherron De Hart, *Sex, Gender and Politics of ERA*, (New York: Oxford University Press, 1990), 68.

17. Maria Bliss to Jim Hunt, Raleigh, November 11, 1976; Nancy Snowden, Hendersonville, to Jim Hunt, Raleigh, December 6, 1976; 1977 ERA File, Hunt Papers, NCDAH; Matthews and De Hart, *ERA*, 80.

18. Mrs. Julius Aker to Jim Hunt, Raleigh, February 26, 1977, ERA File, Hunt Papers, NCDAH.

19. Mrs. Allie C. Phillips to Jim Hunt, Raleigh, February 18, 1977, ERA File, Hunt Papers, NCDAH.

20. Reverend Emerson E. Woodell, Sr., Raleigh, to Jim Hunt, Raleigh, February 4, 1977; Mrs. Ola Johnson, Selma, NC, to Jim Hunt, Raleigh, July 7, 1976, ERA File, Hunt Papers, NCDAH.

21. The Reverend Charles E. Keith, Durham, to Jim Hunt, Raleigh, February 25, 1977; Deborah Waller, Wade, to Jim Hunt, Raleigh, February 16, 1977, ERA File, Hunt Papers, NCDAH.

22. Ossie Fredericks, Salisbury, to Jim Hunt, Raleigh, March 7, 1977; Gordon Hanes, Winston-Salem, to Jim Hunt, March 3, 1977, ERA File, Hunt Papers, NCDAH.

23. Anne Saker, "Madame Chief Justice," *News and Observer*, August 22, 1999, 11; Martin Donsky, "Susie Sharp Calls to Protest ERA," *News and Observer*, March 2, 1977, 6.

24. Matthews and De Hart, *ERA*, 88.

25. *Ibid.*, 89, "All Eyes on NC ERA Vote," *News and Observer*, March 1, 1977, 2; Martin Donsky, "ERA Factions Held Senators in Tug-of-War," *News and Observer*, March 3, 1977, 1; Senator Bobby Lee Combs, Raleigh, to President Jimmy Carter, Washington, D. C., March 2, 1977, and Marshall Rauch, Raleigh, to President Carter, Washington, D. C., undated, North Carolina File, Jimmy Carter Papers, Jimmy Carter Presidential Library, Atlanta (hereinafter cited as JCL).

26. Joseph Grimsley, interview by author, September 26, 1999.

27. James B. Hunt, Jr., interview by author, December 14, 1999; Rowland Evans and Robert Novak, "State Sen. John Henley Switched to Oppose ERA Despite Rosalyn Carter's Call," *Greensboro Daily News*, March 9, 1977, ERA File, Hunt Papers, NCDAH; Mathews, and De Hart, *ERA*, 89.

28. Ruth Mary Meyers, Raleigh, to Jim Hunt, Raleigh, March 4, 1977, ERA File, Hunt Papers, NCDAH.

29. H. Gayle Ward, Raleigh, to Jim Hunt, Raleigh, April 29, 1977, ERA File, Hunt Papers, NCDAH; Hunt, interview by author.

30. "Education Board Votes Green as Interim Chief," *News and Observer*, April 8, 1977; "Green Asks Delay on Education Board Confirmation Vote," *Greensboro Daily News*, April 21, 1977 Press Secretary's File, Hunt Papers, NCDAH.

31. Rob Christensen, "Lt. Gov. Urged as Chairman," *News and Observer*, May 19, 1977; "Senate Loyalties Split as Green, Hunt Feud," *News and Observer*, May 26, 1977, Press Secretary's File, Hunt Papers, NCDAH.

32. "Hunt's Senate Backers Lose School Board Fight to Green," *News and Observer*, May 22, 1977; Jack Betts, "Hunt Questions Green Panel's Appointment," *Greensboro Daily News*, May 27, 1977, Press Secretary's File, Hunt Papers, NCDAH.

33. Ken Friedlin, "Rift Between Hunt, Green is Widening," *Winston-Salem Journal*, May 22, 1977; Martin Donsky, "Compromise Offered on Schools Post, *News and Observer*, May 25, 1977; Rob Christensen, "Green Keeps Low Profile, Tight Budget," *News and Observer*, February 21, 1977, 23; David R. Nelson, "Green Confirms Possibility of Governor Quest in 1980," unknown newspaper, Press Secretary's File, Hunt Papers, NCDAH.

34. "Loyalties," *News and Observer*, May 26, 1977, Press Secretary's File, Hunt Papers, NCDAH.

35. Ned Cline, "Deal Got Green Out of Race?" *Charlotte Observer*, June 2, 1977; Brent Hackney, "Final Insurance Bill: Passage Expected," unknown newspaper, June 23, 1977, Press Secretary's File, Hunt Papers, NCDAH.

36. James B. Hunt, Jr., "Statement on Testing in Schools," February 8, 1977, *Papers*, 63.

37. Marc Sosne, "State Politics and Educational Legislation" (Dissertation, University of North Carolina at Chapel Hill, 1978), ii, 54, 65, North Carolina Collection, Louis Wilson Library, University of North Carolina, Chapel Hill, North Carolina (hereinafter cited as NCC-UNC); Betty Owen, interview by author, October 12, 1999.

38. Sosne, "Politics," i.

39. *Ibid.*, 55–56.

40. Claude Sitton, "Hunt Backing Down on Public School Pledge," *News and Observer*, January 21, 1979, Clippings, Hunt Papers, NCDAH; Marsha Van Dyke Krotsing, "To Be or Merely to Seem? Investigating the Image of the Modern Education Governor" (Ph.D. Dissertation, College of William and Mary, 1987), 172, NCC-UNC; "Hunt Defends Test in Iowa," *News and Observer*, November 13, 1979, 23; Owen, interview by author.

41. James B. Hunt, Jr., "State of the State," January 17, 1977, *Papers*, 8; Owen, interview.

42. Grimsley, interview by author.

43. Ferrel Guillory, "Governor Hopefuls Give Views on Major Issues," *News and Observer*, August 8, 1976, 1, 10; Phil Carlton, interview by author, September 12, 2000.

44. Jerry Bledsoe, *Death Sentence: The True Story of Velma Barfield's Life, Crimes and Execution* (New York: Dutton, 1998), 248.

45. Tom Taft to Jim Hunt, memo, September 14, 1972; D. P. Rudisell, Hickory, NC, to Jim Hunt, February 17, 1976; Jim Hunt, Raleigh, to D. P. Rudisill, Hickory, NC, February 20, 1976, Crime File, Hunt Papers, NCDAH.

46. John Webb, Wilson, to Jim Hunt, Raleigh, August 3, 1976, Crime File, and Ned Cline, "Hunt Won't Block Executions in North Carolina," *Charlotte Observer*, May 19, 1977, Press Secretary's File, both in Hunt Papers, NCDAH; Martin Donsky, "Death Penalty, Tax Reform, Split Candidates in TV Debate," *News and Observer*, August 3, 1976, 5.

47. James B. Hunt, Jr., "Legislative Message on Crime," January 31, 1977, *Papers*, 10, 18–19; Martin Donsky, "Governor Holds Back on Tax Reform Plan," *News and Observer*, June 3, 1977, 29; "Hunt Retreats From Big Battle on Veto Power," *Charlotte Observer*, April 24, 1977, Press Secretary's File, Hunt Papers, NCDAH.

48. Leslie Wayne, "Succession, Veto Power Called For," *News and Observer*, March 9, 1973, 9; Tom Gilmore, speech on succession, North Carolina House of Representatives; May 10, 1977, Succession File, Hunt Papers, NCDAH.

49. Gilmore, speech, May 10, 1977; Lenox Rawlings, "Succession Bill Passes: To Go Before Voters," *Winston-Salem Journal*, May 11, 1977, Succession File, Hunt Papers, NCDAH.

50. James B. Holshouser, interview by author, October 20, 1999; Mrs. Gloria Cargill, Rockingham, to Jim Hunt, November 4, 1977, and Tom Bradshaw to Jim Hunt, memo, September 12, 1977, Succession File, Hunt Papers, NCDAH.

51. Sam Erwin, Jr., statement, November 7, 1977, Sam Erwin Papers, Southern Historical Collection, Louis Wilson Library, UNC (hereinafter referred to as SHC-UNC); Lenox Rawlings, "Decision Keeps Anti-Succession Group in Dark," *Winston-Salem Journal*, October 21, 1977; Jack Betts, "Succession Foes Win Round," *Greensboro Daily News*, October 28, 1977, Press Secretary's File, Hunt Papers, NCDAH.

52. Jim Hunt, Raleigh, to Hugh Wilson, Hillsborough, NC, October 13, 1977; Jim Hunt, Raleigh, to Joe Zaytoun, Raleigh, undated letter, Succession File, Hunt Papers, NCDAH.

53. Martin Donsky, "Self Interest Made in Succession Push," *News and Observer*, August 7, 1977, Succession File, Hunt Papers, NCDAH.

54. Carter Wrenn, interview by author, January 16, 2000; Tom Ellis, interview by author, May 17, 2000; Rob Christensen, "Hunt: Succession a Step Up for North Carolina," *News and Observer*, November 9, 1977, Press Secretary's File, Hunt Papers, NCDAH.

Chapter 10

1. Jeffrey Crow, et al., *A History of African Americans in North Carolina* (Raleigh: Division of Archives and History, 1992,) 204–5; John L. Godwin, *Black Wilmington and the North Carolina Way* (New York: University Press of America, 2000), 250; Rick Nichols, "Deaths Follow School Unrest," (Raleigh) *News and Observer*, February 8, 1971, 3.

2. Crow, *African Americans*, 205; "Youth is Killed in Wilmington," *News and Observer*, February 7, 1971, 1; Tom MacRae, "Wilmington Toll 2; Guard is Called Out," *News and Observer*, February 8, 1971, 1.

3. Nichols, "Deaths," 1.

4. Tom MacRae and John Coit, "Officers Search Church," *News and Observer*, February 9, 1971, 1.

5. Wayne King, "The Case Against the Wilmington Ten," *New York Times Magazine*, December 3, 1978, 70.

6. *Ibid.*, 66.

7. King, "Case," 74; Tom MacRae, "Chavis, 10 Others Bound Over," *News and Observer*, April 1, 1972, 1; Indictment of Wilmington Ten, April 24, 1972, Legal Counsel Jack Cozort File, James B. Hunt Papers, State Archives, Division of Archives and History, Raleigh (hereinafter cited as NCDAH).

8. Ann Shepard, Eric Junious, Jerome Mitchell, and Allen Hall, testimony at Wilmington Ten Conviction Hearing, Cozort File, Hunt Papers, NCDAH; Kerry Sipe, "Chavis Given 29 Years," *News and Observer*, October 19, 1972, 8.

9. Hall, testimony, Cozort File, Hunt Papers, NCDAH; King, "Case," 60.

10. "Chavis Transferred to Smaller Prison," *News and Observer*, March 21, 1976, 20; Reverend Ben Chavis, statement, May 2, 1976, Crime File, Hunt Papers, NCDAH.

11. Fred Harwell, *A True Deliverance: The Joan Little Case* (New York: Alfred A. Knopf, 1975), 27; "Extradition: Hunt to Seek Little's Return," *Sanford Herald,* January 5, 1978, Clippings, Hunt Papers, NCDAH.

12. Allen Hall and Jerome Mitchell, testimony, Post-Conviction Hearing, Cozort File, Hunt Papers, NCDAH; King, "Case," 60, 76.

13. Imani Kanzana, Washington, D. C., to Jim Hunt, Raleigh, January 5, 1977, Wilmington Ten File, Hunt Papers, NCDAH.

14. Parren Mitchell, Washington, to Jim Hunt, Raleigh, January 15, 1977; Charles E. Cobb, New York City, to Jim Hunt, Raleigh, January 13, 1977; anonymous writer, France, to Hunt, Raleigh, no date, Wilmington Ten File, Hunt Papers, NCDAH.

15. "60 Minutes," transcript, March 6, 1977, Cozort File, and Olivia Behlen, Clearwater, Fla., to Jim Hunt, Raleigh, February 6, 1977, Wilmington Ten File, both in Hunt Papers, NCDAH.

16. Samuel Hirsch, New York City, to Jim Hunt, Raleigh, March 14, 1977, Wilmington Ten File, Hunt Papers, NCDAH.

17. John Greenwood, Miami, to Jim Hunt, Raleigh, March 2, 1977, Wilmington Ten File, Hunt Papers, NCDAH.

18. Charlotte Steen, New York City, to Jim Hunt, Raleigh, April 1, 1977; Malcolm McLean, Ashland, WI, to Jim Hunt, Raleigh, April 1, 1977, Wilmington Ten File, Hunt Papers, NCDAH.

19. Jay Stroud, Wilmington, to Jim Hunt, Raleigh, February 9, 1977; Jerome Mitchell, testimony, Post-Conviction Hearing, Cozort File, Hunt Papers, NCDAH.

20. Stroud to Hunt, Cozort File, Hunt Papers, NCDAH.

21. George M. Fountain, Order on Post-Conviction Hearing, North Carolina Superior Court, May 1977, Cozort File, Hunt Papers, NCDAH.

22. "Wilmington 10 Mothers Ask Governor for a Pardon," *News and Observer,* July 21, 1977; Martin Donsky, "Hunt Refuses Sunday Meeting on 10," *News and Observer,* December 1, 1977; Martin Donsky, "Hunt Aide, 10 Group Will Meet," *News and Observer,* December 2, 1977, Press Secretary's File, Hunt Papers, NCDAH.

23. Stan Swofford and Jack Betts, "Wilmington 10 Appeal Rejected," *Greensboro Daily News,* January 6, 1978, Clippings, Hunt Papers, NCDAH.

24. Dawn Maria Crayton, "US Attorney Claims '10' Rights Violated," *News and Observer,* January 20, 1978, 1.

25. Betty McCain, interview by author, October 6, 1999.

26. James B. Hunt, Jr., "Statement on the Wilmington Ten," January 23, 1978, *Addresses and Papers of James B. Hunt, Jr., Governor of North Carolina, 1977–1981* (Raleigh: North Carolina Department of Cultural Resources, 1981), 219.

27. Hunt, "Statement," *Papers,* 219–20.

28. Daniel C. Hoover, "'10' Leader Denounces Hunt Action," *News and Observer,* January 25, 1978, 1.

29. Martin Donsky, "Hunt Cuts Wilmington 10 Terms; Eight Could Be Paroled This Year," *News and Observer,* January 24, 1978, 5.

30. Hoover, "Leader," 1.

31. Donsky, "Terms," 5; "Hunt Gets Praise, Criticism," *News and Observer,* January 25, 1978, 1.

32. "Praise," 1.

33. William A. Draves, Manhattan, KS, to Jim Hunt, Raleigh, January 25, 1978, Wilmington Ten File, Hunt Papers, NCDAH.

34. Donsky, "Terms," 5; Mary McGrory, "Hunt Trips on World Stage: Wilmington 10 Will Haunt Him Forever," *Charlotte Observer*, January 23, 1978, Clippings, Hunt Papers, NCDAH.

35. Ferrel Guillory, "Justice Dept. Deciding Its Role," *News and Observer*, March 25, 1978, 6B.

36. Donsky, "Terms," 1, 5; "Praise," 1; John Farris, Rocky Mount, to Jim Hunt, Raleigh, January 24, 1978, Wilmington Ten File, Hunt Papers, NCDAH.

37. Virginia Warren, Lillington, to Jim Hunt, Raleigh, January 25, 1978, Wilmington Ten File, NCDAH.

38. Dr. Walter Bullington, Charlotte, to Jim Hunt, Raleigh, January 24, 1978, Wilmington Ten File, Hunt Papers, NCDAH.

39. President Jimmy Carter, Winston-Salem press conference, March 17, 1978, *Public Papers of the President of the United States, Jimmy Carter, 1978, Volume 1* (Washington, D.C.: U. S. Government Printing Office, 1979), 537.

40. Ferrel Guillory, "Justice Dept. Deciding Its Role," *News and Observer*, January 26, 1978, 6B; Ferrel Guillory, "Carter Hears State's Views," *News and Observer*, March 1, 1978, 1.

41. Elizabeth Abramoutz, Assistant Director for Education and Women's Issues, Domestic Policy Staff, White House, to the Director of the National Conference of Black Lawyers, May 2, 1978, North Carolina file, Jimmy Carter Papers, Jimmy Carter Presidential Library, Atlanta (hereinafter cited as JCL).

42. King, "Case," 60.

43. Doug Huron, White House memo, September 27, 1978; John Conyers, Washington, D.C., to Jimmy Carter, September 8, 1978, North Carolina File, Carter Papers, JCL.

44. Conyers to Carter, North Carolina File, Carter Papers, JCL; Alex Poinsett, *Walking With Presidents: Louis Martin and the Rise of Black Political Power* (Lanham, MD: Madison Books, 1997), 175.

45. Poinsett, *Presidents*, 173–179; Louis Martin, Memo to President Carter, September 8, 1978, North Carolina File, Carter Papers, JCL.

46. Martin, Memo to Carter, September 8, 1978.

47. King, "Case," 62; Ned Cline, "Hunt Perplexed By Ten Case," *Greensboro Daily News*, undated, Clippings, Hunt Papers, NCDAH.

48. King, "Case," 62; J. Christopher Shultz, "The Burning of America: Race, Radicalism, and the 'Charlotte Three' Trial in the 1970s," *North Carolina Historical Review* 75 (1999), 63.

49. Charlotte Three Ad Hoc Defense Committee, "Case of the Charlotte Three," brochure, Charlotte Three File, Hunt Papers, NCDAH; Schultz, "Burning," 49.

50. Shultz, "Burning of America," 50.

51. Sandra Beck, Charlotte, to Jim Hunt, Raleigh, December 14, 1978, Charlotte Three File, Hunt Papers, NCDAH.

52. Patricia S. Funderburk, Raleigh, to Jim Hunt, Raleigh, October 20, 1978; Judy Hogan, Chapel Hill, to Jim Hunt, Raleigh, November 2, 1978, Charlotte Three File, Hunt Papers, NCDAH.

53. L. C. Dorsey to Jim Hunt, Raleigh, November 20, 1978, Charlotte Three File, Hunt Papers, NCDAH.

54. Nicholas Garrin, Raleigh, to Jim Hunt, Raleigh, October 31, 1978, Charlotte Three File, Hunt Papers, NCDAH.

55. Charlotte City Council Resolution, November 6, 1978; Harvey Gantt, Charlotte, to Jim Hunt, Raleigh, October 17, 1978, Charlotte Three File, Hunt Papers, NCDAH.

56. William P. Whitlow, Charlotte, to Jim Hunt, Raleigh, November 8, 1978, Charlotte Three File, Hunt Papers, NCDAH.

57. Linda Bishop, Charlotte, to Jim Hunt, Raleigh, November 13, 1978, Charlotte Three File, Hunt Papers, NCDAH; Schultz, "Burning," 63.

58. Herbert Lape, Asheville, to Jim Hunt, Raleigh, December 11, 1978, Charlotte Three File, Hunt Papers, NCDAH.

59. Joseph Grimsley to Jim Hunt, Undated Memo, Charlotte Three File, Hunt Papers, NCDAH.

60. Governor James B. Hunt, Jr., statement on Charlotte Three Sentence Commutation, July 1979, Charlotte Three File, Hunt Papers, NCDAH.

61. *Ibid.*

62. Marion Ellis and Vanessa Gallman, "Charlotte 3 Sentences Reduced," *Asheville Citizen*, July 26, 1979, Clippings; Barry Nakell, Chapel Hill, to Jim Hunt, Raleigh, July 13, 1979; Loy H. Witherspoon, Charlotte, to Jim Hunt, Raleigh, July 24, 1979, Charlotte Three File, Hunt Papers, NCDAH.

63. Dr. James M. Efird, Durham, to Jim Hunt, Raleigh, May 8, 1979; Dr. Charles R. Robinson, Durham, to Hunt, Raleigh, April 20, 1979, Wilmington Ten file, Hunt Papers, NCDAH; "Hunt Defends Test in Iowa," *News and Observer*, November 13, 1979, 23; A. L. May, "10 Leader Chavis Free on Parole," *News and Observer*, December 15, 1979, 1.

64. "Wilmington Ten Impact Weighed," *News and Observer*, May 12, 1980, 11.

65. Howard Lee, interview by author, October 26, 1999.

66. Ginny Carroll, "Federal Appeals Court Overturns Convictions of Wilmington 10," *News and Observer*, December 5, 1980, 1; Laurie Willis, "Ben Chavis, Civil Rights Work Brought Limelight, Controversy," *News and Observer*, August 22, 1999, 7. In 1993, Ben Chavis succeeded Benjamin Hooks as executive director of the National Association for the Advancement of Colored People (NAACP). However, sixteen months after Chavis's appointment, the NAACP board of directors dismissed him for allegedly using the association's funds to pay a settlement in a sexual harassment suit. Disgusted with the NAACP, he joined the Nation of Islam and changed his name to Minister Benjamin Chavis Muhammad.

Chapter 11

1. Bert Bennett to Phil Carlton, memo, January 28, 1964, Bert Bennett File, Terry Sanford Papers, Southern Historical Collection, Louis Wilson Library, University of North Carolina, Chapel Hill, North Carolina (hereinafter cited as SHC-UNC).

2. James B. Hunt, Jr., press release, January 14, 1974; Jesse Helms, Washington, D. C., to Jim Hunt, Raleigh, January 9, 1974, Agriculture File, Lieutenant Governor James B. Hunt, Jr., Papers, State Archives, Division of Archives and History, Raleigh, North Carolina (hereinafter cited as NCDAH).

3. Hunt, press release, January 14, 1974, Agriculture File, Lieutenant Governor Hunt Papers, NCDAH.

4. Hunt, statement, October 1, 1975, Speech File, Hunt Papers, NCDAH.

5. Joseph Califano, *Governing In America* (New York: Simon and Schuster, 1981), 183, 212, 214; William Link, *William Friday: Power, Purpose, and American Higher Education* (Chapel Hill: University of North Carolina Press, 1995), 284–85.

6. Joseph Califano, Washington, to Jim Hunt, Raleigh, February 25, 1977; Joseph Califano to Jim Hunt, March 28, 1977; Joseph Califano to Jim Hunt, May 5, 1977; Joseph Califano to Jim Hunt, telegram, July 12, 1977; Jim Hunt to Joseph Califano, July 15, 1977, North Carolina Department of Human Resources File, Governor Hunt Papers, NCDAH.

7. Califano, *Governing*, 183–84, 186; Ferrel Guillory, "HEW Launches War on Smokes," *News and Observer*, January 12, 1978, 1.

8. Jim Hunt, "Statement on Proposal Affecting Tobacco Farmers," November 3, 1977, *Addresses and Papers of James Baxter Hunt, Jr., Governor of North Carolina* (Raleigh: North Carolina Department of Cultural Resources, 1982), 172; Dan Lohwasser, "Califano Has 'Gone Too Far'— Hunt," *Reidsville Review*, January 13, 1978, Clippings, Hunt Papers, NCDAH.

9. Jim Hunt, statement to National Association of Farm Broadcasters, November 11, 1977, *Papers*, 184; Jimmy Carter, press conference, January 14, 1978, *Public Papers of the Presidents of the United States, Jimmy Carter, 1978, Volume 1* (Washington: United States Government Printing Office, 1979), 67.

10. Califano, *Governing*, 186, 251; Joseph Califano, interview by William Link, April 5, 1991, SHC-UNC.

11. Jack Watson to President Carter, White House Memo, February 27, 1978, North Carolina File, Jimmy Carter Papers, Jimmy Carter Presidential Library (hereinafter cited as JCL).

12. Ferrel Guillory, "Carter Hears State's Views," *News and Observer*, March 1, 1978, 1, 9; Califano, *Governing*, 188–89.

13. Califano, *Governing*, 190.

14. *Ibid.*, 188, 208; Peter G. Bourne, *Jimmy Carter: A Comprehensive Biography from Plains to Postpresidency* (New York: Scribner, 1997), 78.

15. Califano, *Governing*, 190.

16. Jimmy Carter, press conference, March 17, 1978, *Public Papers, 1978, Vol. 1*, 1386.

17. Carter, *Public Papers, 1978, Vol. 1*, 1386; Califano, *Governing*, 192.

18. Carter, Winston-Salem press conference, March 24, 1978, *Public Papers, 1978, Vol. 1*, 529.

19. Jimmy Carter, North Carolina Democratic party rally, August 5, 1978, *Public Papers, 1978, Vol. 1*, 1387; "Jimmy," White House, to James B. Hunt, Jr., October 5, 1978, North Carolina File, Carter Papers, JCL; James B. Hunt, Jr., interview by author, December 14, 1999.

20. Betty McCain, interview by author, October 6, 1999; "Helms: Only Party

Ties Bar Hunt's Support," *Greensboro Daily News*, November 1, 1978, Clippings, Hunt Papers, NCDAH.

21. Ned Cline, "Is Governor Hunt Really Backing Ingram?" *Charlotte Observer*, October 22, 1978, Clippings, Hunt Papers, NCDAH.

22. Jim Hunt, "Chinese Say 'Future Bright' for NC-China Trade," press release, November 4, 1979; Craig Dunlap, "North Carolina Advised to Shift Trade Emphasis to Pacific," *Journal of Commerce*, December 28, 1979, 3, North Carolina Department of Commerce File, Hunt Papers, NCDAH; Chip Pearsall and Howard Troxler, "Eastern Belt Opens; Prices Top 1978's," *News and Observer*, July 25, 1979, 1; "Hunt Backs Tobacco Trading in Talk with Chinese Leaders," *News and Observer*, November 3, 1979, 5.

23. Ann Todd and Bruce Kirschenbaum, White House Memo, May 28, 1980, North Carolina File, Carter Papers, JCL.

24. Ferrel Guillory, interview by author, December 15, 1999.

25. Califano, *Governing*, 243–46.

26. Califano, *Governing*, 249–51; Link, *Friday*, 292.

27. Link, *Friday*, 292; William Friday, interview by author, December 29, 1999.

28. Friday, interview by author.

29. William A. Johnson, Lillington, to Jim Hunt, Raleigh, August 22, 1977; Jim Hunt, Raleigh, to Joseph Califano, Washington, September 2, 1977, United States Department of Health, Education, and Welfare Case, Jack Cozort File, Hunt Papers, NCDAH.

30. Califano, interview by Link.

31. *Ibid.*

32. Ferrel Guillory, "Carter Hears State's Views," *News and Observer*, March 1, 1978, 1, 9; Califano, *Governing*, 188–89.

33. Jim Hunt, Statement on UNC-HEW Agreement, May 12, 1978, *Papers*, 292.

34. Link, *Friday*, 314–15; Jim Hunt, Conference for Board of Governors and Trustees, January 11, 1979, *Papers*, 448–49.

35. Jim Hunt, Conference for Board of Governors and Trustees, January 11, 1979, *Papers*, 448–49; Link, *Friday*, 319.

36. Califano, *Governing*, 254.

37. *Ibid.*, 255; Link, *Friday*, 320; Califano, interview by Link; Joseph Califano to President Carter, undated memo, North Carolina File, Carter Papers, JCL.

38. Link, *Friday*, 323.

39. Link, *Friday*, 332.

40. *Ibid.*

41. Stu Eizenstat and Jack Watson to President Jimmy Carter, April 10, 1979, North Carolina File, Carter Papers, JCL.

42. Califano, *Governing*, 252.

43. *Ibid.*, 257; William Friday to Dick Robinson, Memo, April 19, 1979, William Friday Papers, SHC-UNC; Link, *Friday*, 333.

44. Bill Friday to Jim Hunt, telegram, April 19, 1979, Friday Papers, SHC-UNC; Link, *Friday*, 334.

45. Link, *Friday*, 334–35; Friday to Board of Governors, April 20, 1979, Fri-

day Papers, SHC-UNC; Stuart Eizenstat and Jack Watson to President Carter, May 11, 1979, and Joseph Califano to Carter, May 11, 1979, both in North Carolina File, Carter Papers, JCL.

46. William Friday, Statement to the UNC Board of Governors, April 20, 1979, UNC Board of Governors File, Hunt Papers, NCDAH.

47. *Ibid.*; Califano, *Governing*, 258; Joseph Califano to President Carter, May 11, 1979, Carter Papers, JCL; Rob Christensen, "Federal Judge Restrains HEW from Cutting Funds to UNC," *News and Observer*, April 28, 1979, 1; Jim Hunt, Statement on University-HEW Controversy, April 20, 1979, *Papers*, 521.

48. Stu Eizenstat and Jack Watson to President Carter, May 12, 1979, and Califano to Carter, May 11, 1979, both in North Carolina File, Carter Papers, JCL; Link, *Friday*, 343.

49. Jimmy Carter, *Keeping Faith: Memoirs of a President* (New York: Bantam Books, 1982), 115.

50. Califano, *Governing*, 414, 432; McCain and Hunt, interviews by author.

51. "Carter Sounds Trumpet," *News and Observer*, July 17, 1979, 1; Califano, *Governing*, 426, 431.

52. Califano, *Governing*, 432; Bob Woodward, *The Wars of Watergate* (New York: Simon and Schuster, 1999), 86–87.

53. "Politics Led to Ouster, Ex–HEW Official Said," *News and Observer*, July 20, 1979, 5A; Califano, *Governing*, 443.

54. John Robinson, "Departure Raises Cheers," *News and Observer*, July 20, 1979, 1.

55. Joe Rauh, Jr., Washington, to Patricia Harris, Washington, August 10, 1979, North Carolina File, Carter Papers, JCL.

56. Link, *Friday*, 344–46; Friday, interview by author.

57. Hunt, interview by author.

58. Jimmy Carter, remarks to Forsyth County residents, Winston-Salem, October 9, 1980, *Public Papers, Jimmy Carter, 1980–81, Vol. 3*, 2141.

59. Link, *Friday*, 362–64.

Chapter 12

1. Paul Luebke, Stephen Peters and John Wilson, "The Political Economy of North Carolina," *High Hopes for High Tech: Microelectronics Policy in North Carolina* (Chapel Hill: University of Chapel Hill Press, 1985), 314–16.

2. Quentin Lindsey, interview by author, October 7, 1999; James B. Hunt, "Nepal: A Test Ground for Economic Theories," *North Carolina State Alumni News*, September–October 1963, 7, University Archives, North Carolina State University, Raleigh (hereinafter referred to as NCSU); Ferrel Guillory, "NC Senator OKs Tax Package," *News and Observer*, April 4, 1974, 5.

3. "Hunt Tells Views on Textile Issues," *News and Observer*, October 6, 1972, 8.

4. Michael I. Luger, "The States and High-Technology Development: The Case of North Carolina," *High Tech*, 312.

5. Paul Luebke, *Tar Heel Politics 2000* (Chapel Hill: University of North Carolina Press, 1998), 34.

6. Carter Wrenn, interview by author, January 16, 2000.

7. Luebke, *Politics*, 34.

8. "Faircloth Appointment Debatable," *News and Observer*, January 4, 1977, 4, and Ken Friedlin, "Faircloth Tells It Like He Sees It," *Winston-Salem Journal*, May 8, 1977, both in Clippings, Governor James B. Hunt, Jr., Papers, State Archives, Division of Archives and History, Raleigh (hereinafter cited as NCDAH).

9. Jim Hunt, Raleigh, to Lauch Faircloth, Clinton, August 13, 1974, unprocessed Hunt Papers, NCDAH; Betty McCain, interview by author, October 6, 1999; Joseph Grimsley, interview by author, September 26, 1999.

10. Jean G. Marlowe, "North Carolina's Economic Development Program Charges Into the Future," *Wachovia*, Spring 1978, Vol. 65, No. 2, 18, North Carolina Collection, Louis Wilson Library, University of North Carolina at Chapel Hill (hereinafter cited as NCC-UNC).

11. Jim Hunt, press conference, October 5, 1977, North Carolina Department of Commerce File, Hunt Papers, NCDAH.

12. Paul Essex, interview by author, December 7, 1999.

13. Martin Donsky, "Business Community Makes Its Peace With Hunt," *News and Observer*, January 23, 1978, 3; Marlowe, "Development," *Wachovia*, 18, NCC-UNC.

14. "Hunt Proposes Change in Inventory Tax," *Charlotte Observer*, January 12, 1978, 1.

15. Marlowe, "Development," 19–20, NCC-UNC; Cynthia Wilkes Smith to Fran Yoorde, White House Memo, March 6, 1978, North Carolina File, Jimmy Carter Papers, Jimmy Carter Presidential Library, Atlanta (hereinafter cited as JCL); Luger, "States," *High Tech*, 197.

16. Marlowe, "Development," 20; "Hunt Announces That Charlotte Named Foreign Trade Zone," press release, April 29, 1980, Commerce File, Hunt Papers, NCDAH; Paul Essex, interview by author; Stu Eizenstadt, Washington, D.C., to Paul Essex, Raleigh, September 15, 1978, North Carolina File, Carter Papers, JCL; Interview of Jimmy Carter, October 13, 1978, *Public Papers of the Presidents of the United States, Jimmy Carter, 1978, Vol. 2* (Washington: United States Government Printing Office, 1979), 1782.

17. "Hunt, Symphony Go Wooing in Midwest," *Greensboro Daily News*, October 18, 1978, Clippings, and Jim Hunt, remarks transcribed from a mini-cassette tape, September 5, 1980, Commerce File, both in Hunt Papers, NCDAH.

18. Michael I. Luger, "States," *High Tech*, 192.

19. Herbert Ludwigshafen, West Germany, to Hunt, September 11, 1979; Rudolf Escherich, West Germany, to Hunt, September 5, 1979; Jim Hunt, European Trade Mission Report, April 20, 1978; "Governor Hunt Announces New Plant in Thomasville," press release, February 28, 1980, Commerce File, Hunt Papers, NCDAH.

20. Jim Hunt, "Statement on International Development," March 1, 1978, *Addresses and Papers of Governor James Baxter Hunt, Jr., Volume 1, 1977–1981* (Raleigh: North Carolina Department of Cultural Resources, 1982), 252; "North Carolina Delegation Seeks Major Japanese Firms," press release, October 30, 1979;

Craig Dunlap, "North Carolina Advised to Shift Trade Emphasis to Pacific," *Journal of Commerce*, December 27, 1979, 3; Jim Hunt, Raleigh, to Mike Mansfield, Tokyo, April 3, 1980, Commerce File, Hunt Papers, NCDAH.

21. Nell Perry, "Starring North Carolina," *Raleigh Times*, no date, Commerce File, Hunt Papers, NCDAH.

22. Wanda Dell, Tri-Star Pictures, Atlanta, to Jim Hunt, Raleigh, August 14, 1979; Jim Hunt, memo, February 19, 1980; Jim Hunt, Raleigh, to James Taylor, New York, no date; "Hunt Says State is Prepared, Eager to Serve Motion Picture Industry," November 20, 1980, Commerce File, Hunt Papers, NCDAH.

23. "Hunt Announces Major Movie To Be Filmed in North Carolina," press release, November 22, 1980, Commerce File, Hunt Papers, NCDAH.

24. "Interview: North Carolina Jim Hunt," *North Carolina*, January 1981, 18, NCC-UNC; Lindsey, interview by author; Dale Whittington, intoduction, *High Tech*, 3, 13–14; Randal Rothenburg, *The Neoliberals: Creating the New American Politics* (New York: Simon and Schuster, 1984), 194.

25. Gregory Sampson, "Employment and Earnings in the Semiconductor Electronics Industry: Implications for North Carolina," *High Tech*, 287.

26. Lindsey, interview by author; Sampson, "Employment," *High Tech*, 287; "Interview," *North Carolina*, 19, NCC-UNC.

27. Jim Hunt, "Statement on Industrial Growth," *Papers*, July 13, 1978, 325.

28. North Carolina's Economic Report of the Governor, 1979, 1, NCC-UNC; Jack Betts, "A Hard Job Ahead' to Improve Income," *Greensboro Daily News*, no date; Stan Swofford, "Hunt Doesn't Seek Top Industry," *Greensboro Daily News*, no date, Clippings, Hunt Papers, NCDAH.

29. Luger, "High-Technology," *High Tech*, 194; Jim Hunt, "AFL-CIO Convention," September 21, 1978, *Papers*, 379; *Ad Magazine in German and in American*, Commerce File, Hunt Papers, NCDAH; "Interview," *North Carolina*, 17, NCC-UNC.

30. Wilbur Hobby, Durham, to Jim Hunt, Raleigh, October 1, 1974, unprocessed Lieutenant Governor James B. Hunt Papers, NCDAH; Joe Grimsley, interview by author; Luebke, *Politics*, 35, 111–12.

31. Walton Jones, Chapel Hill, to Jim Hunt, Raleigh, October 14, 1977, North Carolina Board of Governors File, Hunt Papers, NCDAH; Luebke, *Politics*, 116–17.

32. Luebke, *Politics*, 117–18.

33. Luebke, *Politics*, 99–100; Ted Vaden, "Hunt Backs Unionized Company," *News and Observer*, July 22,1977, Scrapbook, Hunt Papers, NCDAH.

34. Luebke, *Politics*, 100; Grimsley, interview with author, April 15, 2001.

35. "Hunt Tells Truckers He Can't Do Any More," *Charlotte Observer*, July 3, 1979, 1; Gary Pearce, "Governor James B. Hunt, Jr.," *Papers*, xxvii.

36. Luebke, *Politics* 113–14; Jim Hunt, "Outline of Remarks of Welcome of DePoortere Corporation," *Papers*, 153.

37. Luebke, *Politics*, 123–24; Elizabeth Wheaton, *Greenkill: The 1979 Greensboro Killings* (Athens: University of Georgia Press, 1987), 52; Howard Covington and Stephen R. Kelly, "Hunt's Brown Lung Plan Draws Fire," *Asheville Citizen*, December 13, 1979, 1; Jim Hunt, "Statement on Brown-Lung Cases," December 12, 1979, *Papers*, 641.

38. Luebke, "Economy," *High Tech*, 325.

39. C. E. Bishop, et al., *The State of the South 2000* (Chapel Hill: MDC, Inc., 2000), 40–41, 44, 94–95.

40. *Ibid.*, 40.

Chapter 13

1. Howard Lee, interview by Jack Bass, December 13, 1973, Southern Historical Collection, Wilson Library, University of North Carolina at Chapel Hill, Chapel Hill, North Carolina (hereinafter referred to as SHC-UNC).

2. Lee, interview by Bass, SHC-UNC.

3. Paul Horvitz, "Lee Brings Moderate Approach to Resource Post," (Raleigh) *News and Observer*, January 22, 1977, 3D; Howard Lee, interview by Joseph Meisner, May 5, 1995, SHC-UNC; Howard Lee, interview by author, October 26, 1999.

4. Lee, interviews by Bass and Meisner, SHC-UNC; William R. Richardson, Chapel Hill, to Gene Simmons, Tarboro, September 10, 1970, North Carolina Democratic Executive Committee File, Governor Robert Scott Papers, State Archives, Division of Archives and History, Raleigh (hereinafter cited as NCDAH).

5. Baren Rosen, "Black Registers Lift Lee's Hopes," *News and Observer*, April 20, 1972, 12; Lee, interview by author.

6. Howard Lee, mailgram to Jim Hunt, March 1, 1976, unprocessed Lieutenant Governor James B. Hunt, Jr., Papers, and Ralph Scott, Burlington, to Jim Hunt, Raleigh, September 7, 1979, James B. Hunt, Jr., File, Ralph Scott Papers, both in NCDAH; Lee, interview by author.

7. Lee, interview by Meisner, SHC-UNC.

8. Paul Luebke, *Tar Heel Politics 2000* (Chapel Hill: University of North Carolina Press, 1999), 150.

9. Lee, interview by author.

10. Joe Grimsley to Hunt Campaign County Keys, October 6, 1976, Jim Hunt File, Ralph Scott Papers, NCDAH.

11. Lee, interview by Meisner, SHC-UNC; Lee, interview by author.

12. Lee, interview by Meisner, SHC-UNC.

13. *Ibid.*

14. *Ibid.*

15. *Ibid.*

16. Lee, interview by author.

17. Martin Donsky, "Political Aftermath of Decision," *News and Observer*, January 25, 1978, 1.

18. Lee, interview by author.

19. *Ibid.*

20. "Governor Supports Judge Facing Primary Challenge," *Durham Herald*, February 9, 1978, "Ruffin Named to Hunt Post," *Durham Herald*, February 14, 1978, Scrapbook, Hunt Papers, NCDAH; Lee, interview by author.

21. Eva Clayton, interview by Joseph Meisner, May 30, 1995, SHC-UNC.

22. Betsy Warren Harrison, interview by author, October 23, 2002; data submitted from the office of Senator Howard Lee, October 2002.

23. Jim Hunt, "Meeting with Mayors," *Addresses and Papers of North Carolina Governor James B. Hunt, 1977–1981* (Raleigh: Department of Cultural Resources, 1982), 88.

24. Lee, interview by Meisner, SHC-UNC.

25. Harrison, interview by author.

26. *Ibid.*

27. "Secretary Lee Fires Head of CETA Program," *News and Observer*, August 24, 1977, 1, 2; Ted Vaden, "State Lags in CETA Audits," *News and Observer*, August 31, 1978, 1.

28. Vaden, "Audits," 1.

29. "Under the Dome," *News and Observer*, September 2, 1978, 1.

30. Bruce Siceloff, "Spill Leaves Residents Feeling Sick, Worried," *News and Observer*, September 9, 1978, 1.

31. Lee, interview by Meisner, SHC-UNC.

32. Lee, interview by Meisner, SHC-UNC.

33. *Ibid.*; Jim Hunt, "Statement on PCB Spills in Eastern North Carolina," August 17, 1978, *Papers*, 349–50; Patricia Harris, Washington, to Jim Hunt, Raleigh, September 29, 1978, North Carolina File, Jimmy Carter Papers, Jimmy Carter Library, Atlanta (hereinafter cited as JCL); A. L. May and Bruce Siceloff, "State Eyes Treatment of PC on Roadside," *News and Observer*, January 26, 1979, 1.

34. Charles B. Parker, memo to Bill Calhoun, December 18, 1978; Howard Lee, memo to Jim Hunt, February 15, 1980; Assistant Director Eva Clayton, memo to Bill Calhoun, June 1, 1979, Jack Cozort File, Hunt Papers, NCDAH.

35. Henry Bridges, Raleigh, to Howard Lee, Raleigh, August 1, 1979; Lee to Hunt, memo, February 15, 1980, Cozort File, Hunt Papers, NCDAH; "Firing of Lee Asked By Lake," *Raleigh Times*, March 14, 1980, 6; "Indictments of Four Allege Misuse of CETA Funding," *News and Observer*, November 15, 1979, 24; Daniel Hoover, "Job Center Funds Probed," *News and Observer*, August 31, 1979, 1; Lee, interview by author.

36. Wilbur Hobby, interview by Jack Bass, December 1973, SHC-UNC.

37. Bert Bennett, memo to Phil Carlton, April 15, 1964, Bert Bennett File, North Carolina Governor Terry Sanford Papers, SHC-UNC.

38. Pat Stith and Daniel Hoover, "Union Boss Quite An Entrepreneur," September 9, 1979, *News and Observer*, 1; "Under the Dome," *News and Observer*, April 14, 1972, 6.

39. Stith and Hoover, "Boss," 4; Elizabeth Leland, "Official Says Hobby Sought Report Change," *News and Observer*, December 12, 1981, 23; "Hobby Expects To Get Records," *News and Observer*, November 2, 1979, 5A.

40. "Under the Dome," *News and Observer*, September 15, 1979, 1; "Under the Dome," *News and Observer*, November 12, 1979, 8; Daniel C. Hoover, "Indictments of Four Allege Misuse of CETA Funding," *News and Observer*, November 15, 1979, 23; Ralph Scott, Burlington, to Jim Hunt, Raleigh, September 7, 1979, Ralph Scott Papers, NCDAH.

41. Beverly Lake, Jr., interview by author, October 9, 1999; A. L. May, "Hunt Snubs Lake's Barbs in Debate," *News and Observer*, September 9, 1980, 1; "Cleaning CETA's House," *News and Observer*, September 9, 1981, 4; Lee, interview by author.

42. Pat Stith, "NC Demands Hobby's Firm Pay CETA Contract Funds," *News and Observer*, September 27, 1980, 1.

43. A.L. May and Pat Stith, "Hunt Withdraws Attempt to Shift CETA Investigation," *News and Observer*, September 5, 1980, 1; "Hunt's Timely Whistle," *News and Observer*, September 6, 1980, 1.

44. Lee, interview by author.

45. Lee, interview by author; Clayton and Lee, interviews by Meisner, UNC.

46. A.L. May, "Reed Violated Travel Ban, Hunt Says," *News and Observer*, August 27, 1981, 1; Daniel Hoover, "Bradshaw to Give Up DOT Post," *News and Observer*, May 13, 1981, 1; David McKinnon, "Roads Official Fired After Acquittal," *News and Observer*, April 18, 1981, 1; Dan Hoover, "Inside Help Suspected On Road Bids," *News and Observer*, August 17, 1980, 1.

47. A.L. May, "Governor Announces Grimsley to Succeed Lee as NRCD Chief," *News and Observer*, July 29, 1981, 1; Lee, interview by author.

48. Lee, interview by Meisner, SHC-UNC.

49. Jim Hunt, "Dinner Honoring Howard Lee," July 23, 1981, *Addresses and Papers of James Baxter Hunt, Jr., Governor of North Carolina, Volume II, 1981–1985* (Raleigh: Division of Archives and History, 1987), 146.

50. *Ibid.*, 146; James B. Hunt, Jr., interview by author, December 14, 1999.

51. Leland, "Report," 23; Elizabeth Leland, "Hobby Guilty of CETA Abuse," *News and Observer*, December 20, 1981, 1; Lee, interview by Meisner, SHC-UNC; Lee, interview by author; data from Lee's staff, submitted October 2002.

Chapter 14

1. "Hunt's Rating 64% in Carolina Poll," *Greensboro Daily News*, November 19, 1978, Clippings, Jim Hunt Papers, State Archives, Division of Archives and History, Raleigh (hereinafter cited as NCDAH).

2. Martin Donsky, "Hunt Boxed in By Tax Vow," (Raleigh) *News and Observer*, January 9, 1978, 1. "General Assembly Supports Tax Break, But Not Hunt's," *Wilmington Star*, December 17, 1978; A. L. May, "Hunt Considers Permanent Tax Cut," *News and Observer*, January 1, 1979, Clippings, Hunt Papers, NCDAH.

3. "Hunt Right to Freeze Jobs," *Asheville Citizen*, October 1, 1979, Clippings, Hunt Papers, NCDAH; Jim Hunt, "Governor's Conference on Fighting Inflation," February 1, 1979, *Addresses and Papers of Governor James B. Hunt, Jr., 1977–1981* (Raleigh: Department of Cultural Resources, 1982), 459.

4. Paul Krause, "Do-Little Assembly Reflecting Mood?" *Raleigh Times*, March 23, 1979; Krause, "Governor Pleased by Assembly Work," *Raleigh Times*, June 8, 1979, Clippings, Hunt Papers, NCDAH.

5. Jim Hunt, "State of the State," January 15, 1979, *Papers*, 26–38.

6. "Scott Says His Stand's on Hunt's Plan Same," *Fayetteville Observer*, December 20, 1979, Scrapbook, Hunt Papers, NCDAH; Jim Hunt, *Raising A New Generation: The North Carolina Story* (Raleigh: Department of Human Resources, 1978), 1.

7. Sherry Johnson, "Hunt Defends New Generation as Vital Program for

Children," *News and Observer*, November 17, 1979, Clippings, Hunt Papers, NCDAH.

8. Mary Odom, statement, NCUERA Board of Director's meeting, October 11, 1978; Rosalina Whelon, memo to President Carter, November 30, 1978, North Carolina file, Jimmy Carter Papers, Jimmy Carter Presidential Library, Atlanta (hereinafter cited as JCL).

9. Sarah Weddington to Gretchen Poston, White House memo, January 9, 1979, and Sarah Weddington to President Carter, White House memo, undated, both in North Carolina file, Carter Papers, JCL.

10. Rosalina Whelon, White House memo, November 30, 1979; Interdepartmental Task Force on Women, undated memo, North Carolina File, Carter Papers, JCL.

11. Donald G. Mathews and Jane Sherron De Hart, *Sex, Gender and Politics of ERA* (New York: Oxford University Press, 1990), 98–102.

12. Paul Krause, "ERA Forces Took Calculated Risk," *Raleigh Times*, February 16, 1979, Clippings, Hunt Papers, NCDAH; Mathews and De Hart, *Politics*, 110; "Karolina," NCUERA, to "Eileen and Sheila," undated, North Carolina File, Carter Papers, JCL.

13. "Hunt Raps Assembly for Inflationary Hikes," *News and Observer*, June 14, 1979; "Hunt Helps Carter Defend Inflation Plan," *News and Observer*, December 10, 1978, Clippings, Hunt Papers, NCDAH; William Welch, "White House Embarrasses Governor," September 10, 1979, Jim Hunt File, Wilson County Library, Wilson, NC.

14. A.L. May, "Hunt Rode His Campaign Pledges to Enactment," *News and Observer*, February 10, 1980, Clippings, North Carolina Collection, University of North Carolina (hereinafter cited as NCC-UNC).

15. A.L. May, "1,500 Folks Show Support For Governor Hunt," *News and Observer*, August 19, 1979, 1; "Committee Says Hunt Should Run," *Greensboro Daily News*, December 5, 1979, "Gov. Hunt Campaign Kitty Hits $600,000," *Fayetteville Times*, December 6, 1979, Clippings, Hunt Papers, NCDAH.

16. Elizabeth Wheaton, *Codename Greenkill: The 1979 Greensboro Killings* (Atlanta: University of Georgia Press, 1987), 1–93; "500 Troops, 400 Police to Patrol Funeral March," *News and Observer*, November 9, 1979, 1; Daniel C. Hoover, "Scott Critical of Hunt's Trip," *News and Observer*, November 13, 1979, 23.

17. J. F. Gillimore, Columbus, NC, to Jim Hunt, Raleigh, NC, undated, Ku Klux Klan File, Hunt Papers, NCDAH.

18. James Harris, Germantown, NC, to Jim Hunt, Raleigh, November 8, 1979; Anne Rove to Jim Hunt, Raleigh, May 27, 1980, T. Holmen, Seattle, to Jim Hunt, Raleigh, December 4, 1979, Ramon Leganeche, Seattle, undated, to Jim Hunt, Raleigh, Ku Klux Klan File, Hunt Papers, NCDAH.

19. Wheaton, *Greenkill*, 224; Paul O'Connor, "Hunt Urges Watch on Extremists," *Raleigh Times*, December 19, 1979; "CWP: Hunt Promotes KKK," *Raleigh Times*, December 21, 1979, Clippings, Hunt Papers, NCDAH; "CWP Disrupts Press Conference," *News and Observer*, July 24, 1980, Clippings, NCC-UNC.

20. "Disrupts," NCC-UNC; Jim Hunt, Raleigh, to the Reverend Charles Whitaker, September 18, 1980, Communist File, Hunt Papers, NCDAH.

21. Eddie Knox, interview by author, September 12, 2000; Martin Donsky,

"Hunt, Green Going Abroad to Recruit Industry," *News and Observer*, March 2, 1978; Jack Betts, "Greener Pastures," *Greensboro Daily News*, June 18, 1978, Clippings, Hunt Papers, NCDAH.

22. "Governor Has Too Much Power, Green Says," *Charlotte Observer*, January 9, 1979; William Welch, "Hunt Sits in 1980 Driver's Seat," March 12, 1979, Clippings, Hunt Papers, NCDAH.

23. Sherry Johnson, "Crime Rises 11.14 Per Cent in 5 Cities," *News and Observer*, December 19, 1979, Scrapbook, Hunt Papers, NCDAH; "Under the Dome," *News and Observer*, November 2, 1979, 2; "Look Who's Running For Governor," *Tar Heel*, Volume VII, No. 7, November/December 1979, 29, NCC-UNC.

24. Robert Scott, Haw River, to author, received January 13, 2000; Memory F. Mitchell, editor, *Addresses and Papers of Robert Scott, Governor of North Carolina, 1969–1973* (Raleigh: North Carolina Department of Cultural Resources, 1978), 210–11; Jean Speck, *The Gentleman from Haw River* (Raleigh, NC: Edwards and Broughton, Inc., 1990), 148; "Jim Hunt: Man in Politics with a Longtime Ambition," *Durham Morning Herald*, December 5, 1974, Clippings, NCC-UNC.

25. "Ex-Gov. Scott Interested In Job for Carter," *News and Observer*, January 7, 1977, 33; Joseph Grimsley, interview by author, September 26, 1999; Jimmy Carter, Nomination of Robert Scott, *Public Papers of the Presidents of the United States, Jimmy Carter, 1977, Volume 1* (Washington: United States Government Printing Office, 1978), 1026; Betty McCain, interview by author, October 6, 1999; "Hunt Asks Consideration for Scott for College Job," *Fayetteville Times*, February 1, 1979; Rob Christensen, "Scott Raps Hunt's Role in Filling Colleges Post," *News and Observer*, February 2, 1979, Clippings, Hunt Papers, NCDAH.

26. L. May, "Bert Bennett: Power Behind the Candidates," *News and Observer*, Clippings, Hunt Papers, NCDAH; Scott to author, received January 13, 2000.

27. "Say It Again, Bob," *News and Observer*, April 4, 1979; A. L. May, "Criticism By Scott New Worry for Hunt," *News and Observer*, April 5, 1979, Clippings, Hunt Papers, NCDAH.

28. Ned Cline, "Hunt Offers Critic's Wife Job," *Charlotte Observer*, April 5, 1979, Clippings, Hunt Papers, NCDAH.

29. Scott to author, January 13, 2000; Daniel Hoover, "Scott Says He Will Oppose Hunt in May Gubernatorial Primary," *News and Observer*, October 12, 1979, Hunt File, Wilson County Library, Wilson; "Under the Dome," *News and Observer*, March 12, 1980, 1.

30. Hoover, "Primary."

31. May, "Criticism."

32. "Scott Fakes Left, Veers to Right," *Charlotte Observer*, December 24, 1979; "Scott Attacks Hunt, But Hunt Looks to November," *News and Observer*, May 1, 1980; "Scott Enters Race with Blast at Machine," William M. Welch, (Pilot, Virginia) *Ledger Star*, Ferrel Guillory, "Beyond Being Anti-Hunt, Bob Scott Lacks Campaign Theme," *News and Observer*, November 23, 1979, Clippings, Hunt Papers, NCDAH.

33. Pat Stith and Daniel Hoover, "Union Boss Quite An Entrepreneur," *News and Observer*, September 9, 1979, 1; Daniel Hoover, "Memos of Political Tips Were Sent to Hunt," *News and Observer*, January 29, 1980, 1; A. L. May and Daniel Hoover, "Hunt Apologizes for Political Reports," *News and Observer*, January 31,

1980, 1; Daniel Hoover, "Hunt Knew of Memos, Scott Says," *News and Observer,* March 7, 1980, 33.

34. Bert Bennett, interview by author, October 12, 1999.

35. Scott to author, received January 13, 2000.

36. Grimsley, interview by author.

37. Carter Wrenn, interview by author, January 16, 2000; Tom Ellis, interview by author, May 17, 2000; Daniel C. Hoover, "Helms Club Breakout," *News and Observer,* November 12, 1979, 12.

38. Sherry Johnson, "Hunt Defends New Generation as Vital Program for Children," *News and Observer,* November 17, 1979, Clippings, Hunt Papers, NCDAH.

39. Bruce Siceloff, Sherry Johnson, "Conservative Groups Attacking Child-Care Act," *News and Observer,* December 6, 1979; Claude Sitton, "Hunt Opponents Resort to Smear Campaign," *News and Observer,* December 9, 1979, Clippings, Hunt Papers, NCDAH.

40. Daniel C. Hoover, "TV Evangelist Calls His Flock to Politics," *News and Observer,* November 3, 1979, 1; Wayne Greenhaw, *Elephants in the Cotton Fields* (New York: Macmillan, 1987), 166.

41. Jesse Helms Newsletter, 1978, Jim Hunt File, Ralph Scott Papers, NCDAH; Wrenn, interview by author.

42. Beverly Lake, Jr., interview by author, October 9, 1999; Howard E. Covington and Marion Ellis, *Terry Sanford: Politics, Progress and Outrageous Ambitions* (Durham and London: Duke University Press, 1999), 220–21, 230–36, 338–45; I. Beverly Lake, Jr., to Jim Hunt, September 21, 1975, unprocessed Hunt Papers, NCDAH.

43. "CP&L to Pass on Escalating Fuel Costs," *News and Observer,* February 7, 1974, 12; Steve Berg, "Utilities Commission Gets Public's Scrutiny," *News and Observer,* March 25, 1974, 1; "Utility Bill Survives Lake's Attack," *News and Observer,* March 16, 1975, 4D; Gary Pearce, "Criticism Outrages Utility Bill Sponsor," *News and Observer,* March 13, 1975, 1; Paul Klause, "Hunt Outlines 'Presumed Sentence' Plan," March 8, 1979, *Raleigh Times,* Clippings, Hunt Papers, NCDAH; Lake, interview by author.

44. Lake, interview by author.

45. Jim Hunt, "Western North Carolina Appreciation Day," October 6, 1979, *Papers,* 613; Dan Hoover, "Hunt Suggests Stripping Lake of Chairmanship," *News and Observer,* Clippings, Hunt Papers, NCDAH; "Lake Switches to GOP, Enters Governor's Race," October 5, 1979, Hunt File, Wilson County Library.

46. Lake, interview by author, "Demos Believe Lake Used," *Raleigh Times,* October 5, 1979, Clippings, Hunt Papers, NCDAH; Carter Wrenn, interview by author.

47. "Hunt Plans Media Campaign," *News and Observer,* September 9, 1980, 1; "Hunt Takes Efforts to the Air Waves," *News and Observer,* October 2, 1980, 1.

48. Jim Hunt for Governor Campaign, Memo to Ralph Scott, July 8, 1980, Jim Hunt File, Ralph Scott Papers, NCDAH; "Information on Lake Offered," *News and Observer,* August 19, 1980, 1; "Hunt Bars Data Release," *News and Observer,* August 20, 1980, 1.

49. "Higher Voter Turnout Predicted for North Carolina," *News and Observer,* November 4, 1980, 1; Lake, interview by author.

50. "Hunt Snubs Lake's Barbs in Debate," *News and Observer*, September 9, 1980, 1.

51. "Snubs," 1.

52. A.L. May and Daniel Hoover, "President Pledges Aid on Tobacco," *News and Observer*, October 8, 1980, 1; Jack Watson, White House, to Jim Hunt, Raleigh, December 1, 1980, North Carolina File, Carter Papers, JCL; Wrenn, interview by author.

53. A.L. May, "Hunt Outdistances Other Democrats," *News and Observer*, November 5, 1980, 1.

54. *Ibid.*; Paul Luebke, *Tar Heel Politics 2000* (Chapel Hill, University of North Carolina Press, 1999), 36.

55. Editorial, *News and Observer*, November 6, 1980, 8.

56. May, "Outdistances," 1.

Chapter 15

1. William D. Snider, *Helms and Hunt; The North Carolina Senate Race, 1984* (University of North Carolina Press: Chapel Hill and London, 1985), 80, 109–10, 171–72.

2. "Hunt's Mark on History," *Wilson Daily Times*, December 16–17, 2000, 3D.

Bibliography

Manuscript Collections

Atlanta, Georgia. Jimmy Carter Presidential Library: Jimmy Carter Presidential Papers.

Chapel Hill, North Carolina. North Carolina Collection, University of North Carolina at Chapel Hill: Clipping File, 1976–1989; James B. Hunt, Jr., Articles; Interview with Five North Carolina Governors, WUNC-TV; North Carolina's Economic Report to the Governor, 1979.

Chapel Hill, North Carolina. Southern Historical Collection, University of North Carolina at Chapel Hill: Sam Erwin Papers; William Friday Papers; Terry Sanford Papers; Southern Oral History Collection.

Raleigh, North Carolina. North Carolina Department of Archives and History: Equal Rights Amendment Papers; Lieutenant Governor James B. Hunt, Jr., Papers; Governor James B. Hunt, Jr., Papers; North Carolina Board of Education Papers; Governor Kerr Scott Papers; North Carolina State Senator Ralph Scott Papers; Governor Robert Scott Papers.

Raleigh, North Carolina. North Carolina State University Archives: *Agromeck* Yearbook; James B. Hunt, Jr., File; North Carolina State College Student Senate Minutes; (North Carolina State College) *Technician*.

Wilson, North Carolina. Wilson County Library: James B. Hunt, Jr., File.

Books

Ambrose, Stephen. *Nixon: The Triumph of a Politician, 1962–1972*. New York: Simon and Schuster, 1989.

Baker, Betty. *Henry Hunt: Family and Descendants of Virginia and North Carolina*. Raleigh: Betty Baker, 1994.

Bartley, Numan. *The New South, 1945–1980*. Baton Rouge: Louisiana State University Press, 1995.

Bass, Jack and Walter DeVries. *The Transformation of Southern Politics: Social Change and Political Consequences.* Athens: University of Georgia Press, 1995.

Bishop, C. E., Ferrel Guillory, Sarah Rubin, and Leah D. Totten. *The State of the South 2000.* Chapel Hill: MDC, Inc., 2000.

Black, Earl and Merle Black. *How Presidents Are Elected.* Cambridge: Harvard University Press, 1992.

Bledsoe, Jerry. *Death Sentence: The True Story of Velma Barfield's Life, Crimes, and Execution.* New York: Dutton, 1998.

Bourne, Peter G. *Jimmy Carter: A Comprehensive Biography from Plains to Post-presidency.* New York: Scribners, 1997.

Burns, August M. and Julian M. Pleasants. *Frank Porter Graham and the 1950 Senate Race in North Carolina.* Chapel Hill: University of North Carolina Press, 1990.

Bush, George. *All the Best, George Bush: My Life in Letters and Other Writings.* New York: Scribners, 1999.

Califano, Joseph. *Governing In America.* New York: Simon and Schuster, 1981.

Carter, Dan T. *The Politics of Rage: George Wallace, The Origins of the New Conservatism, and the Transformation of American Politics.* Baton Rouge: Louisiana State University, 1995.

Carter, Jimmy. *Keeping Faith: Memoirs of a President.* New York: Bantam Books, 1982.

_____. *Public Papers of the Presidents of the United States, Jimmy Carter, 1977, Volume 1.* Washington: United States Government Printing Office, 1978.

_____. *Public Papers of the President of the United States, Jimmy Carter, 1978, Volume 1–2.* Washington, D. C.: U. S. Government Printing Office, 1979.

_____. *Public Papers of the President of the United States, Jimmy Carter, 1980–81, Volume 3.* Washington, D. C.: U. S. Government Printing Office, 1981.

Cecelski, David S. and Timonty Tysons, eds. *Democracy Betrayed: The Wilmington Riot of 1898 and Its Legacy.* Chapel Hill: University of North Carolina Press, 1998.

Chafe, William. *Never Stop Running: Allard Lowenstein and The Struggle to Save American Liberalism.* New York: Basic Books, 1993.

_____. *The Unfinished Journey: America Since World War II, Second Edition.* New York: Oxford University Press, 1991.

Clancy, Paul R. *Just a Country Lawyer.* Bloomington, IN: Indiana University Press, 1974.

Cohadas, Nadine. *Strom Thurmond and the Politics of Southern Change.* New York: Simon & Schuster, 1993.

Covington, Howard E., Jr., and Marion Ellis. *Terry Sanford: Politics, Progress and Outrageous Ambitions.* Durham: Duke University Press, 1999.

Crow, Jeffrey. *A History of African Americans in North Carolina.* Raleigh: North Carolina Department of Archives and History, 1992.

Davis, Ruth J. *History of the County of Wilson.* Wilson: Ruth J. Davis, 1985.

De Hart, Jane Sherron, and Donald G. Mathews. *Sex, Gender and the Politics of ERA.* New York: Oxford University Press, 1990.

Drescher, John. *The Triumph of Good Will.* Jackson, MS: University Press of Mississippi, 2000.

Evers, Charles. *Have No Fear: The Charles Evers Story.* John Wiley and Sons, Inc., 1998.

Fitzgerald, Gayle Lane. *Remembering a Champion*. Raleigh: Edwards & Broughton, Inc., 1988.

Gardner, Ava. *Ava: My Story*. New York: Bantam Books, 1990.

Genovese, Eugene D. *The Slaveholders Dilemma: Freedom and Progress in Southern Conservative Thought, 1820–1860*. Columbia, SC: University of South Carolina Press, 1992.

Glad, Betty. *Jimmy Carter: In Search of the Great White House*. New York: W. W. Norton and Company, 1980.

Godwin, John L. *Black Wilmington and the North Carolina Way*. New York: University Press of America, 2000.

Greenhaw, Wayne. *Elephants in the Cotton Fields*. New York: Macmillan, 1987.

Hamrick, Grace Rutledge and Jenneale Coulter Moore. *The First Ladies of North Carolina*. Charlotte: Heritage Printers, Inc., 1981.

Harwell, Fred. *A True Deliverance: The Joan Little Case*. New York: Alfred A. Knopf, 1975.

Holshouser, James Eubert. *Addresses and Public Papers of James Eubert Holshouser, Governor of North Carolina, 1973–1977*. Raleigh: North Carolina Division of Archives and History, 1978.

Hunt, James B., Jr. *Addresses and Public Papers of James B. Hunt, Jr. Governor of North Carolina, 1977–1981*. Raleigh: North Carolina Division of Archives and History, 1982.

_____. *Addresses and Papers of James Baxter Hunt, Jr., Governor of North Carolina, Volume II, 1981–1985*. Raleigh: North Carolina Division of Archives and History, 1987.

_____. *Raising A New Generation: The North Carolina Story*. Raleigh: North Carolina Department of Human Resources, 1978.

Key, V. O., Jr. *Southern Politics in State and Nation*. Knoxville: University of Tennessee Press, 1949.

Konkle, Burton Alva. *John Motley Morehead and The Development of North Carolina*. Philadelphia, PA: William J. Campbell, 1927.

Lal Joshi, Leo Bhuwan. *Democratic Innovations in Nepal: A Case Study of Political Acculturation*. Berkeley: University of California Press, 1966.

Lieberman, Joseph. *The Power Broker: A Biography of John M. Bailey*. Boston: Houghton-Mifflin Co., 1966.

Link, William. *William Friday: Power, Purpose And American Higher Education*. Chapel Hill: University of North Carolina Press, 1995.

Luebke, Paul. *Tar Heel Politics 2000*. Chapel Hill: University of North Carolina Press, 1998.

Luebke, Paul, Michael Luger, Stephen Peters, Gregory Sampson, and John Wilson. *High Hopes for High Tech: Microelectronics Policy in North Carolina*. Chapel Hill: University of North Carolina Press, 1985.

McLean, Angus. *Papers and Letters of Governor Angus Wilton McLean, 1925–29*. Raleigh: North Carolina Printers, 1931.

Morrison, Cameron. *Letters and Papers of Cameron Morrison, Governor of North Carolina, 1921–25*. Raleigh: North Carolina Printers, 1927.

Morrison, Joseph. *Governor O. Max Gardner*. Chapel Hill: University of North Carolina Press, 1971.

Noblin, Stuart. *Leonidas Polk: Agricultural Crusader.* Chapel Hill: University of North Carolina Press, 1951.

Orr, Oliver, Jr. *Charles Brantley Aycock.* Chapel Hill: University of North Carolina Press, 1961.

Parajulee, Ranjee. *The Democratic Transition in Nepal.* New York: Rowman and Littlefield Publishers, Inc., 2000.

Poinsett, Alex. *Walking with Presidents: Louis Martin and the Rise of Black Political Power.* Lanham, MD: Madison Books, 1997.

Raper, Horace. *William W. Holden: North Carolina's Political Enigma.* Chapel Hill: University of North Carolina Press, 1985.

Reagan, Alice. *North Carolina State University: A Narrative History.* Ann Arbor, MI: Edwards Brothers, 1987.

Rothenberg, Randall. *The Neoliberals: The New American Politics.* New York: Simon & Schuster, 1984.

Scott, Robert. *Addresses and Papers of Robert Scott, Governor of North Carolina, 1969–1973.* Raleigh: North Carolina Division of Archives and History, 1978.

Scott, W. Kerr. *Address and Papers of W. Kerr Scott, Governor of North Carolina, 1949–1953.* Raleigh: North Carolina Archives, 1955.

Schoenbaum, Thomas J. *Islands, Capes, and Sounds.* Winston-Salem: John F. Blair, 1982.

Snider, William D. *Helms and Hunt: The 1984 North Carolina Senate Race.* Chapel Hill: University of North Carolina Press, 1985.

Sydnor, Charles. *Development of Southern Sectionalism, 1819–1848.* Baton Rouge: Louisiana State University Press, 1948.

Tucker, Glenn. *Zeb Vance: A Champion of Personal Freedom.* Indianapolis, IN: Bobbs-Merrill Company, 1965.

Turner, Herbert Snipes. *The Dreamer: Archibald DeBow Murphy, 1777–1832.* Verona, VA: McClure Printing Company, 1971.

Wheaton, Elizabeth. *Greenkill: The 1979 Greensboro Killings.* Athens: University of Georgia Press, 1987.

Witcover, Jules. *Marathon: Pursuit of the Presidency, 1972–1976.* New York: Viking Press, 1977.

Woods, Randall Bennett. *Fulbright: A Biography.* New York: Cambridge University Press, 1999.

Woodward, Bob. *The Wars of Watergate.* New York: Simon and Schuster, 1999.

Zelnick, Bob. *Gore: A Political Life.* Washington, D. C.: Regnery Publishing, Inc., 1999.

Articles

Abrams, Douglas C. "A Progressive-Conservative Duel: The 1920 Democratic Gubernatorial Primaries in North Carolina." *North Carolina Historical Review* 55 (Winter 1978): 421–43.

Alderman, Edwin. "Charles Brantley Aycock: An Appreciation." *North Carolina History Review* 1 (July 1924): 243–50.

Bratton, Mary Jo Jackson. "Cradled in Conflict: Origins of East Carolina University." *North Carolina History Review* 63 (January 1986): 74–103.

Eaton, Clement. "Edwin A. Alderman: Liberal of the New South." *North Carolina Historical Review* 23 (April 1946): 206–21.

Faulkner, Walt, and Janice Faulkner. "Look Who's Running for Governor." *Tar Heel* 7 (November/December 1979): 28–30.

"Four Men for the New Season" and "New Day A'Coming in the South." *Time* (May 31, 1971): 16–20.

Green, Elma C. "Those Opposed: The Anti-Suffragists in North Carolina, 1900–1920," *North Carolina Historical Review* 67 (July 1990): 315–333.

Hunt, James B., Jr. "From Your Editor." *The Agriculturalist* 31 (October 1957): 5.

_____. "From Your Editor." *The Agriculturalist* 31 (March 1958): 10, 14.

_____. "From Your Editor." *The Agriculturalist* 31 (May 1958): 5–6.

_____. "Is There Any Future in Farming?" *The Agriculturalist* 31(December 1957): 5.

_____. "Nepal: A Test Ground for Economic Theories." *North Carolina State Alumni News* 38 (September–October 1965): 4–7.

_____. "A Student Grange for State College." *The Agriculturalist* 30 (April 1957): 16, 19.

_____. "Together We Stand." *The Agriculturalist* 30 (October 1956): 10, 19.

_____. "YDC Program for Victory in 1968." *Tar Heel Democrat* 4 (Winter 1968): 1.

Hunt, James L. "The Making of a Populist: Marion Butler, Part One." *North Carolina Historical Review* 62 (Spring 1985): 53–77.

_____. "The Making of a Populist: Marion Butler, Part Two." *North Carolina Historical Review* 62 (Summer 1985): 179–202.

Ireland, Robert E. "Prison Reform, Road Building, and Southern Progressivism: Joseph Hyde Pratt and the Campaign for 'Good Roads and Good Men.'" *North Carolina Historical Review* 68 (April 1991): 125–57.

Jeffrey, Thomas. "Internal Improvements and Political Parties in Antebellum North Carolina, 1836–1860." *North Carolina Historical Review* 55 (Spring 1978): 111–56.

"Jim Hunt: Our Man in Raleigh." *New East* 1 (November/December 1973): 12, 29.

Jones, Graham. "Keep Your Eye on Him! A Nuts and Bolts Man." *North Carolina State Alumni News* 42 (May/June 1970): 7–9.

King, Wayne. "The Case Against the Wilmington Ten." *New York Times Magazine* (December 3, 1978): 60–79.

Linder, Suzanne Cameron. "William Louis Poteat and the Evolution Controversy." *North Carolina Historical Review* 40 (Spring 1963): 135–57.

Link, Arthur S. "The Wilson Movement in North Carolina." *North Carolina Historical Review* 23 (October 1946): 483–94.

Logan, Frenise. "The Movement in North Carolina to Establish a State Supported College for Negroes." *North Carolina Historical Review* 35 (July 1958): 167–80.

Marlowe, Jean G. "North Carolina's Economic Development Program Charges Into the Future." *Wachovia* 65 (Spring 1978): 18–19.

McLaurin, Melton. "The Knights of Labor in North Carolina Politics." *North Carolina Historical Review* 49 (Summer 1972): 298–315.

"North Carolina Interview: Governor Jim Hunt." *North Carolina* (January 1981): 16–20.

Nosstrom, Kathryn. "'More Was Expected Of Us': The North Carolina League of

Women's Voters and the Feminist Movement in the 1920s." *North Carolina Historical Review* 68 (July 1991): 307–19.

Olsen, Otto. "Albion Tourgee, Carpetbagger." *North Carolina Historical Review* 40 (Autumn 1963): 434–54.

Payne, Peggy. "Jim Hunt: Ag Grad to Governor." *North Carolina State Alumni News* 49 (November/December 1976): 6–7.

Rose, Charlie. "YDC Report." *North Carolina Democratic Executive Committee Progress* (May 9, 1969): 3.

Sellers, Charles. "Walter Hines Page and the Spirit of the New South." *North Carolina Historical Review* 24 (October 1952): 481–99.

Shultz, J. Christopher. "The Burning of America: Race, Radicalism, and the 'Charlotte Three' Trial in the 1970s." *North Carolina Historical Review* 75 (1999): 43–65.

Steelman, Joseph F. "Edward J. Justice: Profile of a Progressive Legislator, 1899–1913." *North Carolina History Review* 48 (April 1971): 147–60.

_____. "The Progressive Democratic Convention of 1914 in North Carolina." *North Carolina History Review* 46 (Spring 1969), 83–104.

Trelease, Allen W. "The Fusion Legislatures of 1895 and 1897: A Roll Call Analysis of the North Carolina House of Representatives." *North Carolina Historical Review* 57 (July 1980): 280–309.

Watson, Elgiva D. "The Election Campaign of Governor Jarvis, 1880: A Study of the Issues." *North Carolina Historical Review* 48 (Summer 1971): 276–300.

Watson, Richard L. "Southern Democratic Primary: Simmons vs. Bailey in 1930." *North Carolina Historical Review* 42 (Spring 1965): 21–46.

Newspapers

Asheville Citizen
Chapel Hill Newspaper
Charlotte Observer
(University of North Carolina at Chapel Hill) *Daily Tar Heel*
Durham Morning Herald
Fayetteville Observer
Greensboro Daily News
Hickory Record
(New York) *Journal of Commerce*
(Pilot, VA) *Ledger Star*
(Raleigh) *News and Observer*
Raleigh Times
Reidsville Review
(North Carolina State College) *Technician*
(North Carolina State University) *Technician*
Wilson Daily Times
Winston-Salem Journal

Interviews by Author

Allen, Gordon. July 12, 2000, Raleigh. Tape recording.

Bennett, Bert. October 12, 1999, Winston-Salem, North Carolina. Tape recording.

Carlton, Phil. September 8, 2000, Pinetops, North Carolina. Author's notes.

Ellis, Tom. May 17, 2000, Raleigh. Author's notes.

Essex, Paul. December 7, 1999, Raleigh. Tape recording.

Flaherty, David. October 13, 1999, Raleigh. Tape recording.

Friday, William. December 29, 1999, Chapel Hill. Tape recording.

Gilmore, Thomas. December 10, 2000, Julian, North Carolina. Author's notes.

Grimsley, Joseph. September 26, 1999, Clayton, North Carolina. Tape recording.

_____. June 17, 2000, Clayton, North Carolina. Tape recording.

_____. April 15, 2001, Rockingham, North Carolina. Author's notes.

Guillory, Ferrel. December 15, 1999, Raleigh. Tape recording.

Harrison, Betsy Warren. October 2002. Telephone interview. Author's notes.

Henley, Carl. January 25, 2000. Author's notes.

Holshouser, James. October 20, 1999, Southern Pines, North Carolina. Tape recording.

Holtzman, Abraham. December 9, 1999, Raleigh. Tape recording.

Hunt, James B., Jr. December 14, 1999, Raleigh. Tape recording.

Hunt, James Baxter, Sr. December 27, 1999, Lucama, North Carolina. Tape recording.

Hunt, Pearl Johnson. December 27, 1999, Lucama, North Carolina. Tape recording.

Hunt, Robert. September 26, 1999, Raleigh. Author's notes.

Knox, Eddie. September 12, 2000, Charlotte. Author's notes.

Lake, I. Beverly, Jr. October 9, 1999, Raleigh. Tape recording.

Lee, Howard. October 26, 1999, Raleigh. Tape recording.

Lindsey, Quentin. October 7, 1999, Raleigh. Tape recording.

McCain, Betty. October 6, 1999, Raleigh. Tape recording.

Owen, Betty. October 7, 1999, Raleigh. Tape recording.

Scott, Robert. January 13, 2000. Questionnaire.

Webb, John. December 7, 1999, Raleigh. Tape recording.

Wrenn, Carter. January 16, 2000, Raleigh. Author's notes.

Interviews by Others

Clayton, Eva. Interview by Joseph Meisner, May 30, 1995. Tape recording, Southern Oral History Collection, Louis Wilson Library, University of North Carolina, Chapel Hill, North Carolina.

Eure, Thad. Interview by Jack Bass, December 12, 1973. Transcript, Southern Oral History Collection, University of North Carolina, Chapel Hill, North Carolina.

Guillory, Ferrel. Interview by Joseph Meisner, April 29, 1996. Transcript, Southern Oral History Collection, University of North Carolina, Chapel Hill, North Carolina.

Hobby, Wilbur. Interview by Jack Bass, December 1973. Transcript, Southern Oral History Collection, Louis Wilson Library, University of North Carolina, Chapel Hill, North Carolina.

Hunt, James B., Jr. Interview by William Friday, December 31, 1999, *North Carolina People*, WUNC-TV. Videotape.

Lee, Howard. Interview by Jack Bass, December 13, 1973. Transcript, Southern Oral Historical Collection, Louis Wilson Library, University of North Carolina, Chapel Hill, North Carolina.

_____. Interview by Joseph Meisner, May 5, 1995. Tape recording, Southern Oral History Collection, Louis Wilson Library, University of North Carolina, Chapel Hill, North Carolina.

Michaux, H. M. Interview by Jack Bass, November 20, 1974. Transcript, Southern Oral History Collection, Louis Wilson Library, University of North Carolina, Chapel Hill, North Carolina.

Scott, Ralph. Interview by Jack Bass, December 20, 1973. Transcript, Southern Oral History Collection, Louis Wilson Library, University of North Carolina, Chapel Hill, North Carolina.

Theses and Dissertations

Grimsley, Joseph Wayne, Jr. "Challenges to the North Carolina Speaker Ban Law, 1963–1968." M. A. thesis, North Carolina State University, 1994.

Hunt, James B., Jr. An Economic Analysis of Optimum Flue-Cured Tobacco Production Practices Under Acreage Control and Poundage Control." M. A. thesis, North Carolina State College, 1962.

Krotsking, Marsha Van Dyke. "To Be or Merely to Seem? Investigating the Image of the Modern Education Governor." Dissertation, College of William and Mary, 1987.

Sosne, Marc. "State Politics and Educational Legislation." Dissertation, University of North Carolina at Chapel Hill, 1978.

Index